In loving memory of Lisa, and for our families: Donna, David, Jake, Halley, Scott, Chris, Leslie, Jacob, Eliana, Cindy, Alex, and Chris

BRIEF CONTENTS

CONTENTS

Teaching Students to Solve Problems[1]

by Luke Froeb

When I started teaching MBA students, I taught economics as I had learned it, using models and public policy applications. My students complained so much that the dean took me out to the proverbial woodshed and gave me an ultimatum, "improve customer satisfaction or else." With the help of some disgruntled students who later became teaching assistants, I was able to turn the course around.

The problem I faced can be easily described using the language of economics: the supply of business education (professors are trained to provide abstract theory) is not closely matched to demand (students want practical knowledge). This mismatch is found throughout academia, but it is perhaps most acute in a business school. Business students expect a return on a fairly sizable investment and want to learn material with immediate and obvious value.

One implication of the mismatch is that teaching economics in the usual way—with models and public policy applications—is not likely to satisfy student demand. In this book, we use what we call a "problem-solving pedagogy" to teach microeconomic principles to business students. We begin each chapter with a business problem, like the fixed-cost fallacy, and then give students just enough analytic structure to understand the cause of the problem and how to fix it.

Teaching students to solve real business problems, rather than learn models, satisfies student demand in an obvious way. Our approach also allows students to absorb the lessons of economics without as much of the analytical "overhead" as a model-based pedagogy. This is an advantage, especially in a terminal or stand-alone course, like those typically taught in a business school. To see this, ask yourself which of the following ideas is more likely to stay with a student after the class is over: the fixed-cost fallacy or that the partial derivative of profit with respect to price is independent of fixed costs.

ELEMENTS OF A PROBLEM-SOLVING PEDAGOGY

Our problem-solving pedagogy has three elements.

1. Begin with a Business Problem

Beginning with a real-world business problem puts the particular ahead of the abstract and motivates the material in a straightforward way. We use narrow, focused problems whose solutions require students to use the analytical tools of interest.

2. Teach Students to View Inefficiency as an Opportunity

The second element of our pedagogy turns the traditional focus of benefit–cost analysis on its head. Instead of teaching students to spot and eliminate inefficiency, for example, by changing public policy, we teach them to view each underemployed asset as a money-making opportunity.

3. Use Economics to Implement Solutions

After you find an underemployed asset, moving it to a higher-valued use is often hard to do, particularly when the inefficiency occurs within an organization. The third element of our pedagogy addresses the problem of incentive alignment: how to design organizations where employees have enough information to make profitable decisions and the incentive to do so.

Again, we use the tools of economics to address the problem of implementation. If people act rationally, optimally, and self-interestedly, then mistakes have only one of two causes: either people lack the *information* necessary to make good decisions or they lack the *incentive* to do so. This immediately suggests a problem-solving algorithm; ask:

1. Who is making the bad decision?
2. Do they have enough information to make a good decision?
3. Do they have the incentive to do so?

Answers to these three questions will point to the source of the problem and suggest one of three potential solutions:

1. Let someone else make the decision, someone with better information or incentives
2. Give more information to the current decision maker
3. Change the current decision maker's incentives

The book begins by showing students how to use this algorithm, and subsequent chapters illustrate its use in a variety of contexts, for example, extent decisions, investments, pricing, bargaining, principal–agent relationships, and uncertain environments.

USING THE BOOK

The book is designed to be read cover-to-cover as it is short, concise, and accessible to anyone who can read and think clearly. The pedagogy is built around business problems, so the book is most effective for those with some work experience. Its relatively short length makes it reasonably easy to customize with ancillary material.

The authors use the text in full-time MBA programs, executive MBA programs (weekends), healthcare management executive programs (one night a week), and nondegree executive education. However, some of our biggest customers use the book in online business classes at both the graduate and undergraduate levels.

In the degree programs, we supplement the material in the book with online interactive programs like Cengage's *MindTap*. Complete Blackboard courses, including syllabi, quizzes, homework, slides, videos to complement each chapter, and links to supplementary material, can be downloaded from the Cengage website. Our *ManagerialEcon.com* blog is a good source of new business applications for each of the chapters.

In this fifth edition, we have updated and improved the presentation and pedagogy of the book. The biggest substantive change is to Chapter 17, where we present the decomposition of an observed difference between two groups into a treatment effect + selection bias. Michael Ward has been using this in his classes at University of Texas at Arlington, and rewrote the chapter to include it. We are also beginning work to add interactive "activities" to the electronic text in MindTap, Cengage's new learning platform. These activities help comprehension, especially for weaker students. In addition, we continue to rewrite and update the supplementary material: videos, worked video problems, and the test bank. In addition to the other updates throughout the text, Chapter 24 has two new sections.

We wish to acknowledge numerous classes of MBA, executive MBA, nondegree executive education, and healthcare management students, without whom none of this would have been possible—or necessary. Many of our former students will recognize stories from their companies in the book. Most of the stories in the book are from students and are for teaching purposes only.

Thanks to everyone who contributed, knowingly or not, to the book. Professor Froeb owes intellectual debts to former colleagues at the U.S. Department of Justice (among them, Cindy Alexander, Tim Brennan, Ken Heyer, Kevin James, Bruce Kobayahsi, and Greg Werden); to former colleagues at the Federal Trade Commission (among them, James Cooper, Pauline Ippolito, Tim Muris, Dan O'Brien, Maureen Ohlhausen, Paul Pautler, Mike Vita, and Steven Tenn); to colleagues at Vanderbilt (among them, Germain Boer, Jim Bradford, Bill Christie, Mark Cohen, Myeong Chang, Craig Lewis, Rick Oliver, David Parsley, David Rados, Steven Tschantz, David Scheffman, and Bart Victor); and to numerous friends and colleagues who offered suggestions, problems, and anecdotes for the book (among them, Lily Alberts, Olafur Arnarson, Raj Asirvatham, Bert Bailey, Justin Bailey, Pat Bajari, Molly Bash, Sarah Berhalter, Roger Brinner, the Honorable Jim Cooper, Matthew Dixon Cowles, Abie Del Favero, Kelsey Duggan, Vince Durnan, Marjorie Eastman, Tony Farwell, Keri Floyd, Josh Gapp, Brock Hardisty, Trent Holbrook, Jeff and Jenny Hubbard, Brad Jenkins, Dan Kessler, Bev Landstreet [B5], Bert Mathews, Christine Milner, Jim Overdahl, Craig Perry, Rich Peoples, Annaji Pervajie, Jason Rawlins, Mike Saint, David Shayne, Jon Shayne, Bill Shughart, Doug Tice, Whitney Tilson, and Susan Woodward). We owe intellectual and pedagogical debts to Armen Alchian and William Allen[3]; Henry Hazlitt[4]; Shlomo Maital[5]; John MacMillan[6]; Steven Landsburg[7]; Ivan Png[8]; Victor Tabbush[9]; Michael Jensen and William Meckling[10]; and James Brickley, Clifford Smith, and Jerold Zimmerman.[11] Special thanks to everyone who guided us through the publishing process, including Molly Umbarger, Christopher Rader, and Jason Fremder.

END NOTES

1. Much of the material is taken from Luke M. Froeb and James C. Ward, "Teaching Managerial Economics with Problems Instead of Models," in *The International Handbook on Teaching and Learning Economics*, eds. Gail Hoyt and KimMarie McGoldrick (Northampton, MA: Edward Elgar Publishing, 2012).

2. Armen Alchian and William Allen, *Exchange and Production*, 3rd ed. (Belmont, CA: Wadsworth, 1983).

3. Henry Hazlitt, *Economics in One Lesson* (New York: Crown, 1979).

4. Shlomo Maital, *Executive Economics: Ten Essential Tools for Managers* (New York: Free Press, 1994).

5. John McMillan, *Games, Strategies, and Managers* (Oxford: Oxford University Press, 1992).

6. Steven Landsburg, *The Armchair Economist: Economics and Everyday Life* (New York: Free Press, 1993).

7. Ivan Png, *Managerial Economics* (Maiden, MA: Blackwell, 1998).

8. http://www.mbaprimer.com

9. Michael Jensen and William Meckling, *A Theory of the Firm: Governance, Residual Claims and Organizational Forms* (Cambridge, MA: Harvard University Press, 2000).

10. James Brickley, Clifford Smith, and Jerold Zimmerman, *Managerial Economics and Organizational Architecture* (Chicago: Irwin, 1997).

Problem Solving and Decision Making

1 Introduction: What This Book Is About

In 1992, a junior geologist was preparing a bid recommendation for an oil tract in the Gulf of Mexico. She suspected that the tract contained a large accumulation of oil because her company, Oil Ventures International (OVI), had an adjacent tract with several productive wells. Since no competitors had neighboring tracts, none of them suspected a large accumulation of oil. Because of this, she thought that the tract could be won relatively cheaply and recommended a bid of $5 million. Surprisingly, OVI's senior management ignored the recommendation and submitted a bid of $21 million. OVI won the tract over the next-highest bid of $750,000.

If the board of directors asked you to review the bidding procedures at OVI, how would you proceed? Where would you begin your investigation? What questions would you ask?

You'd find it difficult to gather information from those closest to the bidding. Senior management would be suspicious and uncooperative because no one likes to be singled out for bidding $20 million more than was necessary. Likewise, our junior geologist would be reluctant to criticize her superiors. You might be able to rely on your experience—provided that you had run into a similar problem. But without experience, or when facing novel problems, you would have to rely on your analytic ability.

This book is designed to show you how to complete an assignment like this.

1.1 Using Economics to Solve Problems

Solving a problem like OVI's requires two steps: first, figure out what's causing the problem; and second, how to fix it. In this case, you would want to know whether the $21 million bid was too high at the time it was made, not just in retrospect. If the bid was too aggressive, then you'd have to figure out why the senior managers overbid and how to make sure they don't do it again.

Both steps require that you predict how people behave in different circumstances, and this is where the economic content of the book comes in. The one thing that unites economists is their use of the rational-actor paradigm. Simply put, it says that people act rationally, optimally, and self-interestedly. The paradigm not only helps you figure out why people behave the way they do but also suggests ways to get them to change. To change behavior, you have to change self-interest, and you do that by changing incentives.

Incentives are created by rewarding good performance with, for example, a commission on sales or a bonus based on profitability. The performance evaluation metric (revenue, cost, profit, or return on investment, ROI) is separate from the reward structure (commission, bonus, raise, or promotion), but they work together to create an incentive to behave a certain way.

To illustrate, let's go back to OVI's story and try to find the source of the problem. After her company won the auction, our geologist increased the company's oil reserves by the amount of oil estimated to be in the tract. But when the company drilled a well, it was essentially "dry," so the acquisition did little to increase the size of the company's oil reserves. Using the information from the newly drilled well, our geologist updated the reservoir map and reduced the estimated reserves to where they was before OVI won the tract.

Senior management rejected the lower estimate and directed the geologist to "do what she could" to increase the size of the estimated reserves. So, she revised the reservoir map again, adding "additional" (not real) reserves to the company's asset base. The reason behind this behavior became clear when, several months later, OVI's senior managers resigned, collecting bonuses tied to the increase in oil reserves that had accumulated during their tenure.

The incentive created by the bonus plan explains both the overbidding and overestimated reserves as rational, self-interested responses to the incentive created by the bonus. Senior managers overbid because they were rewarded for acquiring reserves, regardless of the price. Their ability to manipulate the reserve estimate made it difficult for shareholders and their representatives on the board of directors to spot the mistake.

To fix this problem, you would have to find a way to better align managers' incentives with the company's goals, perhaps by rewarding management for increasing profitability, not just for acquiring reserves. This is not as easy as it sounds because it is typically hard to measure an employee's contribution to company profitability. You can do this subjectively, with annual performance reviews, or objectively, using company earnings or stock price appreciation as performance metrics. But each of these performance measures can create problems, as we'll see in later chapters.

1.2 Problem-Solving Principles

This story illustrates our problem-solving methodology. First, we reduced the problem (overbidding) to a bad decision by someone at the firm (senior management) by asking:

Q1: Who made the bad decision?

Once we know the "who," we can use economics to figure out the "why." If people behave rationally, optimally, and self-interestedly, a bad decision occurs for one of two reasons: either (i) decision makers do not have enough information to make a good decision or (ii) they lack the incentive to do so. This suggests that we can isolate the source of almost any problem by asking two more questions:

Q2: Did the decision maker have enough information to make a good decision?

Q3: Did the decision maker have the incentive to make a good decision?

Answers to these three questions not only point to the source of the problem but also suggest ways to fix it.

S1: Let someone else—someone with better information or better incentives—make the decision,

S2: Give more information to the current decision maker, or

S3: Change the current decision makers' incentives (the performance evaluation metric or the reward scheme).

In OVI's case, we see that (Q1) senior management made the bad decision to overbid; (Q2) they had enough information to make a good bid, but (Q3) they didn't have the incentive to do so. One potential fix (S3) is to change the incentives of senior management so that they are rewarded for increasing profitability instead of oil reserves.

When reading about various business mistakes in the chapters that follow, you should ask yourself these three questions to see if you can find the cause of each problem, and a solution. By the time you finish the book, the analysis should become second nature.

Here are some practical tips that will help you develop problem-solving skills:

Think about the problem from the organization's point of view. Avoid the temptation to think about the problem from the employee's point of view because you will miss the fundamental problem of **goal alignment**: how does the organization give employees enough information to make good decisions and the incentive to do so?

Think about the organizational design. Once you identify a bad decision, avoid the temptation to solve the problem by simply reversing the decision. Instead, think about why the bad decision was made and how to make sure that similar mistakes won't be made in the future.

What is the trade-off? Your solution may solve the problem you identify, but it may cause other problems. In this case, changing the incentives of senior management by giving them limited stock (that they cannot sell for five years) may solve the overbidding problem, but it may also makes their performance dependent on external factors like the global macroeconomy, which are clearly beyond their control. Subject your solution to the same analysis. Ask the same three questions that allowed you to identify the initial problem.

*Don't define the problem as the lack of your solution.** This kind of thinking may cause you to miss the best solution. For example, if you define a problem as "the lack of centralized purchasing," then the solution will be "centralized purchasing" regardless of whether that is the best option. Instead, define the problem as "high acquisition cost," and then examine "centralized purchasing" versus "decentralized purchasing" (or some other alternative) as potential solutions to the problem.

*Avoid jargon** because most people misuse it. Force yourself to spell out what exactly you mean in simple language. It will help you think clearly and communicate precisely. As Einstein said, "If you can't explain it simply, you don't understand it well enough." In addition, almost every scam is "sold" using jargon. If you use jargon, experienced listeners will instinctively mistrust you and your analysis.

1.3 Test Yourself

In 2006, an investigative news program sent a TV reporter with a perfectly good car into a garage owned by National Auto Repair (NAR). The reporter came out with a new muffler and transmission—and a bill for over $8,000. After the story was aired on national TV, consumers began avoiding NAR, and profit plunged. What is the problem, and how do you fix it?

Let's run the problem through our problem-solving algorithm:

Q1: Who made the bad decision?

The NAR mechanic recommended unnecessary repairs.

Q2: Did the decision maker have enough information to make a good decision?

Yes, in fact, the mechanic is the only one with enough information to know whether repairs are necessary.

Q3: Did the decision maker have the incentive to make a good decision?

No, the mechanic receives bonuses or commissions tied to the amount of repair work, which rewards the mechanic for making needless repairs.

Although answers to the three questions clearly point to the source of the problem, solving it proved much more difficult. NAR tried two different solutions, but both failed.

First, the company reorganized into two divisions: one responsible for recommending repairs and the other responsible for doing them. Those who recommended repairs were paid a flat salary, but those who did the repairs were paid based on the amount of work they did.

PAUSE HERE AND TRY TO FIGURE OUT WHY THIS CHANGE DID NOT SOLVE THE PROBLEM.

Mechanics in the two divisions began colluding. In exchange for recommending unnecessary repairs, the service mechanic shared his incentive pay with the recommending mechanic. The unnecessary repairs continued.

NAR then went back to single mechanic who both recommended and performed repairs, but replaced the incentive pay with a flat salary. Although this removed the incentive to do unnecessary repairs, it also removed the incentive to work hard, resulting in what economists call "shirking." Since mechanics made the same amount of money regardless of whether they recommended and performed repairs, they ignored all but the most obvious problems.

Figuring out which solution is most profitable involves weighing the trade-offs associated with various solutions. For example, before implementing the two-division solution, NAR management should have asked whether the new decision maker had enough *information* to make good decisions, as well as the *incentive* to do so. The answer could have alerted NAR management to the potential for collusion between the recommending mechanic and the repairing mechanic. Similarly, this kind of analysis would have identified shirking by the mechanics as a cost of the flat-salary solution.

With the benefit of hindsight, I would have suggested a third potential solution: keep the original organizational design, but use an additional performance metric, based on reports provided by "secret shoppers" who bring good cars into the garage to test whether the mechanics order unnecessary repairs. If so, fire or penalize the mechanics who recommend unnecessary repairs. Secret shoppers are used successfully in other contexts, for example, in restaurants to measure service quality. By measuring and rewarding quality, restaurant chains are able to protect the value of a brand as a signal of quality. Similarly, using secret shoppers may have been able to protect the value of NAR's brand as a signal of reliable service.

1.4 Ethics and Economics

Using the rational-actor paradigm in this way—to change behavior by changing incentives—makes some students uncomfortable because it seems to deny the altruism, affection, and personal ethics that motivate most people. These students resist learning the rational-actor paradigm because they think it implicitly endorses self-interested behavior, as if the primary purpose of economics were to teach students to behave rationally, optimally, and selfishly.

These students would probably agree with a *Washington Post* editorial, "When It Comes to Ethics, B-Schools Get an F,"[1] which blames business schools in general, and economists in particular, for the ethical lapses at FIFA, Goldman Sachs, and other organizations.

> A subtle but damaging factor in this is the dominance of economists at business schools. Although there is no evidence that economists are personally less ethical than members of other disciplines, approaching the world through the dollar sign does make people more cynical.

What these students and the author, a former Harvard ethics professor, do not understand is that to control unethical behavior, we first have to understand why it occurs. When we analyze problems like the one at OVI, we're *not* encouraging students to behave opportunistically. Rather, we're teaching them to anticipate opportunistic behavior and to design organizations that are less susceptible to it. Remember, the rational-actor paradigm is only a tool for analyzing behavior, not advice on how to live your life.

It is also important to realize that these kinds of debates are often debates about value systems. *Deontologists* judge actions as good or ethical by whether they conform to a set of principles, like the Ten Commandments or the Golden Rule. *Consequentialists*, on the other hand, judge actions by their consequences. If the consequences of an action are good, then the action is deemed to be good or moral. We illustrate these contrasting value systems with a story about price gouging.[2]

When Notre Dame entered the 2006 season as one of the top-ranked football teams in the country, demand for local hotels during home games rose dramatically. In response, local hotels raised room rates. According to the *Wall Street Journal*, the Hampton Inn charged $400 a night on football weekends for a room that cost only $129 on non football days. Rates climbed even higher for games against top-ranked foes. For the game against the University of Michigan, the South Bend Marriott charged $649 per night—$500 more than its normal weekend rate of $149.

On a campus founded by priests of the Congregation of Holy Cross, where many students dedicate a year after graduation to working with the underprivileged, these high prices caused alarm. The *Wall Street Journal* quotes Professor Joe Holt, a former priest who teaches ethics in the school's executive MBA program, "It is an 'act of moral abdication' for businesses to pretend they have no choice but to charge as much as they can based on supply and demand." The article further reports Mr. Holt's intention to use the example of rising hotel rates on football weekends for a case study in his class on the integration of business and values.

Deontologists like Professor Holt would object on principle to the practice of raising prices in times of shortage.[3] We might label this the *Spider Man Principle*: with great power comes great responsibility. The laws of capitalism allow corporations to amass significant power; in turn, society should demand a high level of responsibility from corporations. In this case, while property rights give a hotel the *option* of increasing prices, possession of these rights does not relieve the hotel of its *obligation* to be concerned about the consequences of its choices. A simple beneficence argument might suggest that keeping prices low would be better for consumers.

Economics, on the other hand, gives us a *consequentialist* understanding of the practice by comparing high prices to the implied alternative. An economist would show that if prices do not rise, the *consequence* would be excess demand for hotel rooms. Would-be guests would find their rooms rationed, perhaps on a first-come, first-served basis. More likely, arbitrageurs would set up a black market, by making early reservations, and then "selling" their reservations to customers willing to pay the market-clearing price. Not only would consumers end up paying the same price, but these "arbs" would make money that would have otherwise gone to the hotel. Without the ability to earn additional profit during times of scarcity, hotels would have less incentive to build additional rooms, which would make the long-run problems even worse!

Versions of this debate—between those who criticize business on ethical grounds and those who are trying to make money—have been going on in this country since its founding. Although a full treatment of the ethical dimensions of business is beyond the scope of this book, many disagreements are really about whether morality should be defined by *deontology* or *consequentialism*. Once you realize that a debate is really a debate between value systems, it becomes much easier to understand opposing points of view, and to reach compromise with your adversaries. For example, if the government were considering price-gouging laws that made it illegal to raise prices on football weekends, a solution might involve donation of some of the profits earned on football weekends to a local charity. This might assuage the concerns of those who ascribe to the Spider Man principle.

As a footnote to this story, when someone offered our former priest $1,500 for his apartment on home-game weekends, he took the offer and now spends his weekends in Chicago. Apparently, his principles became too costly for him.

1.5 Economics in Job Interviews

If this well-reasoned introduction doesn't motivate you to learn economics, read the following interview questions—all from real interviews of students. These questions should awaken interest in the material for those of you who think economics is merely an obstacle between you and a six-figure salary.

```
-------Original Message-------

From: "Student A"
Sent: Friday, January 2, 2009, 3:57 PM
Subject: Economics Interview Questions

I had an interview a few weeks ago where I was told that
the position paid a very low base and was mostly incen-
tive compensation. I responded that I understood he was
simply "screening out" low productivity candidates
```

[NOTE: low productivity candidates would not earn very much under a system of incentive compensation, and so would be less likely to accept a job with strong incentive compensation].

```
I "signaled" back to him that this compensation struc-
ture was acceptable to me, as I was confident in my abil-
ities to produce value for the company, and for me.
```

[Note: "Signaling" and "screening" are both solutions to the problem of adverse selection, the topic of Chapter 19.]

```
-------Original Message-------

From: "Student B"
Sent: Tuesday, January 18, 2000, 1:22 PM
Subject: Economics Interview Questions

I got a question from Compaq last year for a market-
ing internship position that partially dealt with sunk
costs. It was a "true" case question where the inter-
viewer used the Internet to pull up the actual products
as he asked the question, "I am the product manager for
the new X type server with these great features. It is to
be launched next month at a cost of $5,500. Dell launched
its new Y-type server last week; it has the same features
(and even a few more) for a cost of $4,500. To date, Com-
paq has put over $2.5 million in the development process
for this server, and as such my manager is expecting
above-normal returns for the investment.

My question to you is "what advice would you give to me on
how to approach the launch of the product, that is, do I go
ahead with it at the current price, if at all, even though
Dell has a better product out that is less expensive, not
forgetting the fact that I have spent all the development
money and my boss expects me to report a super return?"

I laughed at the question because it was the very first
thing we spoke about in the interview, catching me off-
guard a bit. He wanted to see if I got caught worry-
ing about all the development costs in giving advice to
scrap the launch or continue ahead as planned. (I'm not
an idiot and could see that coming a mile away ... thanks
to economics, right? ! ! !)
```

[NOTE: the interviewer was testing Student B to see whether he would commit the "sunk-cost fallacy," covered in Chapter 3.]

```
-------Original Message-------

From: "Student C"
Sent: Tuesday, January 18, 2000, 1:37 PM
Subject: Economics Interview Questions

I got questions regarding transfer price within entities
of a company.

What prices could be used and why.
```

[NOTE: the problem of transfer pricing is one of the most common sources of conflict between divisions and is covered in Chapters 22 and 23.]

```
-------Original Message-------

From: "Student D"
Sent: Tuesday, January 18, 2000 1:28 PM
Subject: Economics Interview Questions

You are a basketball coach with five seconds on the
clock, and you are losing by two points. You have the
ball and can take only one more shot (there is no chance
of a rebound). There is a 70% chance of making a two-
pointer, which would send the game into overtime with
each team having an equal chance of winning. There is
only a 40% chance of making a three-pointer (winning if
made). Should you shoot the two- or the three-point shot?
```

[NOTE: This is an example of decision making under uncertainty, the subject of Chapter 17. For those of you who cannot wait, the answer is take the three-point shot because it results a higher probability of winning, 40%, as opposed to $35\% = (70\%) \times (50\%)$ for a two-point shot.]

SUMMARY & HOMEWORK PROBLEMS

Summary of Main Points

- Problem solving requires two steps: (i) figure out why people are making mistakes and then (ii) figure out how to prevent future ones.
- The **rational-actor paradigm** is a model of behavior that which assumes that people act rationally, optimally, and self-interestedly, that is, they respond to incentives.
- Incentives have two pieces: (i) a way of measuring performance and (ii) a compensation scheme to reward good (or punish bad) performance.
- A well-designed organization is one in which *employee incentives are aligned with organizational goals*. By this we mean that employees have (i) enough information to make good decisions and (ii) the incentive to do so.
- You can analyze any problem by asking three questions:
  Q1: Who made the bad decision?
  Q2: Does the decision maker have enough information to make a good decision?
  Q3: Does the decision maker have the incentive to make a good decision?
- Answers to these questions will suggest one of three solutions:
  S1: Let someone else make the decision, someone with better information or incentives.
  S2: Give the decision maker more information.
  S3: Change the decision maker's incentives.

Multiple-Choice Questions

1. Why might performance compensation caps be bad?
   a. Different pay rates promote dissent.
   b. Compensation caps can discourage employees from being productive after the cap.
   c. Compensation caps can discourage employees from being productive before the cap.
   d. Both b and c.
2. What is a possible consequence of a performance compensation reward scheme?
   a. It creates productive incentives.
   b. It creates harmful incentives.
   c. Both a and b.
   d. Neither a nor b.
3. Which of the following is NOT one of the three problem-solving principles laid out in Chapter 1?
   a. Under whose jurisdiction is the problem?
   b. Who is making the bad decision?
   c. Does the decision maker have enough information to make a good decision?
   d. Does the decision maker have the incentive to make a good decision?
4. Why might it be bad for hotels to not charge higher prices when rooms are in higher demand?
   a. Arbitrageurs might establish a black market by reserving rooms and then selling the reservations to customers.
   b. Rooms may be rationed.
   c. Without the profit from these high demand times, hotels would have less of an incentive to build or expand, making the long-run scarcity problem even worse.
   d. All of the above.
5. The rational-actor paradigm assumes that people do NOT
   a. act rationally.
   b. use rules of thumb.
   c. act optimally.
   d. act self-interestedly.

6. The problem-solving framework analyzes firm problems
   a. from the organization's point of view.
   b. from the manager's point of view.
   c. from the worker's point of view.
   d. from society's point of view.
7. Why might welfare for low-income households reduce the propensity to work?
   a. It will not.
   b. It reduces the incentive to work.
   c. It is unfair.
   d. It encourages jealousy.
8. Why might a "bonus cap" for executives be a bad policy for the company?
   a. It isn't. Executives shouldn't make more than a certain amount.
   b. It would sow discontent.
   c. It would encourage shirking after the executives reached the cap.
   d. The cap could be set too high, so executives may work too hard and not reach it.
9. What might happen if a car dealership is awarded a bonus by the manufacturer for selling a certain number of its cars monthly, but the dealership is just short of that quota near the end of the month?
   a. It may sell the remaining cars at huge discounts to hit the quota.
   b. It creates an incentive to sell cars from different manufacturers.
   c. It would ruin the relationship between the dealer and the manufacturer.
   d. Potential buyers will lose buying power at the dealer.
10. Why might a supermarket advertise low prices on certain high-profile items and sell them at a loss?
    a. It is a way for companies to be charitable.
    b. The store will sell other groceries to the same customers, often at a markup.
    c. It would not.
    d. This reduces the incentives of trade.

Individual Problems

1-1 Goal Alignment at a Small Manufacturing Concern

The owners of a small manufacturing concern have hired a vice president to run the company with the expectation that he will buy the company after five years. Compensation of the new vice president is a flat salary plus 75% of the first $150,000 profit, and then 10% of profit over $150,000. Purchase price for the company is set at 4.5 times earnings (profit), computed as average annual profitability over the next five years.

a. Plot the annual compensation of the vice president as a function of annual profit.
b. Assume the company will be worth $10 million in five years. Plot the profit of buying the company as a function of annual profit.

1-2 Goal Alignment at a Small Manufacturing Concern (cont.)

Does this contract align the incentives of the new vice president with the profitability goals of the owners?

1-3 Goal Alignment at a Small Manufacturing Concern (cont.)

Redesign the contract to better align the incentives of the new vice president with the profitability goals of the owners.

1-4 Goal Alignment at New York City Schools

A total of 1,800 New York City teachers who lost their jobs earlier this year have yet to apply for another job despite the fact that there are 1,200 openings. Why not?

1-5 Goal Alignment between Airlines and Flight Crews

Planes frequently push back from the gate on time, but then wait 2 feet away from the gate until it is time to queue up for take-off. This increases fuel consumption, and increases the time that passengers must sit in a cramped plane awaiting take-off. Why does this happen?

1-6 Goal Alignment between Hospitals and the British Government

In 2008, the Labour Party in Britain promised that patients would have to wait for no more than four hours to be seen in an emergency room. The National Health Service started rewarding hospitals that met this goal. What do you think happened? (*HINT*: It was not good.)

Group Problems

G1-1 Goal Alignment with Your Company

Are your incentives aligned with the goals of your company? If not, identify a problem caused by goal misalignment. Suggest a change that would address the problem. Compute the profit consequences of the change.

G1-2 Contracts at Your Company

Identify a contract between your company and a supplier or customer. Does it align the incentives of the parties? If not, suggest a change that would address the problem. Compute the profit consequences of the change.

END NOTES

1. Amitai Etzioni, "When It Comes to Ethics, B-Schools Get an F," *Washington Post*, August 4, 2002.
2. Ilan Brat, "Notre Dame Football Introduces Its Fans to Inflationary Spiral," *Wall Street Journal*, September 7, 2006.
3. We thank Bart Victor for his enumeration of these objections.

2 The One Lesson of Business

In the spring of 2011, Rick Ruzzamenti of Riverside, California, decided to donate his kidney to an organization set up to match donors and recipients. His selfless act set off a domino chain of 60 operations involving 17 hospitals in 11 different states.[1] Donors, unable to help their loved ones because of incompatible antibodies, donated kidneys to others who donated to others, and so on, until the chain ended six months later in Chicago.

The good news is that 30 people received new kidneys and escaped the living hell of dialysis. The bad news is that this complex barter system is the only legal way for Americans to get kidneys.[2] It is so inefficient that only 17,000 of the 90,000 people on waiting lists received kidneys last year.

To understand how complex and cumbersome this process is, imagine trying to use it to find a new apartment. Suppose you wanted to move from Detroit to Nashville. You would first try to find someone moving in the opposite direction, from Nashville to Detroit. Failing that, you might try to find a three-way trade: find someone moving from Nashville to Los Angeles, and another person moving from Los Angeles to Detroit. Then swap the first apartment for the second, the second for the third, and the third for the first. Finding a matched set of trades that have the desired moving times, locations, and types of apartments causes the same kinds of compatibility problems that trading kidneys does.

There are two common, but very different, reactions to this kind of inefficiency. Economists see it as a threat, and something to be eliminated, for example, by replacing this complex barter system with a simple market.

Businesspeople, on the other hand, see this kind of inefficiency as an opportunity to make money. In this case, a creative entrepreneur could borrow $100 million at 20% interest, buy a hospital ship, anchor it in international waters, set up a database to match donors to recipients, broker sales, and fly in experienced transplant teams. If she charges $200,000 and earns 10% on each transaction, the break-even quantity is just 1,000 transplants each year. This represents only 1% of the potential demand in the United States alone.

The goal of this chapter is to show you how to exploit inefficiency as an opportunity to make money. Students who've had some economics training will find that they have a slight head start, but learning how to turn inefficiency into opportunity requires as much creativity and imagination as analytic ability.

2.1 Capitalism and Wealth

To identify money-making opportunities, like those in the kidney market, we first have to understand how wealth is created and destroyed.

Wealth is created when assets move from lower- to higher-valued uses.

An individual's **value** for a good or a service is measured as the amount of money he or she is willing to pay for it.[3] To "value" a good means that you want it and can pay for it.[4]

If we adopt the linguistic convention that buyers are male and the sellers are female, we say that a buyer's "value" for an item is how much he will pay for it, his "top dollar." Likewise, a seller won't accept less than her value, "cost," or "bottom line."

The biggest advantage of capitalism is that it creates wealth by letting people follow their self-interest.[5] A buyer willingly buys if the price is below his value, and a seller sells for the same selfish reason. Both buyer and seller gain; otherwise, they would not transact.

Voluntary transactions create wealth.

Suppose that a buyer values a house at $240,000 and a seller at $200,000. If they can agree on a price—say, $210,000—they both gain. In this case, the seller sells at a price that is $10,000 higher than her bottom line and the buyer buys at a price that is $30,000 below his top dollar.

Formally, the difference between the agreed-on price and the seller's value is called **seller surplus**. Likewise, **buyer surplus** is the buyer's value minus the price. The total surplus or *gains from trade* created by the transaction is the sum of buyer and seller surplus ($40,000), the difference between the buyer's top dollar and the seller's bottom line.

To see how well you understand the wealth-creating process, try to identify the assets moving to higher-valued uses in the following examples:

- Factory owners purchase labor from workers, borrow capital from investors, and sell manufactured products to consumers. In essence, factory owners are intermediaries who move labor and capital from lower-valued to higher-valued uses, determined by consumers' willingness to pay for the labor and capital embodied in manufactured products.
- AIDS patients sometimes sell their life insurance policies to investors at a discount of 50% or more. The transaction allows patients to collect money from investors, who must wait until the patient dies to collect from the insurance company. This transaction moves money across time, from investors (who are willing to wait) to AIDS patients (who want the money now).

- Rover.com is an online service to match dog owners to dog walkers, pet sitters, and overnight boarders. Since its founding in 2011, Rover has become the largest marketplace for pet-sitting services, with over 65,000 registered sitters.
- When consumers purchase insurance, they pay an insurance company to assume risk for them. In this context, you can think of risk as a "bad," the opposite of a "good," moving from a consumer who wants to get rid of it to an insurance company willing to assume it for a fee.
- In video games like Diablo III or World of Warcraft, thousands of people in less-developed countries spend time playing the games to acquire "currency" that can be used to acquire add-ons. These "gold farmers" sell the currency to other players for cash on Web sites outside of the game environment.

Here's a final example that is not so obvious. In 2004, a private equity consortium purchased Mervyn's, a department store located in the western United States. It sold off the real estate on which the stores were located, and the new owners set store rents at market rates. As a consequence, rent payments doubled and the 59-year-old retailer went out of business, throwing 30,000 employees out of work.

PAUSE FOR A MOMENT AND TRY TO FIGURE WHY THIS TRANSACTION CREATED WEALTH.

The private equity group unbundled Mervyn's land-owning activity from its retail activity. Once Mervyn's stores had to pay market rents, it became clear that the retail activity was losing money because its costs were higher than the value it produced. The economy, as a whole, is better off without such money-losing ventures.

How do you create wealth? Which assets do you move to higher-valued uses?

We close this section with a warning against the idea that if one person makes money, someone else must be losing out. This mistake is so common that it even has a name, "the **zero-sum fallacy.**" Policy makers often invoke the fallacy to justify limits on profitability, or prices, or trade. It is a fallacy because the voluntary nature of trade requires that both parties gain; otherwise, the transaction would not occur.

2.2 Does the Government Create Wealth?

Governments play a critical role in the wealth-creating process by enforcing property rights and contracts—legal mechanisms that facilitate voluntary transactions.[6] By making sure that buyers and sellers can keep the gains from trade, our legal system makes trade more likely, which contributes to America's enormous wealth-creating ability.[7]

Conversely, the absence of property rights contributes to poverty. The reasons are simple: without private property and contract enforcement, wealth-creating transactions are less likely to occur.[8] Ironically, many poor countries survive largely on the wealth created in the so-called underground, or black-market economy, where transactions are hidden from the government.

Secure property rights are also associated with measures of environmental quality and human well-being. In nations where property rights are well protected, more people have access to safe drinking water and sewage treatment and they live about 20 years longer.[9] If you give people ownership to their property, they have an incentive to take care of it, invest in it, and keep it clean.

2.3 How Economics Is Useful to Business

Economics can be used by business people to spot money-making opportunities (assets in lower-valued uses). To see this, we begin with "efficiency," one of the most useful ideas in economics.

*An economy is **efficient** if all assets are employed in their highest-valued uses.*

Economists are obsessed with efficiency. They search for assets in lower-valued uses and then suggest public policies to move them to higher-valued ones. A good policy facilitates the movement of assets to higher-valued uses; and a bad policy prevents assets from moving or, worse, moves assets to lower-valued uses.

Determining whether a policy is good or bad requires analyzing all of its effects—the unintended as well as the intended effects. Using this idea, Henry Hazlitt reduced all of economics into a single lesson:[10]

The one lesson of economics: The art of economics consists in looking not merely at the immediate but at the longer effects of any act or policy; it consists of tracing the consequences of that policy not merely for one group but for all groups.[11]

For example, recent proposals to prevent lenders from foreclosing on houses helps the delinquent homeowners, but it also hurts lenders. If lenders cannot foreclose on bad loans, this raises the cost of making loans, which, in turn, hurts prospective home buyers.

Determining whether the policy is good or bad requires that we look not only at the happy faces of the family that gets to stay in a foreclosed home, but also at the sad faces of the family that can no longer afford to buy a house because the cost of borrowing has gone up. The trick to "seeing" these indirect effects is to look at incentives. In this chapter, we apply the rational actor paradigm to the problem of finding money making opportunities.

Making money is simple in principle—find an asset employed in lower-valued use, buy it, and sell it to someone who places a higher value on it.

The one lesson of business: the art of business consists of identifying assets in low-valued uses and devising ways to profitably move them to higher-valued ones.

In other words, each underemployed asset represents a potential wealth-creating transaction. The art of business is to identify these transactions and find ways to profitably consummate them.

For example, once the government banned kidney sales, it simultaneously created an incentive to try to circumvent the ban. Buying a hospital ship and sailing to international waters is just one solution. According to recent research, there is a thriving illegal or "black market" for kidneys in the United States. For about $150,000, organ brokers will connect wealthy buyers with poor foreign donors, who receive a few thousand dollars and the chance to visit an American city. Once there, transplants are performed at "broker-friendly" hospitals with surgeons who are either complicit in the scheme or willing to turn a blind eye. Kidney brokers often hire clergy to accompany their clients into the hospital to ensure that the process goes smoothly.[12]

Anything that impedes asset movement destroys potential wealth. We discuss three such impediments: taxes, subsidies, and price controls. These regulations create inefficiency which also means opportunity.

Taxes

The government collects taxes out of the total surplus created by a transaction. If the tax is larger than the surplus, the transaction will not take place. In our housing example, if a sales tax is 25%, for instance, as in Italy, the tax will be at least $50,000 because the price has to be at least $200,000, the seller's bottom line. Since the tax is more than the surplus created by the transaction, the buyer and seller cannot find a mutually agreeable price that lets them pay the tax.[13]

The *one lesson of economics* tells us that the intended effect of a tax is to raise revenue for the government, but the unintended consequence of a tax is that it deters some wealth-creating transactions.

The *one lesson of business* tells us that these unconsummated transactions represent money-making opportunities. For example, in 1983, Sweden imposed a 1% "turnover" (sales) tax on stock sales on the Swedish Stock Exchange. Before the tax, large institutional investors paid commissions that averaged 25 basis points (0.25%). The turnover tax, by itself, was four times the size of the old trading costs, and it fell most heavily on these big institutional investors.

After the tax was imposed, institutional traders began trading shares on the London and New York Stock Exchanges, and the number of transactions on the Swedish Stock Exchange fell by 40%. Smart brokers recognized this opportunity and profited by moving their trades to London and New York. The Swedish government finally removed the turnover tax in 1990, but the Swedish Stock Exchange has never regained its former vitality.

Subsidies

The opposite of a tax is a subsidy. By encouraging low-value consumers to buy or high-value sellers to sell, subsidies destroy wealth by moving assets from higher- to lower-valued uses—in exactly the wrong direction.

For example, government policies designed to extend credit to low-income Americans increased homeownership from 64% to 69% of the population. Many of these recipients, like Victor Ramirez, were able to afford houses only due to the subsidies. Mr. Ramirez says. "I was a student making $17,000 a year, my wife was between jobs. In retrospect, how in hell did we qualify?"[14]

He qualified due to government subsidies. We know that these subsidies destroy wealth because, without them, the money would have been spent differently. A simple test will tell us whether the subsidy is inefficient: offer each potential homeowner a payment equal to the amount of the subsidy. If they would rather spend the money on something other than a home, then there is a higher-valued use for the money.

The same logic can be used to identify ways to profit from inefficiency. To see this, let's look at health insurance that fully subsidizes visits to the doctor. If you get a cold, you go to the doctor, who charges the insurance company $200 for your care. This subsidy destroys wealth if you would rather self-medicate and keep the $200.

Employers who recognize this are starting to offer insurance that requires a large deductible or copayment. These fees stop low-value doctor visits and dramatically reduce the cost of insurance. Employers can either keep the money or use it to raise workers' wages (by the amount they save on insurance) to attract better workers. These high-deductible policies are becoming more popular with companies like Whole Foods Market that have recognized the inefficiency.

Price Controls

A **price control** is a regulation that allows trade only at certain prices.

There are two types of price controls: **price ceilings,** which outlaw trade at prices above the ceiling, and **price floors,** which outlaw trade at prices below the floor. The prohibition on buying and selling kidneys is a form of price ceiling. Americans are allowed to buy and sell kidneys—but only at a price of zero.

Price floors above the buyer's top dollar or price ceilings below a seller's bottom line deter wealth-creating transactions.[15] In our kidney example, potential kidney sellers are deterred from selling because they can do so only at a price of zero.

To see how to profit from this kind of inefficiency, we turn to the case of taxis, which are regulated with a fixed price. This functions like a price ceiling when you need to get you to the outer reaches of your metropolitan area because the fixed fares won't let taxis recover the cost of return trip. In addition, taxis are often poorly maintained because regulated fares don't allow taxis to charge for better quality. Finally, taxis have a well-deserved reputation for recklessness because there is no way for taxis to increase earnings except by increasing volume, which they do by driving from place to place as fast as possible.

Uber is an alternative to taxis that makes money, in part, by exploiting these regulatory inefficiencies. Flexible pricing and consumer ratings give Uber drivers an incentive to go to distant destinations, to clean their cars, and to drive safely.[16]

Beyond avoiding the inefficiency created by taxi regulation, Uber's success is also due to: (i) a more efficient driver–passenger matching technology; (ii) larger scale, which supports faster matches; and (iii) surge pricing, which allows it to more closely match supply with demand throughout the day. The surge pricing can be thought of as a way around inefficiency of fixed fares mandated by regulation.[17]

2.4 Wealth Creation in Organizations

Companies can be thought of as collections of transactions, from buying raw materials like capital and labor to selling finished goods and services. In a successful company, these transactions move assets to higher-valued uses and thus make money for the company.

As we saw from the story of the oil company in the introductory chapter, a firm's organizational design influences decision making within the firm. Some designs encourage profitable decision making; others do not. A poorly designed company will consummate unprofitable transactions or fail to consummate profitable ones.

The reasons for this are analogous to the wealth-destroying effects of government policies: organizations impose "taxes," "subsidies," and "price controls" within their companies that either deter profitable transactions or encourage unprofitable ones. For example, overbidding at the oil company was caused by a "subsidy" paid to management for acquiring oil reserves. Senior management responded to the subsidy by acquiring reserves, regardless of the price. One solution to the problem was to eliminate the subsidy.

The analogy between the market-level problems created by taxes, subsidies, and price controls and the organization-level problems of goal alignment suggests is that we are using the same economic tools to analyze both types of problems. The target of the analysis changes—from markets to organizations—but the principles are the same.

SUMMARY & HOMEWORK PROBLEMS

Summary of Main Points

- Voluntary transactions create wealth by moving assets from lower- to higher-valued uses.
- Anything that impedes the movement of assets to higher-valued uses, like taxes, subsidies, or price controls, destroys wealth.
- Efficiency means that each asset is employed in its highest-valued use. Each inefficiency implies a money-making opportunity.
- The art of business consists of finding an asset in lower-valued use and devising ways to profitably move it to higher-valued one.

- A company can be thought of as a series of transactions. A well-designed organization rewards employees who identify and consummate profitable transactions or who stop unprofitable ones.

Multiple-Choice Questions

1. An individual's value for a good or service is
   a. the amount of money he or she used to pay for a good.
   b. the amount of money he or she is willing to pay for it.
   c. the amount of money he or she has to spend on goods.
   d. None of the above.

2. The biggest advantage of capitalism is that
    a. it allows the market to self-regulate.
    b. it allows a person to follow his self-interest.
    c. it allows voluntary transactions, which create wealth.
    d. All of the above.
3. Wealth-creating transactions are more likely to occur
    a. with private property rights.
    b. with strong contract enforcement.
    c. with black markets.
    d. All of the above.
4. Which of these actions creates value?
    a. Buying a struggling firm and selling off its assets for more than the purchase price
    b. A baseball slugger drawing paying fans into the ballpark
    c. A student increasing his decision-making ability with an MBA
    d. All of the above
5. Which of the following are examples of a price floor?
    a. Minimum wages
    b. Rent controls in New York
    c. Both a and b
    d. None of the above
6. A price ceiling
    a. is a government-set maximum price.
    b. is an implicit tax on producers and an implicit subsidy to consumers.
    c. will create a surplus.
    d. causes an increase in consumer and producer surplus.
7. Taxes
    a. impede the movement of assets to higher-valued uses.
    b. reduce incentives to work.
    c. decrease the number of wealth-creating transactions.
    d. All of the above.
8. A consumer values a car at $20,000 and it costs a producer $15,000 to make the same car. If the transaction is completed at $18,000, the transaction will generate

    a. no surplus.
    b. $5,000 worth of seller surplus and unknown amount of buyer surplus.
    c. $2,000 worth of buyer surplus and $3,000 of seller surplus.
    d. $3,000 worth of buyer surplus and unknown amount of seller surplus.
9. A consumer values a car at $525,000 and a seller values the same car at $485,000. If sales tax is 8% and is levied on the seller, then the seller's bottom-line price is (rounded to the nearest thousand)
    a. $527,000.
    b. $524,000.
    c. $525,000.
    d. $500,000.
10. Voluntary transactions
    a. always produce gains for both parties.
    b. produce gains for at least one party.
    c. always increase wealth for everyone.
    d. are inefficient.

Individual Problems

2-1 Airline Delays

How will commercial airlines respond to the threat of new $27,500 fines for keeping passengers on the tarmac for more than three hours? What inefficiency will this create?

2-2 Selling Used Cars

I recently sold my used car. If no new production occurred for this transaction, how could it have created value?

2-3 Flood Insurance

The U.S. government subsidizes flood insurance because those who want to buy it live in the flood plain and cannot get it at reasonable rates. What inefficiency does this subsidy create?

2-4 France's Labor Unions Force Early Closing Times

In 2013, France's labor unions won a case against Sephora to prevent the retailer from staying open late and forcing its workers to work "antisocial hours." The cosmetics store does about 20% of its business after 9 P.M., and the 50 sales staff who work the late shift are paid an hourly rate that is 25% higher than the day shift. Many of them were students or part-time workers, who were put out of work by these new laws. Identify the inefficiency, and figure out a way to profit from it.

2-5 Kraft and Cadbury

When Kraft recently bid $16.7 billion for Cadbury, Cadbury's market value rose, but Kraft's market value fell by more. What does this tell you about the value-creating potential of the deal?

2-6 Price of Breast Reconstruction versus Breast Augmentation

Two similar surgeries, breast reconstruction and breast augmentation, have different prices. Breast augmentation is cosmetic surgery not covered by health insurance. Patients who want the surgery must pay for it themselves. Breast reconstruction following breast removal due to cancer is covered by insurance. The price for one of the surgeries has increased by about 10% each year since 1995, whereas the other has increased by only 2% per year. Which of the surgeries has the lower inflation rate? Why?

Group Problems

G2-1 One Lesson of Business

Identify an unconsummated wealth-creating transaction (or a wealth-destroying one) created by some tax, subsidy, price control, or other government policy, and then figure out how to profitably consummate it (or deter it). Estimate how much profit you would earn by consummating (or deterring) it.

G2-2 One Lesson of Business (within an Organization)

Identify an unconsummated wealth-creating transaction (or a wealth-destroying one) within your organization, and figure out how to profitably consummate it (or deter it). Estimate how much profit you would earn by consummating it (or deterring) it.

END NOTES

1. See Kevin Sack, "60 Lives, 30 Kidneys, All Linked," *New York Times*, February 18, 2012.
2. See Sally Satel and Mark J. Perry, "More Kidney Donors Are Needed to Meet a Rising Demand," *Washington Post*, March 7, 2010.
3. An individual's **value** for a good or service is measured as the amount of money he or she is willing to pay for it. It is the ability-to-pay component of value that is behind most critiques of capitalism. Unless you have enough money to purchase an item, you do not value it.

   But other theories of value have even bigger problems. For example, under Communism, a labor theory of value is used. Value depends on how much labor produced it. This definition (the amount of labor embodied in the good), if used to guide decisions, could lead to situations where goods are produced that nobody wants. The defining tenet of Communism is "from each according to his ability; to each according to his need." Communism is bad at creating wealth because it allocates goods according to "needs," not "wants," and because it's tough to gauge how much people need goods. Individuals have great incentive to claim they are "needier" than they really are. In the political arena, groups compete for government funds by claiming they are the "neediest." Economists dislike the word *need* because it is so often used to manipulate others into giving away something. Listen to news reports about proposed government spending cuts. Most often those affected claim they "need" the programs targeted for elimination. That sounds better than saying they "want" the programs. The definitions of value differ because Communism and Socialism are more concerned with the distribution of wealth than with the creation of wealth, which is capitalism's greatest concern. In other words, capitalism is concerned with making the proverbial "pie" as large as possible, while Socialism and Communism are concerned more about how to slice up that pie.

4. This is the idea behind the French phrase laissez-faire (leave them alone).

5. "The only proper functions of a government are: the police, to protect you from criminals; the army, to protect you from foreign invaders; and the courts, to protect your property and contracts from breach or fraud by others, to settle disputes by rational rules, according to objective law." Ayn Rand, *Atlas Shrugged* (New York: Random House, 1957), 977.

6. Tom Bethell, *The Noblest Triumph: Property and Prosperity through the Ages* (New York: St. Martin's Press, 1995).

7. "The inherent vice of capitalism is the unequal sharing of blessings; the inherent virtue of socialism is the equal sharing of miseries" (Winston Churchill).

8. Seth Norton, "Property Rights, the Environment, and Economic Well-Being," in *Who Owns the Environment?* ed. Peter J. Hill and Roger E. Meiners (Lanham, MD: Rowman and Littlefield, 1998).

9. Henry Hazlitt, *Economics in One Lesson* (New York: Crown, 1979).

10. For chilling examples of the unintended consequences of government policy, read Jagdish Bhagwati's book, *In Defense of Globalization* (New York: Oxford University Press, 2004). In 1993, for example, the U.S. Congress seemed likely to pass Senator Tom Harkin's Child Labor Deterrence Act, which would have banned imports of textiles made by child workers. Anticipating its passage, the Bangladeshi textile industry dismissed 50,000 children from factories. Many of these children ended up as prostitutes. Ironically, the bill, which was designed to help children, had the opposite effect.

11. Jeneen Interlandi, "Not Just Urban Legend," *Newsweek*, January, 19, 2009.

12. With a 25% tax, the seller receives 75% of the sales price. If the tax is levied on the seller, her bottom-line price increases to $266,667 = $200,000 / (0.75), which is above the buyer's top dollar of $240,000. If the tax is levied on the buyer, his top dollar decreases to $192,000, which is below the seller's bottom line.

13. David Streitfeld and Gretchen Morgenson, "Building Flawed American Dreams," *New York Times*, October 18, 2008.

14. Price floors below a seller's bottom-line and price ceilings above a buyer's top dollar have no effect.

15. Megan Mcardle, "Why You Can't Get a Taxi," *The Atlantic*, May 2012.

16. Judd Cramer and Alan B. Krueger, "Disruptive Change in the Taxi Business: The Case of Uber," *American Economic Review* 106, no. 5 (2016): 177–182.

3 Benefits, Costs, and Decisions

Big Coal Power Company burns two types of coal from the Southern Powder River Basin in Wyoming: high-energy 8,800 coal and low-energy 8,400 coal. The numbers refer to the amount of energy contained in one pound of coal, for example, 8,400 Btu/lb. Power plants crush the coal, and then burn it to produce electricity.

The 8,400 coal generates about 5% less electricity per ton than 8,800 coal, so when the price of 8,400 fell 20% below the price of 8,800 coal, the plant manager did the obvious thing and switched to the lower-price coal. Not only did this reduce the average cost of electricity but it also increased the manager's compensation because his performance evaluation was based on the average cost of electricity (cost/Btu). Unfortunately, however, the move also reduced company profit.

Because the conveyor belts and crushers were already at capacity, the manager was unable to increase the tonnage going through the plant. Electricity output fell by 5%, the difference between the amount of electricity produced by the two different coals, and the parent company had to replace the lost electricity with higher-cost natural gas. Company profit fell by $5 million, computed as the cost of replacing the lost electricity with natural gas, minus the savings from using lower-price 8,400 coal.

Even though mistakes like this seem obvious in retrospect, spotting them before they occur can be very difficult. The goal of this chapter is to show you how to use benefit-cost analysis not only to spot mistakes but also to identify profitable decisions that should have been made instead.

3.1 Background: Variable, Fixed, and Total Costs

Knowing how costs vary with output allows you to compute the costs associated with the consequence of a decision that changes output.

*Variable costs vary with output, but **fixed costs** do not.*

To illustrate, suppose that you are the manager of a new candy factory. To produce candy, you build a factory, purchase ingredients, and hire employees. Suppose your factory's capital costs are $1 million/year (e.g., a $10 million factory and a 10% cost of capital), employees can be hired for $50,000 each and ingredients cost $0.50/candy bar. If you decide to produce 1,000 candy bars in a year, you need to hire 10 employees, but if you decide to produce 2,000 bars, you need 20 employees. For 1,000 bars, your production costs would be $1,500,500—$1 million for the factory, $500,000 in employee costs, and $500 in ingredient costs. For 2,000 bars, your production costs would be $2,001,000—$1 million for the factory, $1 million in employee costs, and $1,000 in ingredient costs (a total of 1,001,000 in variable costs).

Notice that labor costs and ingredient costs vary with output, but factory capital costs are $1 million regardless of how much you produce. We say that labor costs and ingredient costs are variable, while the capital cost is **fixed**. The distinction is important for decisions on how much to produce and sell.

To illustrate the relationships among these costs, we plot them against output in Figure 3.2. For output levels of zero, both fixed and total costs are greater than zero. Total and variable costs both increase with output, and variable costs appear as the difference between the total cost curve and the fixed cost line.[1]

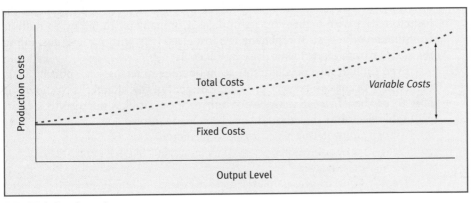

FIGURE **3.2** **Cost Curves**

3.2 Background: Accounting versus Economic Profit

We now leave our fictitious candy manufacturer to talk about a real one. In 1990, Cadbury India offered its employees free housing in company-owned flats (apartments) to offset the high cost of living in Bombay (now Mumbai). In 1991, when Cadbury added low-interest housing loans to its benefits package, employees took advantage of this incentive and purchased their own homes, leaving the company flats empty. The empty flats remained on the company's balance sheet for the next six years.

In 1997, Cadbury adopted Economic Value Added (EVA®), a financial performance metric trademarked by Stern Stewart & Co. The main difference between ordinary **accounting profit** and EVA® is that EVA® includes a capital charge of 15%, representing the return that Cadbury could have made if it had invested the capital tied up in the apartments.

By charging each division within a firm for the amount of capital it uses, EVA® gives division managers an incentive to incur capital expenditures only if they earn more than they cost, for example, by giving division managers an incentive to reduce capital expenditures if they earn less than 15%.

After adopting EVA®, Cadbury India's annual EVA® dropped by £600,000 (15% cost of capital times the £4,000,000 capital tied up in the apartments).[2] In response, senior managers decided to sell the unused apartments as they were earning less than the company's cost of capital.

If the Cadbury managers had a good sense of their factories' variable, fixed, and total costs, why were they holding on to the company-owned flats?

To answer this question, we recognize another important distinction: the difference between accounting costs and what economists call "economic costs." The difference is especially important to big decisions about whether to buy or sell assets. For these decisions, you have to figure out what else you could do with the money if you decide to sell an asset. We measure the cost of using capital on any project by the returns we could get from investing it elsewhere, which accounting costs do not do.

Table 3.1 presents a recent annual income statement for Cadbury.[3] The firm sold over £6 billion in goods for the year, and after subtracting various expenses, it ended up with a profit of £431 million, which represents a return of approximately 6.4% on sales. Expense categories include items such as the following:

- Costs paid to its suppliers for product ingredients
- General operating expenses, such as salaries to factory managers and marketing expenses
- Depreciation expenses related to investments in buildings and equipment
- Interest payments on borrowed funds

TABLE **3.1**

Cadbury Income Statement (amounts in millions of pounds)

Net Sales	£6,738	
Cost of Sales	£3,020	
Gross Profit		£3,718
Operating Expenses		
Selling, General, and Administrative Expenses	£2,654	
Depreciation and Amortization	£215	
Total Operating Expenses		£2,869
Operating Income		£849
Other Income (Expense)		
Net Interest	£(226)	
Other Income	£(3)	
Total Other Income (Expense)		£(229)
Earnings before Provision for Income Taxes		£620
Provision for Income Taxes		£(189)
Net Earnings		£431

These types of expenses are the **accounting costs** of the business.

Economists, however, are interested in all the **relevant costs** of decisions, including the **implicit costs** that do not show up in the accounting statements. For an example of an implicit cost, look at the income statement again. Notice that it lists payments to one class of capital providers of the company (debt holders). **Interest** is the cost that creditors charge for the use of their capital. But creditors are not the only providers of capital. Stockholders provide equity, just as bondholders provide debt. Yet the income statement reflects no charge for equity even though this is an important consideration for investment decisions.

Suppose that Cadbury receives £4 billion in equity financing. If these equity holders expect an annual return of 12% on their money (£480 million), we would subtract this amount from the £431 million in net earnings to get a better idea of the *economic profit* of the business, −£49 million. Negative economic profit means that the firm is earning less than shareholders expect.

Had Cadbury shareholders expected only a 10.77% rate of return, the economic return would have been close to zero, and investors would have been satisfied. However, given that they expected a 12% return, they "lost" money in this investment, relative to what they could have earned elsewhere.

In practical terms, a firm may show an accounting profit while experiencing an economic loss. The two amounts are not the same because economic profit recognizes both explicit and implicit costs of capital. A failure to consider these *hidden* or *implicit* costs is why the Cadbury India managers continued to hold on to flats. By adopting EVA®, the firm made visible the *hidden cost of equity*, and the mangers sold the abandoned flats.

In general, managers should consider all the benefits and costs of a decision. To show you how to do this, we introduce what economists call "opportunity costs."

3.3 Costs Are What You Give Up

When deciding between two alternatives, you obviously want to choose the one that returns the highest profit. Accordingly, we define the "opportunity cost" of one alternative as the forgone opportunity to earn profit from the other.

With this definition, costs imply decision-making rules, and vice versa. If the benefit of the first alternative is larger than its cost—the profit of the second alternative—then choose the first. Otherwise, choose the second. This link is made explicit in Figure 3.3, showing a decision where the profit of A is greater than the cost of A (the profit of B).

The opportunity cost of an alternative is what you give up to pursue it.

Henceforth, when we use the term *cost*, we are referring to *opportunity cost*. Because costs depend on what you give up, and this depends on

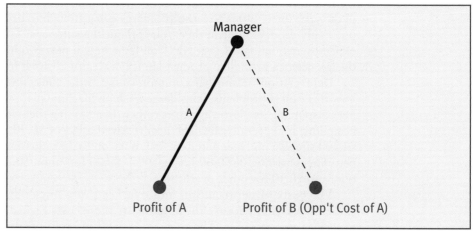

FIGURE **3.3 Opportunity Cost**

the decision that you are trying to make, costs and decisions are inherently linked.

To illustrate the link, consider the company's decision to hold onto the company-owned flats and earn, say, 2%. The *opportunity cost* of the decision is the forgone *opportunity* to invest capital in the company's other operations and earn a >12% return.

3.4 Sunk-Cost Fallacy

The general rule for making decisions is simple.

> *Consider all costs and benefits that vary with the consequence of a decision (If you miss some, that is the **hidden-cost fallacy**.)*

> *But consider only costs and benefits that vary with the consequence of the decision. (If you take account of irrelevant costs or benefits, that is the **sunk- or fixed-cost fallacy**.)*

> *These are the **relevant costs and benefits** of a decision.*

In this section and the next, we examine these two mistakes in more detail.

One of the most frequent causes of the sunk-cost fallacy is the "overhead" allocated to various activities within a company. Because overhead does not vary with most business decisions, it should not influence them. Look back at the income statement in Table 3.1. Overhead costs appear in the line item of Selling, General, and Administrative Expenses. An example of such an overhead expense would be costs associated with the corporate headquarters staff or with the sales force. These costs are considered fixed because output can be increased without the need to increase the corporate staff, like the CFO or CEO.

For example, suppose that you are in charge of a new products division and are considering launching a product that you will be able to distribute through your existing sales force, without incurring extra expenses. However, if you launch the new product, your division will be forced to pay for a portion of the sales force. If this "overhead" charge is big enough to deter an otherwise profitable product launch, then you commit the sunk-cost fallacy. Overhead expenses are analogous to a "tax" on launching a new product. In this case, the tax deters a profitable product launch, a wealth-creating transaction.

Depreciation[4] is another common cause of the sunk-cost fallacy. To see how this causes problems, consider a washing machine plant that is considering outsourcing its plastic agitators rather than making them internally as had been done for several years. The firm received a bid of $0.70 per unit from a trusted supplier and compared the bid to its internal production costs of $1.00 per unit, consisting of $0.60 for material, $0.20 for labor, $0.10 for depreciation, and $0.10 for other overhead.

The costs of depreciation and overhead[5] are not relevant to an outsourcing decision because the firm incurs these costs regardless of whether it decides to outsource. The relevant cost of internal production is $0.80, and the relevant cost of outsourcing is $0.70. Multiply the cost difference by one million agitators/year, and the firms would save $100,000 if it outsourced the part.

In this case, identifying the right decision was easier than implementing it. Six years earlier, the plant had incurred $1 million worth of tooling costs to make molds for the agitators. Following accounting principles, the cost of the tooling was recorded as an "asset" on the plant's balance sheet. Each year, the accountants charged the plant $100,000/year for using this asset, which was expected to last for 10 years. After the first year, the value of the asset had shrunk to $900,000; after the second, $800,000; and so on. This is called "straight-line depreciation."

Six years after incurring the tooling expense, there was still $400,000 worth of undepreciated capital left on the company's balance sheet. Accountants told the manager that if he decided to outsource the agitator, these "assets" would become "worthless," and the manager would be forced to take a charge[6] against his division's profitability. The $400,000 charge would prevent him from reaching his performance goal, and he would have to forgo his bonus. Since the accounting profit was $400,000 lower with outsourcing, the manager decided not to outsource even though outsourcing would have increased company profitability.

The company's incentive compensation scheme that rewarded managers for increasing accounting profit gave the plant manager an incentive to commit the sunk-cost fallacy. This leads to an important lesson:

> *Accounting profit* does not necessarily correspond to economic profit.

In other words, the accounting costs do not necessarily correspond to the relevant costs of a decision. In this case, rewarding employees for increasing *accounting profit* led to a decision (not outsourcing) that reduced *economic profit*.

If you remember the discussion in Chapter 1, a question should immediately occur to you: "How can the company better align the incentives of the plant manager with the profitability goals of the parent company?"

The right answer involves a trade-off: if we allow the plant manager to ignore the sunk-tooling costs, he will make the right outsourcing decision. However, in the future, such a policy tells the manager that he can make sunk-cost investments without worrying about whether they will turn out to be profitable.

On the other hand, if we punish the plant manager for making the bad investment (which is what the accounting performance metric does), then we create incentives for him to forgo profitable outsourcing, that is, to commit the sunk-cost fallacy.

We see a similar tradeoff in the pharmaceutical industry, where drug development programs are very difficult to stop once they get started, and in software development, where companies continue to develop software in-house, even after cheaper and better alternatives become available on the market. In these industries, the employee who can most easily recognize the mistake is often the one who originally made it. Fixing these problems is difficult because the employee with the best information about when to stop development often lacks the incentive to do so.

3.5 Hidden-Cost Fallacy

The second mistake you can make is to ignore hidden costs.

> The *hidden-cost fallacy* occurs when you ignore relevant costs, those costs that do vary with the consequences of your decision.

As a simple example of this, consider a football game. You buy a ticket for $20, but at game time, scalpers are selling tickets for $50 because your team is playing its cross-state rival who has legions of fans willing to pay over $50 to go to the game. Even though you do not value the tickets at $50 (indeed—you value them for much less), you go anyway because you think "These tickets cost me only $20."

By going to the game, you give up the opportunity to scalp the tickets and earn $50, so the opportunity cost of going to the game is $50. Unless you place a value on going to the game that is as at least $50, then yours is not the highest-valued use for the ticket. In this case, you are sitting on an unconsummated wealth-creating transaction. Instead, scalp the tickets and stay home!

The example in the introduction also illustrates the hidden-cost fallacy. There, the plant manager did not consider the hidden cost of replacing the lost electricity from the decision to switch to the lower-priced, but also lower-energy coal.

In fact, the subprime mortgage crisis of 2008 can be traced to a failure to recognize the hidden costs of loans made by dubious lenders, like Long Beach Financial, owned by Washington Mutual (now bankrupt).

> Long Beach Financial was moving money out the door as fast as it could, few questions asked, in loans built to self-destruct. It specialized in asking homeowners with bad credit and no proof of income to put no money down and defer interest payments for as long as possible. In Bakersfield, California, a strawberry picker with an income of $14,000 and no English was lent every penny he needed to buy a house for $720,000.[7]

The credit-rating agencies did not recognize the hidden cost of these very risky loans. As a consequence, Long Beach Financial was able to package and sell these risky loans to Wall Street investors, like Lehman Brothers, who went bankrupt when the loans eventually defaulted.

3.6 A Final Warning

The mistakes in this chapter may seem obvious, but they were all made by sophisticated and experienced managers in some of the best-run companies in the world. It is not much of a stretch to predict that you will make some of the same mistakes, and for the same reasons: either you will lack the information necessary to make a good decision or you won't have the incentive to do so.

When you find yourself struggling with a decision, remember two things: first, recognize the **relevant benefits and costs** of the decision. This is sometimes hard to do because it is easy to get lost in the data. Decision-makers are easily distracted by irrelevant numbers, and often forget why they are analyzing the numbers. They forget the most important lesson of this chapter, that costs are defined by the decisions you are trying to make. When this happens, take a step back and ask "What decision am I trying to make?"

If you begin with the costs, you will always get confused; but if you begin with the decision, you will never get confused.

Second, consider the consequences of the decision from your organization's point of view. Like the washing machine plant manager in this chapter, you may find yourself penalized for doing what's best for the organization. Given the number and types of decisions that managers have to make, it is impossible to design compensation schemes that perfectly align managers' incentives with the organization's goals for each decision. When this happens, and it almost certainly will, consider putting the company's interests ahead of your own. Good supervisors will recognize these sacrifices and try to find ways to reward you.

SUMMARY & HOMEWORK PROBLEMS

Summary of Main Points

- Costs are associated with decisions.
- The **opportunity cost** of an alternative is the profit you give up to pursue it.
- Consider *all costs* and benefits that vary with the consequences of a decision and *only* costs and benefits that vary with the consequences of a decision. These are the relevant costs and relevant benefits of a decision.
- Fixed costs do not vary with the amount of output. Variable costs change as output changes. Decisions that change output change only variable costs.
- Accounting profit does not necessarily correspond to economic profit.
- The fixed-cost fallacy or sunk-cost fallacy means that you consider irrelevant costs. A common fixed-cost fallacy is to let overhead or depreciation costs influence short-run decisions.
- The hidden-cost fallacy occurs when you ignore relevant costs. A common hidden-cost fallacy is to ignore the opportunity cost of capital when making investment or shutdown decisions.

- If you begin by looking at the costs, you will always get confused; if you begin with the decision you are considering, you will never get confused.

Multiple-Choice Questions

1. A business owner makes 1,000 items a day. Each day she contributes eight hours to produce those items. If hired, elsewhere she could have earned $250 an hour. The item sells for $15 each. Production does not stop during weekends. If the explicit costs total $150,000 for 30 days, the firm's accounting profit for the month equals
   a. $300,000.
   b. $60,000.
   c. $450,000.
   d. $240,000.
2. If a firm is earning negative economic profits, it implies
   a. that the firm's accounting profits are zero.
   b. that the firm's accounting profits are positive.
   c. that the firm's accounting profits are negative.
   d. that more information is needed to determine accounting profits.

3. Opportunity costs arise due to
   a. resource scarcity.
   b. lack of alternatives.
   c. limited wants.
   d. abundance of resources.
4. After graduating from college, Jim had three choices, listed in order of preference: (1) move to Florida from Philadelphia, (2) work in a car dealership in Philadelphia, or (3) play soccer for a minor league in Philadelphia. His opportunity cost of moving to Florida includes
   a. the benefits he could have received from playing soccer.
   b. the income he could have earned at the car dealership.
   c. both a and b.
   d. cannot be determined from the given information.
5. Economic Value Added helps firms avoid the hidden-cost fallacy
   a. by ignoring the opportunity costs of using capital.
   b. by differentiating between sunk and fixed costs.
   c. by taking all capital costs into account, including the cost of equity.
   d. none of the above.
6. The fixed-cost fallacy occurs when
   a. a firm considers irrelevant costs.
   b. a firm ignores relevant costs.
   c. a firm considers overhead or depreciation costs to make short-run decisions.
   d. both a and c.
7. Mr. D's Barbeque of Pickwick, TN, produces 10,000 dry-rubbed rib slabs per year. Annually Mr. D's fixed costs are $50,000. The average variable cost per slab is a constant $2. The average total cost per slab then is
   a. $7.
   b. $2.
   c. $5.
   d. impossible to determine.
8. All the following are examples of variable costs, except
   a. hourly labor costs.
   b. cost of raw materials.
   c. accounting fees.
   d. electricity cost.
9. The U.S. government bought 112,000 acres of land in southeastern Colorado in 1968 for $17,500,000. The cost of using this land today exclusively for the reintroduction of the black-tailed prairie dog
   a. is zero, because they already own the land.
   b. is zero, because the land represents a sunk cost.
   c. is equal to the market value of the land.
   d. is equal to the total dollar value the land would yield if used for farming and ranching.
10. When a firm ignores the opportunity cost of capital when making investment or shutdown decisions, this is a case of
    a. fixed-cost fallacy.
    b. sunk-cost fallacy.
    c. hidden-cost fallacy.
    d. none of the above.

Individual Problems

3-1 Concert Opportunity Cost

You won a free ticket to see a Bruce Springsteen concert (assume the ticket has no resale value). U2 has a concert the same night, and this represents your next-best alternative activity. Tickets to the U2 concert cost $80, and on any particular day, you would be willing to pay up to $100 to see this band. Assume that there are no additional costs of seeing either show. Based on the information presented here, what is the opportunity cost of seeing Bruce Springsteen?

3-2 Concert Opportunity Cost 2

You were able to purchase two tickets to an upcoming concert for $100 apiece when the concert was first announced three months ago. Recently, you saw that StubHub was listing similar seats for $225 apiece. What does it cost you to attend the concert?

3-3 Housing Bubble

Because of the housing bubble, many houses are now selling for much less than their selling price just two to three years ago. There is evidence that homeowners with virtually identical houses tend to ask for more if they paid more for the house. What fallacy are they making?

3-4 Opportunity Cost

The expression "3/10, net 45" means that the customers receive a 3% discount if they pay within 10 days; otherwise, they must pay in full within 45 days. What would the seller's cost of capital have to be in order for the discount to be cost justified? (*Hint:* Opportunity Cost)

3-5 Starbucks

Starbucks is hoping to make use of its excess restaurant capacity in the evenings by experimenting with selling beer and wine. It speculates that the only additional costs are hiring more of the same sort of workers to cover the additional hours and costs of the new line of beverages. What hidden costs might emerge?

3-6 Dropping University Courses

Students doing poorly in courses often consider dropping the courses. Many universities will offer a refund before a certain date. Should this affect a student's drop decision?

3-7 Business Costs

A business incurs the following costs per unit: labor $125/unit, materials $45/unit, and rent $250,000/month. If the firm produces 1,000,000 units a month. Calculate the following:
a. Total variable costs
b. Total fixed costs
c. Total costs

Group Problems

G3-1 Fixed-Cost Fallacy

Describe a decision made by your company that involved costs that should have been ignored. Why did your company make the decision? What should it have done? Compute the profit consequences of the change.

G3-2 Hidden-Cost Fallacy

Describe a decision that you or your company made that involved opportunity costs that should have been considered. Why did your company make the decision? What should it have done? Compute the profit consequences of the change.

G3-3 Hidden Cost of Capital

Does your company charge your division for the capital that it uses? If not, does this lead to bad decisions? What can be done to fix the problem? Compute the profit consequences of the change.

G3-4 Sunk Cost of Depreciation or Fixed Cost of Overhead

Does your company make decisions based on depreciation or overhead? If so, does this lead to bad decisions? What can be done to fix the problem? Compute the profit consequences of the change.

END NOTES

1. Note that the shape of the total cost curve is not a straight line as it would have been if we graphed the costs of the candy factory. The reason: per unit variable costs often drop with increasing output—a topic we will discuss in later chapters.
2. We do not know the actual size of the charges—they should be viewed as illustrative.
3. Adapted from the Cadbury Schweppes PLC 2004 Annual Report. Note that this income statement is for worldwide Cadbury operations, not just for the Bombay Division, and is presented for a general illustration of economic versus accounting costs.
4. *Depreciation* is an accounting methodology to allocate the costs of capital equipment to the years over the lifetime of the capital equipment.
5. Labor would not be considered a fixed cost unless the company would keep the workers on payroll regardless of whether the part was produced internally or externally.
6. Taking a "charge" against profitability means that accounting profit would be reduced by the amount of the charge—in this case, $400,000.
7. Michael Lewis and David Einhorn, "The End of the Financial World as We Know It," *New York Times*, January 3, 2009.

4 Extent (How Much) Decisions

In 2016, Georgetown Public Media was trying to decide how to allocate its $120,000 marketing budget across three radio stations.

89.3 WPGL News wanted the budget allocated by audience size. As it is larger than the other two stations, this would give it $60,000: (1) to host panels on topical issues to increase the diversity of its audience and (2) to advertise on buses to reach people where they are listening—in their cars. However, over the past three years, WPGL expenses have risen, and last year they were 40% above revenue.

91.9 WPGK, the independent station (blues, jazz, world music, and Americana), surveyed its listeners and found that they have a passion for live music. Consequently, WPGK wants $40,000: (1) to host a backstage tent at a local music festival where it can do livestream interviews with musicians and (2) to add dates to its successful Winter Wednesday concert series.

90.5 WPOL Classical has the smallest audience of the three, but wants $60,000 in order to collaborate with WPGK Radio on joint marketing events to attract a new and more diverse audience. A recent national study showed tremendous potential for growth because young nonwhite consumers said they love classical music, but had never heard of their local public radio station. In addition, a $10,000 marketing expenditure last year caused a 15% increase in membership.

QUESTION: Obviously, the sum of the three requests is bigger than the advertising budget ($60 + 40 + 60 > 120$). If you were in charge, how would you allocate the money?

ANSWER: First, you have to figure out what you are trying to accomplish. In the case of nonprofit organizations, there is usually a tension between maximizing profit and using the money to "do good." But in this case, there is no conflict because increasing audience size (doing good) also maximizes profit because 15% of new listeners will become members and donate $140 to the organization.

The second step is to figure out where a dollar of advertising will have the biggest impact. The poll results suggest if you could somehow inform young nonwhite listeners about the classical station, they would become listeners. In addition, the effects of WPOL marketing efforts last year suggest that increases in the advertising budget would increase audience size.

Finally, if we want to fully fund the classical station, should you reduce the news advertising budget? The fact that the news station is losing money is irrelevant. We are concerned only with increasing audience size, as each new listener has the same 15% probability of becoming a member. As is common in decisions like this, there is no good evidence on whether allocating less money to news station advertising would affect its audience size.

In this case, Georgetown Public Media decided to fully fund the requests of the alternative and classical stations, and gave only $20,000 to the news station. Based on this allocation, it expects 9,280 new listeners, who are expected to contribute $194,880 to the organization.

The purpose of this chapter is to show you how to make extent decisions like this one.

4.1 Fixed Costs Are Irrelevant to an Extent Decision

In 2005, Memorial Hospital's chief executive officer (CEO) conducted performance reviews of the hospital's departments. As part of this review process, the chief of obstetrics proposed increasing the number of babies being delivered by his department. The CEO examined the department's financial statements and found that the average cost (AC) of deliveries ($5000) was above average revenue ($4300). He asked what seemed like a reasonable question, "Why would we want to do more of something that is losing $700 every time we do it?"

As you should now recognize, the CEO is committing the *fixed-cost fallacy*. As we learned in Chapter 3, the **relevant costs and benefits** of this extent decision ("how many babies should the hospital deliver") are those that vary with the consequences of the decision.

Fixed costs are irrelevant to an extent decision.

If the CEO had started with a question like "Should we increase output from 500 to 501 deliveries?" he might have avoided the mistake. The answer depends only on the extra or *marginal cost* of another delivery, $3000. This is the relevant cost of an extent decision.

4.2 Marginal Analysis

To analyze extent decisions, we break down the decision into small steps and compute the costs and benefits of taking another step. If the benefits of taking another step are greater than the costs, then take another step. Otherwise, step backward.

We call this *marginal analysis*. To illustrate, we use it to answer the question, "Should I sell more?" where marginal analysis applies to both costs and revenues.

Marginal cost (MC) is the additional cost incurred by producing and selling one more unit.

Marginal revenue (MR) is the additional revenue gained from selling one more unit.

If the benefit of selling another unit (MR) is bigger than the MC, then sell another unit.

Sell more if MR > MC; sell less if MR < MC. If MR = MC, you are selling the right amount (maximizing profit).

Marginal analysis works for any extent decision, like whether to change the level of advertising, the quality of service, the size of your staff, or the number of parking spaces to lease. The same principle applies to each decision—do more if MR > MC, and do less if MR < MC.

Note that marginal analysis points you in the right direction, but it does not tell you how far to go. The reason for this is that MC typically rises, and MR falls, with additional steps. So after taking a step, you have to recompute MC and MR to see whether further steps are warranted.

To illustrate how to use marginal analysis, let's return to Georgetown Public Media's problem.

First, let's try to estimate the MR of adding another listener. From the information in the story, the MR of adding another listener can be computed as the probability of becoming a member times the revenue expected from each member, $15\% \times \$140 = \$21$. This is a crude estimate (some listeners may donate more), but it is the only information we have.

As is often the case, even if you have good information about MR or MC, information about the other is harder to come by. In this example, we have only a little bit of information about the MC of adding listeners, from the classical station, when last year's $10,000 increase in advertising led to a 15% increase in listeners. If this 15% represents 2,000 new listeners, then the MC of adding a classical station listener is $5/listener, computed as $10,000/2,000, sometimes called *customer acquisition cost*.

Because MR > MC or $21 > $5, marginal analysis tells you to increase classical advertising, but it doesn't tell you how far to go. Rather, you have to get there by taking steps. In this case, you might double last year's budget and measure the effect.

To see how to do this, look at the following excel spreadsheet (derived from fictitious data). In the first two rows, you can see that doubling the budget increases the number of listeners from 2,000 to 3,386 and the profit from $32,000 to $51,112. Profits are computed in the last column as $21 times the number of customers minus the cost of the advertising. Note also that the customer acquisition cost (the MC of adding a new listener) increases from $5 to $10. Keep increasing advertising, as long as the MC of adding a listener is less than $21.

Advertising	MR	MC	Listeners	Profit
$10,000	$21	$5.00	2000	$32,000
$20,000	$21	$10.00	3386	$51,112
$40,000	$21	$20.00	4773	$60,224
$42,000	$21	$21.00	4870	$60,274
$44,000	$21	$22.00	4963	$60,227

From the table, you can see that the optimal level of advertising is $42,000, where the MC of acquiring a customer ($21) is equal to the MR of acquiring a customer. If you advertise more than this, the number of listeners increases, but profit falls because MC is higher than MR. Note also that as the advertising level increases, its effectiveness drops. This is reflected in the increasing MC of acquiring another customer, which is typical of many extent decisions. You pick the low-hanging fruit first (where the MC is low), and then you move to the more costly, higher-hanging fruit (where the MC is higher).

Typically, MR falls, and MC rises, the more you do.

For another application, suppose you are trying to decide when to cut down a tract of trees. As you know by now, always begin your analysis with a question, "Should I harvest the trees now or wait a year?" Because this is an extent decision, break the decision into steps, where a step is a year. Suppose further that the trees are worth $100 today and are growing at an 8% rate. Next year, they will be worth $108.

If you harvest the trees today you would earn, say $100, from selling the timber. If your investments earn 5%, after a year, you would have $105. On the other hand, if you let the trees grow, and the trees are growing at an 8% rate, after a year you would have timber worth $108. Don't harvest.

In general, if the trees grow faster than your investments you earn more by letting them grow. As trees grow older, their growth rate will eventually fall below what you can make by investing your money. At this point, harvest the trees.

4.3 Deciding between Two Alternatives

Managers often have to decide between competing strategies to achieve the same end. To see how to use marginal analysis in this setting, let's return to the problem facing Georgetown Public Media. Imagine that the manager has $100,000 to split between the news and classical stations.

This question defines the relevant costs: the *opportunity cost* of spending *one more* dollar on advertising for the classical station is the forgone opportunity to spend *that* dollar on advertising for the news station. To increase profit, increase spending on whichever medium has a higher marginal impact and "pay" for the increase by reducing spending on the other. To do this, compute the marginal customer acquisition cost for both alternatives, and then shift spending toward the cheaper one. This will increase profit even if you don't know the benefit of acquiring a customer. All you need to know is whether shifting dollars increases the total number of customers.

In the following table, we vary the amount going to the classical station. In the first row, with only $10,000 going to classical advertising, we see that the MC of adding a listener is $5. In contrast, the MC of adding a news listener is $67.50. Since it is cheaper to add customers by advertising on the classical station, increase the budget to the classical station and pay for it by reducing spending on news. In the second row, after shifting $10,000 to classical advertising, we see that the total number of listeners (last column) increases. Keep shifting dollars from news to classical, until you find the advertising split that maximizes the number of listeners.

The optimal advertising split is $60,000 going to classical and $40,000 going to news. At this split, the MC of adding consumers is the same for each medium, and the audience size is maximized (8,240). Although shifting more than this increases the number of classical listeners, the increase is not enough to offset the decline in news listeners.

Classical			News			Total
Advertising	# Listeners	MC	Advertising	# Listeners	MC	# Listeners
$10,000	3,386	$5.00	$90,000	3,430	$67.50	6,816
$20,000	4,197	$10.00	$80,000	3,273	$60.00	7,470
$30,000	4,773	$15.00	$70,000	3,095	$52.50	7,867
$40,000	5,219	$20.00	$60,000	2,889	$45.00	8,108
$50,000	5,584	$25.00	$50,000	2,646	$37.50	8,229
$60,000	5,892	$30.00	$40,000	2,348	$30.00	8,240
$70,000	6,159	$35.00	$30,000	1,965	$22.50	8,124
$80,000	6,394	$40.00	$20,000	1,424	$15.00	7,819
$90,000	6,605	$45.00	$10,000	500	$7.50	7,105

Of course, it is very rare to have this kind of detailed information about a marginal change. Typically, you will have only the kind of information available to Georgetown Public Media. To gain more information about the effectiveness of your advertising, you might want to increase classical advertising and measure the gain in listeners. Then reduce news advertising, and measure the loss in listeners. By changing the advertising levels separately, you may be able measure the marginal effectiveness of advertising expenditures on each station.

With advertising, there may also be subtle measurement issues. For example, some psychological models of advertising suggest that for fewer than four exposures, advertising has no effect on decisions. The *marginal* effectiveness of that fourth exposure is thus very large, but the *average* effectiveness of the entire advertising budget would be much lower.

For another application of marginal analysis, let's figure out how to reduce costs at a Fortune 50 company that produces textile products at various manufacturing plants in Latin America. The plants operate as cost centers, meaning that plant managers are rewarded for reducing costs of production. To evaluate the performance of its plants, the firm measures production using standard absorbed hours (SAH). For each garment produced, the firm computes the time required to complete each step in the manufacturing process. Complex garments like overalls require more time and thus are assigned a higher SAH (15 minutes) than simple garments like T-shirts (2 minutes). The output of a factory is thus measured in SAH, and each factory is evaluated based on how much it costs to get one hour's worth of production in terms of cost per SAH.

Obviously, measuring output in this way allows managers to identify lower-cost factories. Suppose that a factory in the Yucatan, Mexico operates at $20/SAH, and a factory in the Dominican Republic operates at $30/SAH. As a manager, do you think you could save $10/SAH by shifting production from the Dominican Republic to the Yucatan?

Before answering this question, you might want to remember the big lesson of Chapter 3, that costs are defined by the decision you are trying to make. Here you are trying to decide whether to shift output from one factory to another. If the costs used to compute cost per SAH include overhead that cannot be avoided, then you won't save on overhead as you shift production— overhead is irrelevant for this extent decision. So, first you must adjust the cost per SAH to exclude fixed costs, lest you commit the fixed-cost fallacy.

Second, make sure that cost per SAH is a good proxy for MC. To check whether this is so, make sure that when you reduce output in the Dominican Republic, you really are avoiding close to $30/SAH, and make sure that you are incurring only about $20/SAH as you shift production to the Yucatan. If this is not correct, then cost per SAH is a poor proxy for MC.

If you are convinced that $10 per SAH is a reasonable proxy for difference in MCs between the two factories, you can make money by shifting production. And, as above, marginal analysis tells you what direction to go (shift production to the factory with the lower MC), but it doesn't tell you *how far* to go. Decide how far to go by taking a step and then re-measuring MC to determine whether to take another step.

In this example, the company shifted some production, but not as much as the managers wanted because they needed to maintain good working relationships with politicians in the Dominican Republic who would have been upset if too many local workers lost jobs (another hidden cost!).

4.4 Incentive Pay

How hard to work is an extent decision, so marginal analysis can be used to design incentives to encourage hard work. To illustrate this idea, suppose you are a landowner evaluating two different bids for harvesting a tract of timber containing 100 trees. One bid is for $150 per tree, and the other bid is for $15,000 for the right to harvest all the trees. Which bid should you accept?

Although both bids have the same face value, they have dramatically different effects on the logger's incentives. If you charge a fixed fee of $15,000 for the right to harvest all the trees, the logger treats the price paid to the landowner as a fixed or sunk cost. He should, by the reasoning in Chapter 3, ignore that cost when deciding how many trees to cut down. In other words, under the fixed-fee contract, the marginal payment to the landowner of cutting down another tree is zero. This gives the logger an incentive to cut down trees as long as the value of each tree is greater than the cost of harvesting it. Under this contract, the logger will end up cutting down all the trees that are profitable to cut down.

On the other hand, if you charge the logger a royalty rate of $150 per tree, the logger will cut down only those trees that can generate profit greater than $150. If the forest is a mix of pine worth $200 per tree and fir worth $100 per tree, the logger will harvest only the pine and leave the fir.[1] Consequently, the landowner will receive less money under a royalty contract. The incentive effect of a royalty rate is analogous to that of a sales tax because it deters some wealth-creating transactions, that is, the fir trees are not harvested.[2]

The same idea can be applied to the problem of motivating salespeople. To see this, suppose you are considering two different compensation schemes. One is based on a 10% commission rate, where the salesperson earns 10% on sales she makes. The other pays a 5% commission rate plus a $50,000 per year flat salary. Each year, you expect salespeople to sell about 100 units at a price of $10,000 per unit. Which compensation scheme should you use?

As in our logging example, the two payment schemes have the same face value but dramatically different effects on incentives. If you pay a 10% commission, the marginal benefit to the salesperson of making another sale is $1,000. If you pay a 5% commission, the marginal benefit is only $500. If some sales are relatively easy to make (i.e., the salesperson gives up less than $500 worth of time and effort to make them), and some sales are relatively difficult to make (i.e., they require at least $800 worth of effort), then only the easy sales will be made under the 5% commission. Both the easy and difficult sales will be made under the 10% commission. The $50,000 salary is fixed with respect to sales effort, and so does not affect behavior.

In essence, the sales force responds to the smaller *marginal benefit* of selling with less effort, which we call *shirking*. This kind of shirking is analogous to the decision of the logger to harvest only the high-profit trees when he pays a royalty rate for each tree harvested. The logger responds negatively to the *high marginal cost of logging* just as the salesperson responds negatively to the *low* **marginal benefit** *of selling*. To induce higher effort, use incentives that reduce marginal cost or increase marginal benefit. Fixed cost or benefit does not affect effort.[3]

4.5 Tie Pay to Performance Measures That Reflect Effort

Measuring performance is a critical part of any organization, as the following story illustrates. In 1997, a 50-year-old chief operating officer (COO) with a bachelor's degree in journalism and a law degree managed a consulting firm with 10 account executives. The COO was in charge of keeping clients happy and ensuring that the account executives were working in the best interests of the company. The COO earned a flat salary of $75,000.

After taking classes in human resources, economics, and accounting, the CEO recognized that the usual **accounting profits** were not motivating the COO to work harder. He sat down with his COO, and together they designed a new metric. All revenues counted toward the COO's "profit" goal. But only the expenses that the COO controlled directly—like compensation and office expenses—were "charged" against his profit metric. All overhead items, like rent, were placed in another budget because the COO could not control them; that is, they were "fixed" with respect to his effort.

The CEO and the COO both agreed that, without much effort, the COO could earn[4] $150,000 each quarter. But earning more would take extraordinary effort. To motivate the COO, they agreed on an incentive compensation scheme that paid the COO one-third of each dollar that the company earned above $150,000.

After making the change, the COO's compensation jumped to $177,000—an increase of 136%—but the firm's revenues also jumped from $720,000 to $1,251,000—an increase of 74%. A good economy certainly contributed to the increase, but the compensation plan also helped. Revenue increased because the COO pushed hard to make and exceed earnings goals and, for the first time, he worried about expenses. For example, he attempted to contain costs by asking why phone bills were so high.

Along with changing the COO's compensation scheme, the CEO also moved to a system of incentive pay for the account representatives. This had equally dramatic effects on the account representatives—except for one employee who was going through a divorce. The incentive pay scheme did little to increase his marginal incentives because half of everything he earned went to his estranged wife. In other words, the marginal benefit of extra work for this employee was half as much as that of other employees, and he responded by working less hard.

Although the benefits of incentive pay seem clear, it is not a panacea—especially in cases where it is difficult to measure performance. For example, if you reward software programmers for finding and fixing "bugs" in software, you also create an incentive for the same programmers to deliberately produce bugs so they can be found later on. Research has found that incentive schemes are most effective when "effort matters, there is little intrinsic desire to do the job, and money boosts the recipient's social status."[5]

On a related note, recognize that it is virtually impossible to measure and reward all the different tasks and activities you want an employee to perform. This is especially true of managers, who typically have a wide scope of responsibility. For them, do not put too much faith in monetary incentives alone. Recognize that the success of an organization often depends on managers who exert effort above and beyond the incentives set up for them. Firms should let these managers know that they are appreciated, and promote and reward them as best it can.

4.6 Is Incentive Pay Unfair?

Incentive pay generates inequality simply because more productive workers or those who work harder get paid more. Some employees and managers will resist even well-designed incentive pay schemes because they consider them "unfair." Moreover, incentive pay typically exposes workers to risk beyond their control. For example, even if they work hard, salespeople compensated on sales commission earn less if the macro economy does poorly.

However, these criticisms of incentive pay make the mistake of confusing procedural fairness (everyone has the same opportunity) with outcome fairness (everyone has the same outcome). If you adopt incentive pay, you get higher productivity (procedural fairness) but also greater inequality (outcome unfairness).

The reluctance of people to accept this trade-off can make it difficult for firms to increase productivity. For example, Spain's policy of *finiquito* whereby firms have to pay fired workers 1.5 months of salary for every year worked makes it difficult to motivate long-time employees. The severance pay starts looking so good that long-term employees start trying to get fired. One employee with 17 years' experience speculated in a blog post, "How hard should I really be working?"[6] These kinds of policies are making it very difficult for the southern European countries to grow their way out of the recession.

But countries aren't the only ones who resist incentive pay. Consider this reaction from a "faculty" member in the "corporate learning center" of a Fortune 50 company to a suggestion that his company adopt an incentive compensation plan:

> *Forfeiting our most recently espoused values of equal ownership in Firm X's success is not the answer. I fear that we will be attempting to compete for employees interested in a class-oriented system of compensation. From where I sit, this is the last thing a corporation needing vast, systemic, team-oriented change should be trying to do to compete in the global marketplace. Many folks know I am a staunch opponent of incentive plans, and I often quote Alfie Kohn (1993), whose research shows that rewards punish. Saying "If you do this, you'll get that" differs little from saying "Do this or this will happen to you." Incentives are controlling.*

However, another aspect of the punishment is much more evident in this change of policy: "Not receiving a reward one expects to receive is also indistinguishable from being punished." Just ask all those who don't receive the bonuses they were previously entitled to how they feel about it. The incentive pay policy is overt in its support of class separation over collective team participation. It ignores the premises of modern systems thinking and reverts to the mechanistic theories of Descartes and Newton for justification. A typical business school text from the 1950s would have suggested instituting such an aristocratic policy.

This company has since been acquired.

SUMMARY & HOMEWORK PROBLEMS

Summary of Main Points

- Do not confuse average and marginal costs.
- **Average cost (AC)** is total cost (fixed and variable) divided by total units produced. The fixed cost portion of AC is irrelevant to an extent decision.
- **Marginal cost (MC)** is the additional cost incurred by producing and selling one more unit.
- **Marginal revenue (MR)** is the additional revenue gained from selling one more unit.
- MR and MC are the relevant costs of an extent decision, like selling. Sell more if MR > MC; sell less if MR < MC. If MR = MC, you are selling the right amount (maximizing profit).
- An incentive compensation scheme that increases MR or reduces MC will increase effort. Fixed fees have no effects on effort.
- A good incentive compensation scheme links pay to performance measures that reflect effort.

Multiple-Choice Questions

1. When economists speak of "marginal," they mean
   a. opportunity.
   b. scarcity.
   c. incremental.
   d. unimportant.

2. Managers undertake an investment only if
   a. marginal benefits of the investment are greater than zero.
   b. MCs of the investment are greater than marginal benefits of the investment.
   c. marginal benefits are greater than MCs.
   d. investment decisions do not depend on marginal analysis.

3. A firm produces 500 units per week. It hires 20 full-time workers (40 hours/week) at an hourly wage of $15. Raw materials are ordered weekly, and they cost $10 for every unit produced. The weekly cost of the rent payment for the factory is $2,250. How do the overall costs break down?
   a. Total variable cost is $17,000; total fixed cost is $2,250; and total cost is $19,250.
   b. Total variable cost is $12,000; total fixed cost is $7,250; and total cost is $19,250.
   c. Total variable cost is $5,000; total fixed cost is $14,250; and total cost is $19,250.
   d. Total variable cost is $5,000; total fixed cost is $2,250; and total cost is $7,250.

4. Total costs increase from $1,500 to $1,800 when a firm increases output from 40 to 50 units. Which of the following is true if MC is constant?
   a. FC = $100
   b. FC = $200
   c. FC = $300
   d. FC = $400

5. A manager of a clothing firm is deciding whether to add another factory in addition to one already in production. The manager would compare
   a. the total benefits gained from the two factories to the total costs of running the two factories.
   b. the incremental benefit expected from the second factory to the total costs of running the two factories.
   c. the incremental benefit expected from the second factory to the cost of the second factory.
   d. the total benefits gained from the two factories to the incremental costs of running the two factories.

6. A firm is thinking of hiring an additional worker to their organization who can increase total productivity by 100 units a week. The cost of hiring him is $1,500 per week. If the price of each unit is $12,
   a. the MR of hiring the worker is $1,500.
   b. the MC of hiring the worker is $1,200.
   c. the firm should not hire the worker since MR < MC.
   d. all of the above.

7. A retailer has to pay $9 per hour to hire 13 workers. If the retailer only needs to hire 12 workers, a wage rate of $7 per hour is sufficient. What is the MC of the 13th worker?
   a. $117
   b. $9
   c. $33
   d. $84

8. If a firm's AC is rising, then
   a. MC is less than AC.
   b. MC is rising.
   c. MC is greater than AC.
   d. the firm is making an economic profit.

9. A company is producing 15,000 units. At this output level, MR is $22, and the MC is $18. The firm sells each unit for $48 and average total cost is $40. What can we conclude from this information?
   a. The company is making a loss.
   b. The company needs to cut production.
   c. The company needs to increase production.
   d. Not enough information is provided.

10. Food Fanatics caters meals where its cost of producing an extra meal is $25. Each of its meals sells for $20. At this rate, what should the company do?
   a. Produce more meals and increase its profit.
   b. Produce fewer meals and increase its profit.
   c. Not change production.
   d. None of the above.

Individual Problems

4-1 Extent versus Discrete Problems

Identify which of the following are extent decisions.

a. Decide whether to expand an existing product into a new region.
b. What discount should be given on products during the upcoming holiday sale?
c. Should the advertising budget be changed for the upcoming year?
d. Should you develop a new product for an existing product line?

4-2 Game Day Shuttle Service

You run a game day shuttle service for parking services for the local ball club. Your costs for different customer loads are 1: $30, 2: $32, 3: $35, 4: $38, 5: $42, 6: $48, 7: $57, and 8: $68. What are your MCs for each customer load level? What is the AC? If you are compensated $10 per ride, what customer load would you want?

4-3 Paid for Grades

Children in poor neighborhoods have bleak outlooks on life and do not see much gain to studying. A recent experiment is paying children in poor neighborhoods $100 for each "A" they earn in a six-week grade reporting cycle. How does this affect the children's behavior?

4-4 Supplier Bids

Your company is contemplating bidding on an RFP (request for proposal) for 100,000 units of a specialized part. Why might the amount be more than the requesting company actually wants?

4-5 Processing Insurance Claims

Your insurance firm processes claims through its newer, larger, high-tech facility and its older, smaller, low-tech facility. Each month, the high-tech facility handles 10,000 claims, incurs $100,000 in fixed costs and $100,000 in variable costs. Each month, the low-tech facility handles 2,000 claims, incurs $16,000 in fixed costs and $24,000 in variable costs. If you anticipate a decrease in the number of claims, where will you lay off workers?

4-6 Copier Company

A copier company wants to expand production. It currently has 20 workers who share eight copiers. Two months ago, the firm added two copiers, and output increased by 100,000 pages per day. One month ago, it added five workers, and productivity also increased by 50,000 pages per day. Copiers cost about twice as much as workers. Would you recommend it hire another employee or buy another copier?

Group Problems

G4-1 Extent Decision

Describe an extent decision made by your company. Compute the MC and marginal benefit of the decision. Was the right decision reached? If not, what would you do differently? Compute the profit consequences of the change.

G4-2 Contracts

Does your firm use royalty rate contracts or fixed-fee contracts? Describe the incentive effects of the contracts. Should you change the contract from one to the other? Compute the profit consequences of changing the contract.

END NOTES

1. Alternatively, if the trees differ in their harvesting costs (some are near a logging road, and some are not), the logger will cut down only those trees that yield a profit of at least $150.
2. Recall that we noted in Chapter 2 that when a sales tax is larger than the surplus of a transaction, it deters that transaction. Similarly, when the royalty rate is larger than the surplus here, it deters the wealth-creating transaction (the harvesting of the fir tree).
3. The point of discussing these different compensation schemes is not to argue that one or the other is the optimal design but rather to simply note that incentives will affect behavior.
4. *Earnings* refers to company profit.
5. Tyler Cowen, *Discover Your Inner Economist: Use Incentives to Fall in Love, Survive Your Next Meeting, and Motivate Your Dentist* (New York: Dutton, 2007).
6. http://www.lostinsantcugat.com/2010/01/nonperformance-incentive-pay.html.

Investment Decisions: Look Ahead and Reason Back

In the summer of 2007, Bert Mathews was contemplating the purchase of a 48-unit apartment building in downtown Nashville. The building was 95% occupied and generated $500,000 in annual profit. His investors were expecting a 15% return, and the bank had offered to loan him 80% of the purchase price at a rate of 5.5% interest. He computed his *weighted average cost of capital* or WACC as $0.2 \times (15\%) + 0.8 \times (5.5\%) = 7.4\%$. Mr. Mathews used his cost of capital to figure out how much he could afford to pay for the property, and still earn enough to satisfy his investors. The answer was $6.75 million, computed as $500,000/($6.75 million) = 7.4%. In other words, if he paid $6.75 million and earned $500,000 each year, he could pay his investors 15% on their invested capital.

Even though the owner was willing to sell at this price, Mr. Mathews decided not to purchase because he was worried about the deteriorating housing market and the rising number of mortgage defaults. This turned out to be a good decision. A year later, the building's occupancy rate fell to 90%, which reduced annual profit to $450,000. In addition, lending standards had tightened considerably. Now, the bank was willing to lend only 65% of the purchase price, and at the higher rate of 7.5%. This raised Mr. Mathews' cost of capital to $10.125\% = 0.35 \times (15\%) + 0.65 \times (7.5\%)$, which reduced the value that he placed on the property. If he was going to earn 10.125%, the most he could afford to pay for the property was $4.4 million, computed as $450,000/($4.4 million) = 10.125%, which the owners rejected as too low.

This story illustrates the effect of the financial crisis on the real estate market, but more importantly for our purposes, the relevant costs and benefits of investment decisions, the topic of this chapter.

5.1 Compounding and Discounting

All investment decisions involve a trade-off between current sacrifice and future gain. Before investing, you need to know whether the future benefits are more than the current costs. *Discounting* is a tool that allows you to figure this out.

The easiest way to understand discounting is to first consider its opposite, *compounding,*

$$(\textit{Future value, one period in the future}) = (\textit{Present value}) \times (1 + r)$$

where *r* is the rate of return. If, for example, you invest $1 today at a 10% rate, then you would expect to have $1.10 in one year. After two years, $1 becomes $1.21 = $1.10 × (1.10); after three years, $1.33; and so on. The general formula for compounding is

$$(\textit{Future value, k periods in the future}) = (\textit{Present value}) \times (1 + r)^k$$

In the following table, we use the above formula to compute the time that it takes an investment to double in value, when left to grow, as in a savings account. We see that higher the interest rates cause money to double in a shorter period of time. In fact, we see that the interest rate multiplied by the time it takes to double equals about 72 (last column). This is the so-called rule of 72[1]

If you invest at a rate of return r, divide 72 by r to get the number of years it takes to double your money.

As you can see from the entries in the "Future Value" column this is not an exact formula, but rather an approximation.

Current Value	Interest Rate	Years	Future Value	Rate*Time
$100	2.00%	36.0	$204	72
$100	4.00%	18.0	$203	72
$100	6.00%	12.0	$201	72
$100	7.20%	10.0	$200	72
$100	10.00%	7.2	$199	72
$100	12.00%	6.0	$197	72
$100	15.00%	5.0	$201	75

Discounting is the inverse of compounding and is defined by the formula,

$$(\textit{Present value}) = (\textit{future value, k periods in the future}) / (1 + r)^k$$

So, for example, at a 10% discount rate, $1 next year is worth only $1/ (1.1) = $0.91 today, $1 two years in the future is worth only $0.83 = $1/(1.1)^2 today, and $1 three years in the future is worth only 0.75 = $1/(1.1)^3 today.

For an example of how to use discounting, we turn to the problem of pensions. Like most U.S. cities, Nashville uses discounting to decide how much to save today to fund its future pension obligations. For a pension that pays out $100,000 in 20 years, Nashville must save $20,485 = $100,000/(1.0825)^{20}$ today, using an 8.25% discount rate. If the city invests the $20,485 and earns 8.25%, the savings will compound and be worth $100,000 in 20 years. If, however, the investments earn less than 8.25% (in fact they have done much worse), then the city will not have saved enough when the future finally gets here.

Of course, a more realistic discount rate, say 6.5%, would mean much higher current savings, $28,380 = $100,000/(1.065)^{20}$ to fund the same future pension. But higher savings means less current spending, and current spending is politically popular. This explains why many politicians prefer higher discount rates,[2] and why most public pensions are underfunded, by 25% on average.

In the following table, we compute how much more the California State Pension Fund (Calpers) must save if it were to reduce its discount rate from 7.5% to 2.56%, the risk-free rate of return.[3]

Future Value	Rate	Years	Present Value
$100	7.50%	20.0	$24
$100	6.50%	20.0	$28
$100	5.50%	20.0	$34
$100	4.50%	20.0	$41
$100	3.50%	20.0	$50
$100	2.56%	20.0	$60

We see that as the discount rate falls from 7.5% to the risk-free rate of 2.56%, the amount that the pension fund must save increases from $24 to $60, an increase of more than 150%. But even more reasonable discount rates, like 5.5%, would require $34, an increase of 42% over what Calpers is currently saving.

5.2 How to Determine Whether Investments Are Profitable

We are now in a position to use discounting to determine whether an investment is profitable. The rule is simple: discount and add up the future benefits of an investment, and compare them to the current cost of the investment. If the difference is positive (called the "net present value"), then the investment earns more than the cost of capital. This intuition can be formalized into a general decision rule, called the **NPV rule**.

If the net present value of the sum of all discounted cash flows is larger than zero, then the project earns more than the cost of capital.

To see how this works, consider the returns on two different projects. The first returns $1,200,000 at the end of year 1, and the second returns

$1,200,000 at the end of year 2. The company would obviously prefer to get money more quickly (if only so that it can invest it and earn more). Intuitively, it makes sense that the first project is more attractive than the second. Projects that return dollars sooner have higher rates of return, all else being equal.

Most projects, however, are more difficult to compare. We illustrate two such projects in Table 5.1. Both projects require an initial investment of $100. Project 1 returns $115 at the end of the first year, whereas Project 2 returns $60 at the end of the first year and $60 at the end of the second. The company's cost of capital is 14%. To determine whether the investments are profitable, we discount all future inflows and outflows to the present so we can compare them to the initial investment.

TABLE **5.1**
NPV Example

Year	Project 1		Project 2	
	Cash Flow	Present Value	Cash Flow	Present Value
0	−100.00	−100.00	−100.00	−100.00
1	60.00	52.63	115.00	100.88
2	60.00	46.17	0.00	0.00
Net Value	20.00	−1.20	15.00	0.88

To compute the present value, cash payouts after year one are divided by 1.14; and payouts after year two are divided by $(1.14)^2$. Looking at the "Net Value" of the two projects in Table 5.1, it's clear that Project 2 earns more than the cost of capital while Project 1 does not.

The NPV rule illustrates the link between "**economic profit**" introduced in Chapter 3 and investment decisions. Projects with positive NPV create economic profit because they earn more than the company's opportunity cost of capital (i.e., the company earns profit above what is required to pay its investors and its debt service). The positive NPV of Project 2 means that Project 2's return is higher than 14%, and the negative NPV of Project 1 means that its return is lower than 14%. We see that projects earning accounting profit (like project one) do not necessarily earn economic profit.

A close cousin of NPV analysis is the internal rate of return (IRR).

IRR is the discount rate that sets NPV equal to zero.

To see how this works, consider a project that requires an upfront payment of $2,000 (now), but pays back $500/year for the next five years. We compute the NPV of this project in the following table for an investor with a 5% cost of capital and see that it has a positive NPV of $164.74. According to the NPV theorem, this project earns economic profit because it earns more than the 5% cost of capital.

Project		
Cost of Capital 5.00%		
Year	Cash Flow	Present Value
0	−2,000.00	−2,000.00
1	500.00	476.19
2	500.00	453.51
3	500.00	431.92
4	500.00	411.35
5	500.00	391.76
Net Value		164.74

To find the IRR, we increase the discount rate, until the NPV falls to zero.

Project		
Internal Rate of Return (IRR) = 7.93%		
Year	Cash Flow	Present Value
0	−2,000.00	−2,000.00
1	500.00	463.26
2	500.00	429.23
3	500.00	397.69
4	500.00	368.47
5	500.00	341.40
Net Value		0.04

At a discount rate of 7.93%, the NPV is only $0.04, very close to zero. We say that the *IRR* of this project is 7.93%. If our cost of capital is less than this, for example, 5%, we would invest in the project.

Note that the IRR and NPV give the same answer to this problem, but IRR can be harder to interpret than NPV analysis. When in doubt, use NPV.

5.3 Break-Even Analysis

In your finance classes, you will learn that NPV analysis is the "correct" way to evaluate investment decisions. A positive NPV is both a necessary and a sufficient condition for an investment to be profitable. However, after doing NPV analysis in a variety of circumstances, you will begin to develop shortcuts and rules of thumb, like payback periods, that give you similar answers. This is potentially dangerous. When using shortcuts, make sure that you understand the context in which the shortcut is being used and that it gives the same answer as NPV analysis.

One of the most popular shortcuts is break-even analysis. Break-even analysis can give you the wrong answer as it ignores the time value of money. However, break-even analysis is easy to do and it generates simple, intuitive answers. To illustrate, let's examine an entry decision. Instead of asking whether entry is profitable, break-even analysis asks an easier question, "Can I sell enough to break even?" If you can sell more than the **break-even quantity**, then entry is profitable; otherwise, entry is unprofitable.

To compute the break-even quantity, we have to distinguish between marginal cost (MC), which varies with quantity, and fixed cost (F), which doesn't. Imagine that you incur a fixed cost to enter an industry and a constant[4] per-unit MC when you begin production. You will find that most of your investment decisions can be analyzed using this very simple cost structure.

The break-even quantity is $Q = F/(P - MC)$,

where F is annual fixed cost, P is price, and MC is marginal cost.

The break-even quantity is the quantity that will lead to zero profit.[5] The logic behind the calculation is simple. Each unit sold earns the *contribution margin* $(P - MC)$, so named because this is the amount that one sale contributes to profit. You have to sell at least the break-even quantity to earn enough to cover fixed costs. If you sell more than the break-even quantity, you have earned more than enough to cover your fixed costs, or to earn a profit.

For example, consider Nissan's 2008 redesign of its Titan pickup truck. The Titan had only two years left on its eight-year product life cycle, and Nissan had to decide whether to redesign it. Complicating the decision was a weakening demand for U.S. trucks, with sales predicted to fall from 1.3 million in 2008 to only 400,000 trucks per year by 2011.

Nissan managers used a rough break-even calculation to evaluate their investment alternatives. It would cost $400 million to design and build a new truck from the bottom up. At a 15% cost of capital,[6] the investment would cost Nissan about $60 million per year. As it earned only $1,500 per truck, Nissan would have to sell at least 40,000 trucks each year to break even. With only a 3% share of the U.S. market, however, Nissan predicted they would sell only 12,000 Titan trucks each year, not enough to break even.

The other option was to pay Chrysler to build the new Titan for Nissan. Chrysler had just made a big investment in updating its Dodge Ram pickup and had enough spare capacity on its Mexican assembly line. If Nissan used the Dodge Ram as the base platform for the new Titan, the required investment to build the new model would fall from $400 million to only $80 million. However, the margin would also fall to $1,250 per truck because Dodge charged a price that was above the MC of building the trucks. This would reduce the annual capital cost to only $12 million, which makes the break-even quantity only 9,600 trucks. In the following table, we illustrate this break-even analysis and see that Nissan sells enough to break even on the Dodge platform, but not on its own platform.

Platform	Nissan	Dodge
Cost of Capital	15%	15%
Capital	$400,000,000	$80,000,000
Margin ($P - $MC)	$1,500	$1,250
Break-Even Sales	40,000	9,600
Predicted Sales	12,000	12,000

Outsourcing the Titan to Chrysler would have made economic sense, but in early 2009, the companies issued a joint statement indefinitely postponing the project due to "declining economic conditions."

5.4 Choosing the Right Manufacturing Technology

In 1986, John Deere was building a capital-intensive factory to produce large, four-wheel-drive farm tractors when the price of wheat dropped dramatically. Demand for these tractors also fell because they're used exclusively for harvesting wheat. In response, John Deere stopped construction of its factory and attempted to purchase Versatile, a Canadian company that assembled tractors in a big garage using off-the-shelf components.

We can characterize John Deere's decision as abandoning their capital-intensive factory, characterized by big fixed cost but small MC, in favor of Versatile's technology, characterized by small fixed cost but big MC. Did John Deere make the right decision?

As you should now begin to realize, the answer is "it depends." In this case, it depends on how much John Deere expected to sell. Suppose that the capital-intensive technology had fixed costs of $100 and MCs of $10, whereas Versatile's technology had fixed costs of $50 but MCs of $20. (*Note:* We're deliberately choosing easy-to-work-with numbers so that we can illustrate the general point.) To answer the question, we compute the break-even quantity—the quantity at which John Deere is indifferent between the two technologies.

In the following table, we see that for a quantity of five units, the total costs of the two manufacturing technologies are the same.

	In-House	Versatile
Quantity	5	5
Fixed Costs/Year	$100	$50
Marginal Cost	$10	$20
Total Cost	$150	$150

If John Deere expects to sell more than five units, it should choose the low-marginal-cost technology; and for less than five units, they should choose the low-fixed-cost technology.

In this case, John Deere decided to acquire Versatile because projected demand was low. However, the antitrust division of the U.S. Department of Justice challenged the acquisition as anticompetitive[7] because John Deere and Versatile were two of just four firms that sold large four-wheel-drive tractors in North America.

We end this section with a warning to avoid a very common business mistake:

Do not use break-even analysis to justify higher prices or greater output.

Managers sometimes reason that they must raise price to cover fixed costs. Similarly, managers sometimes reason that since *average* fixed costs decline with quantity, they must sell as much as they can to reduce average cost. Both lines of reasoning are flawed because, as you know, pricing and production are *extent* decisions that require *marginal analysis*, not *break-even analysis*.

Remember, if you start your analysis by looking at costs you will always get confused. Instead, start your analysis by asking a question. For an extent decision, like how high to price or how much to produce, fixed or sunk costs are irrelevant because they do not vary with the consequence of the decision. For an investment decision, fixed or sunk costs are relevant because they haven't yet been incurred.

5.5 Shut-Down Decisions and Break-Even Prices

To study shut-down decisions, we work with break-even prices rather than quantities. If you shut down, you lose your revenue, but you get back your **avoidable cost**. If revenue is less than avoidable cost, or equivalently, if price is less than average avoidable cost,[8] then shut down.

The break-even price is the average avoidable cost per unit.[9]

The only hard part in applying break-even analysis is deciding which costs are avoidable. For that, we use the Cost Taxonomy, shown in Figure 5.1.[10]

To illustrate how to use the taxonomy, consider the following problem. Fixed cost is $100/year, MC is $5/year, and you're producing 100 units per year. How low can price go before it is profitable to shut down?

Again, the answer is "it depends." In this case, it depends on which costs are avoidable. To make this concrete, think of the fixed cost as a one-year renewable lease and the MC as the cost of production. MC varies with how much you produce so it is avoidable. But until the lease comes up for renewal, it is unavoidable, so you ignore it when deciding whether to shut down.

In the *short run*, only MC is avoidable, so the shut-down price is $5. In the *long run*, fixed cost becomes avoidable, so it becomes relevant to the shut-down decision. In the long run, the shut-down price includes average fixed cost and rises to $6.[11] As more costs become avoidable, the shut-down price increases to reflect this.

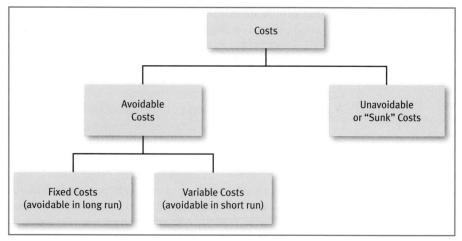

FIGURE **5.1**   **Cost Taxonomy**

5.6 Sunk Costs and Post-Investment Hold-Up

By 2000, Mobil Oil (now ExxonMobil) was the leading supplier of industrial lubricants[12] in the United States. It achieved that position—and a 13% market share—by bundling engineering services with its high-quality lubricants. With twice as many field engineers as its next-largest competitor, Mobil was able to offer custom-designed lubrication programs to complement sales of its lubricants.

One of Mobil's largest customers was TVA, a regional producer of electric power whose annual consumption of lubricants exceeded one million gallons. Early in 2000, Mobil conducted a three-month engineering audit of TVA. This audit included employee training, equipment inspections, and, for each piece of TVA equipment, repair, service, and lubricant recommendations.

TVA made the recommended repairs, but then it gave the lubricant recommendation list to a Mobil competitor that offered lubricants at lower prices. When Mobil failed to match the lower prices, they lost the contract and their three-month investment. Mobil and its managers forgot a basic business maxim.

Before investing, look ahead and reason back.

Economics is often called the "dismal science," partly because of its dark view of human nature. However, this dark view of human nature can protect you against what economists call *post-investment hold-up*. **Sunk costs** are unavoidable, even in the long run, so after you incur them, you become vulnerable to *post-investment hold-up*. In this case, Mobil made the investment in consulting services expecting that they could recoup the investment through their pricing. However, TVA "held them up" by buying lubricants from another vendor.

Let's look more generally at the problem of post-investment hold-up by rewriting profit as a function of the difference between price and average cost.

$$Profit = Rev - Cost = Q * P - Q * (Cost / Q) = Q * (P - AC)$$

If "Cost" includes all your costs, including your opportunity cost of capital, then you are just breaking even (earning zero profit) when $P = AC$. If price falls below AC, then you are losing money.

To see how this affects investment decisions, imagine that you are advising a regional commercial printer, who is negotiating with a magazine, like *National Geographic*. For the magazine, using a regional printer reduces shipping costs. But to print a high-quality magazine, the printer must buy a $12 million roto-gravure printing press. For the sake of clarity, we assume that the press has no resale value and the firm has no capital cost (it can borrow money and pay no interest). Suppose that the MC of printing a single copy is $2 and the printer expects to print one million copies per year over a two-year period.

In the following table, we compute the average cost of printing the magazine over the length of the contract.

Year	Quantity	RFP	
		Sunk Cost	Variable Cost ($2/Unit)
0		$12,000,000	
1	1,000,000		$2,000,000
2	1,000,000		$2,000,000
Total	2,000,000	$12,000,000	$4,000,000
Average		$6	$2
Average Cost		$8	

In the above table, we see that $8 is the average cost of printing magazines over the length of the contract. This is the break-even price for the printer and represents her bottom line in negotiations with the magazine. Before they are incurred, sunk costs are relevant to the negotiation.

QUESTION: Now suppose that the magazine accepts your offer of $8/unit and immediately hands you a purchase order for $8,000,000, for the first-year production. Do you accept the purchase order?

If you said "Yes," you have just been held up. Since the $12M cost of the printer is sunk, the magazine can decide to reduce its second-year price to only $2, and you would have no option but to accept it. Instead, you should instead refuse the purchase order at that price.

If the printer anticipates hold-up, it will be reluctant to deal with the magazine. When this happens, hold-up becomes a problem not just for the potential victim but also for the potential perpetrator. The *one lesson of business* is to figure out how to profitably consummate the transaction between the printer and the magazine.

If possible, the printer will negotiate a contract that penalizes the magazine should it decide to hold them up. With the assurance of a contract, the printer may feel confident enough to incur sunk costs. But contracts are often difficult and costly to enforce. A better solution might be to make the magazine purchase the printing press and then lease it to the printer. In this case, the magazine no longer poses a hold-up threat to the printer because the printer has incurred no sunk costs.[13]

Note that if the cost of the printing press is *fixed*, meaning that it can be recovered by selling the machine, then hold-up is not a problem. If the magazine tries to renegotiate a price less than average cost, the printer will refuse the business, sell the press, and recover its entire investment. Hold-up can occur only if costs are sunk.

In general, many investments are vulnerable to hold-up. Anytime that one party makes a **specific investment**—one that is sunk or lacks value outside of a trading relationship—the party can be held up by its trading partner. If one party anticipates that she is at risk of being held up, she will be reluctant to make relationship-specific investments, or demand costly safeguards, including compensation in the form of better terms from her trading partner. This gives both parties an incentive to adopt contracts or organizational forms, such as investments in reputation or merger, to reduce the risk of hold-up. The goal is to ensure that each party has both the incentive to make relationship-specific investments and to trade after these investments have been made.

Contracts should encourage both investment and trade.

For example, marriages are vulnerable to the same type of post-investment opportunism that plagues commercial relationships. Parties invest time, energy, and money in a marriage, the kinds of investments that differentiate marriages from more casual relationships, which can be thought of as spot-market transactions. These investments are valuable to the marriage parties but are largely specific, in that they have a much lower value outside the relationship. The marriage contract penalizes post-investment hold-up (i.e., divorce), and this makes couples willing to invest more in the marriage.[14]

We close the chapter with the story of an economist and his fiancée who were receiving premarital counseling from a priest before he would marry them. The priest's first question to the couple was "Why do you want to get married?" The economist's fiancée answered, "Because I love him and want to spend the rest of my life with him." As you might imagine, the economist had a different answer, "Because long-term contracts induce higher levels of **relationship-specific investment**."

A year later, trying hard to find the right words to express how he felt about his wife, he wrote an anniversary e-mail—using a cursive font—declaring that his "relationship-specific investment was earning an above-average rate of return."

SUMMARY & HOMEWORK PROBLEMS

Summary of Main Points

- All investment decisions involve a trade-off between current sacrifice and future gain. Before investing, you need to know whether the future benefits are bigger than the current costs. *Discounting* allows you to figure this out.
- Companies, like individuals, have different discount rates, determined by their cost of capital. They invest only in projects that earn a return higher than the cost of capital.
- The **NPV rule** states that if the net present value of the net cash flows from an investment are positive, the project earns **economic profit** (the investment earns more than the cost of capital).
- Although NPV is the correct way to analyze investments, not all companies use it. Instead, they use a variety of shortcuts like pay-back period as they are often easier to do and more intuitive.
- **Break-even quantity** is equal to fixed cost divided by the contribution margin. If you expect to sell more than the break-even quantity, then your investment will be profitable.
- **Avoidable costs** can be recovered by shutting down. If the benefits of shutting down (you get back your avoidable costs) are larger than the costs (you give up your revenue), then shut down. The **break-even price** is average avoidable cost.
- If you incur **sunk costs**, you are vulnerable to **post-investment hold-up**. Anticipate hold-up and choose contracts or organizational forms that give each party both the incentive to make sunk-cost investments and to trade after these investments are made.

Multiple-Choice Questions

1. Which of the following will increase the break-even quantity?
   a. A decrease in overall fixed costs
   b. A decrease in the marginal costs
   c. A decrease in the price level
   d. An increase in price level

2. The higher the discount rates,
   a. the more value individuals place on future dollars.
   b. the more value individuals place on current dollars.
   c. the more investments will take place.
   d. does not affect the investment strategy

3. Assume a firm has the following cost and revenue characteristics at its current level of output: price = $10.00, average variable cost = $8.00, and average fixed cost = $4.00. This firm is
   a. incurring a loss of $2.00 per unit and should shut down.
   b. realizing only a normal profit.
   c. realizing an economic profit of $2.00 per unit.
   d. incurring a loss per unit of $2.00 but should continue to operate in the short run.

4. Sarah's Machinery Company is deciding to dump its current technology A for a new technology B with smaller fixed costs but bigger MCs. The current technology has fixed costs of $500 and MCs of $50, whereas the new technology has fixed costs of $250 and MCs of $100. At what quantity is Sarah's Machinery Company indifferent between two technologies?
   a. 5
   b. 6
   c. 7
   d. 8

5. What is the net present value of a project that requires a $100 investment today and returns $50 at the end of the first year and $80 at the end of the second year? Assume a discount rate of 10%.
   a. $10.52
   b. $11.57
   c. $18.18
   d. $30.00

6. You expect to sell 500 cell phones a month, which have an MC of $50. If your fixed costs are $5,000 per month, what is the break-even price?
   a. $10
   b. $50
   c. $60
   d. $100

7. You are considering opening a new business to sell dartboards. You estimate that your manufacturing equipment will cost $100,000, facility updates will cost $250,000, and on average, it will cost you $80 (in labor and material) to produce a board. If you can sell dartboards for $100 each, what is your break-even quantity?
   a. 1,000
   b. 3,500
   c. 4,375
   d. 17,500

8. If GDP is expected to increase at a steady rate of 3% per year, how many years would it take for living standards to double?
   a. 10
   b. 20
   c. 24
   d. 30

9. Break-even quantity is a point where
   a. the level of profit is maximized.
   b. the level of cost is minimized.
   c. only variable costs are covered.
   d. there are zero profits.

10. In the short run, a firm's decision to shut down should not take into consideration
    a. avoidable costs.
    b. variable costs.
    c. fixed costs.
    d. MCs.

Individual Problems

5-1 George's T-Shirt Shop

George's T-Shirt Shop produces 5,000 custom-printed T-shirts per month. George's fixed costs are $15,000 per month. The MC per T-shirt is a constant $4. What is his break-even price? What would be George's break-even price if he were to sell 50% more shirts?

5-2 Net Present Value

Suppose an initial investment of $100 will return $50/year for three years (assume the $50 is received each year at the end of the year). Is this a profitable investment if the discount rate is 20%?

5-3 Doctor's Human Capital

Probably the most important source of capital is human capital. For example, most medical doctors spend years learning to practice medicine. Doctors are willing to make large investments in their human capital because they expect to be compensated for doing so when they begin work. In Canada, the government nationalized the health-care system and reduced doctors' compensation. Is this a form of **post-investment hold-up**?

5-4 Solar Panel Installation

A university spent $1.8 million to install solar panels atop a parking garage. These panels will have a capacity of 500 kW, have a life expectancy of 20 years and suppose the discount rate is 10%.

a. If electricity can be purchased for costs of $0.10 per kWh, how many hours per year will the solar panels have to operate to make this project break even?
b. If efficient systems operate for 2,400 hours per year, would the project break even?
c. The university is seeking a grant to cover capital costs. How big of a grant would make this project worthwhile (to the university)?

5-5 Toy Trucks

Last year, a toy manufacturer introduced a new toy truck that was a huge success. The company invested $2.5 million for a plastic injection-molding machine (which can be sold for $2.0 million) and $100,000 in plastic injection molds specifically for the toy (not valuable to anyone else). Labor and the cost of materials necessary to make each truck are about $3. This year, a competitor has developed a similar toy that has significantly reduced demand for the toy truck. Now, the original manufacturer is deciding whether it should continue production of the toy truck. If the estimated demand is 100,000 trucks, what is the break-even price for the toy truck? Should the company shut down?

5-6 Running a Hotel during a Recession

In early 2008, you purchased and remodeled a 120-room hotel to handle the increased number of conventions coming to town. By mid-2008, it became apparent that the recession would kill the demand for conventions. Now, you forecast that you will only be able to sell 20,000 room-nights that cost on average $50 per room per night to service. You spent $20 million on the hotel in 2008, and your cost of capital is 10%. The current going price to sell the hotel is $15 million. What is your break-even price?

5-7 Short Run versus Long Run

A firm sells 1,000 units per week. It charges $70 per unit, the average variable costs are $25, and the average costs are $65.

a. What should the firm do in the short run? Why?

b. What should the firm do in the long run? Why?

c. At what price would the firm consider shutting down in the short run?

d. At what price would the firm consider shutting down in the long run?

Group Problems

G5-1 Shut-Down Decision

Describe a shut-down decision your company has made. Compute the opportunity costs and benefits of the decision (using break-even analysis if appropriate). Did your company make the right decision? If not, what would you do differently? Compute the profit consequences of the decision.

G5-2 Investment Decision

Describe an investment decision your company has made. Compute the opportunity costs and benefits of the decision. Did your company make the right decision? If not, what would you do differently? Compute the NPV of the investment.

G5-3 Post-Investment Hold-Up

Describe an investment or potential investment your company (or one of your suppliers or customers) has made that is subject to post-investment hold-up. What could or does your company do to solve the hold-up problem and ensure the investment gets made? Compute the profit consequences of the solution.

END NOTES

1. The rule of 72 applies in most situations. There is also a rule of 69 for continuous compounding of interest. Neither is precise enough for actual contracts and should only be used for on-the-spot mental calculations.

2. If voters were perfectly rational, they would recognize that most cities are not saving enough to fund their future pension obligations. That they don't seem to care enough about the future has long been recognized by psychologists, who have named this "hyperbolic discounting." In other words, they place too much weight on the present and not enough weight on the future. Businesses, like politicians, take advantage of this irrationality by, for example, offering a low "teaser" price and raising price in the future, or by offering a low price on a

consumer durable, like a pod-coffee maker, and then charging a high price on the consumables, like the pod. Hyperbolic discounting implies that when deciding whether to purchase the pod-coffee "system," consumers place too much weight on the "current" low price of the machine, and discount too heavily the "future" high price of the pods. By shifting most of the price to the future, where consumers discount them too heavily, the company can increase demand for the system.

3. http://www.nytimes.com/2016/09/18/business/dealbook/a-sour-surprise-for-public-pensions-two-sets-of-books.html.

4. In later chapters, we will analyze situations in which marginal costs are not constant.

5. 0 = Profit
0 = Revenue − Total Costs
0 = Revenue − Variable Costs − Fixed Costs
$0 = (P \times Q) - (MC \times Q) - F$
$0 = Q(P - MC) - F$
$F = Q(P - MC)$
$F/(P - MC) = Q$
$Q = F/(P - MC)$.

6. If you invest in an asset that loses its value after some period (like designing a new model truck that will become obsolete after eight years), you can adjust your cost of capital to account for the finite life of the investment by using what is known as a Debt constant = $r/(1-(1/(1+r)^n))$, where r is the cost of capital and n is the number of years before the investment loses its value. For example, if the investment loses its value after eight years, then the debt constant is approximately 15% for a 5% cost of capital.

7. This was the first big case for one naive but enthusiastic young economist.

8. Profit = Revenue − Cost
$= (P \times Q) - (AC \times Q)$, where AC = Average Cost = (Total Cost)/Q. Note that if price is less than average cost, profit will be negative.

9. Revenue < Avoidable cost ↔
Revenue/Q < (Avoidable Cost)/Q ↔
Price < (Avg. Avoidable Cost)

10. Ivan Png, *Managerial Economics* (Maiden, MA: Blackwell, 1998).

11. Average Avoidable Cost = (Fixed Cost + Average Avoidable Cost × Q) IQ = ($100 + $5 × 100)/100 = $6.

12. Industrial lubricants are very costly to produce. One 55-gallon barrel of oil yields just two quarts of lubricant.

13. However, now the magazine can be held up by the printer and may be reluctant to buy the machine unless the printer can reassure the magazine that it will not be held up.

14. The weakening of the marriage contract in the United States (reduced penalties for post-investment hold-up) allows a test of this contractual view of marriage. Following the change, we would expect less relationship-specific investment, like the investment in children. Corresponding to the weakening of the contract, women are having fewer children and having them later in life, when it is easier to drop in and out of the labor market. They act as if they are responding rationally to the increased risk of post-investment hold-up.

SECTION 2

Pricing, Costs, and Profits

6 Simple Pricing

In 1968, Mattel introduced the inexpensive and wildly popular Hot Wheels line of toy cars. Forty years and four billion cars later, the suggested retail price of the classic Hot Wheels car had never budged above $1 even as production costs continued to climb, squeezing margins. Eventually, some interns working for Mattel suggested that they double both the wholesale price and suggested retail price of the cars.

Initially, Mattel executives balked, fearing that a price increase could devastate sales. Eventually, Mattel did increase its prices slightly to test the waters and evaluate the wisdom of price adjustments. Shortly following the move, Mattel reported one of its most successful quarters, with revenues unchanged from a year earlier but profits rising by 20%.[1]

Pricing is a powerful but oft-neglected tool. We all know that Profit = $(P - AC) \times Q$, but many businesses seem to focus on Q or AC and forget about P. Think about companies you've worked for—I suspect they spent most of their time thinking about how to sell more or how to reduce costs and not much time thinking about how to raise price. This is a mistake. According to Roger Brinner, Chief Economist at The Parthenon Group, most companies can make money simply by raising price.[2] Theory suggests that he is correct. For a company with a pretax profit margin of 8.6% (the average for the S&P 500, including fixed costs), quantity would have to increase by 4% to have the same profit effect as a 1% increase in price.

In this chapter, we consider "simple pricing," the case of a single firm, selling a single product, at a single price. Although this kind of pricing is rare because most firms sell multiple products, at different prices, and in competition with rivals, it is important to understand simple pricing before moving on to pricing in more complex settings. In addition, the simple pricing model has become part of the business vernacular, and it is important to understand it if you are to communicate well. In this chapter, we introduce demand curves, show you how to use marginal analysis to choose the most profitable price. We finish by showing how firms price in practice.

6.1 Background: Consumer Values and Demand Curves

Let's consider a simplified relationship between price and quantity purchased by a single consumer, using some good, like a slice of pizza.

Suppose consumers are pretty much the same, and that they value the first slice at $5, the second at $4, the third at $3, and so on. This is the marginal value. Knowing the value that consumers place on each subsequent slice allows us to construct Table 6.1, which shows the marginal value and total value for the various quantities. For the first slice, the total and marginal values are the same, both equal to $5. For the second slice, the marginal value is $4, while the total value of consuming two slices is $9 = $5 + $4. For the third slice, the marginal value is $3, and the total value is $12 = $5 + $4 + $3, and so on.

TABLE **6.1**

Pizza Value Table

Slices Purchased	Marginal Value ($)	Total Value ($)
1	5	5
2	4	9
3	3	12
4	2	14
5	1	15

The consumer uses marginal analysis to decide how much to consume because it is an extent decision. If the marginal value of consuming another unit is above the price, the consumer consumes another unit. For example, at a price of $5, the consumer purchases only one slice because the second slice has a value ($4) that is below the price.

At a price of $4, the consumer purchases two slices; at a price of $3, three slices; at a price of $2, four slices; and at a price of $1, five slices. The consumer's decision of how much to buy at each price is a demand curve, listed in Table 6.2.

TABLE **6.2**

Pizza Demand Schedule

Slice Price ($)	Slices Purchased
5	1
4	2
3	3
2	4
1	5

A **demand curve** tells you how much consumers will purchase at a given price.

It is easy to see from Table 6.2 that the consumer purchases more as price falls, which is called the **first law of demand**. This makes intuitive sense. Consider the value you, a hungry consumer, receive from the first slice of pizza—it is likely to be substantial. The additional value you receive from eating the second slice is a bit less, and by the time you have eaten four slices, the additional value of the fifth is fairly small. The marginal, or additional, value of consuming each subsequent slice diminishes the more you consume.

In Table 6.3, we show how much surplus consumers get at each price. At a price of $5, there is no surplus as the consumer pays a price exactly equal to his total value. But as price declines, **consumer surplus,** the difference between total value and amount paid, increases. Note that the additional value of consuming the last slice is only $1.

TABLE **6.3**
Pizza Consumer Surplus

Price ($)	Slices Purchased	Total Amount Paid ($)	Total Value ($)	Surplus ($)
5	1	5	5	0
4	2	8	9	1
3	3	9	12	3
2	4	8	14	6
1	5	5	15	10

To describe the buying behavior of a group of consumers, we add up all the individual demand curves to get an **aggregate demand curve.** The simplest way to show this is to consider the case where each consumer wants only a single item (i.e., the marginal value of a second unit is zero). To construct a demand curve that describes the behavior of seven buyers, we simply arrange the buyers by what they are willing to pay (e.g., $7, $6, $5, $4, $3, $2, and $1). At a price of $7, one buyer will purchase;[3] at a price of $6, two buyers will purchase; at $5, three buyers; and so on. At a price of $1, all seven buyers will purchase the good. An *aggregate or market demand curve* is the relationship between the price and the number of purchases made by this group of consumers. In Figure 6.1, we plot this demand curve.

Note that price—the independent variable—is on the "wrong" axis. There are good reasons for this that will become apparent, but for now, just accept that economists like to do things a little differently. Note also that economists have special jargon describing the response of demand to price. We say that as price decreases, "quantity demanded" increases. If something other than price causes an increase in demand, we instead say that the "demand shifts" to the right, or "demand increases," such that consumers purchase more at the same price. We'll discuss factors that shift demand in a later chapter.

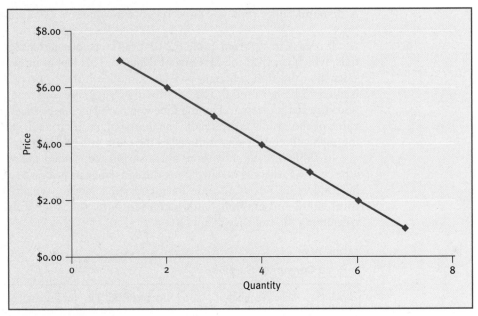

FIGURE **6.1** **Demand Curve**

To determine the quantity demanded at each price using the demand curve, look for the quantity on the horizontal axis corresponding to a price on the vertical axis. At a price of $6, buyers demand two units; at a price of $5, three units; and so on. As price falls, quantity demanded increases.

6.2 Marginal Analysis of Pricing

Demand curves present sellers with a dilemma. Sellers can raise price and sell fewer units, but earn more on each unit sold. Or they can reduce price and sell more, but earn less on each unit sold. This trade-off is at the heart of pricing decisions.

We use demand curves to change the pricing decision ("what price should I charge") into a quantity decision ("how much should I sell?") that we already know how to solve. If marginal revenue (MR) is greater than marginal cost (MC),[4] sell more, and you do this by reducing price. Reduce price (sell more) if MR > MC. Increase price (sell less) if MR < MC.

To see how to use marginal analysis to increase profit, examine Table 6.4. The columns list the Price, Quantity, Revenue, MR, MC, and total Profit for a simple demand curve. Suppose that the product costs $1.50 to make. At a price of $7, one consumer would purchase, so revenue would be $7. Cost would be $1.50, so profit on the first sale would be $5.50.

TABLE **6.4**
Optimal Price

Price ($)	Quantity	Revenue ($)	MR ($)	MC ($)	Profit ($)
7	1	7	7	1.50	5.50
6	2	12	5	1.50	9.00
5	3	15	3	1.50	10.50
4	4	16	1	1.50	10.00
3	5	15	−1	1.50	7.50
2	6	12	−3	1.50	3.00
1	7	7	−5	1.50	−3.50

If we sell a second unit, we have to reduce price to $6, and revenue increases from $7 to $12. We say that the MR of the second unit is $5. This is bigger than the MC of the second unit, so it pays to sell the second unit. In the last column, we see that profit increases from $5.50 to $9.00.

If we sell a third unit, we have to reduce price to $5, and revenue increases from $12 to $15. The MR of the third unit is $3, which is bigger than the MC of the third unit, so it pays to sell the third unit. In the last column, we see that profit increases from $9.00 to $10.50.

So far, all these changes have been profitable because MR has been greater than the MC. We earned $5.50 on the first unit, $3.50 on the second unit, and $1.50 on the third unit. These **marginal profits** sum to a total profit of $10.50, as indicated in the last column of Table 6.4.

However, if we sell a fourth unit, total profit decreases because the MR is only $1, which is less than the $1.50 MC. Selling three units, at a price of $5 is "optimal" because it makes the most profit.

After going through your analysis to compute the optimal price, suppose your boss looks at you and says, "This is the stupidest thing I've ever seen! Since the price is $5, and the cost of producing another good is only $1.50, we're leaving money on the table." What do you tell her?

Your boss has confused *average* revenue or price with *marginal* revenue. They're easy to confuse. Here's why. As long as price is greater than average cost, it appears that an increase in quantity would increase profit.[5] However, this reasoning is incorrect because you cannot sell more without reducing the price on *all* goods, and not just on the extra units your boss wants to sell.

Tell your boss that you are already making all profitable sales—those for which MR exceeds MC. Marginal analysis, not average analysis, tells you where to price or, equivalently, how many units to sell.

6.3   Price Elasticity and Marginal Revenue

Unfortunately, you're never going to see a demand curve like the one in Figure 6.1. In general, it is very difficult to get information about demand at prices away from the current price. In fact, if anyone—particularly an economic consultant—ever tries to show you a complete demand curve, don't trust it; the consultant probably has only a very rough estimate as to what demand looks like away from current prices.

At this point you may be shaking your head and wondering why you have to learn about things you will never see. Table 6.4 shows us that we don't need the entire demand curve to know how to price—all we need is information on MR and MC. If MR > MC, reduce price; if MR < MC, increase price. As we saw earlier, marginal analysis points you in the right direction, but it doesn't tell you how far to go. You get to the best price by taking steps and then by re-computing MR and MC to see whether you should take another step.

So how do we estimate MR? The answer involves measuring quantity responses to past price changes, essentially "experimenting" with price changes, or surveying potential consumers to see how much they would buy in response to a price change. If you do get useful information about demand away from the current price, it's likely to be about the **price elasticity** of demand, which we denote by e.

$$e = \%\Delta Quantity\ Demanded \div \%\Delta Price$$

where %Δ means "percentage change in." Price elasticity measures how sensitive demand is to a change in price. A demand curve for which quantity changes more than price is said to be **elastic**, or sensitive to price; and a demand curve for which quantity changes less than price is said to be **inelastic**, or insensitive to price.

If $|e| > 1$, demand is elastic; if $|e| < 1$, demand is inelastic.

Since price and quantity move in opposite directions—as price goes up, quantity goes down, and vice versa—price elasticity is *always* negative (the first law of demand requires it); that is, $e < 0$. Because it is negative, many people will just drop the negative sign. To avoid confusion, we will usually refer to elasticity using its absolute value, denoted by $|e|$.

To show how to estimate elasticity, consider this 1999 "experiment" at MidSouth, a medium-sized retail grocery store. The store's managers decreased the price of three-liter Coke (diet, caffeine-free, and classic) from $1.79 to $1.50 because they wanted to match a price offered at a nearby Walmart. In response to the price drop, the quantity sold doubled, from 210 to 420 units per week.

To compute elasticity, simply take the percentage quantity increase and divide it by the percentage price decrease. Some confusion inevitably occurs because we can compute percentage changes in several different ways, depending on whether we divide the changes by their initial or final values. Usually, the best estimate comes from dividing by the midpoint of price $(P_1 + P_2)/2$ and the midpoint of quantity $(Q_1 + Q_2)/2$.[6]

$$e = [(Q_1 - Q_2) \div (Q_1 + Q_2)] \div [(P_1 - P_2) \div (P_1 + P_2)]$$

In the three-liter Coke example, the calculation works like this:

$$-3.8 = [(210 - 420) \div (210 + 420)] \div [(1.79 - 1.50) \div (1.79 + 1.50)]$$

In this case, the estimated price elasticity is −3.8, indicating an elastic demand, where a 1% decrease in price of three-liter Coke leads to a 3.8% increase in quantity.[7] The change in revenue associated with the change is

$$(\$1.50 \times 420) - (\$1.79 \times 210) = \$630 - \$375.90 = \$254.10$$

This experiment illustrates the relationship between elasticity and revenue,

for an elastic demand, a decrease in price leads to an increase in revenue.

In general, we can express the revenue change as the sum of quantity and price changes:[8]

$$\%\Delta Revenue \approx \%\Delta Quantity + \%\Delta Price$$

If quantity increases by more than price decreases (which it does for elastic demand), then revenue increases, and *vice versa*. The results in Tables 6.5 and 6.6 summarize the relationship.

TABLE **6.5**
  For *Elastic* Demand

Price increase → Revenue decrease
Price decrease → Revenue increase

TABLE **6.6**
  For *Inelastic* Demand

Price increase → Revenue increase
Price decrease → Revenue decrease

To illustrate the relationship between price, revenue, and elasticity, let's look at former mayor Marion Barry's tax increase on gasoline sales in the District of Columbia (DC). Before the tax was put into law, DC gas station owners argued against it, predicting that the 6% price increase would reduce quantity by 40%. Essentially, gas station owners were arguing that the price elasticity of demand for gasoline sold in the District was −6.7 = 40% ÷ 6%. Because of this very elastic demand, the gas station owners predicted that a tax increase would cause gasoline revenue, and the taxes collected out of revenue, to decline.

In fact, after the tax was levied, quantity fell by 38%, very close to what gas station owners had predicted. More importantly, tax revenue fell, as would be predicted by the top row of Table 6.5.

The exact numerical relationship between MR (change in revenue) and elasticity is MR $= P(1-1/|e|)$.[9] We can use this formula to express the marginal analysis rule using price elasticity and margins place of MR and MC:

$$MR > MC \text{ implies that } (P - MC)/P > 1/|e|$$

This expression has an intuitive interpretation. The left side of the expression is the *current margin* $(P - MC)/P$, whereas the right side is the *desired margin*, which is the inverse elasticity, $1/|e|$. If the current margin is greater than the desired margin, reduce price because MR $>$ MC. Intuitively, the more elastic demand becomes ($1/|e|$ becomes smaller), the less you can profitably raise price because you will lose too many customers.

For example, after MidSouth Grocery reduced the price of three-liter Coke to $1.50, its actual margin was 2.7%, which is much less than the desired margin of 26% $=1/|3.8|$. In other words, the price was much too low according to our simple model of pricing (one product, one firm, one price). Ordinarily, a profit-maximizing store manager would raise the price in such a situation. In this case, however, the managers were using three-liter Coke as a *loss leader*, deliberately pricing too low as a way to attract customers to the store. Why? Because they hoped that customers would spend money on other items once they got there. Our simple pricing model does not take account of the effect of a low Coke price on sales of other products. We will discuss this, and other more complex pricing strategies, in later chapters.

To see how to use elasticity to set price, consider the following spreadsheet. The first two columns represent a demand curve, with price determining how much quantity is sold. In the third column, we compute the price elasticity. In the first row, at a price of $4.8, quantity is 7.0, and elasticity is -1.4. The actual margin is 0.46, and the desired margin is 0.71 $= 1/(1.4)$. Since the actual margin is less than the desired margin, produce less, and you do this by increasing price.

In the second row, price goes up to $5.0, the actual margin increases to 0.48, and the desired margin decreases to 0.59 because demand becomes more elastic. At a price of 5.2, we see that profit is maximized at $16, and the desired margin (0.5) is equal to the actual margin. At the optimal price of 6.2 and a 50% margin, it is easy to compute MC (MC $= 2.6$).

Price ($)	Quantity	Elasticity	(P − MC)/P	1/|Elas|	Profit ($)
4.8	7.0	−1.4	0.46	0.71	15.50
5.0	6.6	−1.7	0.48	0.59	15.88
5.2	6.2	−2.0	0.50	0.50	16.00
5.4	5.7	−2.3	0.52	0.43	15.88
5.6	5.2	−2.7	0.54	0.37	15.52
5.8	4.7	−3.1	0.55	0.32	14.96
6.0	4.2	−3.5	0.57	0.29	14.22

6.4 What Makes Demand More Elastic?

Given the importance of price elasticity to pricing—the more elastic is demand, the lower is the profit-maximizing price—it's worthwhile to understand what makes demand more or less elastic. In this section, we list five factors that affect demand elasticity and optimal pricing.

Products with close substitutes have more elastic demand.

Consumers respond to a price increase by switching to their next-best alternative. If their next-best alternative is a very close substitute, then it doesn't take much of a price increase to induce them to switch. This is why revenues fell when Mayor Barry raised the price of gasoline by 6%. Since DC has many commuters, they began purchasing gasoline near their homes in Virginia and Maryland, close substitutes for gasoline in DC.

In a similar vein, we see that individual brands, such as Nike, have closer substitutes (other brands) than do aggregate product categories, like running shoes. This leads to our next factor.

Demand for an individual brand is more elastic than industry aggregate demand.

As a rough estimate, brand price elasticity is approximately equal to industry price elasticity divided by the brand share. For example, if the elasticity of demand for all running shoes is −0.4%, and the market share of Nike running shoes is 20%, price elasticity of demand for Nike running shoes is −0.4/(0.20) = −2. Using our optimal pricing formula, this would give Nike a desired margin of 50%.

If you search the Internet, you'll find industry price elasticity estimates that you can combine with market share estimates to get an estimate of brand elasticity. And you can use this estimate to gain a general idea of whether your brand price is too high or too low.

Products with many complements have less elastic demand.

Individual products that are consumed as part of a larger bundle of complementary goods—say, computers, operating systems, and the applications that run on them—have less elastic demand. One of the reasons that iPhones have such a low price elasticity of demand (and such a high margin) is due to the number of applications (apps) that run on them. If the price of an iPhone increases, you are less likely to substitute to another product, due to the complementary apps.

Another factor affecting elasticity is time. Given more time, consumers are more responsive to price changes. They have more time to find substitutes when price goes up and more time to find new uses for a good when price goes down. This leads to our fourth factor:

In the long run, demand curves become more elastic.

This phenomenon could also be explained by the speed at which price information is disseminated. As time passes, information about a new price becomes more widely known, so more consumers react to the change.

As an example, consider automatic teller machine (ATM) fees. In 1997, a bank in Evanston, Indiana, ran an experiment to determine the elasticity of demand for ATMs with respect to ATM fees. At a selected number of ATMs, the bank raised user fees from $1.50 to $2.00. When informed of the fee increase, users typically completed the current transaction (the short run) but avoided the higher-priced ATMs in the future (the long run).

Our final factor relates elasticity to the price level. As price increases, consumers find more alternatives to the good whose price has gone up. And with more substitutes, demand becomes more elastic.

As price increases, demand becomes more elastic.

For example, high-fructose corn syrup (HFCS) is a caloric sweetener used in soft drinks. For this application, sugar is a perfect substitute for HFCS. However, import quotas and price supports have raised the U.S. price of sugar to about twice that of HFCS. All soft drink bottlers have switched to HFCS from sugar. Because bottlers have no close substitutes for *low-priced* HFCS, its demand is less elastic. But if the price of HFCS were to rise to that of sugar, sugar would become a perfect substitute for HFCS. In other words, demand for *high-priced* HFCS becomes very elastic as it approaches the price of sugar.

As a strategy, many firms would like to make demand for their products less elastic (less sensitive to price). One way to do this is to create a brand identity that makes consumers less sensitive to price. A good example of this is Harley Davidson whose motorcycle brand has become synonymous with freedom, individualism, and the American Way. To build and maintain the brand the firm supports user groups (H.O.G., Harley Owners' Group) and sponsors motorcycle rallies (e.g., in Sturgis).

6.5 Forecasting Demand Using Elasticity

We can also use elasticity as a forecasting tool. With an elasticity and a percentage change in price, you can predict the corresponding change in quantity:[10]

$$\%\Delta Quantity \approx e(\%\Delta Price)$$

For example, if the price elasticity of demand is -2, and price goes up by 10%, then quantity is forecast to decrease by 20%.

Remember that price is only one of many factors that affect demand. Income, prices of substitutes and complements, advertising, and tastes all affect demand. To measure the effects of these other variables on demand, we define a factor elasticity of demand:

Factor elasticity of demand = (%ΔQuantity Demanded) ÷ %ΔFactor

Factors can be anything that affects demand, such as temperature, other prices, or incomes. For example, demand for bottled water, iced tea, and carbonated soft drinks is strongly influenced by temperature. If the temperature elasticity of demand for beverages is 0.25, then a 1% increase in temperature will lead to a 0.25% increase in quantity demanded.

Income elasticity of demand measures the change in demand arising from changes in income. Positive income elasticity means that the good is **normal;** that is, as income increases, demand increases. Negative income elasticity means that the good is **inferior**; that is, as income increases, demand declines. The decreasing incomes associated with the financial crisis of 2008 provided a number of examples of inferior goods. Although most retailers saw dramatic sales declines in 2008, Walmart's sales increased. Sales of Spam, a low-priced meat product, shot up in 2008, leading Hormel to add a second shift at its Minnesota factory.

Cross-price elasticity of demand for Good A with respect to the price of Good B measures the change in quantity demanded for A caused by a change in the price of B. A positive cross-price elasticity means that Good B is a **substitute** for Good A: as the price of a substitute increases, demand increases.

Negative cross-price elasticity means that Good B is a **complement** to Good A: as the price of a complement increases, demand decreases. Computers, for example, are complements to operating systems that run on them. We can trace part of Microsoft's initial success with its DOS operating system to its strategy of licensing DOS to competing computer manufacturers. That strategy helped keep the price of computers low, which stimulated demand for Microsoft's operating system.

We can estimate factor elasticities by using a formula analogous to the estimated price elasticity formula, and we can use factor elasticities to forecast or predict changes over time or even changes from one geographic area to another.

Suppose you're trying to compare the year-to-year performance of one of your regional salespeople over a period in which income grew by 3%. If demand for your products has an income elasticity of 2, you would expect quantity to increase by 6%. You don't want to reward the salesperson for increases in quantity that are largely unrelated to her effort. A performance measure more closely related to effort would subtract 6% from the actual growth because that is the growth related to income, and not to sales effort.

6.6 Stay-Even Analysis, Pricing, and Elasticity

Stay-even analysis is a simple two-step procedure that tells you whether a given price increase, for example, 5%, will be profitable.

1. In the first step, you compute how much quantity you can afford to lose before the price increase becomes unprofitable. This "stay-even quantity" is a simple function of the size of the price increase and the contribution margin, $\%\Delta Q = \%\Delta P/(\%\Delta P + \text{margin})$, where margin $= (P - MC)/P$.[11]
2. In the second step, you predict how much quantity will go down if you raise price by the given amount.

The decision rule is simple:

If the predicted quantity is less than the stay-even quantity, then the price increase will likely be profitable, and vice versa.

The analysis gives you a quick answer to the question of whether changing price is profitable. It uses the same information as does the marginal analysis of Section 6.4, but it does so in a simpler, intuitive way.

To illustrate, let's go back to the Mattel's pricing question from the beginning of this chapter: should they double the price of their Hot Wheels cars? Imagine that it costs Mattel $0.50 to manufacture, package, and distribute a car, which it currently sells to retailers for $0.75. If Mattel were to double the wholesale price to $1.50, the margin would increase *fourfold* from $0.25 to $1.00. This means that Mattel could lose three-fourths of its customers and still earn the same profit that it earned prior to the price increase. Thus, Mattel's stay-even quantity for a 100% increase in price is a 75% decrease in quantity. Since quantity fell by much less than 75%, the price increase was profitable.

6.7 Cost-Based Pricing

Our expressions for optimal pricing, $MR=MC$ or $(P-MC)/P=1/|elasticity|$ use information about consumer demand and a firm's cost structure to find the optimal price. Yet, many companies set prices based only on costs, ignoring demand entirely. For example, cost-plus pricing arrives at a price by adding a fixed dollar margin to the cost of each product, while mark-up pricing multiplies the cost by a fixed number greater than 1. It doesn't take much analysis to see that ignoring consumer demand leads to suboptimal pricing—just imagine cost-based pricing applied to diamonds, wine, movie tickets, or bottled water. Without comparing costs to demand, we cannot know if goods are priced optimally.

To understand why cost-based pricing persists, we apply the second question in our problem-solving paradigm: does the decision maker have enough information to make a good decision? In one survey of managers, most reported that they are well informed about their own costs, but less than half reported being well informed about demand.[12] Part of the reason for this is historical accident. Tax compliance required firms to have cost accountants, and since these cost data were there anyway, pricing managers used them. A firm that takes its profitability (and pricing) seriously needs a "demand accounting" (market research) division, too.

SUMMARY & HOMEWORK PROBLEMS

Summary of Main Points

- Individual demand describes how many units an individual will purchase at a given price.
- **Aggregate demand**, or market demand, is the total number of units that will be purchased by a group of consumers at a given price.
- Pricing is an extent decision. Reduce price (increase quantity) if $MR > MC$. Increase price (reduce quantity) if $MR < MC$. The optimal price is where $MR = MC$.
- **Price elasticity of demand,**
  $e = (\%\text{change in quantity demanded}) \div (\%\text{change in price})$
  1. Estimated price elasticity $= [(Q_1 - Q_2) / (Q_1 + Q_2)] \div [(P_1 - P_2) / (P_1 + P_2)]$ is used to estimate demand elasticity from a price and quantity change.
  2. If $|e| > 1$, demand is **elastic;** if $|e| < 1$, demand is **inelastic.**

- %ΔRevenue ≈ %ΔPrice + %ΔQuantity
- Elastic demand ($|e| > 1$): Quantity changes more than price.

	ΔRevenue
Price ↑	−
Price ↓	+

- Inelastic demand ($|e| < 1$): Quantity changes less than price.

	ΔRevenue
Price ↓	−
Price ↑	+

- MR > MC implies that $(P - MC) / P > 1/|e|$; that is, the more elastic is demand, the lower the optimal price.
- Five factors affect elasticity:
  1. Products with close **substitutes** have more elastic demand.
  2. Products with many **complements** have less elastic demand.
  3. Demand for brands is more elastic than industry demand.
  4. In the long run, demand becomes more elastic.
  5. As price increases, demand becomes more elastic.
- **Income elasticity, cross-price elasticity,** and advertising elasticity are measures of how changes in these other factors affect demand.
- It is possible to use elasticity to forecast changes in demand: %ΔQuantity = (Factor elasticity)(%ΔFactor).
- **Stay-even analysis** can be used to determine the quantity change required to offset a price change. The stay-even quantity is %ΔQ = %ΔP/(%ΔP + margin). A proposed price increase is profitable if the predicted quantity loss is less than the stay-even quantity.

Multiple-Choice Questions

1. Jim has estimated elasticity of demand for gasoline to be −0.7 in the short run and −1.8 in the long run. A decrease in taxes on gasoline would
   a. lower tax revenue in both the short and long run.
   b. raise tax revenue in both the short and long run.
   c. raise tax revenue in the short run but lower tax revenue in the long run.
   d. lower tax revenue in the short run but raise tax revenue in the long run.

2. Its lunch time, you are hungry and would like to have some pizza. By the law of diminishing marginal value,
   a. you would pay more for your first slice of pizza than your second.
   b. you would pay more for your second slice of pizza than your first.
   c. you would pay an equal amount of money for both the slices since they are identical.
   d. none of the above.

3. Jim recently graduated from college. His income increased tremendously from $5,000 a year to $60,000 a year. Jim decided that instead of renting he will buy a house. This implies that
   a. houses are normal goods for Jim.
   b. houses are inferior goods for Jim.
   c. renting and owning are complementary for Jim.
   d. need information on the price of houses.

4. Which of the following goods has a negative income elasticity of demand?
   a. Cars
   b. Items from Dollar stores
   c. Shoes
   d. Bread

5. An economist estimated the cross-price elasticity for peanut butter and jelly to be 1.5. Based on this information, we know the goods are
   a. inferior goods.
   b. complements.
   c. inelastic.
   d. substitutes.

6. Christine has purchased five bananas and is considering the purchase of a sixth. It is likely she will purchase the sixth banana if
   a. the marginal value she gets from the sixth banana is lower than its price.
   b. the marginal benefit of the sixth banana exceeds the price.
   c. the average value of the sixth banana exceeds the price.
   d. the total personal value of six bananas exceeds the total expenditure to purchase six bananas.

7. Buyers consider Marlboro cigarettes and Budweiser beer to be complements. If Marlboro just increased its prices, what would you expect to occur in the Budweiser market?
   a. Demand would rise, and Budweiser would reduce price.
   b. Demand would fall, and Budweiser would reduce price.
   c. Demand would fall, and Budweiser would increase price.
   d. Demand would rise, and Budweiser would increase supply.

8. Which of the following is the reason for the existence of consumer surplus?
   a. Consumers can purchase goods that they "want" in addition to what they "need."
   b. Consumers can occasionally purchase products for less than their production cost.
   c. Some consumers receive temporary discounts that result in below-market prices.
   d. Some consumers are willing to pay more than the price.

9. A bakery currently sells chocolate chip cookies at a price of $16/dozen. The MC is $8/dozen. The cookies are becoming more popular with customers, and so the bakery owner is considering raising the price to $20/dozen. What percentage of customers must be retained to ensure that the price increase is profitable?
   a. 28.0%
   b. 33.3%
   c. 66.6%
   d. 72.0%

10. Suppose your firm adopts a technology that allows you to increase your output by 15%. If the elasticity of demand is -3, how should you adjust price if you want to sell all of your output?
    a. 5% lower
    b. 0.5% lower
    c. 15% higher
    d. 15% lower

Individual Problems

6-1 Elasticity of T-shirt Sales

George has been selling 5,000 T-shirts per month for $8.50. When he increased the price to $9.50, he sold only 4,000 T-shirts. What is the demand elasticity? If his MC is $4 per shirt, what is his desired markup and what is his initial actual markup? Was raising the price profitable?

6-2 Increasing Movie Ticket Prices

To conduct an experiment, AMC increased movie ticket prices from $9.00 to $10.00 and measured the change in ticket sales. Using the data over the following month, they concluded that the increase was profitable. However, over the subsequent months, they changed their minds and discontinued the experiment. How did the timing affect their conclusion about the profitability of increasing prices?

6-3 Promotional Pricing

An end-of-aisle price promotion changes the price elasticity of a good from -2 to -3.

If the normal price is $10, what should the promotional price be?

6-4 Bar Nuts

Why do bars offer free peanuts?

Group Problems

G6-1 Pricing

Describe a pricing decision your company has made. Was it optimal? If not, why not? How would you adjust price? Compute the profit consequences of the change.

END NOTES

1. Matt Townsend, "Mattel Surges Most Since 2009 as Prices Fuel Profit," *Bloomberg*, July 17, 2012, www.bloomberg.com/news/2012-07-17/mattel-surges-most-since-2009-as-prices-fuel-profit.html.
2. See Roger Brinner, "Pricing: The Neglected Orphan," *Parthenon Perspectives*.
3. Don't get distracted by the fact that at a price of $6, the buyer is being charged a price exactly equal to his or her value and is thus earning no surplus. At a price of $6, the buyer is exactly indifferent between buying and not buying. This is a result of using whole numbers to describe prices and values. For convenience, imagine that the value is a fraction above the price, so that the buyer will purchase.
4. **Marginal profit** $= MR - MC$ and is the extra profit from selling one more unit.
5. Profit $=$ Revenue $-$ Cost $= Q*(P - AC)$, where AC is average cost.
6. In computing the midpoints, we use the formulas $(Q_1 + Q_2)/2$ and $(P_1 + P_2)/2$. Since 2 divides both denominator and numerator, the formula simplifies, as here.
7. Note that if we used the initial price and quantity to compute the percentage changes, the calculation would be $[(210 - 420)/210]/[(\$1.79 - \$1.50)/\$1.79]$ or $-100\% / 16.2\%$; that is, -6.2.
8. This is a first-order approximation and will work well for small changes. The approximation does not work well for large changes.
9. $MR = \Delta\text{Revenue}/\Delta Q = \Delta(PQ)/\Delta Q = (\Delta PQ + \Delta QP)/\Delta Q = P(1 - 1/|e|)$. The symbol Δ means "change in."
10. This is a first-order approximation and will work well for small changes. The approximation does not work well for large changes.
11. This is just one of many equivalent formulas. The important thing to note is that any stay-even formula ensures that the profit before and after the price change is the same.
12. Robert J. Doan and Hermann Simon, *Power Pricing* (New York: Simon & Schuster, 1996).

7 Economies of Scale and Scope

In 1906, three entrepreneurs launched the French Battery Company in Madison, Wisconsin. The company's early growth was driven by the demand for radio batteries, and its most successful product was the Ray-O-Vac battery, leading the firm to change its name to Rayovac in 1930. Over the next 60 years, it grew to become one of the top three battery producers in the United States along with Duracell and Energizer.

In 1996, the company was acquired by the Thomas H. Lee Company, a Boston-based private equity firm. After making an initial public offering the following year, the company took advantage of easy credit availability to expand via acquisition. It purchased battery manufacturers such as BRISCO GmbH, ROV Limited, VARTA AG, Direct Power Plus, and Ningbo Baowang in order to take advantage of "efficiencies and economies of scale." Company managers expected that as they produced more of the same good, average costs would fall.

In 2003, Rayovac purchased Remington Products (electric razors); in 2005, it purchased United Industries Corporation (lawn and garden care, household insect control, and pet supplies) and Tetra Holding GmbH, a German supplier of fish and aquatic supplies. To reflect its position as a provider of a broad portfolio of products, the company changed its name to Spectrum Brands in 2005. Managers often justified the company's expansions into these new areas with claims of cost savings. For example, as part of its acquisition of United Industries, Spectrum's managers anticipated "that there would be synergies, better performance, and all that." As is often the case, it is much easier to describe synergies than it is to capture them, and although it's not clear whether this was the case for Spectrum, the company declared bankruptcy in 2009.[1] Since emerging from bankruptcy, Spectrum has delivered impressive performance, and it has continued to pursue synergies via acquisitions of businesses like the Hardware & Home Improvement Group of Stanley Black & Decker in 2012 and Armored AutoGroup in 2015.

In this chapter, we examine the two types of synergies described in the above story, economies of scale and scope, and show you how to exploit them.

This is especially important if your company is following a cost leadership strategy, but managers should always be looking for ways to cut costs, regardless of whether it is the company's primary strategy. A reduction in average cost translates to an immediate increase in profit (recall that Profit = (Price − Average Cost)*Quantity). If marginal cost (MC) goes down as well, you get an "extra" increase in profit from the increase in output; remember that if MC falls below marginal revenue (MR), it becomes profitable to increase output.

Many business decisions, like break-even analysis, can be made using very simple characterizations of cost (like a fixed cost plus a constant per-unit cost). With economies of scale or scope, however, decision making may require more complex (and realistic) cost functions. In this section, we will examine decision making in the presence of economies of scale and scope.

7.1 Increasing Marginal Cost

Most firms will eventually face increasing average costs as they try to increase output. The firm finds that each extra unit of output requires more inputs to produce than previous units, an outcome described as the *law of diminishing marginal returns.*

> The *law of diminishing marginal returns* states that as you try to expand output, your marginal productivity (the extra output associated with extra inputs) eventually declines.

Diminishing marginal returns occur for a variety of reasons, among them are the difficulty of monitoring and motivating larger workforces, the increasing complexity of larger systems, or the fixed nature of some factors. In popular jargon, these are known as "bottlenecks." Bottlenecks often arise when more workers, or any variable input, must share a fixed amount of a complementary input. When productivity falls from bottlenecks, costs increase.

Diminishing marginal productivity implies increasing marginal cost.

If more inputs are needed to produce each extra unit of output, then the cost of producing these extra units—the marginal cost—must increase. And once the marginal cost rises above the average cost, the average will rise as well. Say, for example, the average cost to produce the first 100 units of a product is $50 per unit. If the marginal cost of the 101st unit is more than $50, overall average cost will increase.

Increasing marginal costs eventually lead to increasing average costs.

Just as a baseball player's season batting average will rise if his game batting average is above his season batting average, so too does average cost rise if marginal cost is above the average.

In Figure 7.1, the rising average cost of production implies that marginal cost is above average cost.

In the presence of fixed costs, increasing marginal cost gives you a U-shaped average cost curve (shown in Figure 7.2). The curve initially falls due to the presence of fixed costs, but then it rises due to increasing marginal costs.

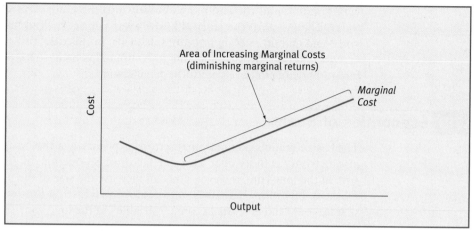

FIGURE **7.1**   **Diminishing Marginal Returns**

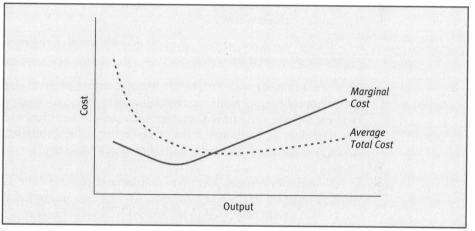

FIGURE **7.2**   **U-Shaped Average Cost Curve**

Knowing what your average costs look like will help you make better decisions. Here's a famous example. In 1955, Akio Morita brought his newly invented $29.95 transistor radio to New York. He shopped it around, and after turning down an original equipment manufacturer (OEM) deal from Bulova, he eventually found a retailer that would sell it under his "Sony" brand name. The problem was that the retailer had a chain of around 150 stores and wanted to buy 100,000 radios, 10 times more than Mr. Morita's capacity. Mr. Morita turned the offer down. He knew that he would lose money producing 100,000 units because increasing output would require hiring and training more workers and an expansion of facilities, raising his average cost or break-even price.

After being turned down, the retailer agreed to settle for 10,000 units at the lowest unit price, and the rest is history. The Sony brand radios became very popular, and the company evolved into the giant electronics firm it is today. The moral of the story is know what your costs look like—otherwise, you could end up making unprofitable deals. In this case, using a more realistic cost function, Morita was able to compute his break-even prices, allowing him to bargain effectively with the retail chain.[2]

7.2 Economies of Scale

The law of diminishing marginal returns is primarily a short-run phenomenon arising from the fixity of at least one factor of production, like capital or plant size. In the long run, however, you can increase the size of the plant, hire more workers, buy more machines, and remove production bottlenecks. In other words, your "fixed" costs become "variable" in the long run.

If long-run average costs are constant with respect to output, then you have **constant returns to scale**.

If long-run average costs rise with output, you have **decreasing returns to scale** *or* **diseconomies of scale**.

If long-run average costs fall with output, you have **increasing returns to scale** *or* **economies of scale**.

Economies of scale can result from a variety of areas. Larger firms can benefit more from capital equipment like machinery: average costs decrease as volume increases and fixed costs are unchanged. Larger firms may also benefit from purchasing economies if they receive discounts for buying in larger quantities. Average costs associated with shared administrative services can also fall as output increases.

Economies of scale have had a dramatic effect on the structure of the poultry industry in the United States.[3] In 1967, a total of 2.6 billion chickens and turkeys were processed in the United States. By 1992, that number had increased to nearly seven billion. Despite this large increase, the number of processing facilities dropped from 215 to 174. The share of shipments of plants with over 400 employees grew from 29% to 88% for chicken production and from 16% to 83% for turkey production over the same period. The shift in the structure of the industry was due largely to changes in technology, which reduced costs of processing poultry in larger plants.

Taking advantage of economies of scale is also critical in ocean shipping. The *Maersk McKinney Moller* entered service in July of 2013 with the largest cargo capacity of any container ship in the world. The ship is over 1,300 feet long and has a cargo capacity of over 18,000 TEU containers (TEU is the acronym for a 20-foot equivalent unit, which is a stackable, 20-foot-long cargo container.) The enormous size of the ship reflects the value of economies of scale in this industry. On a standard shipping route, the daily operating expenses (in dollars per TEU) for a 2,000 TEU capacity ship are about $20. Increasing the capacity of that ship to 14,000 TEU, however, cuts the daily operating expenses per TEU to just over $12.[4]

It is important to realize, however, that the same factors (i.e., the fixity of some input) that cause diminishing marginal returns in the short run can also cause decreasing returns to scale in the long run. Often, the managerial structure of the company does not scale beyond a certain point. Management is an important input into the production processes. As the company grows, so do the problems of coordination, control, and monitoring. Managers often behave as if they have a fixed amount of decision-making capability, so giving them more decisions often leads to managerial bottlenecks that raise costs.

Knowing whether your long-run costs exhibit constant, decreasing, or increasing returns to scale can help you make better long-run decisions. If your long-run costs exhibit increasing returns to scale, securing big orders allows you to reduce average costs.

7.3   Learning Curves

Learning curves are characteristic of many processes. As you produce more, you learn from the experience, and this experience helps you produce future units at a lower cost. Learning curves mean that current production lowers future costs, which has important strategic consequences. Here the maxim "Look ahead and reason back" is particularly important.

For example, every time an airplane manufacturer doubles production, marginal cost decreases by 20%. If the first plane costs $100 million, then the second will cost $80 million, the fourth will cost $64 million, the eighth will cost $51.2 million, and so on. In Table 7.1, we illustrate such a learning curve. Note that marginal cost is below average cost at all levels of production beyond the first plane, indicating economies of scale.[5]

TABLE **7.1**
Airplane Manufacturing Costs

Quantity	Marginal Cost ($M)	Total Cost ($M)	Average Cost ($M)
1	100.0	100.0	100.0
2	80.0	180.0	90.0
3	70.2	250.2	83.4
4	64.0	314.2	78.6
5	59.6	373.8	74.8
6	56.2	429.9	71.7
7	53.4	483.4	69.1
8	51.2	534.6	66.8
9	49.3	583.9	64.9
10	47.7	631.5	63.2

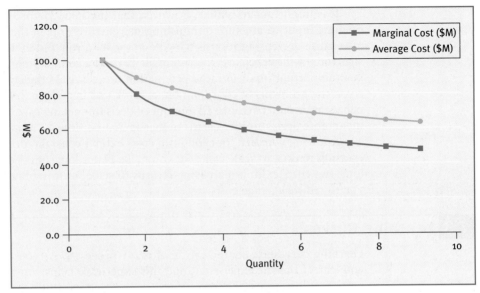

FIGURE 7.3 Airplane Manufacturing Learning Curve

To see how learning curves affect decision making, put yourself in American Airlines' place during negotiations with Boeing to purchase airplanes. From Boeing's point of view, a big order from the world's largest airline would allow it to "walk down its learning curve," as shown in Figure 7.3, and reduce the costs of future production. However, American knows that its order will allow Boeing to reduce costs for future sales and wants to capture some of Boeing's increased profit.

If American knew exactly how many planes Boeing would make over the lifetime of the airplane, it could offer a price at Boeing's average cost. For example, if Boeing expected to produce eight units, American could offer $66.8 million per plane, and Boeing would break even on the order over the lifetime of the model. But if the lifetime production is not known, then American must pursue other strategies. For example, American could ask for "kickbacks" on sales of future Boeing planes; however, this request may violate European or U.S. antitrust laws. Alternatively, since stock prices reflect future earnings, American could ask for a percentage of the increase in Boeing's stock market value following announcement of the deal; such a request would be equivalent to buying call options to purchase Boeing stock before beginning negotiations. When Boeing's stock value increased because of the order, the value of the call options would also increase. These strategies may violate securities laws on insider trading, so be sure to get legal advice before trying something like this.

Instead, American offered to purchase planes exclusively from Boeing over the next 30 years in exchange for a very favorable price. By offering exclusivity, American guaranteed Boeing a big chunk of demand that would lower costs. Boeing was willing to give American a very good deal in exchange for such a guarantee.

As a strange footnote to this story, in 1998, Boeing tried to acquire rival McDonnell-Douglas. The European Commission antitrust authority objected because Boeing's large European competitor, Airbus, objected to the long-term exclusive contracts as anticompetitive. Airbus claimed Boeing's exclusive contracts prevented it from competing for American's business. To complete its purchase of McDonnell-Douglas, Boeing agreed not to enforce its exclusive contracts with American, leaving American free to purchase from Airbus if it so chose.

7.4 Economies of Scope

Gibson Guitar traditionally used rosewood for fingerboards on its less expensive Epiphone guitars and reserved ebony for its high-end Gibson brand. Both rosewood and ebony are excellent tone woods, but ebony is preferred for its distinct sound and pure black appearance. A significant number of ebony fingerboard blanks are rejected for use on the Gibson brand guitars because carving of the fingerboard reveals brown streaks in the otherwise pure black wood. The percentage of fingerboards rejected has increased steadily over the past 10 years as the world supply of streak-free ebony has shrunk.

Gibson Guitar began installing these streaked blanks on its lower-end instruments. The buyers perceive the streaked ebony fingerboard as an upgrade over rosewood. Its ability to use discarded ebony in its Epiphone guitars gives Gibson both a cost and quality advantage over rivals that produce only high-end or only low-end instruments. In this case, we say there are economies of scope between production of high-end and low-end guitars.

If the cost of producing two products jointly is less than the cost of producing those two products separately—that is,

$$\text{Cost}(Q_1, Q_2) < \text{Cost}(Q_1) + \text{Cost}(Q_2)$$

—then there are **economies of scope** between the two products.

Obviously, you want to exploit economies of scope by producing both Q_1 and Q_2. This is a major cause of mergers. For example, about eight years ago, we saw a consolidation in the food distribution business. Companies like Kraft, Sara Lee, and ConAgra sell a variety of meat products, hot dogs, sausage, and lunchmeats because they can derive economies of scope by distributing these products together. Once you set up a distribution network, you can easily pump more products through the network without incurring additional costs.

These low costs put pressure on their competitors, in particular, a regional breakfast sausage manufacturer in 1997. This manufacturer used 18 trucks and a single distribution center that served retail customers located in 21 southern and Midwestern states. Unfortunately, the demand for breakfast sausage is seasonal, with a peak in November and December. During the heavy winter months, the manufacturer had to pay outside carriers a premium to handle excess product, but for the other eight months, half of its trucking fleet sat idle.

Because the firm sold only a single product—breakfast sausage—it could not exploit the scope economies associated with distributing a full product line. The manufacturer had several choices. It could have acquired other companies to have a full product line to distribute. It could have sold out to one of the larger, full-line companies, like ConAgra. Such a company could exploit the scope economies associated with distribution, thus placing a higher value on the firm. Or it could have outsourced its distribution function. Several regional and nationwide distribution companies distribute a variety of food products, and these companies could take advantage of scope economies by distributing a full portfolio of meat products.

Our sausage maker eventually decided to outsource its distribution. However, after it sold its trucking fleet, it was held up by the distributor. Outsourcing was a good idea, but poorly executed.

7.5   Diseconomies of Scope

Production can also exhibit **diseconomies of scope** if the cost of producing two products together is higher than the cost of producing them separately. In this case, you reduce costs by paring down the product line. AnimalSnax Inc. makes pet food on extruder lines in 23 plants. This manufacturer has a variety of customers, from large retailers like Walmart to small mom-and-pop pet stores. Currently, the firm produces 2,500 different products, or stock-keeping units (SKUs), using 200 different formulas. All customers pay about the same price per ton. Recently, however, some of the large customers have demanded price concessions.

These requests worry the firm because of the so-called *80–20 rule*: according to this rule of thumb, 80% of a firm's profit comes from around 20% of its customers. Because big customers (the 20%) order in bulk, the manufacturer can set up its extruders for long production runs. These big orders are much more profitable than smaller orders because all orders require the same setup time regardless of the amount produced and packaged.

To reduce the costs associated with smaller orders, AnimalSnax reduced the variety of its product offerings to 70 SKUs, using only 13 different formulas. The firm also began offering price discounts for larger orders. Although some smaller customers were upset about being forced to use new formulas, most were willing to switch. This allowed the company to consolidate small orders into large ones to reduce setup costs.

Typical savings for one extruder line are illustrated in Figure 7.4. Under the new approach, the same amount of pet food that had been produced in one eight-hour shift could now be produced in just six hours. This dramatic increase in productivity (25%) also allowed the company to close several of its 23 plants.

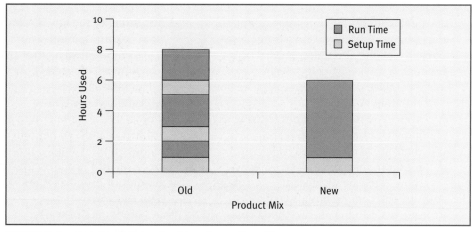

FIGURE **7.4**   **Pet Food Extruder Line Operation Times**

SUMMARY & HOMEWORK PROBLEMS

Summary of Main Points

- The **law of diminishing marginal returns** states that as you increase output, your marginal productivity (the extra output associated with extra inputs) eventually declines.
- Increasing marginal costs eventually cause increasing average costs and make it more difficult to compute break-even prices. When negotiating contracts, it is important to know what your cost curves look like; otherwise, you could agree to unprofitable deals.
- If average cost falls with output, then you have **increasing returns to scale**. In this case you want to focus your strategy on securing sales that enable you to realize lower costs. Alternatively, if you offer suppliers big orders that allow them to realize **economies of scale**, try to share in their profit by demanding lower prices.
- If your average costs are constant with respect to output, then you have **constant returns to scale**. If average costs rise with output, you have **decreasing returns to scale or diseconomies of scale**.

- **Learning curves** mean that current production lowers future costs. It's important to look over the life cycle of a product when working with products characterized by learning curves.
- If the cost of producing two outputs jointly is less than the cost of producing them separately—that is, $\text{Cost}(Q_1, Q_2) < \text{Cost}(Q_1) + \text{Cost}(Q_2)$ —then there are **economies of scope** between the two products. This can be an important source of competitive advantage and can shape acquisition strategy.

Multiple-Choice Questions

1. Microsoft found that instead of producing a DVD player and a gaming system separately, it is cheaper to incorporate DVD playing capabilities in its new version of the gaming system. Microsoft is taking advantage of
   a. economies of scale.
   b. learning curve.
   c. economies of scope.
   d. decreasing marginal costs.

2. As a golf club production company produces more clubs, the average total cost of each club produced decreases. This is because
   a. total fixed costs are decreasing as more clubs are produced.
   b. average variable cost is decreasing as more clubs are produced.
   c. there are scale economies.
   d. total variable cost is decreasing as more clubs are produced.

3. Average costs curves initially fall
   a. due to declining average fixed costs.
   b. due to rising average fixed costs.
   c. due to declining accounting costs.
   d. due to rising marginal costs.

4. What might you reasonably expect of an industry in which firms tend to have economies of scale?
   a. Exceptional competition among firms
   b. A large number of firms
   c. Highly diversified firms
   d. A small number of firms

5. A security system company's total production costs depend on the number of systems produced according to the following equation: Total Costs = $20,000,000 + $4,000* quantityproduced. Given these data, which of the following is a *false* statement?
   a. There are economies of scale.
   b. There are fixed costs associated with this business.
   c. There are diseconomies of scale.
   d. A firm that produces a larger output has a cost advantage over a smaller firm.

6. Following are the costs to produce Product A, Product B, and Products A and B together. Which of the following exhibits economies of scope?
   a. 100, 150, 240
   b. 100, 150, 250
   c. 100, 150, 260
   d. All of the above

7. According to the law of diminishing marginal returns, marginal returns
   a. diminish always prior to increasing.
   b. diminish constantly.
   c. diminish never.
   d. diminish eventually.

8. It costs a firm $90 per unit to produce product A and $70 per unit to produce product B individually. If the firm can produce both products together at $175 per unit of products A and B, this exhibits signs of
   a. economies of scale.
   b. economies of scope.
   c. diseconomies of scale.
   d. diseconomies of scope.

9. A company faces the following costs at the respective production levels in addition to its fixed costs of $50,000:

Quantity	Marginal Cost ($)	Sale Price ($)	Marginal Return ($)
1	10,000	20,000	10,000
2	11,000	20,000	9,000
3	12,000	20,000	8,000
4	13,000	20,000	7,000
5	14,000	20,000	6,000

10. How would you describe the returns to scale for this company?
    a. Increasing
    b. Decreasing
    c. Constant
    d. Marginal

11. Once marginal cost rises above the average cost,
    a. average costs will increase.
    b. average costs are unaffected.
    c. average costs will decrease.
    d. none of the above.

Individual Problems

7.1 Scale and Scope

What is the difference between economies of scale and economies of scope?

7.2 Brand Extensions

Suppose Nike's managers were considering expanding into producing sports beverages. Why might the company decide to do this under the Nike brand name?

7.3 Rangers' T-Shirts

The variety of Riverside Ranger logo T-shirts includes 12 different designs. Setup between designs takes one hour (and $18,000), and, after setting up, you can produce 1,000 units of a particular design per hour (at a cost of $8,000). Does this production exhibit scale economies or scope economies?

7.4 Average and Marginal Costs

Describe the change in average costs and the relationship between marginal and average costs under the following three conditions as quantities produced increase:

	Average Cost	Marginal Cost versus Average Cost
Constant returns to scale	Rising Falling Flat	Higher Lower Equal
Decreasing returns to scale	Rising Falling Flat	Higher Lower Equal
Increasing returns to scale	Rising Falling Flat	Higher Lower Equal

7.5 Learning Curves

Suppose you have a production technology that can be characterized by a learning curve. Every time you increase production by one unit, your costs decrease by $6. The first unit costs you $64 to produce. If you receive a request for proposal (RFP) on a project for four units, what is your break-even price? Suppose that if you get the contract, you estimate that you can win another project for two more units. Now what is your break-even price for those two units?

7.6 Multiconcept Restaurants Are a Growing Trend

A multiconcept restaurant incorporates two or more restaurants, typically chains, under one roof. Sharing facilities reduces costs of both real estate and labor. The multiconcept restaurants typically offer a limited menu, compared with full-sized, stand-alone restaurants. For example, KMAC operates a combination Kentucky Fried Chicken (KFC)/Taco Bell restaurant. The food preparation areas are separate, but orders are taken at shared point-of-sale (POS) stations. If Taco Bell and KFC share facilities, they reduce fixed costs by 30%; however, sales in joint facilities are 20% lower than sales in two separate facilities. What do these numbers imply for the decision of when to open a shared facility versus two separate facilities?

Group Problems

G7-1 Economies of Scale

Describe an activity, process, or product of your company that exhibits economies or diseconomies of scale. Describe the source of the scale economy. How could your organization exploit the scale economy or diseconomy? Compute the profit consequences of the advice.

G7-2 Learning Curves

Describe an activity or process or product of your company characterized by learning curves. Describe the source of the learning curve. How could your organization exploit the learning curve? Compute the profit consequences of the advice.

G7-3 Economies of Scope

Describe two activities inside your organization, or one inside and one outside your organization, that exhibit economies (or diseconomies) of scope. Describe the source of the scope economies. How could your organization exploit the scope economy or diseconomy? Compute the profit consequences of the advice.

END NOTES

1. For more on Spectrum Brands' difficulties, see Elizabeth Woyke and David Henry, "The Buyout Boom's Dark Side," *Business Week*, August 13, 2007.
2. Akio Morita with Edwin M. Reingold and Mitsuko Shimomura, *Made in Japan: Akio Morita and Sony* (New York: Penguin, 1988).
3. Michael Ollinger, James M. McDonald, and Milton Madison. "Technological Change and Economies of Scale in U.S. Poultry Processing," *American Journal of Agricultural Economics* 87 (February 2005): 116–129.
4. Shipping costs from Jean-Paul Rodrigue, Claude Comtois, and Brian Slack, eds., *The Geography of Transport Systems*, 3rd ed. (London: Routledge, 2013).
5. Formula for marginal cost: $100*0.8 \wedge$ (Log (# planes)/Log (2)).

Understanding Markets and Industry Changes

In 1997, the portable electric generator industry was a mildly profitable but not particularly exciting industry. For over a decade, sales of portable electric generators had been pretty stable with average annual growth of around 2%. But all this changed dramatically as the year 2000 (Y2K) approached. Many consumers were afraid that the power grid would collapse because the computer programs that controlled it would not be able to adapt to the change from 1999 to 2000. Anticipating a big increase in demand for portable generators, managers at Akers, MacMillan, and Parlow (AMP) implemented a Y2K strategy that involved doubling production capacity. Other firms in the industry made similar investments.

In 1999, demand for portable generators boomed as expected; industry shipments increased by 87%, and prices increased by 21%. But the following year was a bust. Demand fell back to 1998 levels, and prices tumbled to below the 1998 level. Industry profit dropped dramatically, along with capacity utilization rates. AMP's Y2K strategy to increase production capacity turned out to be a big mistake. Along with half the firms in the industry, it declared bankruptcy in 2000.

AMP's managers would have benefited from a better understanding of the changes affecting its industry. In particular, everything that happened to AMP was predictable. If AMP's managers had been able to forecast and interpret these industry-level changes, the topic of this chapter, they would have been able to survive and even prosper. In this chapter, we show you how to do this using aggregate demand and aggregate supply curves.

8.1 Which Industry or Market?

In Chapter 6, we showed you how to set a single price if you are a single firm, selling a single product, facing a group of consumers whose behavior can be described by a demand curve. This is often referred to as a "monopoly" model of pricing because it involves only a single firm. In this chapter, we show you how prices are determined in an industry where many sellers and many buyers come together in a "market" setting, a situation referred to as "perfect competition" because sellers must compete with one another in order to sell to buyers. We characterize the behavior of sellers with what is called a "supply curve" in much the same way that we characterized the behavior of buyers with a demand curve.

One note of caution before we begin the chapter: do not use demand and supply analysis to describe changes facing an individual firm. For example, it makes no sense to talk about the "demand and supply of iPhones" because there is only one seller of iPhones. Rather you use demand and supply to talk about the changes in the overall smart phone industry.

Before you begin analyzing an industry, you must carefully consider what you want to learn from the analysis. Perhaps you want to forecast future changes or to understand past ones. In our example, you might want to know, "Why did the price for portable generators in the United States increase in 1999 and decrease in 2000?" Usually the question will suggest a particular *market definition*. The current question suggests that you should examine the *annual market for portable generators in the United States*. Notice that this market has a time (annual), a product (portable generators), and a geographic (the United States) dimension. Different questions will suggest different markets to study. Although this point may seem obvious, people often overlook it. Avoid confusion by first defining your market or industry.

Demand and supply analysis is especially important if your firm's success or profitability is closely linked to the profitability of your primary industry. If you know how the industry is going to change, it will help you recognize opportunities. For example, many towns are changing zoning laws to make it more difficult to build apartments. This has led some entrepreneurs to anticipate a reduction in future supply that will drive up the price of apartments. To position themselves to take advantage of these changes, they are building new apartments or buying and renovating existing ones.

8.2 | Shifts in Demand

As we've seen, changes in price lead to changes in quantity demanded. In an example from Chapter 6, we showed that when we increase price from $6 to $7, one fewer consumer decides to purchase, so quantity demanded decreases from two units to one unit. This change is called a **movement along the demand curve**.

But price is only one factor that affects demand. In general, it helps to catalog the factors that affect demand into controllable and uncontrollable factors.

> A *controllable factor* is something that affects demand that a company can control.

Price, advertising, warranties, product quality, distribution speed, service quality, and prices of substitute or complementary products also owned by the company are all examples of controllable factors.

A firm can manipulate controllable factors to increase demand for its products. Here's a famous business example. In the late 1970s, Microsoft developed the DOS operating system to control IBM personal computers. Demand for the DOS operating system depended not only on its own price but also on the price and availability of the computers that ran it, as well as on the applications that ran under it, like spreadsheets and word processors.

To increase demand for its DOS operating system, Microsoft manipulated the following controllable factors:

- Microsoft licensed its operating system to other computer manufacturers. The resulting competition between IBM and these new licensees lowered the price of computers—a complementary product.
- Microsoft developed its own versions of word processing and spreadsheet software—Word and Excel—two important complementary products in almost any office.
- Microsoft kept the price for its DOS product relatively low. As more consumers purchased DOS computers, more companies made applications that ran on DOS computers, increasing future demand for DOS software.

In contrast, **uncontrollable factors** include things like income, weather, interest rates, and prices of substitute and complementary products owned by other companies. And as is illustrated by the story in the introduction, *expectations* of future changes can also affect current demand. Consumer expectation of a massive power outage in 2000 was an uncontrollable factor that affected 1999 demand for portable electric generators.

> *An* **uncontrollable factor** *is something that affects demand that a company cannot control.*

Even though you may not be able to control a factor affecting demand, you need to understand how it affects the industry in which you compete because it can affect your own profitability. This requires that you learn how to manipulate demand and supply curves, our next topic.

Because we only have two variables on our demand graph—price and quantity—the only way to represent a change in a third variable is with a **shift of the demand curve**. For example, if the price of a substitute product increases, then industry demand for a product will increase. We represent this as a rightward shift in the demand curve, as shown in Figure 8.1.

In this case, at every price, demand shifts rightward, or increases, by four units. At a price of $8.00, for example, quantity demanded is nine units compared to five previously. Another way to look at this is from the perspective of quantity demanded. For example, seven units were previously demanded at a price of $6.00; this quantity is now associated with a price of $10.00.

In contrast to this increase in demand, a decrease in a substitute's price would decrease demand, shifting the curve leftward where fewer units are demanded at each price.

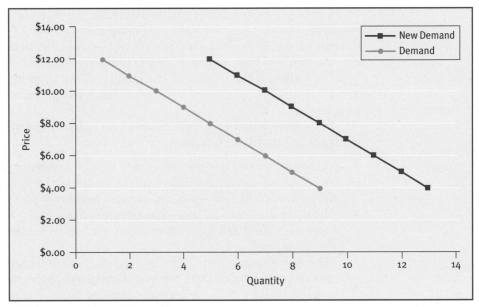

FIGURE **8.1**   **Demand Increase**

8.3 Shifts in Supply

Supply curves describe the behavior of a group of sellers and tell you how much will be sold at a given price.

The construction of supply curves is similar to that of demand curves; we arrange sellers by the prices at which they are willing to sell. Every person willing to sell at or below the given price "supplies" product to the market. For example, suppose we have nine sellers, with values of {$4, $5, $6, $7, $8, $9, $10, $11, $12}; at a price of $4, one seller would be willing to sell; at a price of $5, two sellers; and so on, until, at a price of $12, all nine sellers would be willing to sell. This supply curve describes the aggregate behavior of these nine sellers.

Note that a supply curve requires competition among sellers. As we saw in Chapter 4, a single firm will produce where MR = MC. In contrast, multiple firms facing competition will behave as if they produce where $P - MC$. In this case, price will determine how much is supplied to the market: high prices lead to lots of supply and low prices to smaller supply.

Supply curves differ from demand curves in one very important way:

Supply curves slope upward; that is, the higher the price, the higher the quantity supplied.

In other words, at higher prices, more suppliers are willing to sell. We plot our aggregate supply curve in Figure 8.2.

As with demand curves, we plot supply curves with price on the vertical axis and quantity on the horizontal axis. Also, like demand curves, supply

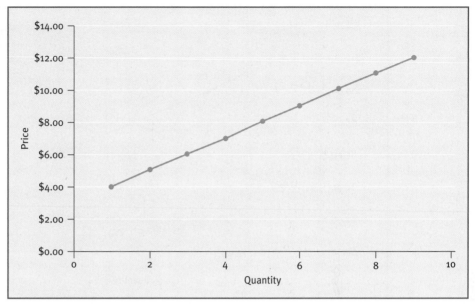

FIGURE **8.2** **Supply Curve**

curves shift when a variable other than price changes. Entry or exit of firms along with changes in costs, technology, and capacity will all result in a **shift of the supply curve**. Consider the effect of increased costs. How would that shift the supply curve? Think about an individual seller first—if that producer now has to pay more to produce the same quantity, he or she will require a higher price to cover those increased costs. If other sellers are situated similarly, the aggregate supply curve will *decrease*, or shift upward (and to the left). This means that higher prices are necessary to induce sellers to supply the same quantities. Alternatively, you could say that a smaller quantity will be made available at the previous price.

8.4 Market Equilibrium

Market equilibrium is the price at which quantity supplied equals quantity demanded.

In other words, at the equilibrium price, the numbers of buyers and sellers are equal, so there's no pressure for prices to change. That's why we call it an "equilibrium." You can see an illustration of market equilibrium in Figure 8.3, where, at a price of $8, five units are demanded and five units supplied.

To understand why this is an equilibrium, consider what happens at prices higher or lower than $8. For example, at a price of $11, the quantity demanded (2) is less than the quantity supplied (8), meaning that eight sellers are trying to sell to only two buyers. The sellers will compete with one another by offering to sell at a lower price. We say that *excess supply* exerts downward pressure on price.

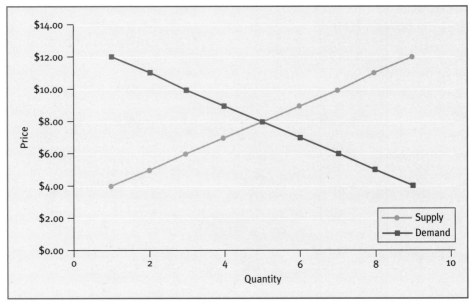

FIGURE **8.3 Market Equilibrium**

At a price of $6, the quantity demanded (7) is greater than the quantity supplied (3)—seven buyers are chasing just three sellers, a case of *excess demand*. In this case, we say that *excess demand* exerts upward pressure on price. Only at a price of $8 are the numbers of buyers and sellers equal, exerting no pressure on price to change. This is why we call $8 an *equilibrium price*.

At the equilibrium price, only buyers with values of $8 and above buy, and only sellers with values $8 and below sell. No one else wants to buy or sell.

> *In market equilibrium, there are no unconsummated wealth-creating transactions.*

Another way of thinking about this is that the market has identified the high-value buyers and the low-value sellers, brought them together, and set a price at which they can exchange goods. The market moves goods from lower- to higher-valued uses and thus creates wealth. Economists often personify market forces by saying that the market works with an "invisible hand."[1]

> *RIDDLE: How many economists does it take to change a light bulb?*

> *ANSWER: None. The market will do it.*

8.5 Predicting Industry Changes Using Supply and Demand

We can use supply and demand curves to describe changes that occur at the industry level. In Table 8.1 and Figure 8.4, we begin with a simple example of how an increase in demand changes price and quantity. This increase in demand could arise from an increase in income, a decrease in the price of a complement, or an increase in price of a substitute.

TABLE **8.1**
Market Equilibrium Analysis

	Price ($)	Demand	Supply	New Demand
	12	1	9	5
	11	2	8	6
Equilibrium 2	10	3	7	7
	9	4	6	8
Equilibrium 1	8	5	5	9
	7	6	4	10
	6	7	3	11
	5	8	2	12
	4	9	1	13

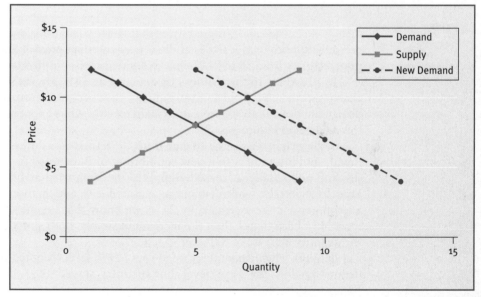

FIGURE 8.4   Market Equilibrium Following Demand Shift

We see the initial equilibrium of $8, where quantity demanded equals quantity supplied (5 units) in the first three columns of Table 8.1, as indicated by the shaded numbers in the fifth row. After the demand shift, the new equilibrium is $10, where quantity demanded equals quantity supplied (7 units). The shaded numbers in columns 1, 3, and 4 of the third row show this new equilibrium.

Again, the mechanism driving price to the new equilibrium is competition among buyers to buy and competition among sellers to sell. At the old price of $8,

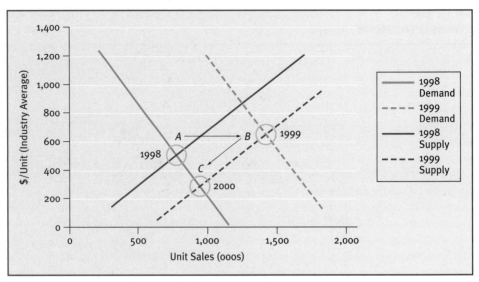

FIGURE **8.5** Demand-Supply in U.S. Generator Business

there is excess demand—more buyers than sellers. This imbalance puts upward pressure on price until it settles at the new equilibrium price of $10. Notice that price increases from $8 to $10, while quantity increases from 5 to 7 units.

To illustrate the usefulness of demand and supply, let's return to the changes in the electric generator industry that occurred around 1999. Using demand-supply analysis, we can explain exactly what happened. We can see this analysis in Figure 8.5.

In the graph, we see the change from 1998 to 1999 as the change from the initial equilibrium of A to a new equilibrium of B (denoted A → B) after both demand and supply increased. Supply shifted outward as firms invested in capacity increases, while demand increased due to anticipation of power outages. Because price increased by 21%, we know that the increase in demand must have been bigger than the increase in supply. Both shifts contributed to the quantity increase of 87%.

In 2000, when demand returned to its 1998 level (denoted B → C), prices dropped below the 1998 level, but quantity stayed above the 1998 level because of the supply increase. Although it is relatively easy to predict these kinds of *qualitative* changes, predicting exact *quantitative* changes is much more difficult. For accurate quantitative predictions, you'd need information about the exact magnitudes of the supply and demand shifts, and information about the slopes of the supply and demand curves, information that is very hard to get. In fact, you should be very suspicious of consultants who claim they can provide accurate quantitative forecasts because it is difficult to precisely estimate the parameters necessary to construct a forecast.

Nevertheless, we can learn a lot from simple qualitative analysis. AMP's managers should have been able to predict the general movement in price and quantity A → B → C, as shown in Figure 8.5; and they could have taken steps to prepare for the changes. For example, because the demand shift was temporary, they could have hired temporary workers, or even outsourced the extra production, instead of investing in their own capacity expansion. Alternatively, like John Deere's managers in Chapter 5, they could have chosen a low-fixed-cost technology, thereby better positioning themselves to make money once price dropped below its 1998 levels.

8.6 Explaining Industry Changes Using Supply and Demand

The preceding analysis has asked you to predict what happens to price and quantity following increases or decreases in supply and demand, or both. This kind of analysis is relatively simple, as there are only four changes that can occur: an increase or decrease in supply and an increase or decrease in demand. A slightly more difficult, but still very useful, analysis involves using supply and demand to explain industry changes. You look at a change in price and quantity, and then describe what must have happened to either supply and demand or both.

For example, the price of soybeans increased by 50% from mid-2007 to early 2008. From what we've learned so far, you should know that an increase in price could have been driven by an increase in demand, a decrease in supply, or both. In this case, both factors appear to have been influencing price. Demand has increased thanks to rising world population and incomes. Supply has contracted because many farmers decided to switch production to substitute products, like corn, that can be turned into biofuels. Both an increase in demand and a decrease in supply caused the dramatic price increase.

Let's test our understanding of the analysis thus far. Try to explain the increase in the quantity of mobile phones and the decline in price over the past decade using shifts in the demand or supply curves.

-------TAKE A MOMENT AND TRY TO COME UP WITH THE ANSWER-------

To answer this question, you have to explain two points in time. On a graph, the initial point has a high price and small quantity. The final point has low price and large quantity. You can explain these data with a simple increase (rightward shift) in the supply curve. In Figure 8.6, as supply increases, the equilibrium price falls from P_0 to P_1 and the equilibrium quantity increases from Q_0 to Q_1.[2]

We end this section by asking you to explain a very significant increase in price and decline in the quantity of short-term commercial loans that occurred during September 2008. These short-term loans are used by virtually every major business to balance the inflows of revenue with the outflows of costs and are behind many major transactions.

In what follows we are going to talk about the 30-day U.S. commercial loan market, where the "price" of a loan is the annualized interest rate on the loan, for instance, 0.5%.

In the second week of September 2008, the quantity of these loans declined dramatically, and the price (interest rate) on these loans shot up from 3% to 5%.

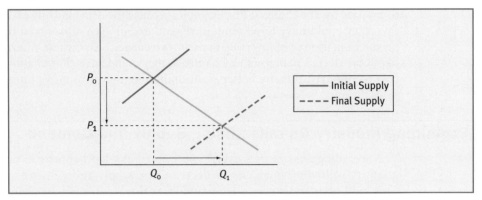

FIGURE **8.6** Demand-Supply Shifts in the Mobile Phone Industry

These changes spooked Treasury Secretary Henry Paulson and Federal Reserve Chairman Ben Bernanke, and they were characterized as a "freeze" in the market for short-term lending. What could have accounted for these changes?

-------TAKE A MOMENT AND TRY TO COME UP WITH THE ANSWER-------

The changes could be explained by a simple decrease in the supply of loans. In fact, following the bankruptcy of Lehman Brothers, the troubles at Fannie Mae and Freddie Mac, and the first bailout of AIG, commercial lenders became increasingly worried that borrowers would not be able to repay these loans. In other words, lenders became less willing to lend, and the resulting decrease in supply caused both an increase in the price of borrowing (the interest rate) and a decline in the amount of lending. As a footnote to this story, the Federal Reserve guaranteed these short-run financial transactions to remove the fear of default, which increased supply, and the interest rates came back down.

Many students report that demand and supply analysis is especially useful in job interviews as it gives them a way to show off their analytical expertise by explaining industry changes.

8.7 Prices Convey Valuable Information

Markets play a significant role in collecting and transmitting information between buyers and sellers. In a sense, prices are the primary mechanism that market participants use to communicate with one another. Buyers signal their willingness to pay, and sellers signal their willingness to sell, with prices.

To illustrate how this communication occurs, let's examine the changes that occurred when a pipeline carrying gasoline to Phoenix broke.[3] The break could have been disastrous because Arizona has no refineries of its own; it receives gasoline primarily through two pipelines. One of these pipelines starts in El Paso and supplies gasoline from refineries in Texas and New Mexico. Upon entering Arizona, that pipeline travels first to terminals in Tucson and then to terminals in Phoenix.

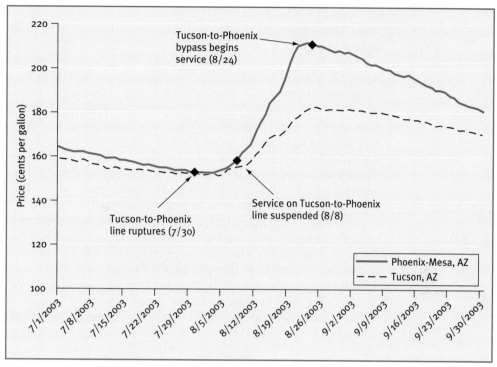

FIGURE **8.7**   Phoenix and Tucson Gas Prices

On July 30, 2003, the Tucson-to-Phoenix section of the pipeline from El Paso ruptured, closing that section of the line from August 8 to August 23, when partial service resumed.

Using supply-demand analysis, you should now be able to analyze what happened in the daily market for gasoline in Phoenix. Following a decrease in supply to Phoenix, the price should go up and quantity should go down. Indeed, the Phoenix price went from less than $1.60 to over $2.10 per gallon. What is less obvious is why the *Tucson* price also increased as shown in Figure 8.7. Given the location of the pipeline break, it would seem that Tucson should now have an excess supply, which would reduce Tucson prices. Instead, Tucson prices increased from about $1.60 to $1.80 per gallon.

What happened? The tank wagon owners who normally deliver gas from the Tucson terminal to Tucson gas stations discovered that delivering gas to Phoenix was more profitable than delivering it to Tucson. Tucson and Phoenix tank wagons waited for as much as six hours at the terminal in Tucson to buy gasoline to deliver to Phoenix. The high prices in Phoenix conveyed information to sellers in Tucson that it was more profitable to sell in Phoenix. So, the supply actually decreased in Tucson—resulting in a price increase in that city.

Next time you hear a politician complaining about the "high price of gas," tell her that without those high prices, consumers would consume too much, and suppliers would supply too little. If politicians set prices instead of markets, prices would not convey the information that provides incentives for buyers to conserve and for sellers to increase supply. Without higher prices, shortages would occur, and gasoline would not move from lower- to higher-valued uses.

A similar situation occurred in Nashville in 2016 when a gas pipeline burst in Alabama. Anticipating a shortage, drivers flocked to gas stations to fill up, and prices rose. In response, tank wagon owners increased deliveries to the Nashville market. Tennessee Governor Bill Haslam also stepped in with an attempt to help the situation. But, rather than calling for price controls, he took another approach, issuing State of Tennessee Executive Order No. 56 that declared a temporary state of emergency. This declaration meant that regulations limiting the number of hours for commercial truck drivers delivering fuel were suspended during the emergency conditions.

The information conveyed by prices is especially important in financial markets, where each market participant possesses a little piece of information about the prospects for a traded security. By trading, they reveal their information to the market. For example, the price of a stock is a good predictor of the discounted flow of profit that will accrue to the stockholder. Likewise, prices of S&P futures are good predictors of the future level of the S&P 500 stock market index, and foreign exchange futures are good predictors of future exchange rates. The information contained in these prices has obvious uses to companies and individuals trying to make decisions based on an uncertain future.

In fact, market prices are so good at forecasting the future that companies like Hewlett Packard, Eli Lilly, and Microsoft are setting up internal markets to help forecast demand for their products.[4] They set up automated trading platforms and let employees buy and sell contracts that pay off according to how much the company will earn or sell in the future. The prices of the contracts tend to be much more accurate predictors than traditional forecasting methods and are being used to plan production. The accuracy of these prices in forecasting future sales can also help firms design compensation schemes for salespeople; for example, salespeople could be rewarded for increasing sales above the forecast quantity.

8.8 Market Making

In the supply-demand analyses in this chapter, we've been ignoring the costs of making a market. Buyers and sellers don't simply appear in a trading pit and begin transacting with one another. Instead, someone has to incur costs to identify high-value buyers and low-value sellers, bring them together, and devise ways of profitably facilitating transactions among them. The economies of Chicago, New York, London, and Tokyo depend largely on the profit earned from making markets. These profits are the "costs" of making a market that, when significant, can prevent prices from moving to equalize demand and supply.

In this section, we show exactly how a "market maker" makes a market— by buying low and selling high. Consider a market maker facing the demand and supply curves shown in Figure 8.8: nine buyers have values {$12, $11,

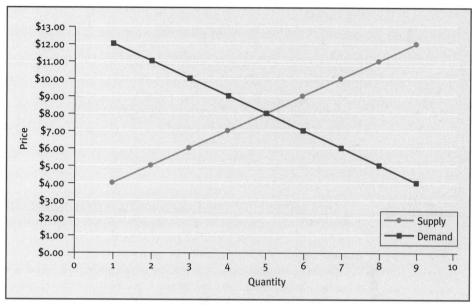

FIGURE **8.8**   Market-Making Supply and Demand Curves

$10, $9, $8, $7, $6, $5, $4}, and nine sellers are willing to sell at the same prices. If there were only a single (monopoly) market maker, how much would she offer the sellers (the bid), and how much would she charge the buyers (the ask)? How many transactions would occur?

If the market maker does not want to be left in either a long (holding inventory) or short (owing inventory) position, then she has to pick prices (the bid and the ask) that equalize quantity supplied and quantity demanded. Note that if the market maker bought and sold at the competitive price ($8), she would earn zero profit. To earn profit, the market maker must buy low (at the bid) and sell high (at the ask). For example, if the market maker were going to engage in, say, three transactions, she would offer sellers $6 (from the supply curve, we see that three sellers will sell if the price is at least $6) and charge buyers $10 (from the demand curve, we see that three buyers are willing to pay at least $10). Consequently, there are five obvious bid-ask price combinations:[5]

- Buy at $4 and sell at $12 (one transaction).
- Buy at $5 and sell at $11 (two transactions).
- Buy at $6 and sell at $10 (three transactions).
- Buy at $7 and sell at $9 (four transactions).
- Buy at $8 and sell at $8 (five transactions).

Note that the market maker faces a familiar trade-off. She can consummate fewer transactions but earn more on each transaction; or she can consummate more transactions but earn less on each transaction. In Table 8.2, we calculate the optimal bid-ask spread for the market maker: either buy at $6 and sell at $10, or buy at $5 and sell at $11. Both earn profit of $12.

TABLE **8.2**
Optimal Spread in Market Making

Bid ($)	Ask ($)	Quantity	Profit ($)
8	8	5	0
7	9	4	8
6	10	3	12
5	11	2	12
4	12	1	8

Now suppose that competition among several market makers forces the bid-ask spread—the price of a transaction—down to the costs of market making, which we suppose to be $2 per transaction. Now what is the competitive bid and ask?

In this case, each market maker would buy at $7 and sell at $9. Those offering worse prices wouldn't make any sales, and those offering better prices wouldn't cover costs. In this case, competition forces price down to cost, thereby raising the number of transactions from three to four.

SUMMARY & HOMEWORK PROBLEMS

Summary of Main Points

- A market has a product, geographic, and time dimension. Define the market before using supply-demand analysis.
- *Market demand* describes buyer behavior; *market supply* describes seller behavior in a competitive market.
- If price changes, *quantity demanded* increases or decreases (represented by a *movement along* the demand curve).
- If a factor other than price (like income) changes, we say that demand curve increases or decreases (a *shift* of the demand curve).
- Supply curves describe the behavior of sellers and tell you how much will be sold at a given price.
- **Market equilibrium** is the price at which quantity supplied equals quantity demanded. If price is above the equilibrium price, there are too many sellers, forcing price down, and vice versa.
- Prices convey valuable information; high prices tell buyers to conserve and sellers to increase supply.
- Making a market is costly, and competition between market makers forces the bid-ask spread down to the costs of making a market. If the costs of making a market are large, then the equilibrium price may be better viewed as a spread rather than a single price.

Multiple-Choice Questions

1. Changes in prices of a good causes
   a. movement along the demand curve.
   b. movement along the supply curve.
   c. no movement along either curve.
   d. both a and b.

2. If the market for a certain product experiences an increase in supply and a decrease in demand, which of the following results is expected to occur?
   a. Both the equilibrium price and the equilibrium quantity could rise or fall.
   b. The equilibrium price would rise, and the equilibrium quantity could rise or fall.
   c. The equilibrium price would fall, and the equilibrium quantity could rise or fall.
   d. The equilibrium price would fall, and the equilibrium quantity would fall.

3. When demand for a product falls, which of the following events would you *not* necessarily expect to occur?
   a. A decrease in the quantity of the product supplied
   b. A decrease in its price
   c. A decrease in the supply of the product
   d. A leftward shift of the demand curve

4. Suppose a recent and widely circulated medical article has reported new benefits of cycling for exercise. Simultaneously, the price of the parts needed to make bikes falls. If the change in supply is greater than the change in demand, the price will _____ and the quantity will _____.
   a. rise, rise
   b. rise, fall
   c. fall, rise
   d. fall, fall

5. Suppose there are nine sellers and nine buyers, each willing to buy or sell one unit of a good, with values {$10, $9, $8, $7, $6, $5, $4, $3, $2}. Assuming there are no transactions costs, what is the equilibrium price in this market?
   a. $5
   b. $6
   c. $7
   d. $8

6. If the government imposes a price floor at $9 (i.e., price must be $9 or higher) in the above market, how many goods will be traded?
   a. Five
   b. Four
   c. Three
   d. Two

7. Say the average price of a new home in Lampard City is $160,000. The local government has just passed new licensing requirements for housing contractors. Based on possible shifts in demand or supply and assuming that the licensing changes don't affect the quality of new houses, which of the following is a reasonable prediction for the average price of a new home in the future?
   a. $140,000
   b. $150,000
   c. $160,000
   d. $170,000

8. Suppose a new employer is also relocating to Lampard City and will be attracting many new people who will want to buy new houses. Assume that the change in licensing requirements mentioned in Question 7 occurs at the same time. What do you think will happen to the equilibrium quantity of new homes bought and sold in Lampard City?
   a. It will decrease substantially.
   b. It will decrease but not by much.
   c. It will increase.
   d. Not enough information.

9. The price of peanuts increases. At the same time, we see the price of jelly (which is often consumed with peanut butter) rise. How does this affect the market for peanut butter?
   a. The demand curve will shift to the left; the supply curve will shift to the left.
   b. The demand curve will shift to the left; the supply curve will shift to the right.
   c. The demand curve will shift to the right; the supply curve will shift to the left.
   d. The demand curve will shift to the right; the supply curve will shift to the right.

10. Holding other factors constant, a decrease in the tax for producing coffee causes
    a. the supply curve to shift to the left, causing the prices of coffee to rise.
    b. the supply curve to shift to the right, causing the prices of coffee to rise.
    c. the supply curve to shift to the left, causing the prices of coffee to fall.
    d. the supply curve to shift to the right, causing the prices of coffee to fall.

Individual Problems

8.1 Widget Market

The widget market is competitive and includes no transaction costs. Five suppliers are willing to sell one widget at the following prices: $30, $29, $20, $16, and $12. Five buyers are willing to buy one widget at the following prices: $10, $12, $20, $24, and $29. What is the equilibrium price and quantity in a competitive market?

8.2 Cotton Prices

The "A" index is a proxy for the world price of cotton. From January to October of 2010, the price reflected by the "A" index increased about 80%.

Provide two separate explanations for this price increase using shifts in supply or demand.

What one piece of information would allow you to decide which of the two is a better explanation?

8.3 Hand Sanitizer

Due to the H1N1 flu outbreak, the demand for hand sanitizer has tripled. Should Johnson & Johnson increase production of their Purell hand sanitizer? Should it invest in doubling production capacity?

8.4 Chocolate Candy Bars Market

a. In the accompanying diagram (which represents the market for chocolate candy bars), the initial equilibrium is at the intersection of S_1 and D_1. Circle the new equilibrium if there is an increase in cocoa prices.

b. In the same diagram, the initial equilibrium is at the intersection of S_1 and D_1. Circle the new equilibrium if there is rapid economic growth.

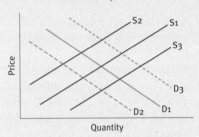

Graph for Problem 8-4
Chocolate Candy Bars Market

8.5 Demand Shifts

Indicate whether the following changes would cause a shift in the demand curve for Product A and, if so, the direction of the shift.

Change	Demand Curve Shift?	Direction of Shift?
Increase in price of complementary product	Yes No	Increase Decrease N/A
Increase in the price of the Product A	Yes No	Increase Decrease N/A
Launch of effective advertising campaign for Product A	Yes No	Increase Decrease N/A

8.6 Valentine's Day

On Valentine's Day, the price of roses increases by more than the price of greeting cards. Why? (*Hint*: Consider what makes roses and cards different and how that difference might affect supply's responsiveness to price.)

Group Problem

G8-1 Supply and Demand

Using shifts in supply and demand curves, describe a change in the industry in which your firm operates. The change may arise from a change in costs, entry/exit of firms, a change in consumer tastes, a change in the macroeconomy, a change in interest rates, or a change in exchange rates. Label the axes, and state the geographic, product, and time dimensions of the demand and supply curves you are drawing.

Explain what happened to industry price and quantity by making specific references to the demand and supply curves. If more than one change occurred, then decompose the change into smaller pieces so that your explanation has a step-by-step character to it. (*Hint and warning:* Demand and supply curves are used at the industry level, not at the firm level.) Describe how your company could profitably use the analysis.

END NOTES

1. Credit for the invisible hand metaphor goes to Adam Smith and his renowned *The Wealth of Nations*.
2. Note that an increase in demand could explain the increase in quantity but not the decrease in price.
3. Federal Trade Commission, *Gasoline Price Changes: The Dynamic of Supply, Demand, and Competition* (Washington, DC: U.S. Government Printing Office, 2005).
4. Barbara Kiviat, "The End of Management?" *Time*, July 12, 2004, "Inside Business" section.
5. Note that it makes sense to make this market only for five transactions or fewer. For quantities greater than this, the demand curve lies below the supply curve. So to complete seven transactions, for example, the market maker would have to offer sellers $10 (see the supply curve) and charge buyers $6 (see the demand curve) for a net loss of $4 per transaction.

9 Market Structure and Long-Run Equilibrium

Jim Collins's book *Good to Great* has sold over four million copies since it was published in 2001, making it one of the most successful business advice books of all time. It has been translated into 35 languages and has appeared on the best-seller lists of the *New York Times*, *Wall Street Journal*, and *Business Week*. Collins and his research team examined over 1,000 established companies and found 11 companies that made the jump from average or below-average performance to great results. From the experiences of these 11 "good-to-great" companies, Collins created a list of general management principles that he argued would help other companies make similar leaps.

Anyone familiar with the 2008 mortgage crisis should easily recognize one of the good-to-great companies, Fannie Mae. Shares of Fannie Mae were valued at around $70 per share in mid-2001, the year Collins's book was published. By 2009, government regulators had seized the company, and its shares were trading below $1. Another one of the companies, Circuit City, declared bankruptcy in 2008 and was liquidated. Overall, none of the 11 good-to-great companies outperformed the market over the years following the book's publication.

So where did the analysis go wrong?

The book ran into two serious problems. The first was to confuse correlation with causation. Just because you observe successful firms behaving in a particular way does not mean that the behavior caused the success. We will return to this theme in Chapter 17 when we examine decision making under uncertainty. Until we do, beware of consultants peddling "best practices" of successful firms.

The second problem of *Good to Great* was to ignore the long-run forces that tend to erode profit. It's incredibly difficult to sustain great performance. High profit draws attention to the value that a firm creates, and customers, suppliers, competitors, substitutes, and new entrants will try to capture some of the values. How and why this occurs is the topic of this chapter.

In contrast to Chapter 8, where we analyzed short-run industry-level changes within a single market or industry, in this chapter, we analyze how changes in one industry affect other industries. In particular, the ability of capital and labor to move between two industries implies that the prices and profits of one industry are related to prices and profits in another.

<hr>

9.1 Competitive Industries

To understand the relationship between industries, we first consider the extreme case of a **perfectly competitive industry** where:

- firms produce a product or service with very close substitutes, meaning demand is very elastic;
- firms have many rivals and no cost advantages;
- the industry has no entry or exit barriers.

The demand curve for the output of a perfectly competitive firm is flat (perfectly elastic). A competitive firm cannot affect price, so there is little a competitive firm can do except react to industry price. If price is above marginal cost (MC), it sells more; if price is below MC, it sells less. In sum, a competitive firm's fortunes are closely tied to those of the industry in which it competes.

No industry is "perfectly" competitive because it is a theoretical benchmark, although several industries, such as formal stock exchanges or agricultural commodities, come close. We use the benchmark because it helps us see the long-run forces that determine long-run industry performance.

Here's an example. Suppose industry demand suddenly increases for a product in a competitive industry. From Chapter 8, you should know that price goes up following the increase in demand. At the higher price, firms in the industry earn above-average profit—but only for a while. This "for a while" is the period that economists call the "short run." Above-average profit lasts only for a while because profit attracts capital to the industry; existing firms expand capacity, or new entrants come into the industry. This increases industry supply, which leads to a decrease in price. Entry and capacity expansion continue, and price keeps falling until firms in the industry are no longer earning above-average profit. At this point, capital stops flowing into the industry, and we say that the industry has reached **long-run equilibrium**. The length of the short run depends on how quickly assets can move into or out of the industry. It could be as short as a few seconds in highly liquid financial markets or as long as several years in industries where it takes a lot of time and effort to move assets.

In the long run, no competitive industry earns more than an average rate of return. If it does, firms will enter the industry or expand, increasing supply until the profit rate returns to average. To a business student trying to make money, this seems like terrible news. But it's not all bad news: In the long run, no competitive industry can earn less than an average rate of return. If it does, firms will exit the industry or reduce capacity, decreasing supply until the profit rate returns to average.

A competitive firm can earn positive or negative economic profit in the short run but only until entry or exit occurs. In the long run, competitive firms earn only an average rate of return.

When firms are in long-run equilibrium, economic profit is zero (including the opportunity cost of capital), firms break even, and price equals average cost. Recall that profit is equal to $(P - AC)^*Q$; so if price equals average cost, and cost includes a capital charge for the opportunity cost of capital, there's no reason for capital to move because it cannot earn a higher rate of return elsewhere.

Competitive industries will experience demand and supply shocks that result in short-run price increases and decreases, but **economic profit** tends to revert to zero. Another way to say this is that profit exhibits **mean reversion** where the mean is zero economic profit. According to reported estimates, profit moves back toward an average rate of return at a speed of about 38% per year.[1] For example, if profit is 20% above the mean one year, it will be only 12.4% above the mean in the following year.[2] A separate analysis of more than 700 business units found that 90% of both above-average and below-average profitability differentials disappeared over a 10-year period. Return on investment, as shown in Figure 9.1, revealed a strong tendency to revert to the mean level of approximately 20% for both over- and underperformers.

Be careful not to confuse short- and long-run analysis. If we are analyzing an increase in demand in an industry, price and quantity will increase in

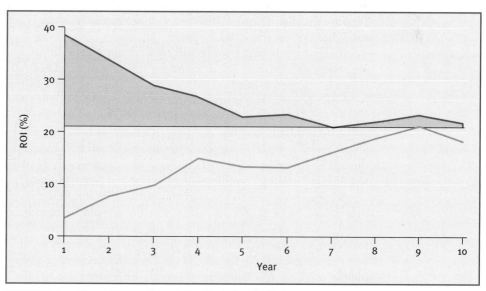

FIGURE **9.1**   **Mean Reversion of Profitability (ROI, Return on Investment)**

the short run, and firms will earn above-average profit. In the long run, these above-average profits will attract new assets into the industry, which will increase supply until profits fall back to the average. Make sure to distinguish between the short run and the long run. For example, do not say things like "demand creates its own supply." Instead, analyze the changes more precisely by separating them into short- and long-run changes.

9.2 The Indifference Principle

We have begun to see the role of entry and exit, or *asset mobility*, as the major competitive force driving profit to zero (remember that economic profit includes a cost of capital, so economic profit is normally zero). Positive profit attracts entry, and negative profit leads to exit. The ability of assets to move from lower- to higher-valued uses is the force that moves an industry toward long-run equilibrium. Such asset mobility leads to what Steven Landsburg[3] calls the **indifference principle**:

> *If an asset is mobile, then in long-run equilibrium, the asset will be indifferent about where it is used; that is, it will make the same profit no matter where it goes.*

Labor and capital are generally highly mobile assets. They flow into an industry when profits are high and out of an industry when profits are negative. Once this long-run equilibrium is reached, capital is indifferent about where it goes because it earns the same return (its opportunity cost) regardless of the industry.

To show you how the forces of asset mobility link markets together, let's apply long-run equilibrium analysis to the problem of deciding where to live. Suppose that San Diego, California, is more attractive than Nashville, Tennessee. What do you think will happen?

If labor is mobile, people will move from Nashville to San Diego. This migration will increase the demand for housing in San Diego, driving up San Diego house prices while simultaneously reducing demand (and prices) for Nashville houses. The process will continue until the higher price of housing makes San Diego just as unattractive as Nashville. At that point, migration will stop, and we say that the two cities are in long-run equilibrium. Both places are now equally attractive, meaning consumers are indifferent between them. The lower housing costs in Nashville compensate Nashvillians for the less attractive living conditions like the hot and humid summers.

Wages also adjust to restore equilibrium. The indifference principle tells us that in long-run equilibrium, all professions should be equally attractive, provided labor is mobile. If school teaching is more attractive than truck driving, for example, some truck drivers will become school teachers, increasing supply and reducing the wage for school teachers, but decreasing supply and increasing the wage for truck drivers. When all professions are equally attractive, the migration stops, and the wages stop moving. It may take a long time for entry to move wages to an equilibrium level, especially in professions that require a long period of training. In these industries, the long run might be very long.

Once equilibrium is reached, differences in wages, called **compensating wage differentials**, reflect differences in the *inherent* attractiveness of various professions. Why do embalmers make almost 20% more than rehabilitation counselors?[4] Assuming the two industries are in long-run equilibrium, the higher wages compensate embalmers for working in a relatively unattractive profession. In the same way that lower-cost housing compensates Nashvillians for living in Nashville, embalmers' higher wages compensate them for working with dead bodies.

As demand and supply shocks change price in one industry, region, or profession, assets move in and out of industries, regions, and professions, until a new equilibrium is reached. In this way, the forces of competition allocate resources to where they are most highly valued and allow our economy to adapt rapidly to shocks.

One of the concerns following the housing meltdown in the late 2000s was its potential impact on labor mobility. In previous recessions, there was a relatively rapid migration from locations where the jobs were disappearing (e.g., the Rust Belt) to areas where they were being created (e.g., the Sun Belt). But this time, the decline in housing values made it difficult for people to move (unless they walked away from their mortgages) because they were reluctant to sell houses at a loss. This reduced the flexibility of the U.S. economy and slowed down the adjustment to a new long-run equilibrium.

We can apply the same long-run analysis to gain insight into some fundamental relationships in finance. We start with the common sense observation that investors prefer higher returns and lower risk. If one investment earns the same return as another but is less risky, investors will move capital from the more risky investment to the less risky investment and bid up the price of the less risky investment. The higher price decreases its expected rate of return[5]—its expected price change—until the higher-risk investment is just as attractive as the less risky investment. In equilibrium, the risky investment will earn a higher rate of return to compensate investors for bearing risk.

We can illustrate this relationship with a simple example. Suppose that two stocks are trading at the same $100 price. Research analysts tell us that in a year, the first stock will increase in value to $120 with probability 0.5 or maintain its current value of $100 with probability 0.5. The expected price of the stock next year is $110, and the expected return is 10%. Likewise, a similarly priced second stock will increase in value to $130 with probability 0.5 or decrease in value to $90 with probability 0.5. Although the second stock has the same expected price ($110) and expected return (10%), it is more risky because the return has a higher variance (next year value of $90 or $130). Investors will sell the risky stock and buy the less risky stock. This increases the price of the first stock, reducing its expected return; it also decreases the price of the second stock, increasing its expected return.

The higher return on a risky stock is called a **risk premium**, and this premium is analogous to a compensating wage differential. Just as higher wages compensate embalmers for preserving cadavers, higher expected rates of return compensate investors for bearing risk.

In equilibrium, differences in the rate of return reflect differences in the riskiness of an investment.

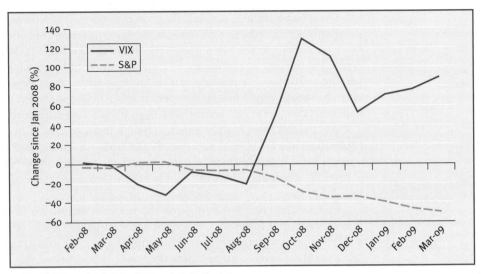

FIGURE **9.2** **Stock Volatility and Returns**

We can see this relationship in Figure 9.2, which plots the Chicago Board Options Exchange Volatility Index (VIX) against the price of the S&P 500 stock index. The VIX measures the implied riskiness of the index, as computed from options prices. From the fall of 2008 to the spring of 2009, the stock market declined by about 50% while the VIX increased by about 100%. Whatever was making stocks more volatile was also reducing the stock prices, thereby increasing expected returns in order to compensate investors for bearing more risk. In other words, investors had to be offered lower prices in order to be willing to take on the added risk.

Since government bonds are thought to be risk-free, investors often benchmark expected stock returns against the returns from holding government bonds. Over the last 50 years in the United States, annual bond returns have averaged 6.97%, whereas annual stock returns have averaged 11.29%. The difference is a risk premium that compensates investors for holding risky stocks. The historical equity risk premium (of stocks over bonds) has varied over the last 50 years as shown in Figure 9.3.[6]

If you can predict how risk changes, you can make a lot of money by anticipating asset price changes. In late 2006, for example, risk premia became very small. Not only was the difference between expected returns on stocks versus bonds small; so were the differences between expected returns on low- versus high-quality stocks and between emerging market debt versus U.S. debt. Small spreads between risky and less risky assets meant either that the world had become less risky or that investors were simply ignoring risk in search of higher returns. In hindsight, it looks like risk was being ignored. If you had been smart enough to recognize this, you would have moved out of risky assets and into less risky assets, like bonds. When risk returned in late 2007, the stock market began a 50% decline, and you would have earned a lot of money.

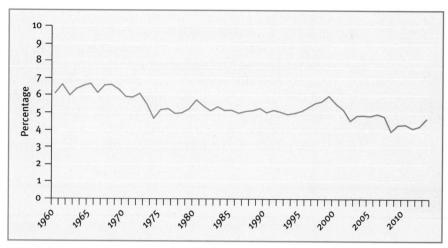

FIGURE 9.3   Historical Equity Risk Premium

You also could have made a lot of money using a similar approach with European debt. Figure 9.4 shows the yields on 10-year government bonds for Greece and Germany since 1997. In late 1997, yields on Greek bonds were over 10% compared to the yields of around 5% for German bonds. This spread disappeared in 2002, with yields of around 5% in both countries, when Greece joined the European Union. In 2008, the risk premium began to reappear. Yields on Greek bonds eventually reached nearly 30% in February 2012, whereas German yields fell to under 2%. If you can anticipate changes in risk premia like this, you can make money. A prescient "risk-off" trade would have been to short Greek debt and buy German debt in 2007, and sell in 2012.

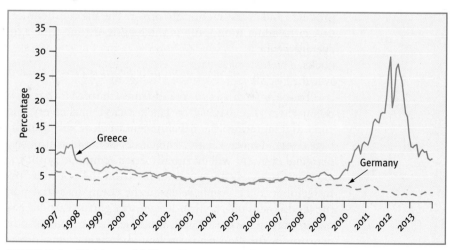

FIGURE 9.4   Yields on 10-Year Government Bonds

Conversely, a prescient "risk-on" trade would have been to buy Greek debt and short German debt in 1997, and sell in 2001.[7]

In fact, today's volatile stock market has given rise to a new jargon, the so-called risk-on and risk-off investing, where investors attempt to profit by increasing their risk exposure when they expect favorable macro developments, and decreasing it when they foresee unfavorable developments. This can be easily understood as an application of the idea of long-run equilibrium. For example, if you expect a reduction (or increase) in the risk that the European Union will dissolve, it makes sense to buy (or sell) assets with exposure to this risk.

9.3 Monopoly

If competitive firms live in the worst of all possible economic worlds, **monopoly** firms live in the best. Monopolies have attributes that protect them from the forces of competition.

- Monopolies produce a product or service with no close substitutes.
- Monopolies have no rivals.
- Barriers to entry prevent other firms from entering the industry.

An example of a monopoly firm is a biotechnology company that develops and then patents a new variety of crop plant without any substitutes. Without rivals and with patent protection preventing others from entering, the firm will enjoy a period of protection from the forces of competition.

Unlike a competitive firm, a monopoly firm[8] can earn positive profit— an above-average rate of return—for a relatively long time. This profit is a reward for doing something unique, innovative, or creative—something that gives the firm less elastic demand.

But even monopolies are not permanently protected from the forces of entry and imitation. No barrier to entry lasts forever. Eventually other firms develop substitutes or invent new products that compete with the monopoly's products and erode monopoly profit. The main difference between a competitive firm and a monopoly is the length of time that a firm can earn above-average profit.

In the long run, even monopoly profit is driven to zero.

To see why this is so, recall from Chapter 6 that a firm will price at the point where $(P - MC)/P = 1/|\text{elasticity}|$. In the very long run, the forces of entry and imitation (the development of close substitutes) make the monopolist's demand more elastic. The elastic demand will push price down toward marginal cost and will eventually drive economic profit to zero.

Here is a well-known example from the portable music player industry. In October 2001, Apple released the company's first portable music player, the iPod. The iPod's stylish design, straightforward user interface, and generous storage space gave Apple a unique, user-friendly product. The elasticity of demand for the iPod was very low, and the margins for the product were very high. Over the next several years, however, rivals like SanDisk, Samsung, and

Microsoft released competing music players. The development of these rival products made demand for iPods more elastic. The higher elasticity reduced the iPod's price-cost margin, and Apple's profit eroded.

Of course, Apple didn't stand still. Its managers keep improving the product, keeping it innovative and different from rival products—in a word, unique. The fact that Apple is still making iPods is testament to the company's ability to innovate.

SUMMARY & HOMEWORK PROBLEMS

Summary of Main Points

- A firm in a **competitive industry** can earn positive or negative profit in the short run until entry or exit occurs. In the long run, competitive firms earn only an average rate of return.
- Profit exhibits **mean reversion** or "regression toward the mean."
- If an asset is mobile, then in equilibrium the asset will be indifferent about where it is used (i.e., it will make the same profit no matter where it goes). This implies that unattractive jobs will pay **compensating wage differentials**, and risky investments will pay compensating risk differentials (or a risk premium).
- The difference between stock returns and bond yields is a compensating risk premium. When risk premia become too small, some investors view this as a time to get out of risky assets because the market may be ignoring risk in pursuit of higher returns.
- **Monopoly** firms can earn positive profit for a longer period of time than competitive firms, but entry of competing firms and imitation eventually erode their profit as well.

Multiple-Choice Questions

1. In the long run, which of the following outcomes is most likely for a firm?
   a. Zero accounting profits but positive economic profits
   b. Zero accounting profits
   c. Positive accounting profits and positive economic profits
   d. Zero economic profits but positive accounting profits

2. At the individual firm level, which of the following types of firms faces a downward-sloping demand curve?
   a. Both a perfectly competitive firm and a monopoly firm
   b. Neither a perfectly competitive firm nor a monopoly firm
   c. A perfectly competitive firm but not a monopoly firm
   d. A monopoly firm but not a perfectly competitive firm

3. Which of the following types of firms are guaranteed to make positive economic profit?
   a. Both a perfectly competitive firm and a monopoly
   b. Neither a perfectly competitive firm nor a monopoly
   c. A perfectly competitive firm but not a monopoly
   d. A monopoly but not a perfectly competitive firm

4. What is the main difference between a competitive firm and a monopoly firm?
   a. The number of customers served by the firm.
   b. Monopoly firms are more efficient and therefore have lower costs.
   c. Monopoly firms can generally earn positive profits over a longer period of time.
   d. Monopoly firms enjoy government protection from competition.

5. Which of the following products is closest to operating in a perfectly competitive industry?
   a. Nike shoes
   b. Cotton
   c. Perdue Chicken
   d. Restaurants

6. A firm in a perfectly competitive market (a price taker) faces what type of demand curve?
   a. Unit elastic
   b. Perfectly inelastic
   c. Perfectly elastic
   d. None of the above

7. A competitive firm's profit-maximizing price is $15. At MC = MR, the output is 100 units. At this level of production, average total costs are $12. The firm's profits are
   a. $300 in the short run and long run.
   b. $300 in the short run and zero in the long run.
   c. $500 in the short run and long run.
   d. $500 in the short run and zero in the long run.

8. What would happen to revenues if a firm in a perfectly competitive industry raised price?
   a. They would increase.
   b. They would increase but profit would decrease.
   c. They would increase along with profit.
   d. They would fall to zero.

9. If a firm in a perfectly competitive industry is experiencing average revenues greater than average costs, in the long run
   a. some firms will leave the industry and price will rise.
   b. some firms will enter the industry and price will rise.
   c. some firms will leave the industry and price will fall.
   d. some firms will enter the industry and price will fall.

10. A sudden decrease in the market demand in a competitive industry leads to
   a. losses in the short run and average profits in the long run.
   b. above-average profits in the short run and average profits in the long run.
   c. new firms being attracted to the industry.
   d. demand creating supply.

Individual Problems

9-1 Faculty Housing Benefits

At a university faculty meeting in 2012, a proposal was made to increase the housing benefits for new faculty to keep pace with the high cost of housing. What will likely be the long-run effect of this proposal? (*Hint*: Think indifference principle.)

9-2 Snacks, Beer, and Marijuana

Snack food vendors and beer distributors earn some monopoly profits in their local markets but see them slowly erode from various new substitutes. When California voted on legalizing marijuana, which side would you think that California beer distributors were on? What about snack food venders? Why?

9-3 Entry and Elasticity

Suppose that new entry decreased your demand elasticity from −2 to −3 (made demand more elastic). By how much should you adjust your price of $10?

9-4 Competitive Industries

Relative to managers in more monopolistic industries, are managers in more competitive industries more likely to spend their time on reducing costs or on pricing strategies?

9-5 Economic Profit

Describe the difference in economic profit between a competitive firm and a monopolist in both the short and long run. Which should take longer to reach the long-run equilibrium?

9-6 Economics versus Business

Describe an important difference in the way an economist and a businessperson might view a monopoly.

Group Problem

G9-1 Compensating Wage Differential

Give an example of a compensating wage differential, a risk premium, or some kind of long-run equilibrium price difference your company faces. How can your company profitably exploit this difference?

END NOTES

1. Eugene Fama and Kenneth French, "Forecasting Profitability and Earnings," *Journal of Business*, April 2000.
2. Profitability at time $t + 1$ = Profitability at time $t - (0.38 \times$ Profitability at time t); 12.4% = 20% − 7.6%.
3. Steven Landsburg, *The Armchair Economist: Economics and Everyday Life* (New York: Free Press, 1993).
4. Median salary of embalmers equals $40,410, and median salary of rehabilitation counselors equals $34,390 according to May 2015 National Occupational Employment and Wage Estimates from the Bureau of Labor Statistics.
5. The percentage return on an investment that is held for one period is equal to $(P_{t+1} - P_t)/P_t$, where P_t is the initial price of the investment. P_{t+1} is the expected price in the next period, so the difference is the expected return. If the current price increases (i.e., P_t increases), then the expected return decreases.
6. Adapted from information provided by Aswath Damodaran at http://www.stern.nyu.edu/~adamodar/pc/datasets/histretSP.xls.
7. Example inspired by Don Marron at http://dmarron.com/2011/12/21/the-most-imporant-economic-chart-of-the-year/.
8. In contrast to price takers (competitive firms), monopoly firms are price searchers. These firms face a downward-sloping demand curve; as price increases, quantity sold drops and vice versa. A price searcher "searches" for the optimal price–quantity combination.

Strategy: The Quest to Keep Profit from Eroding

In 1971, three partners opened a coffee shop in Seattle's Pike Place Market. Two of the partners wanted to name the store after the ship *Pequod* from *Moby Dick*, but the third disagreed. Eventually they agreed to name the store after the *Pequod*'s first mate. The company enjoyed mild growth until 1988 when the partners agreed to sell the company to their former director of retail operations and marketing. Over the following 20-plus years, that director has overseen the expansion of the company to over 23,000 worldwide stores as of 2015 and revenues of over $19 billion. And in case you haven't put it all together yet—Starbuck was the first mate on the *Pequod* and that former director of retail operations is Howard Schultz, who recently stepped down as CEO of the world's largest coffee retailer, Starbucks.

What has been the key to the company's success? According to Schultz:[1] "Starbucks is the quintessential experience brand and the experience comes to life by our people. The only competitive advantage we have is the relationship we have with our people and the relationship they have built with our customers." The ability to create this unique experience draws on distinctive capabilities the company has developed in both producing high-quality coffee and establishing a relationship-oriented culture among its employees and customers. In a 2012 study of U.S. consumer sentiments expressed through social media outlets, Starbucks was ranked as the most loved restaurant-related brand,[2] and the company generated over $3.6 billion in 2015 operating income despite operating in a very competitive industry.

Succeeding in the face of competition requires that you first find a way to create an advantage and then figure out how to protect that advantage. How important is creating and sustaining advantage? Here's how one financial columnist summarized the view of one of the most respected investors of our time:

> *Warren Buffett was once asked what is the most important thing he looks for when evaluating a company. Without hesitation, he replied, "Sustainable competitive advantage."*

I agree. While valuation matters, it is the future growth and prosperity of the company underlying a stock, not its current price that is most important. A company's prosperity, in turn, is driven by how powerful and enduring its competitive advantages are.

Powerful competitive advantages (obvious examples are Coke's brand and Microsoft's control of the personal computer operating system) create a moat around a business such that it can keep competitors at bay and reap extraordinary growth and profit. Like Buffett, I seek to identify—and then hopefully purchase at an attractive price—the rare companies with wide, deep moats that are getting wider and deeper over time. When a company is able to achieve this, its shareholders can be well rewarded for decades. Take a look at some of the big pharmaceutical companies for great examples of this....

It is extremely difficult for a company to be able to sustain, much less expand, its moat over time. Moats are rarely enduring for many reasons: high profit[s] can lead to complacency and are almost certain to attract competitors, and new technologies, customer preferences, and ways of doing business emerge. Numerous studies confirm that there is a very powerful trend of regression toward the mean for high-return-on-capital companies. In short, the fierce competitiveness of our capitalist system is generally wonderful for consumers and the country as a whole, but bad news for companies that seek to make extraordinary profit over long periods of time.[3]

In Chapter 9, we discussed how the forces of competition tend to erode high profit; in this chapter, we show you what to do about it. This material will help you formulate long-run strategies to slow your firm's competitive erosion of profit; it will help you figure out how to build a moat around your company so that you can sustain profitability. We'll also evaluate Buffett's investment strategy.

10.1 A Simple View of Strategy

From Chapter 9, you should know that firms would rather be monopolists than competitors. In fact, if you hire management consultants, they should advise you to figure out how to become a monopolist (assuming they're worth the money you are paying them). To keep one step ahead of the forces that erode profit, firms develop strategies. And although there are lots of different definitions of strategy, they all generally tend to emphasize the importance of gaining *sustainable competitive advantage*. For example, in the 2013 book *Playing to Win*, co-author A.G. Lafley, the former CEO of Procter & Gamble, defined strategy as "an integrated set of choices that uniquely positions the firm in its industry so as to create sustainable advantage." Firms have a competitive advantage when they can (a) deliver the same product or service benefits as their competitors but at a lower cost or (b) deliver superior product or service benefits at a similar cost. Firms with a competitive advantage are able to earn positive economic profits.

In some respects, strategy is very simple. Figure 10.1 shows the allocation of economic value for a particular product. The height of the column represents the total value of the product where value is the maximum amount a buyer is willing and able to pay for the product. That total value gets divided among the different players. Cost represents how much value is captured by suppliers. The difference between the price you charge and your cost is profit, and the difference between value and price is surplus captured by the consumer. Here's a simple example. Say a representative consumer values the product at $400, it's priced at $300, and it costs $200 per unit to produce. The box between $300 and $200 (price minus cost) represents $100 of profit to the firm. Consumer surplus is also $100 ($400 less $300).

This simple diagram communicates several important ideas in strategy. First, it highlights that both value creation and value capture are critical. The starting point to strategy is producing a product that a consumer is willing and able to pay for. But, you also have to be able to capture some of that value for yourself as profit. Strategy is ultimately about how to increase the size of the profit box. The box gets bigger if the firm can lower its costs or raise its price. At a very high level, it's really that simple. Strategy is about raising price or reducing cost. Really successful firms manage to do both. Extremely successful firms like Starbucks do it over a long period of time, reflecting a *sustainable competitive advantage.*

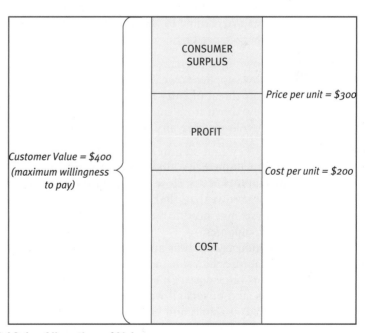

FIGURE **10.1   Allocation of Value**

10.2 Sources of Economic Profit

So what are the keys to competitive advantage and generating sustainable economic profit? Two schools of thought offer differing points of view. The first—the industrial organization (IO) economics perspective—locates the source of advantage at the *industry* level. The second—the resource-based view (RBV)—locates it at the *individual firm* level.

The Industry (External) View

The IO perspective focuses on the industry. According to Michael Porter, "The essence of this paradigm is that a firm's performance in the marketplace depends critically on the characteristics of the industry environment in which it competes."[4] Certain industries are more attractive than other industries because of their structural characteristics. Companies in those industries possess market power, which allows them to keep prices above the competitive level and to earn economic profit. Industry structure includes factors such as barriers to entry, product differentiation among firms, and the number and size distribution of firms. For example, industries with high barriers to entry are more attractive because competitors find it more difficult to enter the industry and drive profit down to competitive levels; firms in industries with differentiated products have less elastic demand and therefore higher profit; and industries with a small number of firms of different sizes are less likely to compete vigorously.

If industry structure is the most important determinant of long-run profitability, then the key to generating economic profit is to operate in the right industry. According to Michael Porter's Five Forces model,[5] the best industries are characterized by

- low buyer power,
- low supplier power,
- low threat of entry (high barriers to entry),
- low threat from substitutes, and
- low levels of rivalry between existing firms.

A key first step in applying the Five Forces model is defining what exactly we mean by "industry." An industry is a group of firms producing products that are close substitutes to each other to serve a market. It's important to realize that firms often operate in multiple industries. So, the analysis may need to be done on a product-by-product basis for multiproduct companies.

Industry analysis and the Five Forces model is largely about which players capture the value in an industry. Just because you are in an industry that creates value doesn't mean that you are going to capture it. Suppliers, industry rivals, and buyers all want to capture value too: suppliers want to charge as much as possible, and buyers want to pay as little as possible. The Five Forces model helps you think about how much of the industry value your firm is likely to capture given the characteristics of the industry. It all depends on the strength of the forces. Let's start with supplier power.

Suppliers can charge higher prices (and capture more of the industry value) when they have greater power. They are the providers of any input to the product or service. Examples include labor, capital, and providers of raw/ partially finished materials. Supplier power tends to be higher when the inputs they provide are critical inputs or highly differentiated. Concentration among suppliers also contributes to supplier power because a firm will have fewer bargaining options. Even if many suppliers exist, power may still be high if there are significant costs to switching between suppliers. The story on buyer power is similar. If buyers are concentrated (consider if your firm were an automotive supplier and your buyers were the major auto manufacturers) or if it is easy for buyers to switch from firm to firm, buyer power will tend to be higher. More power means these buyers will find it easier to capture value (e.g., by bargaining hard to pay a lower price), taking value away from your firm.

Threats from potential entrants are another important force to consider. As we discussed in Chapter 9, economic profits tend to draw new entrants. These entrants will quickly erode the profit of an industry unless barriers prevent or slow their entry. Examples of entry barriers include government protection (e.g., patents or licensing requirements), proprietary products, strong brands, high capital requirements for entry, and lower costs driven by economies of scale.

Substitute products can still erode a firm's ability to capture value even if barriers to entry are high. If close substitutes to a product are available and buyers find it inexpensive to switch to them, it will be hard for a firm to build and maintain high profits.

The final force concerns the rivalry among existing firms, the force most directly related to our typical view of "competition." If a large number of similarly situated firms compete in an industry with high fixed costs and slow industry growth, rivalry is likely to be quite high. Rivalry also tends to be higher when products are not very well differentiated and buyers find it easy to switch back and forth.

The wide differences in profitability across industries in Figure 10.2 support the IO view.[6] The most profitable industry, pharmaceuticals, exhibits relatively high barriers to entry, arising from significant investments in personnel and technology; moreover, successful products enjoy extended periods of patent protection (legal barriers to entry).

Overall, the IO view suggests that the way to earn economic profits is to choose an attractive industry and then develop the resources that will allow you to successfully compete in the industry. But, what about managers who don't have the luxury of choosing a new industry? The tools of industry analysis can still be helpful. First, move beyond a historical analysis of your industry to think about how the five forces might change in the future. Second, and more importantly, think about what actions you can take to make your current industry position more attractive. For example, how can you reduce supplier power? One answer is to increase rivalry among your suppliers. For example, you could do this by using an online procurement auction to purchase raw materials and semifinished inputs. Auctions are the topic of Chapter 17. Steps that

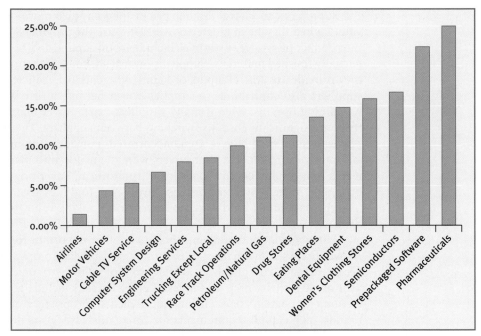

FIGURE **10.2** Profitability Differences between Industries

you take to decrease rivalry with your competitors, reduce buyer power, and build entry barriers will all help improve the attractiveness of your industry position.

It's also important to realize the limitations of tools like the Five Forces. First, this view focuses on value capture—it doesn't really provide any insight into how value gets created in the industry. Second, this view portrays an industry as a zero-sum game; that is, the way you get a bigger piece of the pie is to take it from one of the other participants in the industry. Although this is one way to view competition (and one that is often correct), companies can also work with other industry participants to try to build a larger pie. With a larger pie, everyone's slice grows bigger. Cooperative efforts with rivals, buyers, and suppliers feature prominently in a book by Adam Brandenburger and Barry Nalebuff called *Coopetition* (cooperative competition). The authors remind us that to look beyond the threats to firm profitability, emphasized by Porter's Five Forces analysis, to *opportunities* for cooperation that can enhance firm and industry profitability.

Annabelle Gawer and Michael A. Cusumano offer a similar idea for thinking about strategy in industries like telecommunications where success requires creating an "ecosystem" of complementary products.[7] A company must first decide whether to pursue a "product" or a "platform" strategy; a "product" is proprietary and controlled by one company, whereas a "platform" needs a set of complementary innovations to reach its full potential. One of the biggest mistakes a company can make is to pursue a product strategy and fail to recognize the platform value of their product. The best example of this is perhaps the Macintosh computer, which, due to its early technological lead, could have become the dominant platform for personal computing. Instead they priced high, failed to encourage complementary innovation, and let Microsoft become the dominant platform.

The Resource (Internal) View

If industry structure told the whole story about strategy, we wouldn't expect to find performance differences across firms within industries. These differences do exist, however, and the resource-based view (RBV) gained favor in the 1990s as an explanation for these inter-firm differences.

The RBV explains that individual firms may exhibit sustained performance advantages due to their superior resources, where resources are defined as "the tangible and intangible assets firms use to conceive of and implement their strategies."[8] Resources can be tangible like equipment, real estate, and financial capital as well as intangible like brand, knowledge, and organizational culture.

Two primary assumptions underlie the RBV: resource heterogeneity and resource immobility. The RBV views firms as possessing different bundles of resources that are immobile (the resources resist transfer or copying). These immobile resources are the sources of differential performance within an industry.

Given the differences in resources across firms, the RBV[9] provides further guidance on when these resources may lead to superior performance, where superior performance is defined as the firm's ability to earn above-average profit. If a resource is both valuable and rare, it can generate at least a temporary competitive advantage over rivals. A valuable resource must allow a business to conceive of and implement strategies that improve its efficiency or effectiveness. Examples include resources that let a firm operate at lower costs than its rivals or charge higher prices to its customers. For a resource to be rare, it must not be simultaneously available to a large number of competitors.

Resources that generate temporary competitive advantage do not necessarily lead to a sustainable competitive advantage. For such resources to deliver a sustainable advantage, they must be difficult to substitute for or imitate. Otherwise, any advantages that those resources deliver will be competed away. Imitation and substitution both erode firm profit. In the first, a competitor matches the resource by exactly duplicating it; in the second, a competitor matches the resources by deploying a different but strategically equivalent resource. We can list several conditions that make resources hard to imitate *(inimitability)*:

1. Resources that flow from a firm's unique historical conditions will be difficult for competitors to match.
2. If the link between resources and advantage is unclear, then competitors will have a hard time trying to recreate the particular resources that deliver the advantage.
3. If a resource is socially complex (e.g., organizational culture), rivals will find it difficult to duplicate the resource.

Be wary of any advice you read that claims to identify critical resources or capabilities that successful companies have to develop in order to gain a competitive advantage. You should be skeptical of such advice for two reasons. First, explanations such as these often mistakenly conclude a causal relationship when only a correlation exists. Remember the *Good to Great* companies that we mentioned in Chapter 9. They all had five management principles in common that supposedly drove their success. Their subsequent less-than-great performance raises serious doubts about whether these "best practices" caused their prior superior performance.

The second reason you should question such advice has to do with the nature of competition in general. Publicly available knowledge is *not* going to help you create a competitive advantage. Let's say an author discovers that having a chief managerial economics officer (CMEO) in your company always leads to a competitive advantage in companies and publishes this advice in a new book. You read the book and decide to hire a CMEO for your business and no competitive advantage follows. What happened? Well, your competitor probably read about the CMEO "secret" as well and hired one, too. Now that everyone knows about it, no advantage is possible. Competitive advantage flows from having something that competitors can't easily duplicate, such as an extremely valuable brand like Starbucks. You're not likely to find these on the shelves of your local bookstore. Nor are you likely to get it from a consultant who is selling the same advice that he or she sells to your competitors.

10.3 The Three Basic Strategies

A firm looking to generate superior economic performance, given its industry and resource base, has three basic strategies it can follow to keep one step ahead of the forces of competition:

1. cost reduction,
2. product differentiation, or
3. reduction in competitive intensity.

Most strategies fall into one of these three categories. The first strategy, cost reduction, is pretty self-explanatory. Low-cost strategies are usually found in industries where products are not particularly differentiated and price competition tends to be fierce. Walmart and Southwest are two famous examples of companies that have been very successful in developing low-cost strategies. Note, however, that cost reductions generate increases in long-run profitability *only* if the cost reduction is difficult to imitate. If others can easily duplicate your actions, cost reduction will not give you sustainable competitive advantage.

The third strategy, reducing competitive intensity, is also self-evident. If you can reduce the level of competition within an industry and keep new competitors from entering, you may be able to slow the erosion of profitability. (In the chapter on strategic interaction, we'll use game theory to develop strategies that reduce the intensity of competition.) One easy way to reduce rivalry is to ask the government to do it for you. This is what the bookselling industry in Germany does. Discounting of new books by German booksellers is illegal, essentially making price competition a crime. U.S. washing machine manufacturers have benefited from regulation as well. A 2000 Department of Energy regulation banned the sale of low-priced washing machines under the guise of increasing energy efficiency. Who were the biggest supporters of the ban? It was not the consumers, who by a margin of six-to-one preferred to purchase lower-priced machines. It was the washing machine manufacturers—because now they would be able to sell expensive "front-loading" models at an average price of $240 more than the banned machines.[10]

We can interpret the second strategy, product differentiation, as a reduction in the elasticity of demand for the product. Less-elastic demand leads to an increase in price because the optimal margin of price over marginal cost is related to the elasticity of demand; that is, $(P - MC)/ P = 1/ |e|$. When your product is effectively differentiated from other products, demand is less elastic, leading to a higher margin of price over marginal cost. Starbucks is an excellent example of a company that has successfully pursued a differentiation strategy for over 40 years. And they have pursued differentiation in both the product (coffee) and the overall experience as well.

Another successful example of a product differentiation strategy is Perdue Chicken. Frank Perdue took an essentially homogeneous product—chicken—and turned it into a branded product, Perdue Chicken. He did this by exercising quality control over the entire supply chain, from the feed to the final product. Consumers perceive his branded chickens to be of higher quality. Thus, they have less-elastic demand, allowing Perdue to charge a higher price. Economies of scale (cost reduction) also have played a part in Perdue's success.

Prelude Lobster's[11] managers tried a product differentiation strategy similar to Perdue's. Although they advertised their superior after-catch handling of the lobsters, customers correctly perceived that, for lobsters, unlike chicken, the supply chain is largely uncontrollable. Prelude was eventually forced out of business by lower-cost competitors who did not advertise.

With the benefit of hindsight, it is easy to identify successful strategies (and the reasons for their success) or failed strategies (and the reason for their failures). It's much more difficult to identify successful or failed strategies before they succeed or fail. But this is what you have to do in order to invest successfully, or to build successful strategies.

To illustrate the importance of this idea, let's return to the wisdom of investing in companies with a sustainable competitive advantage. This strategy leads to sustained, above-average profitability for the company, but remember that the stock price also determines the return from investing. If the stock price is high relative to its discounted future earnings, the investment is a bad one, regardless of whether the company has a sustainable competitive advantage. Warren Buffett, for instance, makes money by acquiring companies whose potential future earnings are high relative to their current stock price. He then helps develop strategies to help them realize their high potential earnings by creating a sustainable competitive advantage. He doesn't make money simply by investing in companies with a current competitive advantage. Instead, his success is due to his ability to help these companies craft successful long-run strategies.

SUMMARY & HOMEWORK PROBLEMS

Summary of Main Points

- Strategy is simple—to increase performance, figure out a way to increase P (price) or reduce C (cost).
- The industrial organization (IO) economics perspective assumes that the industry structure is the most important determinant of long-run profitability.
- The Five Forces model is a framework for analyzing the attractiveness of an industry. Attractive industries have low supplier power, low buyer power, low threat of entry, low threat of substitutes, and low rivalry.
- According to the resource-based view (RBV), individual firms may exhibit sustained performance advantages because of their superior resources. To be the source of sustainable competitive advantage, those resources should be valuable, rare, and difficult to imitate/substitute.
- Strategy is the art of matching the resources and capabilities of a firm to the opportunities and risks in its external environment for the purpose of developing a sustainable competitive advantage.
- Be wary of any advice you read that claims to identify critical resources or capabilities that successful companies have to develop in order to gain a competitive advantage.
- To stay one step ahead of the forces of competition, a firm can adopt one of three basic strategies: cost reduction, product differentiation, or reduction in the intensity of competition.

Multiple-Choice Questions

1. An industry is defined as
   a. a group of firms producing the exact same products and services.
   b. firms producing items that sell through the same distribution channels.
   c. firms that have the same resources and capabilities.
   d. a group of firms producing products that are close substitutes.
2. Attractive industries have all the following, except
   a. high supplier power.
   b. low buyer power.
   c. high entry barriers.
   d. low rivalry.
3. Which of the following is *not* an example of an entry barrier?
   a. Government protection through patents or licensing requirements
   b. Strong brands
   c. Low capital requirements for entry
   d. Lower costs driven by economies of scale
4. Buyers have higher power when
   a. their suppliers sell a highly differentiated product.
   b. they are not a significant purchaser of their supplier's output.
   c. switching costs are low.
   d. the buyer industry is highly fragmented (buyers are not concentrated).
5. Which of the following is *not* a factor that contributes to higher rivalry in an industry?
   a. Numerous competitors
   b. High fixed costs
   c. Fast industry growth
   d. Low switching costs for buyers
6. The concept that describes firms possessing different bundles of resources is
   a. resource heterogeneity.
   b. resource immobility.
   c. barriers to entry.
   d. imitability.
7. If a firm successfully adopts a product-differentiation strategy, the elasticity of demand for its products should
   a. increase.
   b. decrease.

   c. become marginal.
   d. be unaffected.
8. When a resource or capability is valuable and rare, a firm may gain a
   a. sustainable competitive advantage.
   b. competitive parity.
   c. cost advantage.
   d. temporary competitive advantage.
9. Which of the following is critical for a firm adopting a long-term cost-reduction strategy?
   a. The firm must also differentiate its product or service.
   b. The strategy reduces costs by at least 10%.
   c. The strategy is focused on reducing internal production costs.
   d. The methods of achieving cost reductions are difficult to imitate.
10. When a resource or capability is valuable, rare, hard to imitate, and nonsubstitutable, firms may gain
   a. a temporary competitive advantage.
   b. a complex competitive advantage.
   c. competitive parity.
   d. a sustainable competitive advantage.

Individual Problems

10-1 High Rivalry

For each category, indicate which condition is associated with higher rivalry among competitors.

Number of firms	High	Low
Fixed costs	High	Low
Level of product differentiation	High	Low
Industry growth	High	Low
Buyer switching costs	High	Low

10-2 Increasing Customer Value

To increase a company's performance, a manager suggests that the company needs to increase the value of its product to customers. Describe three ways in which this advice might be incorrect (*Hint:* Think about what else might or might not change that affects profit.)

10-3 Intangible Resources

Why might intangible resources like human capital and intellectual assets be a more likely source of sustainable competitive advantage than tangible resources?

10-4 Five Forces and the Airline Industry

Examine the U.S. passenger airline industry using the Five Forces model. Is this an attractive industry? Why or why not?

10-5 Smartphone Market

The smartphone market has been dominated by Apple, but recently the Droid has been able to leverage Google's information services into market gains while Blackberry, known for its secure business-oriented network, has attempted to become more attractive with a "friendlier" interface. At the same time, a number of less capable fringe firms are emerging. How do these features fit into an industrial organization (IO) view of the market versus a resource-based view (RBV)?

10-6 Salons and Teeth Whitening

Salon owners have recently started offering teeth whitening services to clients in addition to their more standard services. In a number of states, regulators have ordered the salon owners to stop, claiming that this service constitutes the practice of illegal dentistry. What group would you expect to be behind the state's efforts to ban salons from providing teeth whitening services? Why?

Group Problems

G10-1 Strategy

What strategy is your company following (try to classify it into one of the three strategies in the text)? How is your strategy working—how long will it allow you to maintain a competitive advantage?

G10-2 Resources

What are your firm's key resources and/or capabilities? How do these translate into a competitive advantage?

END NOTES

1. See http://www.forbes.com/sites/carminegallo/2011/03/25/starbucks-ceo-lesson-in-communication-skills/.

2. See http://www.digitalcoco3.com/brand-love-infographic/.

3. Whitney Tilson, "Boring Portfolio" column on the Motley Fool site, February 28, 2000, http://www.fool.com/boringport/2000/boringport000228.htm.

4. Michael Porter, "The Contributions of Industrial Organization to Strategic Management," *Academy of Management Review* 6 (1981): 609–620.

5. Michael Porter, *Competitive Strategy* (New York: Free Press, 1980).

6. Profitability measured by operating income divided by assets over the period 1988–1995. Adapted from Pankaj Ghemawat and Jan W. Rivkin. "Creating Competitive Advantage." Harvard Business School Background Note 798-062, February 2006 (revised from original January 1998 version).

7. Anabelle Gawer and Michael A. Cusumano, "How Companies become Platform Leaders," *Sloan Management Review* 49 (2008): 28–35. Michael Porter also recognizes the importance of considering complements in an industry, although he argues that the presence of complements is not necessarily bad or good for an industry. He suggests that complements affect industry profitability through the way they influence the other five forces.

8. Definition from Jay B. Barney and Asli M. Arikan, "The Resource-Based View: Origins and Implications," in *The Blackwell Handbook of Strategic Management*, edited by Michael A. Hitt, R. Edward Freeman, and Jeffrey S. Harrison (Oxford: Oxford University Press, 2001), 138.

9. For an overview of the resource-based view, see Jay Barney, "Firm Resources and Sustained Competitive Advantage," *Journal of Management* 17 (1991): 99–120. The explanation contained here draws from that description.

10. For more on how companies use the legal and regulatory process to further their competitive strategies, see Richard Shell, *Make the Rules or Your Rivals Will* (New York: Crown Business, 2004). For more on regulation, see S. E. Dudley, *Primer on Regulation* (Mercatus Policy Series, George Mason University, November 2005), available at http://mercatus.org/publication/primer-regulation.

11. Harvard Business School case number 9-373-052, "Prelude Corp." Harvard Business School case number 9-373-052, "Prelude Corp."

11 Foreign Exchange, Trade, and Bubbles

When the business plan for the new Nissan Rogue was developed in September 2005, a dollar was worth 115 yen. At this exchange rate, the contribution margin for models sold in the United States was projected to be 18%.

When the Rogue was launched 21 months later, the dollar had *appreciated* to 124 yen. For the U.S. division of Nissan, this was good news because the Rogue was produced in Japan, but sold in the United States. Consequently, the revenue they earned (in dollars) had gone up relative to the costs they incurred (in yen). The contribution margin jumped to 20%. We illustrate this change in Figure 11.1.

As you can see in the figure, Nissan's good fortune did not last long. In 2008, the dollar started falling in value. By June 2011, the dollar had fallen to 77 yen and this caused the Rogue's margin to fall to 12%.

At that time, Nissan had planned on increasing the "domestic content" of its vehicles sold in the United States. Greater domestic content means that costs, and profit, are affected less by exchange rate movements. Higher domestic content can also increase domestic demand by appealing to consumers who want to "Buy American."

But higher domestic content has costs, as well. One can imagine a Japanese company in Indiana paying an American worker $16/hour to assemble items that were manufactured in Mexico by a worker who makes only $4/hour. For equal amounts of work, this would imply an 80% domestic content, but also much higher costs. As of 2016, Nissan had made some progress toward increasing the domestic content of their cars, for example, their Frontier Truck had the highest domestic content in its class (50%).

In this chapter, we show you (1) how exchange rates are determined and (2) how changes in exchange rates affect firms and consumers. We also tell you what little we know about "bubbles," prices that are not determined by the usual forces of supply and demand. The bursting of an asset bubble can have a big effect on exchange rates, so we include bubbles in this chapter.

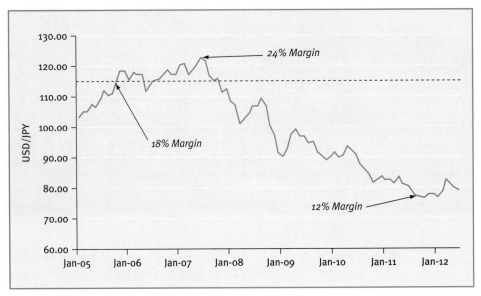

FIGURE **11.1** YEN/USD Exchange Rate

11.1 The Market for Foreign Exchange

To illustrate exchange rate movements, we examine the curious case of Iceland. The story begins in 2001, when all three of Iceland's recently privatized banks decided to enter the high-risk world of investment banking. They borrowed from other banks, and used the funds to buy Beverly Hills condos, British soccer teams, and Danish airlines. At that time, the prices of the assets they purchased were rising faster than the interest rates they were paying, so the banks made a lot of money.

Buoyed by the belief that asset prices would keep rising, Iceland's banks borrowed more and bought more. By 2006, the banks were finding it difficult to borrow from other banks, so they started borrowing through the Internet, mostly from depositors living in the United Kingdom. In just two years, the number of depositors lending money to Iceland's banks outnumbered the entire population of Iceland and the amount they borrowed was bigger than Iceland's entire national income.

By 2008, some of the assets purchased by the banks began to decline in value. In response, the credit rating agencies downgraded the banks' creditworthiness, and foreign depositors rushed to withdraw their money. As deposits came home to the UK, not only did the banking sector crash, but the krona plunged in value and prices of imported goods soared.[1]

Although these changes caused a lot of pain in Iceland, there is an upside to a weak currency—Iceland's exports began looking a lot less expensive to foreign buyers. Exports (and tourism) increased, and employment eventually recovered.

Greece had a similar crash, at about the same time, but its response has been very different. Because Greece does not have its own currency (it abandoned the drachma when it joined the Eurozone in 2001), their exchange rate is "fixed" with respect to their major trading partners. Consequently, Greece's exports still look expensive, and its economy has yet to recover. As of 2016, unemployment was still over 20% and national income was shrinking.

To understand these changes, we begin with a simple question, "Why do people want to trade one currency for another?" To answer it, imagine that an Icelander wants to buy a Land Rover built in the United Kingdom. Before she can purchase an imported car, imagine that our Icelandic consumer must pay for the car in pounds. While not literally true (it could be anyone in the vertical supply chain, for example, the manufacturer, exporter, or local car dealer), the exposition is simpler if we pretend that the consumer exchanges krona (ISK) for pounds (GBP) and then buys the imported car herself.

In words that should now be familiar, we say that the Icelander "demands" pounds in order to purchase British goods. Iceland's aggregate demand for British pounds includes everyone in Iceland who wants to purchase British goods and services, or who wants to invest in Britain. To do so, they have to "sell" krona to "buy" pounds. Every time you see the word "sell," think of supply, and every time you read the word "buy," think of demand.

On the other side of the transaction are those who want to "sell" pounds to "buy" krona. The "supply" of pounds includes everyone in Great Britain who wants to buy Icelandic goods and services or who wants to invest in Iceland. The market for **foreign exchange** brings together the demanders of pounds and the suppliers of pounds, and the equilibrium price is the exchange rate, or the price of a pound measured in krona.[2]

We plot the price of a pound measured in krona in Figure 11.2. The financial symbol for this exchange rate is GPB/ISK. We see that the price of a pound

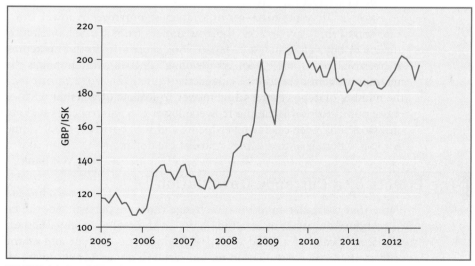

FIGURE **11.2** **GBP/ISK Exchange Rate**

increased from 125 krona in 2008 to about 200 krona in 2012. We say that the pound *appreciated*, or that that krona *depreciated*.

To figure out why these changes occurred, apply the tools of Chapter 8 to the market for foreign exchange. Here is how to do it. When UK depositors withdrew their krona deposits, they *sold krona to buy pounds*. This represented an *increase in demand* for pounds that made the price of a pound *appreciate* against the krona.

Alternatively, we could analyze these movements by using the supply and demand for krona. The trick is realizing that supply of pounds (those who sell pounds to buy krona) is also demand for krona. Similarly, demand for pounds (those who sell krona to buy pounds) is also the supply of krona. And the price of a krona, measured in pounds, is the inverse of the price of a pound measured in krona. When the pound *appreciated* from 125 to 200 krona, we could also say that the krona *depreciated* from 0.008 pounds to about 0.005 pounds, or about half a penny.

If this sounds complicated, it is. The difficult part is keeping track of your frame of reference. If you are looking at it from the point of view of pounds, it is a demand increase that leads to a pound appreciation, but if you are looking at it from the point of view of krona, it is a supply increase that leads to a krona depreciation. Since the pound appreciation is a krona depreciation, both frames give you the same answer.

Now let's test your understanding: try to figure out how a decrease in U.S. interest rates affects the exchange rate of the dollar against a foreign currency, like the yen. This is the kind of question you might get in a job interview at Nissan.

To answer it, we use dollars as our frame of reference and start from first principles. A lower U.S. interest rate would make investing in the United States appear less attractive to a Japanese investor, who has to sell yen to buy dollars to invest in the United States. Consequently, a lower U.S. interest rate would decrease Japanese demand for U.S. dollars, which would make the dollar depreciate against the yen.

Now analyze the behavior of a Japanese borrower. A lower U.S. interest rate makes the "carry trade" (borrow dollars from a U.S. bank and then sell dollars to buy yen to invest in Japan) look more attractive. This represents an increase in the supply of dollars ("selling" dollars), which makes the dollar depreciate against the foreign currency.

Notice that we get the same answer regardless of whether we look at the foreign investors or foreign borrowers: lower U.S. interest rates will make U.S. investors look overseas for investments and U.S. borrowers look domestically for loans. Both lead to a depreciation of the dollar.

11.2 The Effects of a Currency Devaluation

Now that we understand how exchange rates are determined, the next step is to figure out what effects they have on the real economy. We begin with the simple case of a good with 100% domestic content and examine the effects of currency devaluation on four groups: domestic consumers, domestic producers, foreign consumers, and foreign producers.

Golf courses may have close to 100% domestic content, so we are going to use them to illustrate the effect of a peso devaluation. After the devaluation, golf in Mexico looks less expensive to U.S. consumers and makes golf in the United States look more expensive to Mexican consumers. The net effect of a peso devaluation is a reduction demand for U.S. golf and increase in demand for Mexican golf. The supply of golf, with 100% domestic content, is unaffected.

We represent these changes on the left side of Figure 11.3. As above, the key to understanding them is to keep track of your frame of reference. A peso devaluation increases the demand for golf in Mexico but does not affect supply. As a result, the price of Mexican golf goes up, measured in pesos. The higher price helps Mexican golf course owners (producers) but hurts Mexican golfers (consumers).

The peso devaluation (dollar appreciation) has the opposite effect in the United States. In general, a devaluation reduces U.S. demand and price, measured in dollars. U.S. golfers (consumers) benefit but U.S. golf course owners (producers) are harmed.

A currency devaluation helps domestic suppliers and foreign consumers but hurts domestic consumers and foreign suppliers.

Things get more complicated when, as is common, firms do not produce items with 100% domestic content. In general, firms that export heavily also tend to import heavily. In this case, a currency devaluation will increase export demand but also reduce supply because it raises the cost of imported parts. What this means is that our simple message that currency devaluations benefit domestic firms and harm domestic consumers is muted to the extent that the domestic content falls below 100%.

With this caveat, let's return to the effects of an appreciation of the pound relative to the Iceland krona. First, it increased export demand, for example,

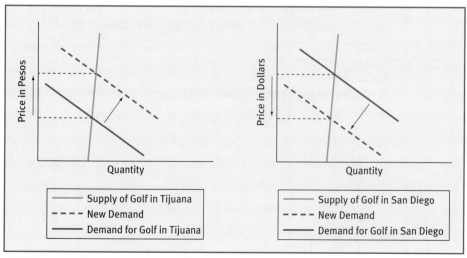

FIGURE **11.3**   Demand-Supply Analysis of a Peso Devaluation

for fish in Iceland. As a consequence, the domestic price of fish (in krona) went up. These changes helped Icelandic producers but hurt Icelandic consumers.

Similarly, the appreciation of the pound decreased export demand for foreign goods sent to Iceland, which caused a drop in the price of, for example, British cars (in pounds). These changes hurt British producers but helped British consumers.

11.3 Bubbles

From 1980 to about 2008, the economies of the developed world experienced steady growth, low unemployment, and mild inflation. Things were so good, for so long, that this period has been called the "great moderation." When it ended, it was sudden, dramatic, and unexpected. Very few economists predicted the crash, but since it happened, many of us have tried to come up with satisfactory explanations for it. With this chapter, we take a tentative step into the controversial area of bubble-ology, the study of prices not determined by the usual forces of demand and supply.

Our explanation has to do with the self-fulfilling role of expectations. During the great moderation, people began to expect that things would continue as they had for so long. To see how this could affect price, imagine that buyers and sellers see a price increase in one year and expect a similar price increase in the following year.

If buyers expect a future price increase, they would accelerate buying to avoid it, just as sellers would delay selling to take advantage of it. We illustrate these changes in Figure 11.4, which shows an increase in demand and a decrease in supply. Both changes tend to increase price. In other words, once people form expectations about future price increases, these expectations tend to become self-fulfilling. This is often what economists mean when they talk about "bubbles."

In addition, if buyers expect prices to increase faster than the interest rate, it makes sense to borrow and buy now in order to sell in the future. In fact, an increase in leverage, or borrowing, often accompanies bubbles.

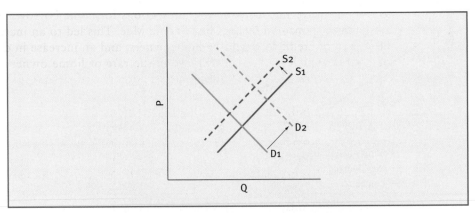

FIGURE **11.4** **Effects of Expectations on Demand and Supply**

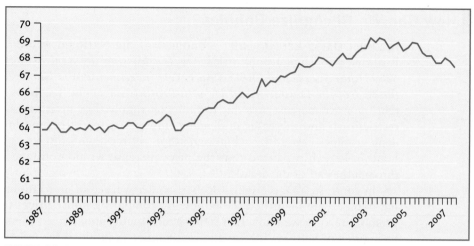

FIGURE **11.5** **U.S. Home Ownership Rate**

There are certain characteristics of bubbles that economists have documented.[3]

1. Bubbles emerge when investors disagree about the importance of big economic events. Because it is easier to place financial bets on higher prices, optimistic investors dominate.
2. Bubbles involve very large increases in trading volume.
3. Bubbles may continue even when many suspect a bubble. The bubble won't pop, however, until a sufficient number of skeptical investors act simultaneously. So far, no one has figured out how to predict when this is likely to occur.

To illustrate these phenomena, let's look at the housing market in the United States. The increase in prices began in 1993 when the government enacted policies designed to encourage low-income homeowners to buy houses. The government reduced qualifications for home borrowing from government-sponsored lenders like Fannie Mae. This led to an increase in the supply of credit to would-be homeowners, and an increase in demand for houses, which lead to an increase in the rate of home ownership, as shown in Figure 11.5.[4] This is the "big economic event" that started the bubble.

Especially in areas where the supply was limited by strict zoning laws (e.g., East Coast, California, and Florida), prices increased dramatically. Because many market participants expected housing prices to continue to increase, they borrowed heavily to buy bigger and sometimes even second houses. The bankers who lent them money thought that the loans were "safe" because the price of the underlying asset had always gone up in the past. As a consequence, banks were willing to lend on very favorable terms.[5]

11.4 How Can We Recognize Bubbles?

In 2006, David Lereah, chief economist of the National Association of Realtors, published a book titled *Are You Missing the Real Estate Boom? Why Home Values and Other Real Estate Investments Will Climb Through the End of the Decade—And How to Profit from Them.* The book argued that the price increase was due to limits on supply (low inventories, zoning restrictions) and increases in demand (low mortgage rates, and favorable demographics caused by a big increase in retirees, who often buy second homes). Lereah predicted that the price increase would continue at least through the end of the decade.

In contrast, Yale economist Robert Shiller warned of an irrational housing bubble.[6] He identified the bubble by comparing house prices to rents. From Chapter 9, we know that in long-run equilibrium, homeowners should be indifferent between buying and renting. For example, if the price of renting becomes much less expensive than buying, we would expect that buyers would turn to renting which would reduce demand for owning and eventually bring the price down.

In Figure 11.6, we plot the relationship between the cost of renting and the cost of owning a house, we see that owning became much more expensive than renting (70% more in 2006). We also see the dramatic decline in house prices beginning in 2006. So, Professor Shiller was right about house prices being too high, but he was a couple years early with his call.

So why did the bubble pop? If you believe the bubble-ologists, it was because there were enough skeptical investors, like Professor Shiller, who started betting on house prices to fall. But the truth is that we don't know. Without a more complete theory of bubbles, one would tell us when they were going to pop, it is impossible to test for the existence of bubbles.

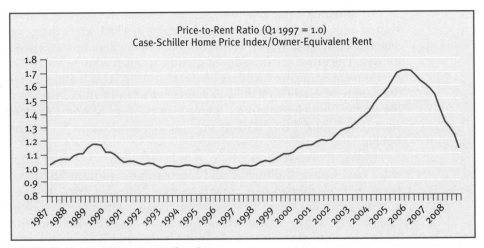

FIGURE **11.6** **Renting versus Owning**

Interestingly, this was not Professor Shiller's first good call on a price bubble. In 2000, he made what is perhaps the best prediction in stock market history when his book *Irrational Exuberance* was released at the same time that the "Internet" or "tech" bubble began to burst. He identified the bubble by looking at the long-run equilibrium relationship between stock prices and earnings or profit. If prices are rational, then they should equal the discounted flow of future earnings. Obviously, we cannot observe future earnings, so Professor Shiller plotted current stock prices against a 10-year trailing average of past earnings.

In Figure 11.7, we update Professor Shiller's analysis and plot the Price/Earnings ratio of the S&P 500 index (and comparable predecessor indices) going back to 1882. The average of the ratio is about 16, which means that, on average, a stock's price is about 16 times its trailing earnings. Equivalently, if you hold a typical stock for 16 years, earnings will just cover the purchase price, on average.

So what do bubbles have to do with exchange rates? Looking at Shiller's graph, we see that from 2003 to 2007, the stock market was over-valued, relative to its long-run average. In fact, there are only two other episodes in history where stock prices have been this high (1929 and 2000), relative to earnings. In both of these cases, prices crashed after reaching these heights.

Shiller's methodology also tells us that Icelandic banks began borrowing and investing at a time when asset prices (including house prices) were very

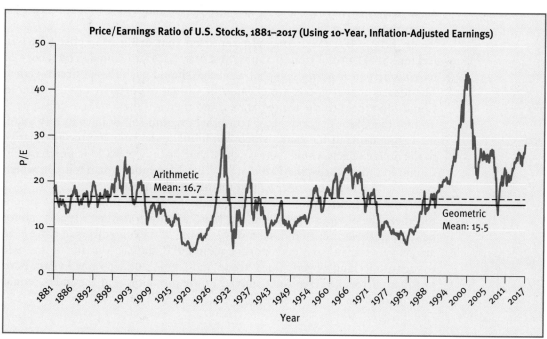

FIGURE **11.7**   Stock Price/Earnings Ratio

expensive. Once the asset prices began to come down, depositors lost faith in the banks' ability to pay them back. When they withdrew their deposits, and sold krona to buy pounds, the krona depreciated relative to the pound, which hurt Icelandic consumers.

If you look closely at the graph, you will also see that 2017 stock prices are as expensive as they were in 2007. This suggests to some that the stock market is over-valued, but others say that the valuation is justified given the very low discount (interest) rates. Remember that when you buy a stock, you receive the discounted flow of future profit. If the discount rate is very low, discounted future profits are bigger, which should drive up the price of the stock relative to its earnings.

The difficulty of testing whether stocks are really over-valued (in a bubble) is why bubble-ology is so controversial. Besides, if someone really knew that a bubble were going to burst, he probably wouldn't waste time telling you (they would trade on the information instead). And he certainly wouldn't waste time writing textbooks.

11.5 Purchasing Power Parity

So is there a similar long-run relationship that would tell us when a currency is over-valued? The answer is *purchasing power parity*, the idea that, in the long run, exchange rates and/or prices should adjust so that tradable goods cost the same no matter where you buy them. If they didn't, exporters could make money by buying the good in one country and selling it in another. This is referred to as "*arbitrage.*"

In July 2007, the *Economist* reported that a Big Mac cost $7.61 in Iceland, $3.41 in the United States, and only $1.45 in China. The theory of *purchasing power parity* says that arbitrage should push these prices together. The idea is that if goods are cheaper in China, exporters can buy them in China, ship them to the United States, and then sell them to U.S. consumers. To buy the Chinese goods, U.S. consumers would sell dollars to buy yuan, increasing demand for yuan, which would make the yuan appreciate relative to the dollar, which would increase the dollar price of a Big Mac purchased in China. In other words, the *Economist*'s "Big Mac Index"[7] can tell you which currencies are over- or under-valued relative to the dollar.

Now there are some problems with the theory linking these prices together. The obvious one is that Big Macs are not traded goods and cannot be shipped thousands of miles. However, many of the ingredients in a Big Mac are actively traded (so it may work) and, in 2007, the Big Mac Index was able to identify Iceland's over-valued krona and China's under-valued yuan. Both of those currencies have since moved in the direction that the index would have predicted.

SUMMARY & HOMEWORK PROBLEMS

Summary of Main Points

- In the market for foreign exchange between England and Iceland, the supply of pounds includes everyone in Britain who wants to *sell* pounds to *buy* krona in order to buy Icelandic goods, or invest in Iceland.
- The *demand* for pounds includes everyone in Iceland who wants to *sell* krona to *buy* pounds in order to buy British goods, or invest in Britain.
- The demand for pounds is equal to the supply of krona, and *vice-versa*.
- Exchange rates are prices determined by supply and demand. An increase in demand for pounds or a decrease in supply of krona will appreciate the pound relative to the krona.
- A decline in U.S. interest rates will induce foreign borrowers to borrow in dollars, *sell* the dollars to *buy* a foreign currency, and then invest in the foreign country (the so-called "carry trade"). Such an increase in the supply of dollars causes a dollar depreciation.
- A decline in U.S. interest rates would have a similar effect on domestic investors who would look to international investments with higher rates of return. They would *sell* dollars to *buy* the foreign currency, and then invest in the foreign country. Such an increase in the supply of dollars causes a dollar depreciation.
- Devaluations help domestic producers and foreign consumers, but hurt domestic consumers and foreign producers.
- Expectations about the future play a role in price bubbles. If buyers expect a future price increase, they will accelerate their purchases to avoid it. Similarly, sellers will delay selling to take advantage of it. In this respect, the expectations become self-fulfilling.

- You can potentially identify bubbles by using the "indifference principle" of Chapter 9 to tell you when market prices move away from their long-run equilibrium relationships.

Multiple-Choice Questions

1. The intersection between demand for dollars and the supply of dollars is known as the
   a. inflation rate.
   b. exchange rate.
   c. price.
   d. quantity.

2. An individual in the United States wants to buy office equipment from England that costs 2,800 pounds. If the exchange rate is $1.92, how much will it cost in dollar terms?
   a. $2,800
   b. $5,376
   c. $1,458
   d. Need more information

3. If the Chinese yuan devalues relative to the U.S. dollar, then
   a. U.S. producers will benefit; Chinese consumers will benefit.
   b. U.S. producers will benefit; Chinese consumers will be hurt.
   c. U.S. producers will be hurt; Chinese consumers will benefit.
   d. U.S. producers will be hurt; Chinese consumers will be hurt.

4. Following a peso appreciation relative to the dollar, which of the following results is expected to occur?
   a. Prices in the United States would rise, and prices in Mexico would rise.
   b. Prices in the United States would rise, and prices in Mexico would fall.
   c. Prices in the United States would fall, and prices in Mexico would rise.
   d. Prices in the United States would fall, and prices in Mexico would fall.

5. Following a peso appreciation relative to the dollar, which of the following results is expected to occur?
   a. U.S. consumers would benefit, and Mexican producers would benefit.
   b. U.S. consumers would be hurt, and Mexican producers would benefit.
   c. U.S. consumers would benefit, and Mexican producers would be hurt.
   d. U.S. consumers would be hurt, and Mexican producers would be hurt.

6. Following an increase in Mexican interest rates relative to U.S. interest rates (which causes Mexican investors to borrow abroad to invest domestically), which of the following is expected to occur?
   a. The dollar would appreciate relative to the peso, and Mexican prices would increase.
   b. The dollar would appreciate relative to the peso, and Mexican prices would decrease.
   c. The dollar would depreciate relative to the peso, and Mexican prices would increase.
   d. The dollar would depreciate relative to the peso, and Mexican prices would decrease.

7. Following an increase in Mexican interest rates relative to U.S. interest rates, which caused U.S. investors to invest in Mexican bonds, which of the following would occur?
   a. The dollar would appreciate relative to the peso, and Mexican prices would increase.
   b. The dollar would depreciate relative to the peso, and Mexican prices would decrease.
   c. The dollar would depreciate relative to the peso, and Mexican prices would increase.
   d. The exchange rate would not be affected, and neither would Mexican prices.

8. In July 2014 the price of a Big Mac was $4.80 in the United States, while in China it was only $2.73 at market exchange rates. So the "raw" Big Mac index says that the yuan was under-valued by 43% at that time. How would domestic inflation in China affect the Big Mac Index?
   a. The Big Mac Index would indicate that the Chinese currency is less under-valued.
   b. The Big Mac Index would indicate that the Chinese currency is more under-valued.
   c. The Big Mac Index is not affected by inflation.
   d. The Big Mac Index would indicate that the Dollar is more under-valued.

9. If the U.S. economy strengthens, consumer incomes increase, and consumers buy more imported goods and services. How will this affect exchange rates?
   a. The dollar will appreciate relative to the yuan, and U.S. prices will increase.
   b. The dollar will appreciate relative to the yuan, and U.S. prices will decrease.
   c. The dollar will depreciate relative to the yuan, and U.S. prices will increase.
   d. The dollar will depreciate relative to the yuan, and U.S. prices will decrease.

10. If buyers expect future price increases, they will _____ their purchases to avoid it. Similarly, sellers will _____ selling to take advantage of it.
    a. accelerate; accelerate
    b. accelerate; delay
    c. delay; accelerate
    d. delay; delay

Individual Problems

11-1 The Carry Trade

In 2014, the euro was trading at $1.35 on the foreign exchange market. By 2015, the rate had fallen to $1.10, due to falling European interest rates. Explain the fall in the price of a euro using supply and demand curves, and in words.

11-2 Brexit Fears

When Great Britain voted to leave the Eurozone, the pound depreciated 17% against the dollar. It also raised fears that the Eurozone would fall apart. Explain how this fear would affect the euro/dollar exchange rate.

11-3 Effects of the Pound Devaluation on Tourism and Bank Profits

Explain the effects of the pound devaluation on (1) imports and tourism to Great Britain and (2) profits of U.S. bank with European trading subsidiaries in London (which earn profit in pounds).

11-4 The Effects of a Pound Depreciation on Whirlpool

Most of the appliances that Whirlpool sells in the UK, are built in the EU. What is the effect of a pound depreciation on Whirlpool's profit margin.

11-3 Domestic Content

Explain the effect of a dollar depreciation on domestic firms and domestic consumers for goods with less than 100% domestic content.

11-4 Dollar Devaluation

How will a dollar devaluation affect businesses and consumers in the twin cities of El Paso, the United States, and Juarez, Mexico?

11-5 Effect of Expectations on the Exchange Rate

If market participants expect the krona to appreciate relative to the dollar, what will happen?

Group Problems

G11-1 Exchange Rate Effects on Industry

Using shifts in supply and demand curves, describe how a change in the exchange rate affected your industry. Label the axes, and state the geographic, product, and time dimensions of the demand and supply curves you are drawing. Explain what happened to industry price and quantity by making specific references to the demand and supply curves. How can you profit from future shifts in the exchange rate? How do you predict future changes in the exchange rate?

G11-2 Exchange Rate Effects on Your Firm

Describe how a change in the exchange rate affected your firm. Explain what happened to your price and quantity. How can you profit from future shifts in the exchange rate? How do you predict future changes in the exchange rate?

END NOTES

1. We are very grateful to Olafur Arnarson for his guidance and feedback on our discussion of the financial crisis in Iceland. We recommend his book on the subject to anyone who reads Icelandic.
2. To analyze these changes, we assume that there are only two countries (Iceland and Great Britain) trading goods and investing in each other's countries. Trade is easier to explain with a two-country example, so we ignore trade that runs through third-party countries.
3. Justin Lahart, "Bernanke's Bubble Laboratory," *Wall Street Journal*, May 16, 2008.
4. David Streitfeld and Gretchen Morgenson, "Building Flawed American Dreams," *New York Times*, October 18, 2008, http://www.nytimes.com/2008/10/19/business/19cisneros.html
5. Edward L. Glaeser, Joseph Gyourko, and Albert Saiz, "Housing Supply and Housing Bubbles," NBER Working Paper 14193, July 2008, https://www.nber.org/papers/w14193
6. Jonathan R. Laing, "The Bubble's New Home," *Barron's*, June 20, 2005, http://www.barrons.com/articles/SB111905372884363176
7. See "Big Mac Index," *The Economist*, http://www.economist.com/content/big-mac-index

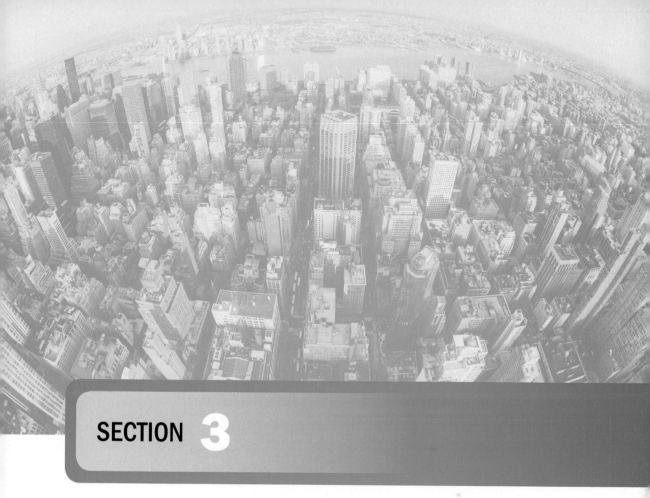

SECTION 3

Pricing for Greater Profit

12 More Realistic and Complex Pricing

In July of 2007, Scholastic Publishing released *Harry Potter and the Deathly Hallows*, the final installment of the smash Harry Potter book series, the best-selling book series in history. Sales expectations were high, as the previous book in the series had sold over seven million copies in the first 24 hours. Scholastic set a suggested retail price of $34.99 and was rumored to be selling the book to retailers at a wholesale price of $18.99, a margin of 45.7%.[1] From Chapter 6, you would expect retailers to set the price somewhere above $18.99—specifically, at the point where the markup equals the inverse demand elasticity, $(P - MC) / P = 1/ |e|$.

Instead, Costco and Walmart offered the book for $18.18 and $17.87, respectively. Online retailer Amazon was even more aggressive. Those who preordered the book paid only $17.99, and also received a $5 gift certificate and free shipping.

At this point, three potential conclusions about pricing might occur to you: (1) book retailers aren't interested in maximizing profit; (2) we gave you bad advice with the $(P - MC) / P = 1/ |e|$ pricing rule; or (3) real-world pricing is more complex than we have let on. In fact, there are a lot of times when you want to move beyond the simple pricing rule of Chapter 6 because you can make more money by doing so.

We have seen this kind of pricing before, when the grocery store in Chapter 6 put a low price on three-liter Coke to generate additional foot traffic. Whatever the grocery store lost on three-liter Coke, it made up in sales on other items. Amazon was following a similar tactic. By pricing low, Amazon sold over two million copies of *The Deathly Hallows*. Some buyers were new customers, who would purchase books from Amazon in the future, and some purchased additional items at the same time that they purchased *The Deathly Hallows*. In fact, Amazon estimated that about 1% of its $2.89 billion second-quarter revenue was due to this effect.

Both the grocery store and the bookstore were pricing where MR < MC, or equivalently where $(P - MC) / P < 1/|e|$. They did so because they were trying to maximize *total* profit, not profit on an individual product.

In this chapter, we show you how to move beyond the simple, single-product analysis of Chapter 6 to more complex and realistic settings, like those involving commonly owned products. In fact, the MR = MC pricing rule applies only to a single-product firm setting a single price on a single product. In more complex settings, the rule may not apply.

12.1 Pricing Commonly Owned Products

Commonly Owned Substitutes

Commonly owned products add a level of complexity to pricing that we can easily understand by using marginal analysis. To see this, let's examine the recently announced acquisition of SABMiller, the owner of Miller brands of beer, by Anheuser-Busch InBev, which owns the Budweiser brands. Many consumers consider Miller and Budweiser to be close substitutes. How would this acquisition change the pricing of the two brands?

With just one brand, the pricing decision is simple. You trade-off the benefits of a lower price (more units sold) against the costs of a lower price (less earned on each unit). Marginal analysis balances these two effects and suggests a price at the point where MR = MC to maximize profit.

Common ownership of two substitutes changes this simple pricing calculus. Now, an increase in the sales of one brand (through a price reduction) will "steal" some sales from the other. Before you owned the rival brand, you didn't care where your additional sales came from, but now that you own both brands, you don't want to steal sales from a brand that you already own. This is sometimes called "cannibalizing" the sales of one product with increased sales of the other. After the acquisition, you will find it profitable to eliminate such cannibalization. You do this by raising price on each brand.

Formally, common ownership of two substitute products reduces the marginal revenue of each product, since some of the revenue gain for one product comes at the expense of the other. With a single product, you price at MR = MC. After acquiring a substitute product, MR falls below MC. As a consequence, the post-acquisition firm finds it profitable to cut back output or, equivalently, increase price. We summarize this intuition in the following maxim:

After acquiring a substitute good, raise price on both goods.

Anticipating some pushback from the Antitrust Division of the U.S. Department of Justice, the merging parties agreed to sell the Miller brands in the United States to a rival, Molson Coors. Only with the assurances that Miller brands would stay under separate ownership did the Department of Justice allow the merger to go forward in July 2016.

Another way to see why acquisitions raise price is to focus on the change in perspective that joint ownership confers. Your concern changes from earning profit on an individual good to earning profit on both goods. Remember from Chapter 6 that aggregate demand (for both goods) is less elastic than the individual demands that comprise the aggregate. With less elastic demand, prices should increase.

So far we haven't said anything about which price to raise more; but here, again, marginal analysis can give us some guidance. Recall that the optimal price for a single product is set so that the margin is lower on more elastic products because consumers are more sensitive to the price of these products. If you could somehow switch these consumers to the higher-margin product, you'd increase profit. You can do this by raising the price on the low-margin good.

After acquiring a substitute product, raise price on both goods, but raise price more on the more elastic (low-margin) product.

As you raise price on the low-margin product, some consumers switch to the higher-margin substitute, thereby increasing profit.

This tells you which direction to go (raise price on both and raise it more on the low-margin product), but it doesn't tell you by how much. You get there by taking small steps. After raising price, recalculate MR and MC—or simply check to make sure that profit increases—to see if further change is profitable.

After acquiring a substitute product, you can also try to reduce cannibalization by *repositioning* the products so that they don't directly compete with each other—provided that repositioning isn't too expensive. For example, post-merger, Anheuser-Busch InBev could reposition some of its larger portfolio as "craft" or "imported" beers so that they don't directly compete with Budweiser.

Commonly Owned Complements

Common ownership of complementary products leads to the opposite advice. Suppose a concert venue purchases the profitable parking garage next to the venue. Before the purchase, both the parking garage and the concert venue set prices without considering the effect of their prices on each other's demand.

But after the acquisition, a price decrease at the concert venue will increase the number of customers at the concert venue *and the parking garage.* Common ownership of the concert venue and parking garage increases MR at each because increasing sales of one product (by reducing price) increases demand for the other. When MR rises above MC, output should increase, or, equivalently, optimal price should fall. We summarize this intuition in the following maxim:

After acquiring a complementary product, reduce price on both products to increase profit.

12.2 Revenue or Yield Management

Products like cruise ships, parking lots, hotels, and stadiums have several characteristics that affect their pricing. First, the costs of building capacity are mostly fixed or sunk. Second, these costs are large relative to marginal costs. Third, firms in these industries typically face capacity constraints; that is, they can increase output only up to capacity, but no further.

To understand how prices are set in these industries, let's begin with the decision of how much capacity to build. This is an extent decision, so we use marginal analysis. The owners have an incentive to keep adding capacity (more parking spaces, more hotel rooms, more cruise ship cabins, more seats in a stadium) as long as *long-run* marginal revenue is greater than *long-run* marginal cost, LRMR > LRMC. The owners stop building additional capacity when LRMR = LRMC. Here, the term *long-run marginal revenue* refers to the expected additional revenue that another parking space, hotel room, ship cabin, or stadium seat would earn over the life of the capacity. Likewise, *long-run marginal cost* is the expected additional cost of building, maintaining, selling, and using another unit of capacity over the life of the capacity.

Once construction is finished, we know from Chapter 3 that we should ignore sunk or fixed costs when setting price to avoid committing the sunk-cost fallacy. The relevant costs and benefits of setting price are the *short-run* marginal revenue (MR) and *short-run* marginal cost (MC). Since short-run marginal cost is likely to be much smaller than long-run marginal cost, while short-run marginal revenue is likely to be close to long-run marginal revenue, you want to price to fill capacity, assuming that capacity was set correctly equating long-run marginal cost to long-run marginal revenue. This leads to the rather obvious advice:

If MR > MC at capacity, then price to fill available capacity.

Because MR > MC, the firm's managers would like to reduce price in order to sell more, but cannot because the firm is limited by capacity. So the firm sells as much as it can, or prices to fill capacity.

If demand is known, this is relatively easy to do. For example, to set price for a parking lot in a downtown business district, you look to see what time the lot fills up. If the lot fills up before 9 a.m., then raise price; if the lot is still empty at 9 a.m., then reduce price. If the lot fills up near 9 a.m., the price is just right.

In contrast, if demand is hard to predict, pricing to fill capacity becomes much more difficult. For example, each time a cruise ship sails, no one knows what demand will be. To determine optimal price, the cruise line's managers balance the costs of overpricing (lost profit on unfilled cabins) against the cost of underpricing (lower margins on filled cabins).

In this case, an optimal price would minimize the expected costs of these two errors. If the lost profit from these two pricing errors is symmetric, then the firm should price so that expected (predicted) demand is just equal to capacity. We call this the "target price." However, if the lost profit from over-pricing is less than the lost profit from underpricing, then the firm should overprice, or price above the target price, and vice versa. This will lead, on average, to more overpricing errors than underpricing errors, but the cost of these errors is lower.

If the cost of overpricing (unused capacity) is smaller than the cost of underpricing (lower margins), then price higher than would fill capacity on average, and vice versa.

The precise degree of underpricing or overpricing depends not only on these costs, but also on the probability of each type of error, which depends on what demand we think is likely to happen. We will illustrate this difference more clearly in Chapter 17 when we discuss pricing under uncertainty.

Obviously, with better demand forecasts, you will make fewer errors, which will raise profit because the ship is filled as close to capacity as possible and at the best possible price. To better match demand to available capacity, cruise ship managers often adjust prices up until the time the ship sails. If it looks like capacity is going unused, they reduce price; and if it looks like capacity will be more than filled, they raise price.

But charging different prices to passengers who purchase at different times raises other problems. First, a slew of websites (from Hopper and Cayole to Google Flights) now help consumers forecast future prices on flights and cruises. If consumers realize that they may get a lower price if they wait to purchase, then you create an incentive for them to wait. This makes it more difficult for airlines to match demand to capacity—the whole point of adjusting price. To eliminate the incentive to time purchases, many cruise-line managers reduce price only slightly or reduce price only by offering cabin upgrades, so that consumers don't realize that they're paying less. Second, if some passengers realize they paid more than their fellow passengers who booked at different times, they may become angry and demand a refund or disparage the cruise line to future customers. We discuss this phenomenon in a section of the chapter on price discrimination titled "Only Schmucks Pay Retail." No one wants to be a schmuck.

12.3 Advertising and Promotional Pricing

In this section, we use marginal analysis to show you how to price in conjunction with advertising or promotional expenditures. The most important thing to realize is that different types of promotional expenditures affect demand in different ways. For pricing, it is most important to know whether promotional expenditures make demand more or less price elastic.[2]

If promotional expenditures make demand more (less) price elastic, then you should reduce (increase) price when you promote the product.

Consider the simplest kind of advertising—information about the price of your product relative to substitute products. Coupons, end-of-aisle displays in grocery stores, and weekly advertising inserts in the newspaper fall into this category. By focusing consumers on prices, you make them more sensitive to price differences, which makes demand more elastic. When you make demand more elastic, you want to reduce price to attract more customers. When you see this kind of promotion, you also typically see a reduction in the price of the promoted good.

On the other hand, advertising designed to increase the attractiveness of the product makes demand less elastic. Advertising the product's high quality or associating the product with a celebrity or desirable activity falls into this category. These promotional campaigns are trying to reduce the customer's sensitivity to price. In this case, it makes sense to *increase* price.

A final cautionary note about pricing and quality: a higher price may influence consumer perceptions about the quality of the product. If you know nothing else about the product except its high price, you may infer that it is of high quality. In this case, you'd want to price high to signal quality. Many wines are priced high for this reason.

12.4 Psychological Pricing

Many pricing strategies are built on the assumption that consumers behave in a rational, calculating way. But, sometimes they don't. Consider Coca-Cola's failed attempt to have vending machines adjust price with the temperature. Because people are willing to pay more for a cold drink when it is hot, the Coca-Cola CEO pronounced that "it is fair that it [a can of Coke] should be more expensive" when heat drives up demand.[3] A consumer outcry (and opportunistic advertising by rival Pepsi) led the company to reverse course. However, the CEO could have easily gained consumer acceptance by explaining that the vending machines will be providing discounts when colder temperature suppresses demand. Even though both statements—higher prices when temperatures are high and lower prices when temperatures are low—are equivalent, they are quite different, behaviorally.

The relatively new field of behavioral economics adds psychological insights to standard economic models. Prospect theory, developed by Nobel Prize winner Daniel Kahneman and his long-time colleague Amos Tversky, identifies several behavioral regularities that are useful in formulating pricing strategy.

First, people perceive how good a price is based on its distance from a "reference price." A reference price is simply how much we *expect* something to cost, given the environment. For example, we might see $4 for a bottle of beer as both unreasonably expensive (at a grocery store) and reasonably cheap (at a restaurant). This means that altering a consumer's price expectation upward can have the same effect on demand as altering the actual price downward, though without sacrificing profit. For example, first presenting a consumer with higher-priced options can drive up price expectations and make later, lower-priced options appear less expensive in comparison.

Managing price expectations is as important as managing price.

Prospect theory implies that consumers are motivated not by the actual price level, but rather by a comparison of the price level to the reference price. The idea is that a consumer will perceive a "win," and is more likely to buy, if the price is below the reference price. It follows that firms should try to "frame" decisions so that consumers perceive them as gains, not losses. By describing its policy as higher prices during warmer weather, Coca-Cola implicitly set a low reference price, during the colder weather. Instead, Coca-Cola should have emphasized the lower prices during cold weather, which would have set a higher reference price, during the warm weather. Similarly, retailers should focus on "cash discounts" rather than "credit card surcharges" and airlines on "discounts for not checking bags" rather than "checked bag fees."

A second behavioral insight is that multiple losses or multiple gains do not obey simple arithmetic. How would you feel if, on your way home today, you lost $20? Now imagine instead you lost $10 and then, minutes later, you lost another $10. Which of these scenarios made you feel worse? To most people, the two losses feel worse even though they amount to the same $20. Similarly, finding two $10 bills makes most people happier than finding one $20 bill. For most of us, losses and gains are superadditive (the happiness from $10 + $10 is greater than the happiness from $20). This has clear implications for pricing:

Integrate losses but separate gains.

Let's reverse the example involving losing $20. If I *have* to lose $20, I'd rather do it all at once than lose a little each step of the way. This is why you rarely see charges for "shipping and handling" quoted separately. This also may account for the popularity of all-inclusive vacations. On the other hand, consider the decision by some airlines in 2008 to begin charging passengers for snacks on flights. At first glance, it seems like a sensible strategy. With a snack charge, only those who really value a snack buy, and the rest of the passengers aren't forced to subsidize their fellow passengers' snacking habits with slightly higher fares. Unfortunately for these airlines, the average consumer did not view it this way. First, the charge was seen as a loss simply because it was new. Second, having passengers face these small charges on top of the ticket price made many feel nickel-and-dimed, with the result that some switched airlines.

Also beware of consumer concerns with fairness. One reason Home Depot would rather face shortages than raise price for snow shovels when it snows is to not be perceived as "unfair." Consumers often have a notion of what they believe to be fair behavior by sellers. If you cross this line, the reaction can be quite strong. You only need to recall the increase in gas prices in 2012 that led to outraged calls for price controls and "windfall profit" taxes from infuriated consumers (although nobody seemed to call for price supports and "insufficient profit" subsidies when prices fell dramatically).

Companies that want to set prices that could be viewed as "unfair" must come up with creative solutions to overcome this concern. One example comes from the music industry. Performers don't want to be perceived as greedy, so they set concert prices well below the market-clearing price. For example, a 2013 Beyoncé concert sold out in seconds because tickets were priced as low as $47. Minutes later, a large number of tickets appeared on secondary sites, like Craigslist and StubHub, at prices of over $2,000 for fairly poor seats. The secondary market prices aren't viewed as unfair because most people think that fans are reselling tickets. But often, the artists or promoters hold back a number of tickets from the initial sale and then resell them on the secondary market. The artist may share in the proceeds from these secondary sales but may avoid blame for the high prices.[4] Of course, this works only as long as consumers don't figure out what's going on.

SUMMARY & HOMEWORK PROBLEMS

Summary of Main Points

- After acquiring a substitute product,
  - raise price on both products to reduce price competition between them.
  - raise price more on the low-margin (more price elastic) product.
  - reposition the products so that there is less substitutability between them.
- After acquiring a complementary product, reduce price on both products to increase demand for both products.
- If fixed costs are large relative to marginal costs, capacity is fixed, and MR > MC at capacity, then set price to fill available capacity.
- If demand is hard to forecast and the costs of underpricing are smaller than the costs of overpricing, then underprice, on average, and vice versa.
- If promotional expenditures make demand more elastic, then reduce price when you promote the product, and vice versa.
- Psychological biases suggest being aware of price expectations and "framing" price changes as gains rather than as losses.

Multiple-Choice Questions

1. After massive promotion of Rihanna's latest music album, the producers reacted by raising prices for her albums. This implies that promotion expenditures made the album demand
   a. more elastic.
   b. unitary elastic.
   c. change due to psychological pricing.
   d. less elastic.

2. All of the following choices are examples of promoting a firm's product, except
   a. celebrity endorsements.
   b. pricing.
   c. discount coupons.
   d. end-of-aisle displays.

3. A firm that acquires a substitute product can reduce cannibalization by
   a. doing nothing.
   b. repositioning a product so that it does not directly compete with the substitute.
   c. setting the same price on both products.
   d. lowering prices on the low-margin products.

4. A shoe-producing firm decides to acquire a firm that produces shoe laces. This implies that the firm's aggregate demand (shoes + laces) will be
   a. less elastic than the individual demands.
   b. more elastic than the individual demands.
   c. equally elastic as the individual demands.
   d. none of the above.

5. After firm A producing one good acquired another firm B producing another good, it lowered the prices for both goods. One can conclude that the goods were
   a. substitutes.
   b. complements.
   c. not related.
   d. none of the above.

6. Firms tend to raise the price of their goods after acquiring a firm that sells a substitute good because
   a. they lose market power.
   b. there is an increase in the overall demand for their products.
   c. the aggregate demand for both goods is more elastic than the demand for the individual goods.
   d. the aggregate demand for both goods is less elastic than the demand for the individual goods.

7. For products like parking lots and hotels, costs of building capacity are mostly fixed

or sunk and firms in this industry typically face capacity constraints. Therefore,

    a. if MR > MC at capacity, then the firms should price to fill capacity.

    b. if MR < MC at capacity, then the firms should price to fill capacity.

    c. if LRMR > LRMC at capacity, then the firms should price to fill capacity.

    d. if LRMR < LRMC at capacity, then the firms should price to fill capacity.

8. A firm started advertising its product and this changed the product's elasticity from -2 to -1.5. If, prior to advertising, the firm charged $10, the firm should

    a. raise price from $10 to $15.00.

    b. reduce price from $10 to $6.67.

    c. raise price from $10 to $13.33.

    d. reduce price from $10 to $7.50.

9. After running a promotional campaign, the owners of a local hardware store decided to decrease the prices for the advertised products sold in their store. One can infer that

    a. the promotional expenditures made the demand for the advertised products more elastic.

    b. the promotional expenditures made the demand for the advertised products less elastic.

    c. the promotional expenditures had no effect on the demand elasticity.

    d. the owners got it wrong. To cover the promotional expenses, they should have raised the prices.

10. On average, if demand is unknown and costs of underpricing are ____ than the costs of overpricing, then ____.

    a. smaller; overprice

    b. smaller; underprice

    c. larger; underprice

    d. none of the above

Individual Problems

12-1 Parking Lot Optimization

Suppose your elasticity of demand for your parking lot spaces is -2, and price is $8 per day. If your MC is zero, and your lot is 80% full at 9 a.m. over the last month, are you optimizing?

12-2 Parking at Cowboys Stadium

What would efficient revenue management imply for the pricing of the Cowboys Stadium parking lot on typical game days? How about for the Super Bowl? How about for the many smaller events that fill less than half the lot?

12-3 Product Store Locations

Some high-end retailers place their most expensive products right in the entryway of the store, where consumers will see them first, and place their more popular, better-selling items further back. Why?

12-4 Macintosh versus iPhone

When the Macintosh computer was introduced in 1982, Apple made it difficult for third-party software developers to develop software for the platform. In contrast, Apple makes it relatively easy for third-party developers to make applications that run on the iPhone. Compare and contrast these two strategies.

12-5 Concert Prices

Concert prices have increased coincidentally with illegal downloading of music off the Internet. Why?

12-6 Radio Stations and Rock Concerts

In 2005, Clear Channel (an owner of multiple popular radio stations) spun off concert promoter Live Nation into an independent company. How would this affect prices for concert tickets or rates for radio programming?

Group Problems

G12-1 Pricing Commonly Owned Products

Evaluate a pricing decision your company made involving commonly owned products. Was it optimal? If not, why not? How would you adjust price? Compute the profit consequences of this adjustment.

G12-2 Yield or Revenue Management

Evaluate a pricing decision your company made that involved a product or service with fixed capacity. Was price set optimally? If not, why not? How would you adjust price? Compute the profit consequences of the change.

G12-3 Promotional Pricing

Evaluate a pricing decision of your company that coincided with a promotional or advertising campaign. Was price set optimally? If not, why not? How would you adjust price? Compute the profit consequences of the change.

G12-4 Psychological Pricing

Evaluate a pricing decision of your company based on psychological pricing. Was price set optimally? If not, why not? How would you adjust price? Compute the profit consequences of the change.

END NOTES

1. Story adapted from Joe Nocera, "Harry and the Strange Logic of Book Discounters," *New York Times*, July 28, 2007, http://select.nytimes.com/2007/07/28/business/28nocera.html.
2. Luke M. Froeb, Steven Tenn, and Steven T. Tschantz, "Mergers When Firms Compete by Choosing Both Price and Promotion," *International Journal of Industrial Organization* 28 (2010): 695–707.
3. Constance L. Hays, "Variable-Price Coke Machine Being Tested," *New York Times*, October 28, 1999, C1.
4. Mark Hefflinger, "Top Artists 'Scalping' Own Tickets on Resale Sites," *Wall Street Journal*, March 12, 2009.

13 Direct Price Discrimination

Pricing Laptops

Dell Inc. sells over 100,000 computer systems per day, more than one every second. The company sells to individual home users, to small businesses, and to every Fortune 100 company. Some of these customers are less price sensitive than others. If Dell could identify these customers and figure out a way to charge them higher prices, it could increase profit.

Pricing Museum Tickets

Once the home of Peter the Great, the enormous green-and-white Winter Palace in Saint Petersburg, Russia, now houses one of the world's most famous art collections. Tourists who fly many miles to Saint Petersburg are unlikely to miss visiting the Hermitage Museum, home to three million works of art. Locals, on the other hand, are poorer than the international tourists who visit their country and have hundreds of other nearby options competing for their expenditures. Charging a single price for admission would require either charging tourists much less than the profit-maximizing price or making the museum prohibitively expensive for many locals.

Potentially, both Dell and the Hermitage could benefit by charging different prices to different consumer groups. Dell could increase profit by charging lower prices to more price-sensitive home and small business users, while the Hermitage could increase profit by offering price discounts to locals.

However, such discriminatory pricing is risky, and sometimes illegal. In this chapter, we discuss ways of profitably designing and implementing price discrimination schemes, in which sellers charge different prices to different consumers, not on the basis of differences in costs but, rather, on the differences in consumer demand. We move beyond the simple pricing of Chapter 6, where a single firm set a single ("uniform") price on a single product by allowing a firm to set multiple prices for the same product.

13.1 Why (Price) Discriminate?

To see how price discrimination increases profit, let's look at the simple aggregate demand curve from Chapter 6 (Table 6.4), where seven consumers are willing to pay $7, $6, $5, $4, $3, $2, and $1 for a good that costs $1.50 to make. There, we saw that the profit-maximizing price is $5. At this price, the company sells three units. We calculate total profit ($10.50) as revenue ($15) minus cost ($4.50).

At the optimal price of $5, low-value consumers—those willing to pay $4, $3, and $2—don't purchase, even though they're willing to pay more than the cost of producing the good. These three consumers represent unconsummated wealth-creating transactions. The one lesson of business tells us to find a way to profitably consummate these transactions.

Suppose you could identify these customers because they live in a certain part of town, because they are older, or because they have children. You could offer them a price reduction by sending discount coupons to residents who live in certain ZIP codes (as Victoria's Secret has done with its catalogs), by offering discounts to senior citizens (as do many restaurants and grocery stores), or by offering discounts for families with children (as airlines do when allowing lap children to fly for free).

To see how this would affect profit, we split the consumers into two different groups and compute the profit-maximizing prices for each group. We do this in Tables 13.1 and 13.2 for the high- and low-value consumers, respectively. In Table 13.1, we compute the profit-maximizing price for the

TABLE **13.1**

Optimal Price for High-Value Consumers

Price ($)	Quantity	Revenue ($)	MR ($)	MC ($)	Total Profit ($)
7	1	7	7	1.50	5.50
6	2	12	5	1.50	9
5	3	15	3	1.50	10.50

TABLE **13.2**

Optimal Price for Low-Value Consumers

Price ($)	Quantity	Revenue ($)	MR ($)	MC ($)	Total Profit ($)
4	1	4	4	1.50	2.50
3	2	6	2	1.50	3
2	3	6	0	1.50	1.50
1	4	4	(2)	1.50	(2)

high-value consumers. The profit-maximizing price is $5, the company sells three units, and total profit ($10.50) is revenue ($15) minus cost ($4.50), the same as computed in Table 6.4. In Table 13.2, we derive demand for low-value consumers by subtracting out the three units demanded by high-value consumers.

If we could charge a separate price to the low-value consumers—those willing to pay $4, $3, $2, and $1—we would face a second demand curve, illustrated in Figure 13.1. We could price at $4 and sell one unit, price at $3 and sell two units, price at $2 and sell three units, or price at $1 and sell four units. Marginal analysis tells us to set a price of $3, sell two units to the low-value group, and earn an extra $3.

This is the motivation for price discrimination: it allows a firm to sell items to low-value customers who otherwise would not purchase because the price is too high.

> ***Price discrimination*** *is the practice of charging different prices to different buyers or groups of buyers based on differences in demand.*

For products with relatively low marginal costs or with less-elastic demand, like software, music, or pharmaceutical drugs, the gap between price and marginal cost is largest. For these products, price discrimination is most profitable because there are more consumers whose values are above the marginal cost of production but below the profit-maximizing price.

Charging lower prices to low-value consumers also means that you charge high-value customers higher prices, making the practice controversial. For example, drug manufacturers sell patented drugs, like Lipitor, Viagra, Zoloft, or Claritin, to different countries at different prices. Drugs sold in Canada and Mexico are less expensive than drugs sold in the United States, at least early in the life cycle of the drug. This has created incentives for U.S. consumers to drive to Mexico and Canada, buy drugs, and bring them back into

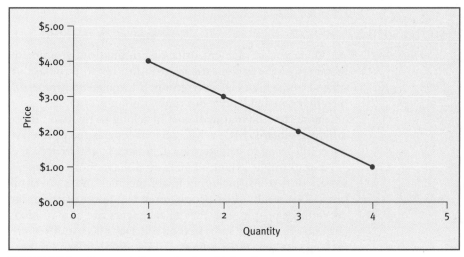

FIGURE **13.1** **Demand Curve for Low-Value Consumers**

the United States. It has also created incentives for pharmacies in Mexico and Canada to offer drugs for sale to U.S. consumers. This so-called drug reimportation emerged as an issue in the 2016 U.S. presidential campaign. If we allow reimportation, what do you think will happen?

We can use our simple example to figure this out. Think of the low-value consumers (those in Table 13.2) as foreign pharmacies. Drug reimportation means that they buy drugs at $3 and then resell them for $5 to U.S. consumers (the high-value group in Table 13.1). Once U.S. drug manufacturers realize that they are losing money by discriminating, they would go back to setting a uniform price of $5. The policy implication is that if we allow drug reimportation, profits of U.S. drug manufacturers would fall, and foreign buyers would face higher prices.

13.2   Direct Price Discrimination

We can draw a distinction between *direct* and *indirect* price discrimination. Under **direct price discrimination**, we can identify members of the low-value group, charge them a lower price, and prevent them from reselling their lower-priced goods to the higher-value group (arbitrage). Under indirect price discrimination, we cannot perfectly identify the two groups or cannot prevent arbitrage, so we must find indirect methods of setting different prices to the two different groups. This distinction will become clearer in Chapter 14 when we describe various methods of achieving indirect price discrimination.

To discriminate directly, you must be able to identify different customer groups with different elasticities. Then, you set an optimal price for each group. Obviously, charge a lower price to the group with the more-elastic demand, and a higher price to the group with the less-elastic demand, according to the pricing formula we derived in Chapter 6.

$$(P_1 - MC_1) / P_1 = 1/ |\text{elasticity}_1|$$

and

$$(P_2 - MC_2) / P_2 = 1/ |\text{elasticity}_2|$$

Once you implement price discrimination, you create an incentive for members of the low-elasticity group to try to purchase at the lower prices offered to the high-elasticity group. If too many customers are able to do this, then they can make price discrimination unprofitable.

Note that the marginal cost of selling to the two different groups can be different—that is, $MC_1 \neq MC_2$. But as long as the price elasticities differ, pricing is still going to be determined, in part, by differences in elasticity.

For example, senior citizens often have more price-elastic demand for a variety of reasons (including lower incomes and a lower opportunity cost of time). As a result, older people often pay lower prices in movie theaters than do younger people. The theater managers are able to recognize a low-value customer by the age indicated on a driver's license. They prevent arbitrage by making sure that those admitted on a senior citizen's ticket do not resell their tickets to younger customers.

Of course, price discrimination need not be limited to just two groups. In the extreme, a firm could tailor prices to each consumer. For example, colleges discriminate between students of different incomes and wealth levels. At America's top universities, fewer than half of all undergraduates pay full price while a majority receive some degree of financial aid. To award scholarships, colleges do not need to identify groups with different elasticities. Instead, colleges tailor prices to each student's family income directly by examining tax returns and bank statements. For example, Harvard and Yale universities both announced that, for middle-class families, college education is priced at about 10% of annual income.

13.3 Robinson-Patman Act

There is a tension in the law about the effects of price discrimination. On the one hand, if a firm offers an array of different prices to consumers, it consummates more transactions and thus creates more wealth. On the other hand, if it charges prices closer to what consumers are willing to pay for a good, it reduces consumer surplus (the difference between what consumers are willing to pay and what they have to pay).

The **Robinson-Patman Act** is part of a group of laws collectively called the *antitrust laws* governing competition in the United States. Under the Robinson-Patman Act, it's illegal to give or receive a price discount on a good sold to another business across state lines. This law does not cover services or sales to final consumers, though a number of states have laws that do. The U.S. Congress passed the Robinson-Patman Act in 1936 in response to complaints from small grocery stores facing competition from lower-cost competitors like A&P, the first grocery store chain. Sometimes called the Anti-Chain-Store Act, the Robinson-Patman Act tries to protect independent retailers from chain-store competition by preventing the chains from receiving supplier discounts. Small retailers have sued book publishers, large book retailers, large drugstore chains, Walmart, and other large retailers (together with their suppliers) for giving or receiving price discounts.[1] There are two ways to defend yourself from a Robinson-Patman lawsuit: you can claim that the price discount was cost-justified or that the price discount was given to meet the competition. This leads to the following legal advice on how to comply with the antitrust laws:

> *Charge all customers the same price, unless the cost of serving them varies. But feel free to cut price to any customer to meet the lower price of a competitor.*[2]

Often, pricing that looks discriminatory (based on demand differences) results instead from the different costs of serving different consumers. Small drugstores, small grocery stores, and small bookstores pay higher prices than do large chains like Walmart at least in part because supplying big customers costs less. Big customers order full truckloads, reducing transportation costs; they also invest in information technology that reduces ordering and inventory costs and simplifies ordering, distribution, and sales. If the higher prices arise from the higher costs of serving small mom-and-pop shops, then the higher prices are not discriminatory.

Antitrust economists have long recognized that the Robinson-Patman Act discourages discounting. If companies have to offer the same price to every customer, they are less likely to reduce price to their most price-elastic customers. Fortunately, many practices, such as offering promotional allowances to large retailers, are similar to discounts, making it relatively easy to comply with the law without risking the loss of your best customers.

13.4 Implementing Price Discrimination

Now that we know how price discrimination works and how legal constraints limit the actual practice, we can discuss how to do it. We focus on the two price discrimination opportunities described in the introduction.

Pricing Laptops

How does Dell identify customers who are less price sensitive and charge them more? The company used to simply ask them. Until a few years ago, visitors of the company's home page would select between shopping for Home, Home Office, Small & Medium Business, or Large Enterprise. Prices for identical products would vary depending on which category you click. In October 2012, you could have purchased a 2.6 GHz Dell Precision M6600 laptop for $3,208 as a large enterprise customer. If instead you clicked on "Home Office," you could have bought the exact same laptop for 40% less. Offering these different prices to different customer groups allowed Dell to increase the overall profitability of selling computers. What's a bit confusing is why large business customers didn't simply order using the "Home Office" or "Small Business" links. Perhaps they eventually learned to do just that. In 2014, Dell seems to have suspended this practice.

Pricing Museum Tickets

Most mornings, there is a long line of customers outside the Hermitage Museum standing in front of a window signed "tickets." Nearby, another line also proclaims tickets—but in Russian and at prices that are 75% less. While proof of citizenship is not required to obtain the "local" tickets, only those asking for tickets in unaccented Russian can get the lower prices. This creates incentives for arbitrage, and many locals have set up small enterprises that buy tickets at local prices and then resell them at a profit. To combat this, the museum staff monitors low-priced ticket holders upon entry into the museum. It has become a game for some foreign visitors to see if they can feign language and mannerisms to pass for a local. Very few succeed.

Foreign tour operators have complained about the discriminatory nature of the pricing at the Hermitage, leading the Russian Travel Industry Union to petition for an end to discriminatory pricing. While the Hermitage initially agreed in 2010, it quickly backed out of the idea, noting that an end to such discriminatory pricing would only lead to everyone paying the higher price.

13.5 Only Schmucks Pay Retail

Consumers don't like knowing that they're paying a higher price than other consumers. This is summed up in popular sayings like "Only schmucks pay retail."[3] If low-elasticity consumers know they're being discriminated against, they may even refuse to purchase. A study of online pricing showed that when shoppers are asked whether they have any discount or coupon codes (thus revealing the existence of price discrimination), a large number of customers abandon their virtual shopping carts, which can make price discrimination unprofitable.[4]

So, if you're price discriminating, it's important to keep it a secret if you can. Otherwise, you may lose your high-value customers to rivals who don't price discriminate (or who hide it better).

SUMMARY & HOMEWORK PROBLEMS

Summary of Main Points

- **Price discrimination** is the practice of charging different people or groups of people different prices based on differences in demand. Typically more people are served under price discrimination than under a uniform price.
- **Arbitrage** can defeat a price discrimination scheme if enough of those who purchase at low prices resell to high-value consumers. This can force a seller to go back to a uniform price.
- If a seller can identify two groups of consumers with different demand elasticities, and can prevent arbitrage between the groups, it can increase profit by charging a higher price to the low-elasticity group.
- **Direct price discrimination** requires that you be able to identify members of the low-value group, charge them a lower price, and prevent them from reselling their lower-priced goods to the higher-value group.
- It can be illegal for a business to price discriminate when selling goods to other businesses unless
  - price discounts are cost-justified, or
  - discounts are offered to meet competitors' prices.
- Price discrimination may outrage customers who discover that others are getting a better price. If you can, keep price discrimination a secret or make sure that customers see the discrimination as fair.

Multiple-Choice Questions

See the end of next chapter for multiple-choice questions.

Individual Problems

See the end of next chapter for individual homework problems.

Group Problems

See the end of next chapter for group homework problems.

END NOTES

1. European and many other countries have laws with similar prohibitions to Robinson-Patman.
2. John H. Shenefield and Irwin M. Stelzer, "Common Sense Guidelines," *The Antitrust Laws: A Primer*, 3rd ed. (Washington, DC: AEI Press, 1998), 123–126.
3. Schmuck (shmŭk) *noun, slang*: a clumsy or stupid person; an oaf.
4. Mikhael Shor and Richard L. Oliver, "Price Discrimination through Online Couponing: Impact on Purchase Intention and Profitability," *Journal of Economic Psychology* 27 (2006): 423–440.

14 Indirect Price Discrimination

Express Lanes

State Route 91 connects the residents of Riverside County, California, to their workplaces in nearby Orange County, on the other side of the Santa Ana Mountains. The freeway is one of the most congested in the United States. Two-hour commutes for a ten-mile stretch are not uncommon. In each direction, drivers face a choice between at least four free public lanes and two tolled express lanes. The express lanes vary in price from around $1.50 in the middle of the night to over $10 on a Friday afternoon.

You might suspect that the express lanes would be popular among impatient drivers. While somewhat true, the express lanes save only a few minutes on an average day. What they do offer is predictability, as delays on the free lanes can vary greatly from day to day. Motorists who value reliability pay the tolls, while those who can afford to be late every now and then don't.[1] The challenge is pricing the toll lanes just right—too high, and even high-value travelers will choose the free lanes; too low, and the "express" lanes will be too popular and congested, decreasing their value.

Airline Travel

Business travelers have less-elastic demand than do leisure travelers, both because they don't pay for their own tickets and because they have fewer alternatives due to very specific time and geographic demands for a flight ("I have to be in Dallas, Texas, at 8:00 a.m. on Tuesday"). Unfortunately for airlines, business and leisure travelers are not easy to identify, making direct price discrimination difficult. Instead, airlines identify leisure travelers by their willingness to plan vacations months in advance. In contrast, business travelers often have to plan trips on very short notice. A ticket purchased a month in advance can often be had for less than half the price of one purchased closer to the flight.

However, if too many business travelers take advantage of such advance-purchase discounts, they can render price discrimination unprofitable.

For example, one manufacturing company found that its 60 regional managers purchased tickets for their biweekly travel just days before takeoff. By standardizing its meeting dates (and purchasing tickets three weeks in advance), the company saved nearly half a million dollars in travel expenses. This, of course, means that the airline lost half a million dollars in revenues.

14.1 Indirect Price Discrimination

When a seller cannot directly identify who has a low or high value, the seller can still discriminate by designing products or services that appeal to different consumer groups. For example, grocery stores use coupons to price discriminate. High-income shoppers are typically less price sensitive than are low-income consumers, at least for low-priced items. They have a high opportunity cost of time, which means they are less likely to clip coupons out of a newspaper or circulars. The grocery store essentially asks low-value consumers to identify themselves by their coupon-clipping behavior.

This **indirect price discrimination** differs from the direct price discrimination of Chapter 13 because high-value customers *could* clip coupons if they wanted. If too many high-value customers (those with a low elasticity of demand) clip coupons, then the attempt at price discrimination becomes unprofitable.

Unlike direct price discrimination, where the seller can identify different groups, indirect price discrimination requires identifying some *feature* that is correlated with value, and then designing products that differ along this feature. The express lanes on State Route 91 differentiate consumer groups based on their value of reliability. Airlines differentiate business customers from leisure customers by their willingness to plan ahead.

Software manufacturers discriminate between high-value and low-value consumers by designing different versions of software to appeal to each group. For example, Adobe used to license its flagship Photoshop product (the leading software for the graphic design industry) for about $300 per year while offering its low-end product, Photoshop Elements, for about $100. Here, the threat is obvious—Adobe must design and price the two versions so that high-value professional editors prefer the full-featured version to the much cheaper version. Adobe did this by omitting some features essential for professional video editing from its low-end version.

To make this concrete, let's go through a numerical example. Suppose your marketing department does a survey (see Table 14.1) of potential users that reveals that commercial users are willing to pay $500 for a full-featured version, whereas home users are willing to pay only $175. This kind of heterogeneity leaves you with the usual trade-off: you can price high ($500) but sell only to the high-value consumers, or price low ($175) and sell to both high- and low-value consumers. Assuming equal numbers of each type of consumer, the profitability of these two strategies is reported in the first two rows of Table 14.2.

Now consider an indirect price discrimination strategy in which we offer both a full-featured version to commercial users and a disabled version to home users. The most we can charge the home users for the disabled version is

TABLE **14.1**
Demand for Software

Software Version	Home Users ($)	Commercial Users ($)
Full-featured version	175	500
Disabled version	150	200

TABLE **14.2**
Potential Software Pricing Strategies

Strategy	Implementation	Total Profit
1. Sell only to commercial users at a single high price.	Price full-featured version at $500; do not sell home version.	$500
2. Sell to all users at a single low price.	Price full-featured version at $175.	$175 + $175 = $350
3. Price discriminate: price high to the commercial users; price low to the home users.	Price disabled version at $150; price full-featured version at $449.	$150 + $449 = $599

$150. The difficult part of implementing indirect price discrimination is pricing the full-featured version to make sure that the high-value customers do not purchase the disabled, and cheaper, software.

Note that if we tried to charge commercial users $500 for the full-featured version, none of them would buy it. This is because consumers will buy the version of the software that gives them more consumer surplus, or value minus price. The disabled version provides $50 of surplus ($200 [value] − $150 [price]), while the full-featured version provides $0 ($500 [value] − $500 [price]). But if we charge $150 for the disabled version and $449 for the full-featured version, high-value consumers gain more surplus by buying the full-featured version ($51 = $500 [value] − $449 [price]) than they do by buying the disabled version. You have to price the full-featured version low enough so commercial users get at least as much consumer surplus as they do from the disabled version. The effect of this price discrimination strategy is shown in the third row of Table 14.2.

This example illustrates the threat of what marketers call *cannibalization*. You could charge $500 for the full-featured software if you did not offer a disabled version. But if you do offer a disabled version of a good, you have to be careful that you do not cannibalize sales of the high-priced version. Specifically, since our commercial users see the full-featured version as $300 better than the disabled version ($500 [value of full-featured version] − $200 [value of disabled version]), the difference in price between the two versions must be less than $300.

Price discrimination is not always profitable. Sometimes, it is better to offer only a single product as the risk of cannibalization is too great. Consider a slight change to our previous example, given in Table 14.3. The only difference is that the commercial users now value even the disabled version highly. As before (Table 14.2), we can sell only to commercial users at a profit of $500, or to all users for a profit of $350. But what if we tried to sell two versions? To attract the home users, the disabled version can be priced no higher than $150. This disabled version gives our commercial users $250 of surplus. Since our commercial user sees only a $100-value difference between the two versions, it cannot be priced higher than $249. But selling the home version at $150 and the commercial version at $249 provides lower profit than selling only the commercial version at $500.

TABLE **14.3**
Demand for Software

Software Version	Home Users ($)	Commercial Users ($)
Full-featured version	175	500
Disabled version	150	400

These examples show that indirect price discrimination is not only a pricing issue, but also a product design issue. We avoid cannibalization by making the lower-priced version as unattractive as possible to commercial users by disabling the features most important to them. For example, only the full-featured Photoshop supports CMYK colors. If you're a home user, you probably don't even know what that is. If you're a professional graphic designer, you probably find CMYK indispensable. Recently, Adobe changed its versioning by dropping its consumer product entirely and instead licensing Photoshop to all customers for $10 per month. A $50 per month plan includes additional software and cloud storage. Effectively, the former full-featured product is now the "disabled" version.

In one of the more infamous examples, IBM released the LaserPrinter E in May 1990, a lower-price alternative to its popular LaserPrinter. The Laser-Printer E printed at a speed of 5 pages per minute compared to 10 pages per minute for the higher-priced LaserPrinter. IBM actually *added* microchips to the LaserPrinter E (at an additional cost) to insert wait states to slow the print speed. This is known as a "damaged goods" strategy.[2] Similarly, Microsoft sold both "server" and "client" versions of its Windows NT operating system at a price difference of $800. It was later revealed that two easily changed lines of code were responsible for the technical differences between the two products.

HP Printers

Hewlett-Packard uses a different strategy to sort consumers into high- and low-value groups. High-value consumers identify themselves by how many ink cartridges they buy. To charge higher prices to the high-value group, HP prices its printers close to marginal cost, but sells cartridges at a 50% margin.

TABLE **14.4**
Pricing Strategies

	Low-Value Consumers $100 Value, 1 Cartridge ($)	High-Value Consumers $200 Value, 2 Cartridges ($)	Total Revenue ($)
Strategy 1: $50 *printer* + $50 cartridge	100	150	250
Strategy 2: $0 *printer* + $ 100 cartridge	100	200	300

To make sure you understand how this works, let's use a numerical example. In particular, suppose that HP's low-value customers consume one cartridge each year and are willing to pay $100 for printing services (printer plus one cartridge), and their high-value customers consume two cartridges each year and are willing to pay $200. What price should HP charge?

We compute the revenue of two different pricing strategies in Table 14.4. In row 1, we compute the revenue from pricing printers at $50 and cartridges at $50. We see that low-value consumers would pay $100, whereas high-value consumers would pay $150. In row 2, we see that the firm could do better by giving away the printer and charging $100 for each cartridge. In this case, the low-value consumers pay $100 and the high-value consumers pay $200.

This pricing strategy works only because the high-value consumers use more cartridges than low-value consumers. Since HP charges a relatively high price for the cartridges, high-value customers end up paying a higher margin on printing services (printer + cartridges) than do low-value consumers.

This pricing strategy, termed *metering*, is used to sell razor blades at higher margins than razors, and famously for the marketing of Barbie products: you give away the dolls and sell the dresses with very high margins. High-value shavers use more razor blades (replacing them more frequently as they become dull), and high-value doll users purchase more Barbie outfits. Lower-value consumers buy fewer razors and fewer doll accessories.

As we described in Chapter 9, profits that flow from successful price discrimination are likely to attract competition. In the case of printer manufacturers, for example, the high markups on ink cartridges create profitable entry for toner refill kits. Printer manufacturers may be tempted to prevent rivals from selling lower-priced cartridges, say, by **tying** the sales of new cartridges to the sales of printers. But such ties can run afoul of the antitrust laws. Here is some advice from a former antitrust prosecutor:[3]

> Do not tie the sale of one product to another. Such arrangements are only legal in a few rare instances—to ensure effective functioning of complicated equipment, to name one. But they are generally against the law.

Instead, HP spends over $1 billion per year on ink research and development, in part to stay a step ahead of generic ink manufacturers. As an alternate strategy, companies like Epson and Canon rely on microchips affixed to their ink cartridges that prevent the use of generic cartridges and ink refills.

14.2 Volume Discounts as Discrimination

So far, we've been discussing ways of price discriminating between different customers—that is, setting different prices to different people or groups of people. Here, we consider the case of a single customer who demands more than one unit of a good. To price discriminate in this case, we have to find a way to set different prices for each unit consumed.

Consider a single customer who's willing to pay $7 for the first unit, $6 for the second, $5 for the third, and so on, as in our earlier demand curve example. If the price is set at $7, this consumer will purchase one unit; if the price is set at $6, two units; $5, three units; and so on. This is an **individual demand curve**.

Note the difference between an individual and an aggregate demand curve. With an aggregate demand curve, each point represents a different consumer with a different value for a single unit of the good. For an individual demand curve, each point represents the value that a single consumer is willing to pay for an additional unit.

Individual demand curves slope downward because the marginal value, the value placed on extra units, declines with each purchase. For example, a retailer who purchases from a manufacturer may find that the first few items are relatively easy to sell, but to sell more, she may have to lower the price, hold the item in inventory for a longer period of time, or spend money on promoting the item. All these activities reduce the value that the customer (here, the retailer) is willing to pay for additional units.

If a seller is setting a single price, it doesn't matter whether she faces an aggregate or an individual demand—the profit calculus is the same. She'll sell all items where MR > MC. If we assume, as before, that marginal cost is $1.50, the profit-maximizing price $5. And, just as in the aggregate demand curve, we see units worth $4, $3, and $2 that are not purchased even though the consumer places a value on these extra units that are higher than the marginal cost of producing them. These three extra units represent unconsummated wealth-creating transactions.

The trick to profitably selling more is to find a way to sell additional units without dropping the prices of the earlier units. There are several ways to do this:

- Offer volume discounts; for example, price the first good at $7, the second at $6, the third at $5, and so on.
- Use two-part pricing, which is both a fixed price and a per-unit price. Charge a per-unit price low enough to consummate all wealth-creating transactions (set it at MC = $1.50), then bargain over how to split the resulting surplus. The consumer's total value for six units is $27 (= $7 + $6 + $5 + $4 + $3 + $2), and six units cost just $9 (= 6 × $1.50) to produce. Bargain over how to split the remaining surplus ($18 = $27 − $9) created by the transaction. This is the "fixed price" part of the transaction.

- Bundle the goods. As we have just seen, the consumer's total value for six units is $27. If you have enough bargaining power, you can capture the entire consumer surplus by pricing a bundle of six goods at just below $27. If not, then bargain over how to split it.

This example illustrates a very important lesson for pricing:

> *When bargaining with a customer, do not bargain over unit price; instead, bargain over the bundled price.*

First, figure out how much the consumer would demand if price were set at marginal cost; then bargain over the bundled price for this amount. This strategy ensures that you're bargaining over how to split the largest possible pie.

14.3 Bundling Different Goods Together

We can also use **bundling** in a slightly different context—when consumers have different demands for different items. Consider a movie theater with two groups of customers whose preferences for two films—a horror film and an adventure film—are different.[4] The theater owners cannot engage in direct price discrimination because they cannot identify the movie preferences of particular consumers ahead of time. But they can bundle the films together in a double feature and accomplish the same thing.

Suppose the theater has 100 potential customers: one half would be willing to pay $12 to see the horror film and $8 to see the adventure film; the other half would pay $8 to see the horror film and $12 to see the adventure film.

If the theater sets the same price for each film, it faces the usual trade-off. It can sell each film to all 100 consumers at a price of $8, leading to a revenue of $800 per film, or it can sell each film to half of the moviegoers at a price of $12, leading to a revenue of $600 per film. In this case, pricing low is more profitable, so each film would be sold at a price of $8 and the theater owner would earn revenue of $1,600 on the two films.

But look what happens when the theater bundles both films together in a double feature. Each customer values the bundle at $20, so the theater can sell to all 100 customers at the bundled price of $20 earning revenue of $2,000 on the two films.

In this case, bundling makes customers more homogeneous (they're willing to pay the same amount for the bundle), so the seller doesn't have to reduce the price of the bundle to sell more tickets. Intuitively, bundling makes it easier for the theater to extract consumer surplus with a single price for the bundle.

Bundled pricing[5] allows a seller to extract more consumer surplus if willingness to pay for the bundle is more homogeneous than willingness to pay for the separate items in the bundle. For example, the bundling of channels allows cable TV providers to extract 65% more consumer surplus than if the channels were priced separately.[6]

SUMMARY & HOMEWORK PROBLEMS

Summary of Main Points

- When a seller cannot identify low- and high-value consumers or cannot prevent arbitrage between two groups, it can still discriminate indirectly by designing products or services that appeal to groups with different price elasticities of demand.
- If you offer a low-value product that is attractive to high-value consumers, you may cannibalize sales of your high-price product.
- Metering is a type of indirect discrimination that identifies high-value consumers by how intensely they use a product (e.g., by how many cartridges they buy). In this case, charge a big markup on the cartridges and a lower markup on the printer.
- When pricing for an individual customer, do not bargain over unit price. Instead, you should
  - offer volume discounts;
  - use two-part pricing; or
  - offer a bundle containing a number of units.
- Bundling different goods together can allow a seller to extract more consumer surplus if willingness to pay for the bundle is more homogeneous than willingness to pay for the separate items in the bundle.

Multiple-Choice Questions

1. A software firm can offer a high-feature version of its software or a stripped-down low-feature version, each with similar production costs. Which of the following cannot be an optimal strategy?
   a. Offer only the high-feature version aimed only at a high-value market segment.
   b. Offer only the low-feature version aimed at all market segments.
   c. Offer both versions targeted to different value segments.
   d. Offer only the high-feature version aimed at all market segments.

2. Which of the following conditions must be satisfied for price discrimination to be successful?
   a. The seller must have a different product for each group of customers.
   b. The seller must be able to identify each customer as having a high or low value.
   c. The seller must be able to prevent arbitrage between the two groups.
   d. None of the above.

3. Perfect price discrimination is when a firm can charge each customer exactly what they are willing to pay. In this case,
   a. the demand curve is very inelastic.
   b. the marginal revenue is the demand curve.
   c. the demand curve is very elastic.
   d. the marginal cost curve is the average cost curve.

Use the following table to answer Questions 4–6. Assume the cost of producing the goods is zero and that each consumer will purchase each good as long as the price is less than or equal to value.

Consumer values are the entries in the following table.

	Consumer A ($)	Consumer B ($)
Good 1	2,300	2,800
Good 2	1,700	1,200

4. Suppose a monopolist only sold the goods separately. What price will the monopolist charge for good 1 to maximize revenues for good 1?
   a. $2,300
   b. $2,800

c. $1,200

d. $1,700

5. What is the total profit to the monopolist from selling the goods separately?
   a. $4,500
   b. $6,300
   c. $7,000
   d. $6,000

6. What is a better pricing strategy for the monopolist? What is the resulting profit?
   a. Bundle the goods at $2,800; Profits = $5,600
   b. Bundle the goods at $4,000; Profits = $8,000
   c. Charge $2,800 for good 1 and charge $1,700 for good 2; Profits = $4,500
   d. Charge $2,300 for good 1 and charge $1,200 for good 2; Profits = $7,000

7. Assume that the price elasticity of demand for movie theatres is −0.85 during all evening shows but for all afternoon shows the price elasticity of demand is −2.28. For the theater to maximize total revenue, it should
   a. charge the same price for both shows, holding other things constant.
   b. charge a higher price for the afternoon shows and lower price for the evening shows, holding other things constant.
   c. charge a lower price for the afternoon shows and higher price for the evening shows, holding other things constant.
   d. Need more information.

8. Arbitrage
   a. is the act of buying low in one market and selling high in another market.
   b. can force a seller to go back to uniform pricing.
   c. can defeat direct price discrimination.
   d. All of the above.

9. Airlines attempt to charge a _____ price to business travelers compared to leisure travelers because business travelers have a _____ demand than leisure travelers.

a. higher; more elastic

b. higher; less elastic

c. lower; more elastic

d. lower; less elastic

10. Metering is
    a. a type of indirect price discrimination.
    b. a type of direct price discrimination.
    c. an evaluation of a product.
    d. an example of bundling.

Individual Problems

14-1 Barbie Dolls and Accessories

Why might Mattel set a much lower margin on its Barbie dolls than on the accessories for the dolls?

14-2 German Brothels

German brothels recently began offering a monthly subscription service for multiple purchasers. If you wished to reduce the incidence of prostitution, would you consider this pricing plan to be a desirable change?

14-3 Selling Salsa

Your family business produces a secret recipe salsa and distributes it through both smaller specialty stores and chain supermarkets. The chains have been demanding sizable discounts but you do not want to drop your prices to the specialty stores. When can you legally accommodate the chains without losing profits from the specialty stores?

14-4 Microwave Ovens

A manufacturer of microwaves has discovered that male shoppers, on average, have lower values for microwave ovens than female shoppers. Additionally, male shoppers attribute almost no extra value to an auto-defrost feature, while female shoppers, on average, value the auto-defrost feature. There is little additional cost to incorporating an auto-defrost feature. The manufacturer is considering introducing two different models. The manufacturer has determined that men value a simple microwave at $70 and one with auto-defrost at $80, while women value a simple microwave at $80 and one with auto-defrost at $150. If there is an equal number of men and women, what pricing strategy will yield the greatest revenue? What if women comprise the bulk of microwave shoppers?

14-5 Music Pricing

The pricing model for iTunes has been to price songs individually. Instead, Spotify opted to offer unlimited song playing for a monthly fee. Would Spotify's pricing model likely yield more profit than pricing songs individually?

14-6 Bundling

At a student café, there are equal numbers of two types of customers with the following values. The café owner cannot distinguish between the two types of students because many students without early classes arrive early anyway (i.e., she cannot directly price discriminate).

	Students with Early Classes ($)	Students without Early Classes ($)
Coffee	0.70	0.60
Banana	0.50	1.00

The marginal cost of coffee is $0.10. The marginal cost of a banana is $0.40. Is bundling more profitable than selling separately? If so, what price should be charged for the bundle?

Group Problems

G14-1 Price Discrimination

Does your company price discriminate? Explain how the practice works (direct or indirect) and estimate the profit consequences of price discrimination relative to charging a single, uniform price. If your company doesn't currently price discriminate, are there opportunities to do so? How would you design the price discrimination? Estimate the profit consequences.

G14-2 Price Discrimination Data[7]

Collect a set of price quotes for no fewer than 30 airplane tickets. Examine how these price quotes change as you vary the tickets—one characteristic at a time.

For instance, suppose you get a price quote for a ticket on United Airlines from Raleigh-Durham to Chicago, departing on May 17 and returning on May 19. Change the following characteristics, one at a time, and get a new price quote:

- Change the time of departure within the same day.
- Change the source of your quote (e.g., from Travelocity to the airline's website).
- Change the predeparture interval date (e.g., compare flights bought a couple of days in advance to months in advance).
- Change the class of the ticket and travel restrictions.
- Change the return date to include a Saturday stay-over.
- Change anything else you can think of.

Make sure you get price quotes from airports where one airline has a dominant presence (e.g., Delta in Seattle) and a route presenting stiff competition from a "discount" carrier such as Frontier or JetBlue.

Describe some of the important differences in pricing you observe. Are the pricing differences consistent with the patterns of indirect or direct price discrimination, or are there other explanations? Original, novel, and thoughtful interpretations of the patterns you see in the data are particularly welcome.

END NOTES

1. Kenneth A. Small, Clifford Winston, and Jia Yan, "Uncovering the Distribution of Motorists' Preferences for Travel Time and Reliability," *Econometrica* 73 (2005): 1367–1382.

2. Raymond J. Deneckere and R. Preston McAfee, "Damaged Goods," *Journal of Economics and Management Strategy* 5 (1996): 149–174.

3. See John H. Shenefield and Irwin M. Stelzer, "Common Sense Guidelines," in *The Antitrust Laws: A Primer*, 3rd ed. (Washington, DC: AEI Press, 1998), 123–126.

4. Adapted from Hal R. Varian, "Sorting Out Bundling and Antitrust Law," *New York Times*, July 26, 2001.

5. Bundling can be accomplished in different ways. *Pure* bundling describes a situation where the commodities in a bundle are not offered for sale separately, whereas *mixed* bundling refers to a pricing strategy where the bundled goods can also be purchased separately.

6. Gregory S. Crawford and Joseph Cullen, "Bundling, Product Choice, and Efficiency: Should Cable Television Networks Be Offered a la Carte?" *Information Economics and Policy* 19 (2007): 379–404.

7. Adapted from Pat Bajari's economics class.

SECTION 4

Strategic Decision Making

15 | Strategic Games

On the island of Bermuda, the Cooper & Sons chain of department stores has been in the same family since 1897. Its largest rival, Gibbons, has been in the hands of another family for nearly as long. Yet, a decade ago, business began to slip. Increasing competition from Internet retailers led revenues to decline by 30% in just a few years. Several competing department stores have shut their doors.

In 2012, competition for the remaining dollars had become fierce. Cooper lowered its prices to try to steal some of Gibbons' customers. Gibbons responded with price cuts of its own. Then Cooper cut prices even more and expanded its store hours.

Short of starting a land war in Asia, few moves are as dumb as starting a price war with a close competitor. Each firm mistakenly believes that it can somehow "win" the war. When this doesn't happen, they find themselves with low profits, consumers who have grown accustomed to low prices, and the problem of how to end hostilities.

In October 2012, Gibbons announced that it would not be undercut. On its face, the announcement—"If you find a better price, we'll match it"—seemed to promise even lower prices, but in fact, it ended the war. Cooper no longer had an incentive to undercut Gibbons' prices because it couldn't gain customers by doing so. Gibbons' customers would stay with Gibbons and demand a price match instead. Quite counterintuitively, a price-matching announcement can end a price war.

In this chapter, we show you how to use game theory to analyze situations like these, where the profit of one firm depends critically on the actions of others. Studying game theory will give you insight into not only where competition with rivals is likely to lead, but also how to change the rules of the game to your advantage.

This chapter can be thought of as a complement to Chapter 10, where we introduced three basic strategies for slowing profit erosion: (1) reducing costs, (2) differentiating your product, and (3) reducing competitive intensity.

Game theory will help you better understand the third strategy.

The likely outcome of a game is a **Nash equilibrium**, named for John Nash, the mathematician (and Nobel laureate in economics) profiled in Sylvia Nasar's 1998 book and the Academy Award-winning 2001 movie, *A Beautiful Mind*.

> *A Nash equilibrium is a pair of strategies, one for each player, in which each strategy is a best response to the other.*

In equilibrium, each player is doing the best that he or she can given what the other player is doing. In what follows, we show how to compute equilibria in each type of game, and how to change the rules of the game to your advantage.

In what follows, we distinguish between two different types of games: sequential-move games and simultaneous-move games.

15.1 Sequential-Move Games

In **sequential-move games**, players take turns, and each player observes what his or her rival did before having to move. To compute the likely outcome of a sequential game, we *look ahead and reason back*, or predict what will happen tomorrow in response to each of our possible actions today. By anticipating how the other player will react tomorrow, we can accurately forecast the consequences of her own moves.

We represent sequential games using the *extensive* or *tree form* of a game, familiar to anyone who has ever used a decision tree. Consider the simple two-move game illustrated in Figure 15.1. An entrant is deciding whether to enter an industry currently controlled by a single incumbent firm. Beginning on the bottom of the left branch of the tree, we see that entry can lead to two different outcomes depending on how the incumbent reacts. The incumbent has two choices: accommodate entry or fight it. Accommodation (e.g., by keeping

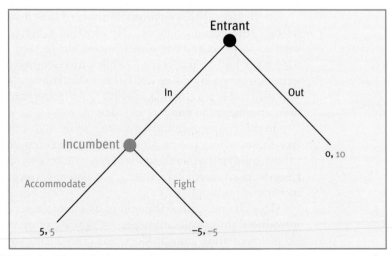

FIGURE **15.1** Entry Game

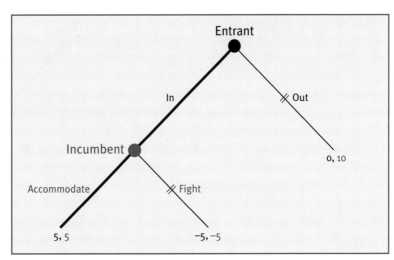

FIGURE **15.2** **Entry Accommodation**

prices high) results in a payoff of $5 million for each firm, whereas fighting (e.g., by pricing low) results in a loss of $5 million for each firm.

Initially, an entrant may fear entry because of the potential loss of $5 million. After all, a gamble between making $5 million and losing $5 million might not appeal to most firms. However, before deciding on a course of entry, the entrant should look forward and reason back. If the entrant decides to enter, the incumbent does better by accommodating. In Figure 15.2, we denote the best response of the incumbent by crossing out the suboptimal strategy.

Once the entrant knows how the incumbent will react, she can compute the profit for both options. If she enters, the incumbent will accommodate, and the entrant earns $5 million. If she stays out, it doesn't matter what the incumbent does—the entrant earns nothing. Comparing $5 million to $0, the entrant will enter. We denote the best strategy of the entrant in Figure 15.2 by crossing out the suboptimal strategy. What remains is the *equilibrium path* of the game, {In, Accommodate}, where each player is maximizing her payoff when taking the actions of subsequent players into account.[1]

The analysis doesn't stop here, however. We don't just want to figure out what's likely to happen; we also want some guidance about how to change the game to our advantage. For example, in this game, if the incumbent could figure out how to deter entry, he could end up on the right branch of the tree and earn $10 million instead of $5 million.

One way to deter entry is to threaten to fight (by slashing prices) if the entrant should enter. We diagram the threat by eliminating one of the branches of the tree in Figure 15.3. If the entrant believes the threat, she'll stay out because entry, combined with an incumbent's low price, would yield a loss of $5 million for the entrant. By eliminating one of his own options, the incumbent has changed the equilibrium of the game to {Out, Fight}. This highlights one of the interesting conclusions of this type of analysis—you can make yourself better off by eliminating one of your options.

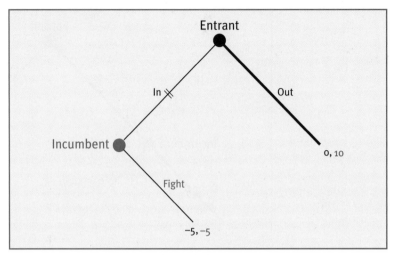

FIGURE **15.3** **Entry Deterrence with Commitment**

The difficult part for the incumbent is convincing the entrant it will price low following entry. Every incumbent would want to claim that he'll fight entry, but this threat, on its own, isn't *credible*. This is because fighting by pricing low is less profitable for the incumbent than pricing high if entry does occur. The incumbent is threatening to act against his own self-interest.

To make a threat credible, you have to change the game. One way to do this is to promise customers that any competitive offer will be beaten by 10%. These promises are legally binding contracts in most jurisdictions. This would credibly signal to potential entrants that the incumbent will reduce its prices if they enter, which would hopefully deter entry.

This is the whole point of studying game theory. Being able to compute the equilibrium tells you where you are likely to end up. But this depends on the payoffs and the rules of the game, neither of which is fixed. While games like Monopoly and checkers have rigid rules, the rules governing business interactions are often more flexible, often dictated by little more than history or inertia. After you compute the equilibrium, try to figure out if you can change it to your advantage.

15.2 Simultaneous-Move Games

In **simultaneous-move games**, each player decides on her strategy before knowing the decisions of other players. To analyze these games, we use the *matrix* or *strategic form* of a game.

How to Find Nash Equilibria

Consider the matrix in Table 15.1. The matrix represents a game between two parolees, Jesse and Frank, who are caught driving together shortly after a nearby bank robbery. The police suspect Jesse and Frank but have no direct evidence tying them to the crime. However, association with other felons is a

TABLE **15.1**

Jesse and Frank

		Frank	
		Confess	Stay Mum
Jesse	Confess	−5, −5	−3, −10
	Stay Mum	−10, −3	−2, −2

violation of parole, so the district attorney (DA) can send them both back to jail to serve the remaining sentences on their previous crimes. The DA puts the two parolees in separate cells and offers to go lighter on the one who confesses.

Jesse (termed the row player because he selects rows of the matrix) has two strategies, Confess and Stay Mum. Frank chooses between the same strategies in the columns of the matrix. The payoff to each (reflecting the number of years in jail) is the two-element entry (row, column) in the corresponding cell. For example, if Jesse chooses "Confess" and Frank chooses "Stay Mum," then Jesse's payoff is −3 (three years in jail) and Frank's payoff is −10.

The game in Table 15.1 describes the three components of a game: the players, their available strategies, and the resulting payoffs. This particular game is about as simple as they come with just two players with two strategies each. To find Nash equilibria, we ask, "Are both players playing a best response to what their rivals are playing?" If so, you have found a pair of strategies that is a Nash equilibrium.

Let's start from Jesse's perspective. For each of Frank's possible strategies, select the row strategy that maximizes Jesse's payoff. If Frank chooses the "Confess" column, Jesse's best row response is to play "Confess," earning a payoff of −5 which is better than his "Stay Mum" payoff of −10. To indicate this, we underline this payoff of −5. If Frank plays "Stay Mum," Jesse's best response is also to play "Stay Mum," earning a payoff of −2. In general, you would continue through all the column player's strategies underlining the best row response, as shown in Table 15.2. In more complex games, best responses might not be unique if two strategies have the same payoff. If two strategies are tied for best response, simply underline both.

TABLE **15.2**

Identifying the Row Player's Best Responses

		Frank	
		Confess	Stay Mum
Jesse	Confess	<u>−5</u>, −5	−3, −10
	Stay Mum	−10, −3	<u>−2</u>, −2

TABLE **15.3**

Identifying the Column Player's Best Responses

		Frank	
		Confess	Stay Mum
Jesse	Confess	$\underline{-5}, \underline{-5}$	$-3, -10$
	Stay Mum	$-10, -3$	$\underline{-2}, \underline{-2}$

We can do the same thing for Frank's best column responses to each row. If Jesse plays "Confess," Frank chooses "Confess" (because -5 is better than -10), and if Jesse plays "Stay Mum," Frank chooses "Stay Mum." This is depicted in Table 15.3.

Recall that a pair of strategies is an equilibrium if both players are playing their best responses. Since we underlined best responses, an equilibrium occurs whenever both payoffs in a box are underlined. In this case, the game has two equilibria, {Confess, Confess} and {Stay Mum, Stay Mum}.

The fact that there are two equilibria (including one in which both stay mum) is a problem for the DA. If she could, the DA would like to change the game to get Frank and Jesse to confess for sure. She does this by increasing the reward to confessing. The DA promises Jesse that if he confesses while Frank stays mum, she will let Jesse go free. She makes the same offer to Frank. Table 15.4 shows how this slight alteration in the payoffs changes the players' best responses.

TABLE **15.4**

Prisoners' Dilemma

		Frank	
		Confess	Stay Mum
Jesse	Confess	$\underline{-5}, \underline{-5}$	$\underline{0}, -10$
	Stay Mum	$-10, \underline{0}$	$-2, -2$

Now there is only one equilibrium. Even if Jesse thinks Frank will stay mum, Jesse's best response is still to confess.[2] The only Nash equilibrium is in the upper-left corner, in which both players confess.

15.3 Prisoners' Dilemma

The situation depicted in Table 15.4 illustrates a tension between conflict (self-interest) and cooperation (group interest). If Frank and Jesse cooperate by both staying mum (lower right), the group would be better off. However, this is not an equilibrium. By following their self-interests, the players both confess and end up in the upper left box.

TABLE **15.5**

Pricing Dilemma

		Gibbons	
		Price Low	Price High
Cooper	Price Low	<u>100</u>, <u>120</u>	<u>400</u>, 0
	Price High	0, <u>480</u>	300, 360

The **prisoners' dilemma** is perhaps the oldest and most studied game in economics, and reflects many business situations. For example, the pricing dilemma in the introduction of this chapter and illustrated in Table 15.5 has the same logical structure as the prisoners' dilemma. Even though Gibbons' profits are higher than Cooper's due to its larger size, both Cooper and Gibbons could make more money if both priced high, but both pricing high is not a Nash equilibrium. Cooper does better by pricing low regardless of what Gibbons does, and Gibbons does better by pricing low regardless of what Cooper does. The only Nash equilibrium is for both to price low, in the upper-left corner.

Price Discrimination Dilemma

You learned in Chapters 13 and 14 that you can often increase profit by price discriminating, provided different consumers have different demand elasticities and you can prevent arbitrage. But when you're competing against other firms, price discrimination may provoke your rivals to retaliate in a way that could make you both worse off. If your rivals begin discriminating in reaction to your decision to discriminate, then everyone's profit can fall below what it would have been had no one price discriminated. For example, firms often discriminate by offering discounts to customers based on where they live. Supermarkets and pizza chains may target promotions to customers who live closer to rival stores.[3] Companies often offer coupons at supermarket checkouts to customers who have purchased competing brands.[4] In each of these attempts to price discriminate, we would expect rivals to react by offering lower prices to these targeted customers as well. The result is that equilibrium prices are lower than they would be without targeted discounts.

In Table 15.6, we see an illustrative game involving two grocery stores. These stores (Kroger and Safeway) are considering whether to offer discount coupons to customers who live farther away—and closer to a competitor's store. These customers have more elastic demand than customers living closer to the store.

If just one grocery store offers such coupons, then its profit increases. However, if its competitor does the same thing, then all the stores wind up with about the same overall sale volume, but at lower prices. In equilibrium, both stores price discriminate, and both are worse off. Intuitively, with a uniform price, the stores compete vigorously for customers only on the boundaries of

TABLE **15.6**
Oligopoly Price Discrimination Dilemma

		Kroger	
		Price Discriminate	Uniform Prices
Safeway	Price Discriminate	0, 0	4, −2
	Uniform Prices	−2, 4	2, 2

their market areas. When they discriminate, they compete vigorously for all customers, no matter where they live, and industry profit suffers. While neither Kroger nor Safeway is a prisoner, they are nevertheless playing a prisoners' dilemma.

Advertising Dilemma

Table 15.7 exhibits an advertising dilemma that again has the same logical structure as the prisoners' dilemma. Rival tobacco manufacturers R.J. Reynolds and Phillip Morris both used to advertise quite heavily on television. Cigarette advertising is predatory; it serves mainly to steal market share from rivals without increasing market size. Thus, both companies could make more money by not advertising, but the lower-right corner in Table 15.7 is not an equilibrium. If the rival doesn't advertise, each firm can do better by advertising and stealing the rival's customers. The only Nash equilibrium is for both to advertise and earn lower profits.

TABLE **15.7**
Advertising Dilemma

		Phillip Morris	
		Advertise	Don't Advertise
R.J. Reynolds	Advertise	30, 30	50, 20
	Don't Advertise	20, 50	40, 40

When the government banned over-the-air cigarette advertising in the early 1970s, the profitability of the cigarette industry increased by nearly 40%.[5] The ban moved the industry from the upper-left corner to the lower-right corner of the payoff matrix. Ordinarily, however, you can't count on the government to help you out of a prisoners' dilemma.

Free-Riding Dilemma

The game in Table 15.8 illustrates the strategic interdependence typical of an MBA study group. It's also typical of the kinds of payoffs you'd expect in any group or team-based activity. Each player has the option of working hard or shirking. The benefit of working hard is that you raise your grade, but the

TABLE **15.8**

Free-Riding Dilemma

		Joe	
		Shirk	Work
Sally	**Shirk**	<u>C+Leisure</u>, <u>C+Leisure</u>	<u>B+Leisure</u>, B
	Work	B, <u>B+Leisure</u>	A, A

downside is that you sacrifice leisure time. If both work, they will earn an A, if only one works, they earn a B, and if both shirk, they earn a C.

To determine the Nash equilibrium of the game, you need to know how study group members rank various outcomes. Assume that students value leisure time more than a one-letter grade improvement, but less than a two-letter grade improvement. Thus, B+Leisure is better than an A which is better than a C+Leisure which is better than a B.

Then, Sally's best response to Joe shirking is to also shirk (C+Leisure is preferable to a B), and Sally's best response to Joe working is again to shirk (B+Leisure is preferable to an A). Because Joe has the same preferences, the Nash equilibrium is {Shirk, Shirk}, where each player receives a C plus leisure time. This outcome is inefficient because students in the group would jointly prefer the A that comes from hard work. However, this outcome is not an equilibrium because once the other group members are working hard, the best response is to shirk.

As in the other prisoners' dilemma games, there is a tension between conflict and cooperation. Successful study groups figure out how to manage this tension, and get out of the low-grade equilibrium.

Getting Out of a Prisoners' Dilemma

The Nash equilibrium of a prisoners' dilemma represents an unconsummated wealth-creating transaction between players. In the pricing dilemma, both players would like to price high. In the advertising dilemma, both would like to advertise less. In the free-riding game, both would like to work harder. However, none of these outcomes is a Nash equilibrium.

The point of studying the prisoners' dilemma is to learn to avoid these bad outcomes or, alternatively, to learn how to consummate these unconsummated wealth-creating transactions among players.

The implication of the prisoners' dilemma for a long-run strategy is clear: try to *avoid* games with the logical structure of a prisoners' dilemma. Instead, work on developing long-run strategies that change the structure of the game to make your own payoffs less dependent on your rivals' actions. If possible, try to differentiate your product or figure out a way to lower your costs.

If you have no other option, try to reduce the intensity of competition without running afoul of the antitrust laws. For example, if Cooper and Gibbons can find a way to coordinate their pricing, they can get out of this dilemma.

However, explicit price coordination is a violation of the antitrust laws, as summed up in the following advice from a former antitrust prosecutor:

> *Do not discuss prices with your competitors. That is one of those black-and-white areas. The enforcement authorities can be counted on to bring a criminal prosecution if they learn that you have met with your competitors to fix prices or any other terms of sale. Jail time is increasingly common.*[6]

Instead, Cooper and Gibbons department stores introduced price matching, reducing the strategic benefits of lowering prices. Effectively, this means that if *either* store charges low prices, both stores in effect do. The only way to improve payoffs is to have both stores charge higher prices.

When Prisoners' Dilemmas Are Repeated

As a general matter, it is easier to get out of a prisoners' dilemma when the game is repeated. For example, suppose our MBA group members were not just playing the free-riding game in Table 15.8 once, but, as is more likely, they were playing it over and over. With repeated games, you can condition your future behavior on your opponent's past behavior with a *trigger* strategy. For example, both could agree to cooperate by working in each period, but adopt the following strategy: if my classmate worked last time, I will work too, but if my classmate shirked, it will trigger me to shirk from now on.

Is this agreement a Nash equilibrium? By working, each player receives an A in each period, but without leisure time (the second best outcome of the four). If one of the players shirks, that player receives a higher payoff in *that* period. But the player knows that his colleague will shirk forever after, leading to a worse outcome. Thus, cooperating leads to the second-best outcome in each period. Cheating leads to a one-time gain followed by worse payoffs in all future periods. The comparison between these depends on the discount rate and on the expected length of the future relationship between MBA students. Low discount rates (where future payoffs are more valuable) and long relationships both make cooperation more likely.

Similarly, the hold-up problem between a supplier and a customer from Chapter 5 can be described as a prisoners' dilemma in which both parties benefit from the transaction but one party cannot help himself from holding up the counter-party once relationship-specific costs are sunk. In a repeated-game context, the likelihood of hold-up is decreased because such an action sacrifices the future value of the relationship. When cooperation is important, devise ways to make the interaction more like a repeated game to avoid "cheating."

To determine the best way to play a repeated prisoners' dilemma, professor of political science Robert Axelrod had a novel idea—he ran a tournament with a cash prize. He asked professors of political science, mathematics, psychology, computer science, and economics to submit strategies as programmable functions, and he then ran simulated tournaments among the programs. Axelrod was able to characterize the features of the strategies that earned the highest profit:

- *Be nice:* Start by cooperating, and don't strike first.
- *Be easily provoked:* Respond immediately to rivals.
- *Be forgiving:* Don't try to punish other players too much if they defect from the cooperative outcome.
- *Don't be envious:* Focus on your own slice of the profit pie, not on your competitor's.
- *Be clear:* Make sure your competitors can easily interpret your actions.

The tit-for-tat strategy—cooperating the first period and then doing what your opponent did last period—won the tournament. It exhibits all of the characteristics of a successful strategy. Tit-for-tat never strikes first and responds immediately to defection, but limits punishment to only a single period. It is focused on maximizing your own profit, and not on limiting your competitor's profits. And finally, it is easily understood by rivals.

15.4 Other Games

Game of Chicken

In the classic game of chicken, two teenage boys—say, James and Dean—drive their cars straight toward each other. If both go straight, they crash and die. If one goes straight while the other swerves, the one who goes straight wins the praise of peers, whereas the one who swerves suffers the humiliation of "chickening out." If both swerve, each suffers humiliation.[7]

Intuitively, you should realize that there are two equilibria to this game. If James goes straight and Dean swerves, then each player is doing the best he can, given what the other player is doing. James cannot improve his payoff by swerving and Dean cannot improve his by going straight (assuming death is worse than humiliation). In Table 15.9, we have attached numerical values to each of the outcomes, and you should verify for yourself that the game of chicken has two equilibria in the off-diagonal entries of the matrix.

TABLE **15.9**

Game of Chicken

		James	
		Go Straight	Swerve
Dean	**Go Straight**	−10, −10	3, 0
	Swerve	0, 3	0, 0

Now that we have analyzed the game and the likely outcomes, the next step is to figure out how to change the game to your advantage. Note that each party prefers one of the equilibria. This implies an obvious strategy: commit to a position, and make sure your rival understands your commitment. Coordination is important here so that the players don't end up killing each other.

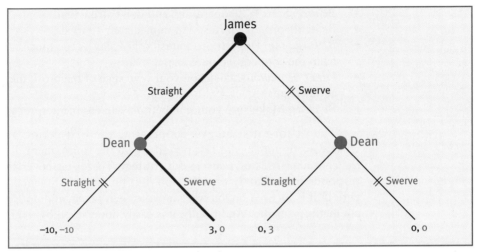

FIGURE **15.4** **First-Mover Advantage in a Game of Chicken**

Commitment changes what is essentially a simultaneous-move game into a sequential-move game. We illustrate this in Figure 15.4. The equilibrium is easy to compute. Dean does better by doing the opposite of whatever James does before him. So if James goes straight, Dean swerves, and vice versa. Once James knows what Dean is going to do, he sees that {Straight, Swerve} gives him a higher payoff than {Swerve, Straight}. The difficult part is convincing the other player that you are committed. One way to do this is to lock the steering wheel in place using an antitheft device, like the Club, and throw away the key. Make sure that the other player sees you do this. Otherwise, he may also commit to going straight, and you could both end up dead.

The game of chicken has business applications as well. Table 15.10 represents the choices faced by competing biotechnology companies who were developing hybrid (disease-resistant) grapes. Each company could afford to tailor the grape variety to only one country, either Italy or South Africa. Both prefer to be the sole entrant in a market, and both prefer Italy—a larger market—to South Africa. This game has the same logical structure as the game of chicken, with two equilibria: {South Africa, Italy} and {Italy, South Africa}.

TABLE **15.10**
Market Entry Game of Chicken

		Firm B	
		Italy	South Africa
Firm A	**Italy**	0, 0	<u>100</u>, <u>50</u>
	South Africa	<u>50</u>, <u>100</u>	−50, −50

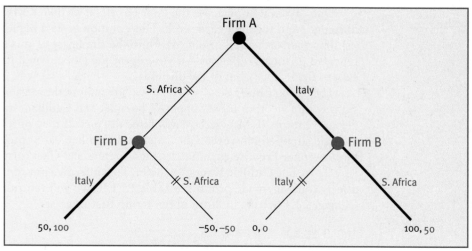

FIGURE **15.5** Sequential Market Entry

If Firm A can move first or commit to going into Italy, it will force Firm B into South Africa. By moving first, Firm A turns the simultaneous-move game into a sequential-move game in which it "chooses" the favorable equilibrium. We graph this outcome in Figure 15.5.

Dating Game

The dating game shares the tension between group interest (cooperation) and self-interest (conflict) inherent in a prisoners' dilemma. The game in Table 15.11 is about a couple with different interests—Sally likes ballet and Joe likes wrestling. But each likes the other's company and would prefer attending events together. The two would be best served if Sally and Joe could agree to attend an event together (total payoff of 5), but neither coordination possibility—both attend the ballet or both attend wrestling match—is a Nash equilibrium. The only Nash equilibrium is the lower left, where Joe goes to the wrestling match and Sally goes to the ballet.[8] This outcome is not optimal, however, since both enjoy spending time together. As in the prisoners' dilemma, the idea is to find a way to change the rules of the game so both players can earn higher payoffs.

TABLE **15.11**
Dating Game

		Joe	
		Wrestling	Ballet
Sally	**Wrestling**	1, <u>4</u>	0, 0
	Ballet	<u>2</u>, <u>2</u>	<u>4</u>, 1

One easy way to increase the joint payoffs is to take turns by attending a different event together each week. This solution gives a higher group payoff (5) than the Nash equilibrium (4). Note the similarity of this solution to the repeated prisoners' dilemma—if you repeat the game, you'll find it relatively easy to figure a way out of the dilemma.

The dating game also gives you a way to analyze the tension between divisions within a corporation. Suppose Chevrolet and Cadillac—two divisions of General Motors (GM)—receive a volume discount if they purchase tires from a single supplier. However, Chevrolet and Cadillac cannot agree on a common supplier because each has its own preference: Chevrolet wants Goodyear Tires, but Cadillac wants Michelin. This interdivision conflict negatively affects company-wide profit (see Table 15.12). We will return to this topic in Chapter 22, "Getting to Work in the Firm's Best Interests."

TABLE **15.12**

Corporate Division Dating Game

		Chevrolet	
		Goodyear Tires	Michelin Tires
Cadillac	**Goodyear Tires**	1, <u>4</u>	0, 0
	Michelin Tires	<u>2</u>, <u>2</u>	<u>4</u>, 1

Interdivision conflict is more likely to arise when the parent company runs each division as a separate profit center. Finding a way to create cooperation for the good of the parent company is the management's problem. In this case, GM might offer some kind of profit sharing or subsidization, such as Cadillac paying Chevrolet to use Michelin tires.

Shirking/Monitoring Game

We can consider the problem of how to manage workers efficiently as a game between an employer and an employee. Game theory helps us understand how best to manage self-interested employees.

Consider the most basic situation: a self-interested employee would prefer to work less (shirk), but shirking is profitable only if his manager is not monitoring what he does. The manager wants the employee to work hard, but must incur costs to monitor the employee's behavior. Table 15.13 represents the game. Try to find an equilibrium before reading on.

TABLE **15.13**

Shirking/Monitoring Game

		Employee	
		Shirk	Work
Manager	**Monitor**	−<u>1</u>, 0	5, <u>5</u>
	Don't Monitor	−10, <u>10</u>	<u>10</u>, 5

If the manager monitors, then the employee does better by working. If the employee works, the manager does better by not spending resources on monitoring. But if the manager doesn't monitor, then the employee does better by shirking. But if the employee shirks, the manager prefers to monitor. And so on. This game has no "pure strategy" equilibrium (meaning that each player selects one of the two strategies and sticks to it), but it does have an equilibrium in "mixed" strategies in which players choose which strategies to play randomly.

An easy way to understand the concept of mixed strategies is to think about a sports contest. Should an American football team run or pass? If the team always runs, the defense will always prepare a good run defense, and the same will happen if the team always passes. The best strategy is to mix between runs and passes to try to keep the defense guessing. The exact probability of running will vary from team to team, depending on its players' abilities, and from game to game, depending on the abilities of rival players. The idea is to use the element of surprise to keep your opponent from taking advantage of your strategy.

In the equilibrium of our monitoring/shirking game, managers randomly monitor employees' behavior, and employees randomly shirk. As the manager's goal is to affect the behavior of the employee, it turns out that the probability of monitoring depends on how much the employee gains by shirking, and the probability of shirking depends on how much it costs the employer to monitor the employee's behavior.

Now that we understand behavior in this game, let's try to figure out how to change the outcome to our advantage. The employer can reduce shirking by combining monitoring with some incentive compensation. When the employer monitors and finds the employee is working hard, the employer can reward the employee with a bonus; or, equivalently, when the employer monitors and finds the employee is shirking, the employer can punish him with a fine, like demotion or dismissal. This combination of monitoring and incentive compensation can reduce the costs of controlling self-interested employees. We'll return to this problem in Chapter 21 when we discuss aligning employee incentives with the goals of the firm.

SUMMARY & HOMEWORK PROBLEMS

Summary of Main Points

- In **sequential-move games**, players observe all prior decisions of the rival before deciding on a strategy.
- In **simultaneous-move games**, players do not observe the rival's decision before deciding on their own strategies.
- A **Nash equilibrium** is a pair of strategies, one for each player, in which each strategy is a best response to the other. These represent the likely outcomes of games.

- When the rules of the game are flexible, change them to your advantage.
- In sequential games, players can change the outcome by committing to a future course of action. Credible commitments are difficult to make because they may require players to threaten to act against their own self-interest.
- In the **prisoners' dilemma**, conflict and cooperation are in tension—self-interest leads the players to outcomes that no one likes. Studying the games can help you find a way to avoid these bad outcomes.

- In repeated games, it is much easier to get out of bad situations. Here are some general rules of thumb:
  - *Be nice:* No first strikes.
  - *Be easily provoked:* Respond immediately to rivals.
  - *Be forgiving:* Don't try to punish other players too much.
  - *Don't be envious:* Focus on your own slice of the profit pie, not on your competitor's.
  - *Be clear:* Make sure your competitors can easily interpret your actions.

Multiple-Choice Questions

1. The prisoners' dilemma is an example of
   a. a sequential game.
   b. a simultaneous game.
   c. a shirking game.
   d. a dating game.
2. A Nash equilibrium
   a. is where one player maximizes his payoff and the other doesn't.
   b. is where each player maximizes his own payoff given the action of the other player.
   c. is where both players are maximizing their total payoff.
   d. is a unique prediction of the likely outcome of a game.

Use the following to answer Questions 3–5:
Consider the following information for a simultaneous-move game: two discount stores (megastore and superstore) are interested in expanding their market share through advertising. The following table depicts the profits of both stores with and without advertising. Payoffs for Megastore are in black.

		Superstore	
		Advertise	Don't Advertise
Megastore	Advertise	$95, $80	$305, $55
	Don't Advertise	$65, $285	$165, $115

3. A Nash equilibrium is
   a. for Megastore to advertise and for Superstore to advertise.
   b. for Megastore to advertise and for Superstore not to advertise.
   c. for Megastore not to advertise and for Superstore to advertise.
   d. for Megastore not to advertise and for Superstore not to advertise.
4. When the stores reach the Nash equilibrium, their profits will be
   a. Megastore $95 and Superstore $80.
   b. Megastore $305 and Superstore $55.
   c. Megastore $65 and Superstore $285.
   d. Megastore $165 and Superstore $115.
5. If collusion were not illegal, then it would be optimal
   a. for Megastore to advertise and for Superstore to advertise.
   b. for Megastore to advertise and for Superstore not to advertise.
   c. for Megastore not to advertise and for Superstore to advertise.
   d. for Megastore not to advertise and for Superstore not to advertise.
6. In a Nash equilibrium,
   a. players are always maximizing their joint profit.
   b. one player is always earning a higher profit than the other.
   c. players must be playing the game sequentially.
   d. None of the above.
7. In repeated games, all of the following make it easier to get out of bad situations except
   a. be nice, no first strikes.
   b. respond immediately to rivals.
   c. punish uncooperative players as much as you can.
   d. make sure your competitors can easily interpret your actions.

Refer to the following strategic form game of price competition for Questions 8 and 9.

		Firm B	
		Low Price	High Price
Firm A	Low Price	0, 0	50, −10
	High Price	−10, 50	25, 25

8. If this game is played once, then
   a. firm A will charge a low price, and firm B will charge a low price.
   b. firm A will charge a high price, and firm B will charge a low price.
   c. firm A will charge a low price, and firm B will charge a high price.
   d. firm A will charge a high price, and firm B will charge a high price.

9. Suppose the game is infinitely repeated. What strategies will each firm likely utilize?
   a. Firm A will charge a low price, and firm B will charge a low price.
   b. Firm A will charge a high price, and firm B will charge a low price.
   c. Firm A will charge a low price, and firm B will charge a high price.
   d. Firm A will charge a high price, and firm B will charge a high price.

10. You, a real-estate developer, own a piece of land in Nassau, Bahamas, next to an equally sized piece of land owned by a competitor. Both of you have the choice of building a casino or a hotel. Your payoffs are as follows:

		You	
		Casino	Hotel
Your	Casino	3, 3	20, 5
Competitor	Hotel	5, 20	2, 2

How much is it worth to you to get your casino building permit first?
   a. $2 million
   b. $3 million
   c. $15 million
   d. $17 million

Individual Problems

15-1 To Vote or Not to Vote

Mr. and Mrs. Ward typically vote oppositely in elections and so their votes "cancel each other out." They each gain two units of utility from a vote for their positions (and lose two units of utility from a vote against their positions). However, the bother of actually voting costs each one unit of utility. Diagram a game in which they choose whether to vote or not to vote.

15-2 To Vote or Not to Vote Part II

Suppose Mr. and Mrs. Ward agreed not to vote in tomorrow's election. Would such an agreement improve utility? Would such an agreement be an equilibrium?

15-3 Compatibility

Microsoft and a smaller rival often have to select from one of two competing technologies. The rival always prefers to select the same technology as Microsoft (because compatibility is important), while Microsoft always wants to select a different technology from its rival. Describe the equilibrium of this game.

15-4 Salary Negotiation

The following figure represents the potential outcomes of your first salary negotiation after graduation.

Assuming that this is a sequential-move game with the employer moving first, indicate the most likely outcome. Does the ability to move first give the employer an advantage? If so, how? As the employee, is there anything you could do to realize a higher payoff?

15-5 Renegotiating Employment Contracts

Every year, management and labor renegotiate a new employment contract by sending their proposals to an arbitrator who chooses the best proposal (effectively giving one side or the other $1 million). Each side can choose to hire, or not hire, an expensive labor lawyer (at a cost of

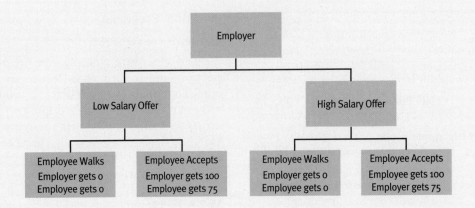

$200,000) who is effective at preparing the proposal in the best light. If neither hires lawyers or if both hire lawyers, each side can expect to win about half the time. If only one side hires a lawyer, it can expect to win three-quarters of the time.

1. Diagram this simultaneous-move game.
2. What is the Nash equilibrium of the game?
3. Would the sides want to ban lawyers?

15-6 Entry Game with Withdrawal

In the text, we considered a sequential-move game in which an entrant was considering entering an industry in competition with an incumbent firm (Figure 15.1). Consider now that the entrant, if fought, has the possibility of withdrawing from the industry (at a loss of 1 for the entrant and a gain of 8 for the incumbent), or staying (at a loss of 5 for each player).

What is the equilibrium of this game? Discuss if the entrant is better off with or without the ability to withdraw.

Group Problem

G15-1 Strategic Game

Describe some interaction your company has with another entity (firms producing complementary or substitute products, upstream suppliers, or downstream customers), or between internal divisions within your firm that can be described as a sequential or simultaneous game. Diagram the strategies, players, and compute payoffs as best you can. Compute the Nash equilibria. What can you do to change the rules of the game to your advantage? Compute the profit consequences of your advice.

END NOTES

1. For sequential games, this is a specific type of Nash equilibrium called a *subgame-perfect* or *rollback* equilibrium.
2. When a player has the same best response to anything that other players might do, it is called a *dominant strategy*. Here, "Confess" is dominant for both Jesse and Frank.

3. Retail scanner data and company loyalty programs sometimes make such discrimination possible. For a detailed analysis of these strategies, see Greg Shaffer and Z. John Zhang, "Competitive Coupon Targeting," *Marketing Science* 14 (1995): 395–416 and Greg Shaffer and Z. John Zhang, "Pay

to Switch or Pay to Stay: Preference-Based Price Discrimination in Markets with Switching Costs," *Journal of Economics and Management Strategy* 9 (2000): 397–424.

4. Examples of these so-called pay-to-switch strategies include Coca-Cola's giving a discount on Diet Coke to purchasers of Diet Pepsi and Chesebrough-Pond's giving a discount on Mentadent Toothpaste to purchasers of PeroxiCare. See Ibid.

5. For more on how the advertising ban actually benefitted the tobacco companies, see James L. Hamilton, "The Demand for Cigarettes: Advertising, the Health Scare, and the Cigarette Advertising Ban," *Review of Economics and Statistics* 54 (1972): 401–411.

6. John H. Shenefield and Irwin M. Stelzer, "Common Sense Guidelines," in *The Antitrust Laws: A Primer*, 3rd ed. (Washington, DC: AEI Press, 1998), 123–126.

7. Actually, the classic version of the game of chicken involved two cars driving toward the edge of a cliff, with the winner being the one who jumped out of the car last. Our updated version preserves the cars as well as the drivers.

8. In an alternate version of the Dating Game, players' preferences for one event over the other are not as strong as their preference to be together. In this case, the game has two equilibria in which both attend the same event.

16   Bargaining

In the summer of 2011, the owners of the National Basketball Association (NBA) were locked in negotiations with the players' union over how to split revenue. The union wanted 57%, equal to its previous contract, but the owners were offering only 50%. Despite some concessions from the players' union, the owners locked out the players, canceling the beginning of the season. After months of finger-pointing and legal threats, the players settled for what the owners had originally offered.

In contrast to the players' union, public sector employee unions have been able to bargain much more successfully. In places like California, with strong unions, public sector workers earn as much as 30% more than their private sector counterparts, by some estimates. In Central Falls, Rhode Island, the city workers were able to win retirement benefits so generous that they bankrupted the city.

A similar contrast appears in the bargaining over drug prices. Hospitals and health maintenance organizations (HMOs) are able to buy drugs at prices that are 10% to 40% less than drugstores pay. What accounts for these differences?

In this chapter, we answer these questions from two different, but complementary, points of view. We begin with a strategic view that characterizes bargaining as a formal *game of chicken* where the ability to commit to a position gives one player bargaining power over its rivals.

The other view of bargaining begins with the observation that real negotiations rarely have rules like the ones that characterize formal games. Under this view of bargaining, it is the alternatives to agreement that determine the terms of agreement, regardless of the precise form of the negotiations. If you can increase your opponent's gain to reaching agreement (or decrease your own), you make your opponent more eager to reach agreement, and this allows you to capture a bigger share of the proverbial pie.

16.1 Strategic View of Bargaining

In this section, we model bargaining as a *game of chicken* where the ability to commit to a position gives one player bargaining power over rivals. To make this concrete, imagine that a company's managers are bargaining with a labor union over a fixed sum and that each player has just two possible strategies: *bargain hard* or *accommodate*. If both bargain hard, they'll fail to reach a deal, and therefore each will earn nothing; if both accommodate, they split the gains from trade. If one player bargains hard and the other accommodates, the player who bargains hard takes 75% of the gains from agreement.

In Table 16.1, we see that this game has the same logical structure as a game of chicken. If both players accommodate, they split the gains from trade (lower right), but this is not an equilibrium because either player can do better by bargaining hard. If both bargain hard, then each earns nothing (upper left), but this is not an equilibrium because either player can do better by accommodating the other. The two equilibria, {Bargain Hard, Accommodate} in the upper-right quadrant and {Accommodate, Bargain Hard} in the lower-left quadrant, are where each party is playing optimally against its rival.

TABLE **16.1**

Labor Negotiation Game

		Management	
		Bargain Hard	Accommodate
Union	**Bargain Hard**	0, 0	<u>75</u>, <u>25</u>
	Accommodate	<u>25</u>, <u>75</u>	50, 50

At this point, you should know what to expect in a game of chicken—both parties will try to steer the game to their preferred equilibrium by committing to a position. If you can convince your rival that you're going to bargain hard, regardless of what your rival does, he will do better by accommodating, and you will get a bigger share of the gains from trade.

To see the value of commitment, we examine the game as a sequential-move game where the party able to make a commitment gets to move first. In this case, imagine that the union makes either a generous offer or a low offer; and then management must either accept or reject the offer. If management accepts the offer, it earns what the union offered; if not, management locks out the union, and each party earns nothing.

We diagram the offers and payoffs in Figure 16.1. To analyze the game, we begin at the second stage, and notice that the management does better by accepting whatever is offered in the first stage. Regardless of whether the union makes a generous offer or a low offer, accepting the offer gives management a higher payout than rejecting it. Realizing this, the union makes a low offer at the first stage and earns 75% instead of 25%. We identify the equilibrium by putting two lines through all the suboptimal options in Figure 16.1.

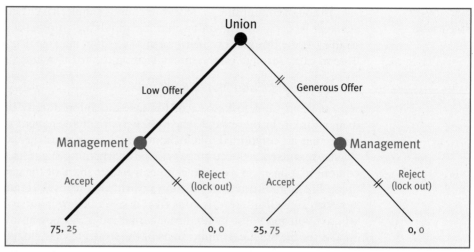

FIGURE **16.1**   Labor Negotiation Game with Union Commitment

This game illustrates a classic *first-mover advantage*—by moving first, or equivalently, by committing to bargain hard, the union can capture most of the gains from trade.

By now you should be able to recognize that the simultaneous-move game is symmetric, which means that if management can commit to lock out the union if it receives a low offer, it can change the outcome of the game. If the union believes management's threat, it will make a generous offer instead of a low one.

As in the entry deterrence game in Chapter 15, by committing to a position, management changes the equilibrium of the game by eliminating an option. We illustrate the new equilibrium in Figure 16.2.

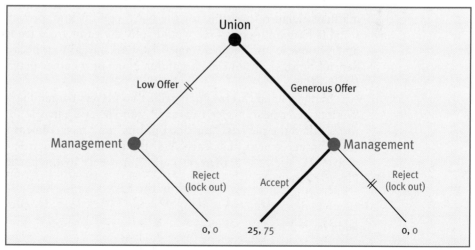

FIGURE **16.2**   Labor Negotiation Game with Management Commitment to Lock Out

Although committing to a lockout sounds simple, it's difficult for the management to persuade the union that it will pursue an otherwise unprofitable strategy. If the threat is not believed by the union, management might actually have to carry through on the threat, leading to the following maxim:

The best threat is one you never have to use.

Lockouts (and strikes) occur because the union doesn't believe management's threat. In these cases, the only way for management to convince the union that it's committed to a lockout is to actually lock the union out.

To summarize: the strategic view of bargaining suggests that if you can commit to a position, you can capture a bigger share of the gains from agreement. But committing to a position is difficult because it requires you to act against your self-interest. If your rival doesn't believe your commitment, she will test you and you may go through a period of no agreement.

To see the practical implications of the strategic view, imagine that you are buying a new car. To get a better price, try to put the car dealer in a position where he is forced to either accept or reject your offer. First, figure out which car you want to buy and exactly which features you want. Then, do some research to find out what the dealer's actual cost is and calculate a price where the dealer can make some, but not too much, money. Bring only one check, preferably a cashier's check that cannot be modified, made out for a specific amount, and threaten to leave if the dealer says anything but "yes" to your offer. If the car dealer believes you, then your offer is likely to be accepted.

16.2 Nonstrategic View of Bargaining

The games just described take a **strategic view of bargaining**, in which the outcome depends on who moves first and who can commit to a position. This dependence of the bargaining outcome on the precise rules of the bargaining game is a little disturbing because real-world bargaining rarely has such well-defined rules. To address this shortcoming, John Nash, the same mathematician responsible for the Nash equilibrium, proved that any reasonable bargaining outcome would split the gains from trade.[1] We call this an "axiomatic" or "nonstrategic" view of bargaining because it does not depend on the rules of the bargaining game or whether players can commit to a position.

To understand this result, imagine two players bargaining with each other. Without agreement, Player 1 earns D_1 and Player 2 earns D_2. These are sometimes called the players' "outside options" or "disagreement values." If they reach an agreement, they earn A. If the gains to trade are positive, that is, if $A - (D_1 + D_2) > 0$, then they are split evenly by the parties. In this case, Player 1 receives

$$D_1 + (A - (D_1 + D_2))/2 = (A + D_1 - D_2)/2,$$

and Player 2 receives

$$D_2 + (A - (D_1 + D_2))/2 = (A + D_2 - D_1)/2.$$

CHAPTER 16 • Bargaining **209**

Notice that each player's split depends not only on how much the agreement is worth (*A*), but also on the players' outside options, or disagreement values (*D₁* and *D₂*). Player 1 receives more if his outside option is better or if Player 2's outside option is worse. This leads immediately to the following advice:

To improve your own bargaining position, improve your outside option, or decrease that of your opponent.

This **nonstrategic view of bargaining** tells you that if you can *decrease* your own gain to reaching agreement by *improving* your outside option, you become a tougher bargainer because you have less to gain by reaching agreement. For example, the best time to ask for a raise is when you already have an attractive offer from another company (*D₁* is big). Because you have a good alternative, your gain to reaching agreement is small, which makes you less eager to reach agreement. Note the similarity of the disagreement value to the idea of *opportunity cost*. The cost of staying in your current job is the offer you give up if you stay. If you have a good alternative offer, the opportunity cost of staying in your job is high, putting you in a stronger bargaining position.

The result also tells us how bargaining is likely to change as circumstances change. Suppose, for example, that Player 1 receives a bonus *B* for reaching agreement. The total gain to reaching agreement has now risen from *A* to *A* + *B*. The nonstrategic view of bargaining tells us that this bonus will be split between the two parties. In essence, Player 1 "gives away" half of his bonus to Player 2. If you increase the first player's gain to reaching an agreement, you make him more eager to reach agreement, and this puts him in a weaker bargaining position.

Bonuses like this are similar to incentive compensation schemes that companies adopt to induce salespeople to increase sales. Offering salespeople bonuses increases their eagerness to reach agreement with their customers, and this makes them weaker bargainers. So, if you give your salespeople an incentive like this, you can expect lower prices when they negotiate with customers. We will come back to this theme in Chapter 21 when we talk about how to align the incentives of salespeople—who typically prefer lower prices so they can make more sales—with the profitability goals of the company.

To understand how advice gleaned from Nash's bargaining outcome differs from advice gleaned from analyzing bargaining as a strategic game, let's return to the union/management game. The strategic view of bargaining emphasized the role of commitment and timing in affecting the outcome of a game. For example, management's commitment to lock out the union in the event of a low offer changes the equilibrium of the game. But strategies play no role in the nonstrategic view of bargaining. Only a strike that hurts management more than it hurts the union can improve the bargaining position of labor. This is why strike threats are more common during seasonal peaks in demand, when it would hurt the firm more than it would hurt the union. By changing the alternatives to agreement for management (bigger loss during a strike), the union can increase management's willingness to reach agreement.

The next time you shop for a car, keep in mind that salespeople typically get paid commissions at the end of the month. So buying a car near the end of the month means that the salesperson earns an immediate commission. This immediacy raises the gain to reaching agreement (remember that current dollars are worth more than future dollars due to the time value of money), increasing the likelihood that you'll receive a better offer. You can also shop for cars at unpopular times, like Black Friday or Christmas Eve, when demand is low. Look at it from the salesperson's point of view: the cost of selling to you is the forgone opportunity to sell to someone else. If there is no one else around, the cost of selling to you is essentially zero; or equivalently, the salesperson's outside alternative is very poor.

Mergers or acquisitions of rivals can also strengthen your bargaining position. Suppose an insurance company is putting together a network of hospitals to serve its client base. The insurance company bargains with individual hospitals over whether to include them in the network and what price they'll charge if included in the network. To get better prices, the insurance company threatens to exclude one hospital in favor of a nearby substitute hospital. But if the two hospitals merge and bargain together, the insurance company's bargaining alternatives become much worse. If the insurance company fails to reach agreement with the merged hospitals, then its managers must go to the third-best alternative, which might be farther away from its client base. This would reduce the attractiveness—and profitability—of the network, and make the insurance company more eager to reach agreement with the merged hospital.

To make this concrete, let's use a numerical example. Suppose an insurance company can market its network to an employer for $100 per subscriber if the network contains one of two hospitals and for $120 if it contains both, but the insurance company cannot market the plan at all without at least one of the hospitals. The insurance company goes to the first hospital and tells them that they are likely to reach agreement with the second. This makes the gain from adding the hospital to its network that already has the other hospital in it only $20. Under the nonstrategic view of bargaining, this $20 is evenly split between the hospital and the insurance company. The insurance company does the same thing to the second hospital. Thus, before a merger, the insurance company plays each hospital against the other, and each hospital gets only $10 for joining the network.

Now suppose the two hospitals merge and bargain together. The insurance company can no longer threaten to drop one of the hospitals in favor of the other, so the gain from striking a bargain with the merged hospitals is the full $120, which is also evenly split in the Nash bargaining solution. The merger increases the total payment to the hospitals from $20 to $60.

16.3 Conclusion

Let's close this chapter by applying the nonstrategic view of bargaining to the different negotiations in the introduction. To do this, we focus on the outside alternatives of each of the parties. Let's begin with the NBA lockout. If the players don't play, they lose not only their salaries (half of the revenue), but they also lose a year of longevity (the average player plays for only five years). In contrast, the owners lose only the contribution margin (half of the revenue minus the variable cost), which is much smaller than what the players lose. Because they have less to gain from reaching agreement, the owners were less eager to reach agreement, and this allowed them to get most of what they asked for.

Public employee unions are particularly good bargainers because they help elect (and defeat) the politicians they bargain against. If a politician fails to reach agreement with the union, she knows that the union can help put her out of a job. This makes the politician more eager to reach agreement and a weaker bargainer. The end result is that public sector unions earn more than private sector workers who have to bargain against bosses whose compensation is typically tied to the profitability of the company.

Finally, let's look at the bargaining between drug companies and two different types of customers, retail drugstores and hospitals. Drugstores typically carry all the competing brands because this is what their customers want. If they fail to stock a drug, the customer will go to a competing drugstore that carries the drug. The drug store will lose not only the profit on sale of the drug, but also the profit on sales of other items that the customer would have bought when buying the drug. For this reason, drugstores are eager to reach agreement on all brands, so they don't get very good prices.

The greater bargaining power of hospitals is due to their ability to "steer" patients toward a particular drug. To do this, they use formularies, which limit the number of brands in each class. For example, they will carry only one nondrowsy allergy drug. This creates price competition among the nondrowsy allergy drug brands to get onto the formulary. As a result, hospitals are able to get better prices.

In this chapter, we have described two different ways of thinking about bargaining. This raises the obvious question, which is better? The answer is that "it depends" on the particular setting in which you find yourself. If you can credibly commit to a position by, for example, making a take-it-or-leave-it offer, then go ahead. If, as is more likely, commitment is costly or not credible, then try to change the alternatives to agreement, as they determine the terms of agreement.

SUMMARY & HOMEWORK PROBLEMS

Summary of Main Points

- The **strategic view of bargaining** envisions bargaining as a game of chicken where the ability to commit to a position allows a player to capture the lion's share of the gains from trade.
- However, credible commitments are difficult to make because they require players to commit to a course of action against their self-interest.

- The **nonstrategic view of bargaining** does not focus on the explicit rules of the game to understand the likely outcome of the bargaining. Rather, it is the alternatives to agreement that determine the terms of any agreement.
- Anything you can do to increase your opponent's gains from reaching agreement or to decrease your own will improve your bargaining position.

Multiple-Choice Questions

1. For threats or commitments to be effective, they must be
   a. irrational.
   b. profitable.
   c. credible.
   d. none of the above.

2. Fred and his employer both know that Fred can generate $200,000 of profit per year for his company. After negotiations, they agree that he will earn $110,000 in annual compensation. What does this imply for the value of his outside or next best alternative?
   a. $0
   b. $5,000
   c. $10,000
   d. $20,000

3. How many pure strategy equilibria does the following game have?
   a. 0
   b. 1
   c. 2
   d. 3

		Labor	
		Bargain Hard	Be Nice
Management	Bargain Hard	0, 0	20, 10
	Be Nice	12, 18	15, 15

4. In the game in Question 3, how much does Labor earn if they can move first?
   a. 10
   b. 15
   c. 18
   d. 20

5. Consider a vendor–buyer relationship. Which of the following conditions would lead to the buyer having more bargaining power?

   a. Lots of substitutes for the vendor's product are available.
   b. There are relatively few buyers and many vendors.
   c. It costs little for buyers to switch vendors.
   d. All of the above.

6. Consider bargaining in which each party increases its outside option by $10,000. Which of the following is a likely result.
   a. The chance of a deal increases.
   b. Each party's share of the bargaining surplus increases by $10,000.
   c. The bargaining split remains the same.
   d. Each party share of the bargaining surplus increases by $5,000.

7. Pete and Lisa are entering into a bargaining situation in which Pete stands to gain up to $5,000 and Lisa stands to gain up to $1,000, provided they reach agreement. Who is likely to have the stronger bargaining position?
   a. Pete
   b. Lisa
   c. They will be equally effective.
   d. These potential gains will have no impact on bargaining.

8. George and KC have been working jobs that pay $60,000 and $30,000 per year, respectively. They are trying to decide whether to quit their jobs and jointly open up a taco stand on the beach, which they estimate can earn $150,000 per year. How will the taco stand proceeds be split?
   a. They won't quit their jobs.
   b. George gets $90,000 and KC gets $60,000.
   c. George gets $75,000 and KC gets $75,000.
   d. George gets $100,000 and KC gets $50,000.

9. The game of chicken has
   a. a second-mover advantage.
   b. a first-mover advantage.
   c. no sequential-move advantage.
   d. potential sequential-move advantages, depending on the players.

10. Two hospitals are bargaining with an insurance company to get into its provider network. The insurance company can earn $100 if it puts one of the hospitals in its network and $200 if it puts both hospitals in its network. If both hospitals merge and bargain jointly, how much more will they earn?
    a. $0
    b. $50
    c. $100
    d. $200

Individual Problems

16-1 Newspaper Bargaining

Two equal-sized newspapers have an overlap in circulation of 10% (10% of the subscribers subscribe to both newspapers). Advertisers are willing to pay $10 to advertise in one newspaper but only $19 to advertise in both, because they're unwilling to pay twice to reach the same subscribers. What's the likely bargaining negotiation outcome if the advertisers bargain by telling each newspaper that they're going to reach an agreement with the other newspaper, so the gains to reaching agreement are only $9? Suppose the two newspapers merge. What is the likely post-merger bargaining outcome?

16-2 Airline Merger

American Airlines and British Airways are proposing to merge. If British pilots and American pilots are represented by different unions, how would this merger affect airline costs?

16-3 House Closing

You've entered into a contract to purchase a new house, and the closing is scheduled for the next week. It's typical for some last-minute bargaining to occur at the closing table, where sellers often try to tack on extra fees. You have three options for the closing: (1) attend yourself, (2) send an attorney authorized to close only per the previously negotiated terms, or (3) presign all the closing documents per the current terms and not attend the closing. Which of these would be most advantageous from a bargaining position?

16-4 A City and Its Unions

Robert G. Flanders Jr., the state-appointed receiver for Central Falls, RI, said his city's declaration of bankruptcy had proved invaluable in helping it cut costs. Before the city declared bankruptcy, he said, he had found it impossible to wring meaningful concessions out of the city's unions and retirees who were being asked to give up roughly half of the pensions they had earned as the city ran out of cash. Why does bankruptcy give the city bargaining power against its unions?

16-5 Entering International Markets

Your pharmaceutical firm is seeking to open up new international markets by partnering with various local distributors. The different distributors within a country are stronger with different market segments (hospitals, retail pharmacies, etc.) but also have substantial overlap.

a. In Egypt, you calculate that the annual value created by one distributor is $60 million per year, but would be $80 million if two distributors carried your product line. How much of the value can you expect to capture?
b. Argentina also has two distributors with values similar to those in Egypt, but both are run by the government. How does this affect the amount you could capture?
c. In Argentina, if you do not reach an agreement with the government distributors, you can set up a less efficient Internet-based distribution system that would generate $20 million in value to you. How does this affect the amount you could capture?

16-6 PBMs

Pharmaceutical Benefits Managers or PBMs are intermediaries between upstream drug manufacturers and downstream insurance companies. They design formularies (list of drugs that insurance will cover) and negotiate prices with drug companies. PBMs want a wider variety of drugs available to their insured populations, but at low prices. Suppose a PBM is negotiating with two nondrowsy allergy drugs, Claritin and Allegra, for inclusion on the formulary. The "value" or "surplus" created by including one nondrowsy allergy drug on the formulary is $100, but the value of including a second drug is only $30.

a. What's the likely bargaining negotiation outcome if the PBM bargains by telling each drug company that they're going to reach agreement with the other drug company?

b. Now suppose the two drug companies merge. What is the likely post-merger bargaining outcome?

Group Problem

G16-1 Bargaining

Describe some bargaining interaction your company has with another entity (firms producing complementary or substitute products, upstream suppliers, or downstream customers), or between internal divisions within your firm. Describe the bargaining as either a strategic or nonstrategic interaction. Compute payoffs as best you can. Compute the Nash equilibria (strategic) or the likely outcome (nonstrategic view). What can you do to change the bargaining to your advantage? Compute the profit consequences of your advice.

END NOTE

1. John Nash, "The Bargaining Problem," *Econometrica* 18, no. 2 (1950): 155–162.

SECTION 5

Uncertainty

Making Decisions with Uncertainty

$\mathbf{X}$YZ makes money by designing and developing software. They start with a number of ideas, recommend the best ones based on market demand, dig deeper into a few, create products, launch them, and then hope their products succeed. Their design process is illustrated in Figure 17.1.

At the "Recommend" phase, the marketing team provides revenue projections for five candidate products. In the "Discover" phase, the technology "department" makes estimates of the cost and complexity for the best two of the five projects.

The company has the capacity to develop only one product at a time, so it is critical that it picks the most profitable. In 2011, based on the data

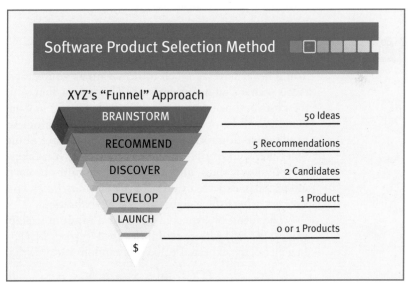

FIGURE 17.1   XYZ Design Process

presented in Table 17.1, the company decided to develop product A because it looked as if it was going to earn $300K more than product B.

TABLE **17.1**
  XYZ Profit Projections

	Product A	Product B
Technology	Complex	Simple
Projected revenue	$1 million	$600,000
Cost	$200,000	$100,000
Profit	$800,000	$500,000

Unfortunately, the product was scrapped prior to launch, which put the company into a financial hole and prompted a formal review of the decision-making process by the board of directors. What the review discovered was a classic trade-off: more technically complex projects had higher potential revenue, but they were also more likely to be scrapped prior to launch, due to their inherent complexity. In fact, a review of last four years of data indicated that only 50% of the more complex products were launched, compared to a 75% launch rate for simpler products.

This mistake could have easily been avoided had XYZ known how to make decisions in the face of uncertainty, the topic of this chapter. In what follows, we show you how to quantify uncertainty by replacing known quantities with *random variables*.[1]

17.1 Random Variables and Probability

You'll never have as much information as you want—especially when you're faced with a significant decision. This means that you cannot simply compute the costs and benefits of a decision (as we did in Chapter 3) because costs or benefits will be uncertain. Instead, we use **random variables** to take account of what we don't know. When we're uncertain about what value a variable will take, we identify the situations in which it takes on different values, list the possible values, and assign a probability to each value. Usually, we are interested in expected values, or *average outcomes*, computed using a weighted average, where the weights are the probabilities.

The mean or expected value of a random variable that can take on two values, $\{x_1, x_2\}$, with probabilities $\{p, 1 - p\}$, is $E[X] = p \times x_1 + (1 - p) \times x_2$. In general, the expected value of a random variable that can take on N values is

$$E[X] = p_1 \times x_1 + p_2 \times x_2 + \cdots + p_N \times x_N$$

where the probabilities sum to one. In this chapter, we will work with discrete random variables, which can assume only a limited number of values.[2]

As a simple example of how to use random variables, suppose you go to a carnival and contemplate playing a game called the Wheel of Cash. The wheel looks like a simple roulette wheel, with three pie-like wedges. On each wedge is a number: $100, $75, and $5. If the cost to play is $50, should you take a chance on the game?

First, note that you have three possible outcomes: $100, $75, and $5. If the wheel is fair—that is, if each outcome has an equal probability of occurring— then the *expected value* of playing the game is $(1/3)(\$100)+(1/3)(\$75)+(1/3)(\$5) = \$60$. So it looks like a really good deal. On average, you'll earn $10 every time you play. But before playing, you should remember this maxim:

If a deal seems too good to be true, it probably is.

If players could really earn, on average, $10 each time they played, we'd expect to see a very long line of players eager to take their chances. Likewise, we'd expect to see the carnival losing money on the game. However, because this is an ongoing operation, we should recognize that it is probably not losing money. What's more likely is that the wheel is *not* fair and that it lands on the $5 wedge more frequently than on the other two wedges. For example, if the wheel is twice as likely to land on the $5 than on the $75 or $100 wedges, then the expected value of playing is only $(1/6)(\$100)+(1/6)(\$75)+(2/3)(\$5) = \$32.50$. On average, you lose (and the carnival earns) $17.50 every time you play.

Now, let's return to the decision facing our software development company, XYZ. If the firm decides to develop the complex product (A), it incurs costs of $200K, and then have a 50% chance of launching, and receiving revenue of $1 million. If the firm decides to develop the simple product (B), it incurs costs of only $100K, and have a 75% chance of launching, but receiving revenue of $600K. What should XYZ do? We diagram the consequences of the decision in Figure 17.2.

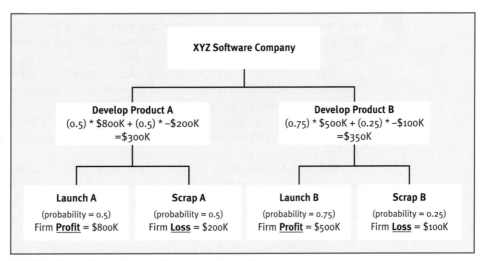

FIGURE **17.2** **Modeling an Uncertain Decision**

Look first at the left branch of the decision tree in Figure 17.2. If XYZ decides to develop product A, it doesn't know whether the product will make it to the launch stage. If it is lucky, it will end up in the first box on the bottom row, and earn $800K (computed as $1,000K revenue minus $200K development cost). If it gets unlucky, the product will not be launched, and the firm will lose the $200K development cost. The firm quantifies its uncertainty by estimating a 50% probability of landing in the first box, and a 50% probability of landing in the second. The expected profit of launching product A is the weighted average of the profit in each box, or $300K. This is computed in the box labeled "Develop Product A."

Now look at the right branch of the decision tree in Figure 17.2. If XYZ decides to develop product B, it doesn't know whether the product will make it to the launch stage. If it is lucky, it will end up in the third box on the bottom row, and earn $500K (computed as $600K revenue minus $100K development cost). If it gets unlucky, the product will not be launched, and the firm will lose the $100K development cost. The firm quantifies its uncertainty by estimating a 75% probability of landing in the third box, and a 25% probability of landing in the fourth. The expected profit of launching product B is the weighted average of the profit in each box, or $350K. This is computed in the box labeled "Develop Product B."

Although more than $50K of expected profit separates the alternatives, you want to make sure that the firm has estimated probabilities precisely enough to distinguish between the two alternatives.

Do not get lulled into a sense of false precision.

A simple way to determine if your probabilities are precise enough is to see how different they would have to be to reverse the decision. If the probability of a successful launch for product B were 67% instead of 75% or if the probability of a successful launch for product A were 55% instead of 50%, the decision would be reversed. If, XYZ Software has no more confidence in one set of probabilities than in the other, the decision is a wash. Thus, XYZ may want to gather more information—perhaps by surveying end users or consulting with outside software engineers in hopes of estimating the probabilities more precisely.

This kind of analysis also clearly identifies the two separate risks that XYZ faces. Since the decision is so close, a next step might be to find a creative way to avoid either possible risk. Perhaps the firm could find a better way to screen potential projects. For example, XYZ may be able to evaluate the software projects sooner, which may reduce the potential loss if they do not launch.

For another example of how uncertainty could change the decision making, let's return to the entry deterrence example in Chapter 15. Suppose that the potential entrant is uncertain about whether the incumbent will price low if it enters, and it quantifies this uncertainty by placing a 40% chance on a low price following entry. So the entrant faces a 60% chance of earning $5, but also a 40% chance of losing $5. The expected value of

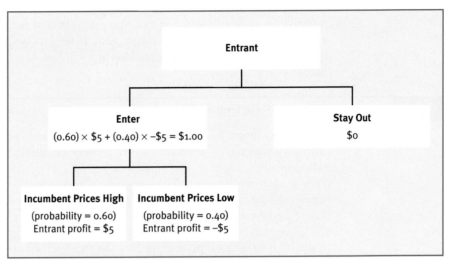

FIGURE **17.3**   **Entry Decision with Uncertainty**

entering is $(0.4)(-\$5) + (0.6)(\$5) = \$1.00$. The expected value of staying out of the industry is \$0. So the expected benefits are \$1.00 larger than the expected costs. We illustrate this decision with a tree in Figure 17.3.

We've seen that using random variables—and their associated probability distributions—rather than exact numbers to do benefit-cost analysis identifies sources of risks and points out ways to mitigate them. But we have another good reason for doing this kind of analysis: if things don't turn out well, you have a good justification for making the wrong decision. By using a distribution that includes a worst-case scenario, you explicitly recognize the possibility that things can turn out poorly. By presenting decision-makers with analyses that account for uncertainty, you allow them to distinguish between bad luck and bad decisions.

To illustrate the final benefit of replacing exact numbers with random variables, let's turn to another example. Suppose an associate invites you to invest in a new business venture. He gives you a prospectus that shows how much money you'll make if you invest. The prospectus is based on estimates of cost and demand. How should you analyze the prospectus?

Your associate has most likely given you a best-case scenario (low costs/ high demand). Add other scenarios (low costs/low demand, high costs/high demand, high costs/low demand), and assign probabilities to each scenario. The appropriate number of scenarios will depend on the specific application. Compute profit under each possible outcome, and calculate expected profit as the weighted sum of the possible outcomes. Almost certainly, your associate will do well under all scenarios; you, however, will do well under only a few.

This analysis exposes an incentive conflict between you (the investor) and your associate. In this case, don't invest unless you can better align his incentives with your own. For example, suggest that he accept a payoff that rewards him only if the venture does well. If he declines, then most likely he doesn't believe his own forecasts. This is a kind of *adverse selection*, a topic that we cover in Chapter 19.

17.2 Uncertainty in Pricing

If you don't know your demand, you face uncertainty in pricing. One of the easiest ways to model uncertainty is to classify the number and type of potential customers. Suppose you run a marketing survey and find you have two types of customers: high-value customers willing to pay $8 and low-value consumers willing to pay just $5. Your survey tells you that there are equal numbers of high- and low-value customers.

Obviously, you have two possible options: price high ($8) and sell only to the high-value group, or price low ($5) and sell to everyone. Which price should you choose? The answer is, "It depends." In this case, it depends on your costs, which we'll set at $3 per unit for illustrative purposes.

We plot the decision tree in Figure 17.4. If you price high, you earn $8 − $3 = $5, provided you get a high-value customer. Since such sales happen only 50% of the time, the expected profit is $2.50. If you price low, you sell all the time, and you earn $5 − $3 = $2. So, price high and sell half as many goods, and earn an *expected* $0.50 more on each unit you sell.

Note that with this high-price strategy, you're left with unconsummated wealth-creating transactions—the low-value customer is willing to pay $5 for a good that costs you $3 to produce. To consummate these transactions, you may want to try price discrimination (see Chapters 13 and 14).

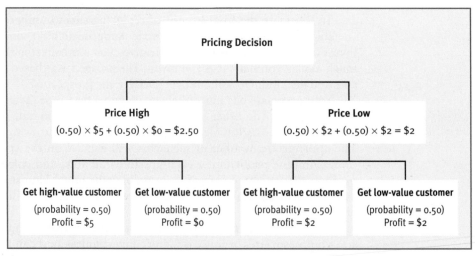

FIGURE **17.4** Pricing Decision with Uncertainty

Price Discrimination

If you can identify the two types of customers, set different prices for each group and prevent arbitrage between them, and then you can price discriminate. Sell at a price of $8 to the high-value customers and at a price of $5 to the low-value customers. A common strategy can exploit observing low-value customers rejecting the high price and leave. Try to offer a discount of $3 before they exit the store.

However, once your customers learn you're discriminating, high-value customers will try to mimic the behavior or appearance of low-value customers to get the lower prices. Figuring out how to correctly identify low- and high-value customers is critical for any price discrimination scheme.

To see how identification matters, consider car salespeople. By making customers wait at the dealership before offering them a price discount, salespeople can identify low-value customers. The longer customers are willing to wait, the bigger the price discount they receive. This discrimination scheme works because the opportunity cost of time is higher for high-value customers. Only low-value customers are willing to wait for better offers.

To defeat this kind of discrimination, try to mimic the behavior of low-value customers. If it's too difficult for you, or if you're too impatient, hire a negotiating agent who can bargain for you.

According to a 1995 article[3] in the *American Economic Review*, new-car salespeople tend to give worse offers (higher prices) to women and minority buyers. The article described a study employing "testers" who were given identical credit histories and bargaining scripts. The study found that women and minority testers received worse offers than their nonminority male counterparts.

Surprisingly, these offers did not vary with the race or gender of the salesperson—minority and female salespeople discriminated against minority and female car buyers, just as their male and nonminority counterparts did. The article concluded that the discrimination did not arise from racial or gender bias but rather, race and gender helped identify the customer's willingness to pay. This kind of "statistical" discrimination is profitable, but also illegal.

Why, then, do salespeople think women and minority buyers are willing to pay more? It could be that nonminority men are better bargainers because they have better access to information about the costs of the car or perhaps they simply have a "taste" for bargaining.

17.3 Data-Driven Decision Making

At the end of her workday, Amy, a young brand manager at Shoebuy.com, found herself in the elevator with the CEO. He asked about online sales of her brand. When Amy admitted that online sales were sluggish, the CEO suggested that displaying product reviews before product features might increase sales. When the elevator opened on the ground floor, Amy said that she had forgotten something and then went back to her office to run an experiment. She set up two sites, one with the product features before product reviews and one with the opposite. Every other online shopper was switched between the two sites. Within 24 hours, Amy had collected enough data to determine which display worked best. Three days later, she e-mailed the CEO to report the results of her experiment: putting the reviews in front of the features increased sales by 3%. Amy received a promotion by year's end, and her "open mind" and "willingness to experiment" were mentioned in her performance review.

Increasingly, firms are hiring "quants" to run experiments to resolve the uncertainty around business decisions. They answer questions like where best to site new facilities or close old ones, how high to set prices, or how to reduce employee turnover. Typically, these are questions about causality, like "Will doing X increase Y?" To answer them, data are collected on outcomes (like sales) from a group exposed to X, the "treatment group," and those not exposed, the "control group." In Amy's case, the customers presented with the new design of product features before product reviews made up the treatment group. Ideally, estimating the casual effect of a treatment X on outcome Y would require us to observe the same group with and without the treatment. Strictly speaking, this is impossible. The same individual cannot be in both groups. Instead, a control group is constructed to be as close an approximation to the treated group as possible. Good analyses are those that are able to construct good controls.

The enemy of a good control is **selection bias**. Selection bias occurs when the treatment group differs systematically from the control group. When this occurs, some of measured effect is due to both the causal effect of the treatment (what we want to estimate) as well as "selection bias" (the underlying difference between the two groups). Unless the selection bias is negligible, our estimate could incorrectly suggest a bad decision.

Observed effect = Treatment effect + Selection bias

Different analytical tools have been developed to construct good controls for different contexts with the goal of eliminating selection bias. Ultimately, a manager will have to evaluate how well they work.

The simplest technique is often the best. In the Shoebuy experiment above, assigning every other user coming to the site is a way to eliminate selection bias. Since there is no reason to think that consumers who arrive near each other differ in any systematic way, any differences between the groups would tend to wash out. Since there is no selection bias, the observed difference between the groups is due solely to the treatment effect. This is why **randomized experiments**, in which the subjects of the experiment are assigned to the treatment group in a random or unbiased way, have come to be regarded as "the gold standard" in data analytics.

Whenever possible, run simple randomized experiments to get unbiased estimates of the treatment effect.

Increasingly, however, firms must use nonexperimental data on choices by consumers, employees, vendors, and so on. This push has led to the new job title of "data scientists" who might use "machine learning" to discern patterns in "big data." No matter the size of the data or how it is processed, selection bias remains the biggest problem. Without an experiment, a control group has to be constructed after the fact. Because it is not randomized, it is possible for unexpected differences between the treatment and control groups to bias the results.

For example, say Shoebuy is trying to decide whether displaying shoe features prominently affects sales. It might be tempting for Amy to try to estimate the benefit of displaying shoe features more prominently by comparing historical sales of shoes when features have been displayed to sales and when features have not been displayed.

To see how selection bias could complicate inference, look at Table 17.2. Each row shows what *would have happened* if we could observe both treatment (features displayed prominently) and control conditions (features not displayed prominently). This is hypothetical because we don't really know what would have happened to the treatment group if it was not treated or the control group if it was treated. The true display effect is $25,000 − $9,000 = $16,000 for the treated group versus $21,000 − $24,000 = −$4,000 for the untreated group. This difference in effects is probably because features are already displayed prominently where they are important (e.g., rubber sole for winter boots or cushioning for running shoes). For the other shoes, displaying these features merely clutters the marketing message and depresses sales.

Amy compares what she does observe, the two diagonal values of $25,000 for the treated and $24,000 for the control to estimate a $1,000 effect. She concludes that displaying features does not help sales very much. The marketing department knows better and now looks suspiciously at any further analyses that Amy produces. Her estimate includes selection bias because the marketing department has already acted on information that Amy wants to test for. It is not uncommon for the analyst to be asked to confirm what the manager already knows and has acted on and this can result in selection bias. The better approach was to run the experiment that Amy ran at the beginning of this section.

TABLE **17.2**

Changing Display Formats

	Sales if Displayed ($)	Sales if Not Displayed ($)	Display Effect ($)
Shoes with Features Displayed Prominently	25,000	9,000	16,000
Shoes without Features Displayed Prominently	21,000	24,000	−4,000

Observed values in **bold** and unobserved values in gray.

An additional problem with data analytics based on the flood of non-experimental data is researcher bias. Sometimes the analyst has the wrong incentives, for example, his or her compensation depends on a certain outcome. Since the comparison group is determined after the data are collected, the analyst has some discretion when deciding which observations belong in the comparison group and which do not. This may create a temptation to admit some selection bias into the analysis in order to generate the desired, but wrong, result. Instead of data driving the decisions, decisions are determining which data are used. When this occurs, you might get severely biased results. For unbiased analyses, analysts should not be compensated based on the results they generate.

17.4 Minimizing Expected Error Costs

Rather than making decisions that maximize *expected* profits (i.e., those whose *expected* benefits are bigger than their *expected* costs), it is sometimes useful to think instead about minimizing *expected* "error costs." This approach is useful when one of your alternatives would work well in one state of the world but not the other, and you are uncertain about which state of the world you are in. For example, XYZ's vice president for new products must decide which products to bring to market and which to pull the plug on. Formally, she wants to know whether the product launch will be profitable. She conducts cost and market research studies to assess the probability, p, that a product launch is profitable.

We illustrate this decision in Table 17.3. The two alternatives are represented by the two rows, and our uncertainty is represented by the columns. In other words, she can choose a row, but she doesn't know which column she is in. If she decides to launch the product and it is profitable, then our column matches the row, and her error cost is zero. Likewise, if she kills the project and it is unprofitable, the column again matches the row. The two errors are represented by the off-diagonal elements in the table: she can kill a profitable product (a "false positive" or "Type I error") that has a cost of C_I; or she can launch an unprofitable product (a "false negative" or "Type II error") with a cost of C_{II}.

TABLE **17.3**

Error Costs of a Product Launch

		REALITY		
		Profitable (Probability = p)	Unprofitable (Probability = $1 - p$)	Expected Error Cost
Decisions	Launch product	0	C_{II}	$(1 - p) \times C_{II}$
	Do not launch product	C_I	0	$p \times C_I$

The optimal decision is to choose the row with the smaller *expected* error costs. If she launches the product, it could be unprofitable, resulting in expected error costs of $(1-p) \times C_{II}$. If she kills the product, there is still a probability p that it would have been profitable and she caused an expected cost of $p \times (C_I)$. Therefore, launch the product if $(1-p) \times C_{II} < p \times C_I$. She needs three pieces of information to make the decision: the size of the two error costs and the probability. Of these, there is often more uncertainty about the probability p.

You can use a type of break-even analysis to determine how high p would have to be before a product launch is profitable. The probability that equates the two expected errors is $\overline{P} = C_I / (C_I + C_{II})$. If p is above $\overline{P}$, approve the project. But will our vice president for product introduction be too cautious? A failed product launch will become all too apparent to everyone, including her superiors. In contrast, a scrubbed product launch that would have been profitable is less apparent simply because we do not observe what did not happen. Since her career advancement is likely to be hindered by noticeable mistakes, she has an incentive to set too high of a value for $\overline{P}$, or be too cautious, so as to avoid the types of mistakes that are most visible.

Another way for her to avoid mistakes is to continue to gather information that will make her more certain that her estimate of p is above P (or below it). With more and better cost studies, focus groups, and pilot studies, she becomes more certain of making the right decision. The value of this information is that the firm will benefit from smaller decision error costs. The important trade-off is usually the cost of delay. Dawdling will cut into a finite product lifecycle or will allow another firm to enter first. Optimally, she would balance the value of more precise information with these costs of delay. However, the same factors that led her to set too high a standard could also lead her to require too much certainty.

This type of analysis is also useful for balancing the risks of overpricing and underpricing errors, which we discussed in Chapter 12. Suppose that a cruise ship faces an uncertain demand. To model the benefits and costs of a pricing decision, consider two states of the world: high demand and low demand. If demand turns out to be high, it would be an error to underprice. If demand turns out to be low, overpricing is a mistake. Predict the probability of demand being high or low, and the costs of under- or overpricing mistakes. Pick the option that minimizes your expected error costs.

17.5 Risk versus Uncertainty

Our approach so far has described uncertainty as something that can be quantified using random variables; that is, you can list the possible outcomes and assign probabilities to each of those outcomes. Some scholars draw a distinction between "risk"—uncertainty that can be modeled with random variables—and "uncertainty," which refers to outcomes that we cannot foresee or whose probabilities we cannot estimate. In other words, *uncertainty* is a way of characterizing what we don't know about the distribution of the random variables themselves.[4]

Understanding the difference between risk and uncertainty can be critical. Risk can be quantified, priced, and traded. It can even be hedged with large pools of assets. Uncertainty, in contrast, is much more difficult to deal with. And, mistaking risk for uncertainty can have devastating consequences because it leads to overconfidence.

At least part of blame for the recent financial crisis can be laid at the feet of bankers who mistakenly thought they were hedging the risk associated with complex financial instruments like collateralized debt obligations (CDOs). This mistaken assumption came from statistical models of risk, constructed from random variables, and tested on data from a period without any extreme events.[5] When the financial crisis hit, it was an outcome far outside the predictions of most statistical models, and the banks found that their hedges could not prevent them from insolvency.

So, how do you deal with uncertainty? Gathering more or better information is often a good place to start. Some companies have turned to prediction markets to help them try to quantify uncertain situations.[6] For example, retailer Best Buy uses dispersed sets of nonexperts to predict a variety of outcomes like holiday sales rates. Google also uses internal prediction markets mostly focused on demand and usage forecasting. Prediction markets gather information from a wide group of people in order to try to turn uncertainty into risk.

Despite our best efforts, we can never be sure that the models we use to quantify risk are the right ones. In other words, uncertainty is something that we cannot eliminate. Consequently, it makes sense to design organizations that can adapt to it—by keeping your options open as long as possible. We leave you with a piece of advice from an organization that is designed to succeed in the most uncertain of environments. The *Warfighting* manual of the U.S. Marines advises us to design flexible, decentralized, organizations to succeed in this "intrinsically unpredictable" environment:

> Because we can never eliminate uncertainty, we must learn to fight effectively despite it. We can do this by developing simple, flexible plans; planning for likely contingencies; developing standing operating procedures; and fostering initiative among subordinates.

SUMMARY & HOMEWORK PROBLEMS

Summary of Main Points

- When you're uncertain about the costs or benefits of a decision, assign a simple probability distribution to the variable and compute expected costs and benefits.
- When customers have unknown values, you face a familiar trade-off: price high and sell only to high-value customers, or price low and sell to all customers.
- If you can identify high-value and low-value customers, you can price discriminate

and avoid the trade-off. To avoid being discriminated against, high-value customers will try to mimic the behavior and appearance of low-value customers.

- Decisions are increasingly being driven by data analytics. When possible run randomized experiments. Otherwise, consider how systematic differences between the control and treatment group might generate selection bias that limits the usefulness of the analysis.

- If you are facing a decision where one of your alternatives would work well in one state of the world but not in the other, and you are uncertain about which state of the world you are in, think about how to minimize expected error costs.
- Because failed initiatives are visible, but never-attempted initiatives are not, guard against employees becoming too cautious.
- Risk can be quantified, estimated, and hedged. Uncertainty cannot. Don't mistake risk for uncertainty, and try to design institutions flexible enough to deal with unforeseen contingencies.

Multiple-Choice Questions

1. You are taking a multiple-choice test that awards you 1 point for a correct answer and penalizes you 0.25 points for an incorrect answer. If you have to make a random guess and there are five possible answers, what is the expected value of guessing?
   a. 0.5 points
   b. 0.25 points
   c. −0.25 points
   d. 0 points

2. A franchise restaurant chain is considering a new store in an unserved part of town. Its finance group estimates an NPV of $10 million if the population growth is 10% (40% probability), an NPV of $4 million if the population does not grow (30% probability), and an NPV of −$4 million if the population shrinks 5% (30% probability). What is the expected value of NPV (to the nearest dollar) for the following situation?
   a. $3.4 million
   b. $4.0 million
   c. $4.6 million
   d. $5.2 million

3. You've just decided to add a new line to your manufacturing plant. Compute the expected loss/profit from the line addition if you estimate the following:

- There's a 50% chance that profit will increase by $100,000.
- There's a 30% chance that profit will remain the same.
- There's a 20% chance that profit will decrease by $15,000.
   a. Gain of $100,000
   b. Gain of $70,000
   c. Loss of $53,000
   d. Gain of $47,000

4. Your software development company is considering investing in a new mobile app. If it goes viral (10% probability), you expect an NPV of $1,000,000; if it is moderately successful (20% probability), you expect an NPV of $200,000; and if it fails (70% probability), you expect an NPV of −$200,000. What is the expected NPV of the product?
   a. $0
   b. $280,000
   c. $333,000
   d. None of the above

5. Suppose an investment project has an NPV of $75 million if it becomes successful and an NPV of −$25 million if it is a failure. What is the minimum probability of success above which you should make the investment?
   a. 1/2
   b. 1/3
   c. 1/4
   d. 1/10

6. To test the effectiveness of two Web advertising agencies, you increase your ad purchase with agency A by 50% without changing your purchase through agency B. The referrals to your website from agency A increased by only 34% but the referrals from agency B fell by 21%. What do you estimate the referrals per dollar are through agency A?
   a. 1.2 referrals per dollar
   b. 1.1 referrals per dollar
   c. 1.0 referrals per dollar
   d. 0.9 referrals per dollar

7. Your company has a customer list that includes 3,000 people. Your market research indicates that 90 of them responded to the coupon. If you send a coupon to one customer at random, what's the probability that he or she will use the coupon?
   a. 0.03
   b. 0.09
   c. 0.30
   d. 0.90

8. Your production line has recently been producing a serious defect. One of two possible processes, A and B, could be the culprit. From past experience you know that the probability that A is causing the problem is 0.8, but investigating A costs $100,000 while investigating B costs only $20,000. What are the expected error costs of shutting down process B first?
   a. $80,000
   b. $20,000
   c. $16,000
   d. $4,000

9. You have two types of buyers for your product. Forty percent of buyers value your product at $10 and 60 percent value it at $6. What price maximizes your expected revenue?
   a. $10
   b. $6
   c. $7.60
   d. $8

10. You are considering entry into a market in which there is currently only one producer (incumbent). If you enter, the incumbent can take one of two strategies, price low or price high. If he prices high, then you expect a $60K profit per year. If he prices low, then you expect $20K loss per year. You should enter if
   a. you believe demand is inelastic.
   b. you believe the probability that the incumbent will price low is greater than 0.75.
   c. you believe the probability that the incumbent will price low is less than 0.75.
   d. you believe the market size is growing.

Individual Problems

17-1 Global Expansion

You're the manager of global opportunities for a U.S. manufacturer who is considering expanding sales into Asia. Your market research has identified the market potential in Malaysia, Philippines, and Singapore as described next:

	Success Level		
	Big	Mediocre	Failure
Malaysia			
Probability	0.3	0.3	0.4
Units	1,200,000	600,000	0
Philippines			
Probability	0.3	0.5	0.2
Units	1,000,000	320,000	0
Singapore			
Probability	0.7	0.2	0.1
Units	700,000	400,000	0

The product sells for $10 and has unit costs of $8. If you can enter only one market, and the cost of entering the market (regardless of which market you select) is $250,000, should you enter one of these markets? If so, which one? If you enter, what is your expected profit?

17-2 Game Show Uncertainty

In the final round of a TV game show, contestants have a chance to increase their current winnings of $1 million to $2 million. If they are wrong, their prize is decreased to $500,000. A contestant thinks his guess will be right 50% of the time. Should he play? What is the lowest probability of a correct guess that would make playing profitable?

17-3 Ad Agencies

The residential division of Prism's high-speed Internet service uses one advertising agency while its commercial division uses another. Two analysts, Andy and Brad, are asked to test evaluate the effectiveness of the two agencies. Andy proposes an A/B test that compares the click-through rates per ad for the two agencies. Brad proposes a difference-in-difference test in which the budgets for both agencies are increased by 50% and the percent change in click-through rates are compared. What might be the sources of selection bias for the two proposals? Which is likely to be smaller?

17-4 Disposing of Used Assets

Your company has a customer who is shutting down a production line, and it is your responsibility to dispose of the extrusion machine. The company could keep it in inventory for a possible future product and estimates that the reservation value is $250,000. Your dealings on the second-hand market lead you to believe that there is a 0.4 chance a random buyer will pay $300,000, a 0.25 chance the buyer will pay $350,000, a 0.1 chance the buyer will pay $400,000, and a 0.25 chance it will not sell. If you must commit to a posted price, what price maximizes profits?

17-5 Saint Petersburg Gambles

You are offered the following gamble based on coin flips. If the first head occurs on the first flip, you get $2. If the first head occurs on the second flip you get $4, and so on, so that if the first head is on the Nth flip, you get $2N. The game

ends only when a flip of the coin results in heads. What is the expected value of this gamble? When offered, most people say they would only pay less than $10 to play this game. What are two reasons why people are willing to pay so much less than the expected value?

17-6 Hiring

The HR department is trying to fill a vacant position for a job with a small talent pool. Valid applications arrive every week or so, and the applicants all seem to bring different levels of expertise. For each applicant, the HR manager gathers information by trying to verify various claims on resume, but some doubt about fit always lingers when a decision to hire or not is to be made. What are the Type I and II decision error costs? Which decision error is more likely to be discovered by the CEO? How does this affect the HR manager's hiring decisions?

Group Problem

G17-1 Uncertainty

Describe a decision your company has made when facing uncertainty. Compute the expected costs and benefits of the decision. Offer advice on how to proceed. Compute the profit consequences of the advice.

END NOTES

1. All of the insights we develop can be gleaned from discrete random variables that typically take on only a few possible values. A continuous random variable assumes an infinite number of values corresponding to the points on an interval (or more than one interval).
2. A continuous random variable assumes an infinite number of values corresponding to the points on an interval (or more than one interval).
3. Ian Ayres and Peter Siegelman, "Race and Gender Discrimination in Negotiation for the Purchase of a New Car," *American*

Economic Review 84 (1995): 304. For a further discussion of the results, see http://islandia.law.yale.edu/ayers/carint.htm.
4. The distinction between risk and uncertainty traces back to the work of economist Frank Knight. See F. H. Knight, *Risk, Uncertainty and Profit* (New York: Augustus Kelley, 1921).
5. Felix Salmon, "Recipe for Disaster: The Formula That Killed Wall Street," *Wired*, February 23, 2009.
6. Renee Dye, "The Promise of Prediction Markets," *McKinsey Quarterly*, April 2008.

18 Auctions

Over 700,000 tons of fish move annually through Tokyo's Tsukiji market, the world's largest, busiest fish market. Tourists line up before 3 A.M. to gain a glimpse at the market's centerpiece, the daily sale of dozens of large tuna, each weighing hundreds of pounds. The tuna do not carry price tags. Instead, wholesalers, restaurant owners, and fish stores bid against each other. A frenzied cloud of hand signals can lead the price on a desirable fish to skyrocket in seconds. The first auction of 2017 saw one prized bluefin tuna (about 10,000 pieces of sushi) sell for over $600,000.

Half a world away, just outside of Amsterdam, sits the 128 acre building that houses the Aalsmeer Flower Auction, the second largest building by footprint in the world. Each day, a majority of the world's wholesale flowers are sold here. Rather than bidders competing to increasing the price, however, a large display shows a decreasing price on each lot of flowers. The first bidder to accept the current price by pressing a button provided to each bidder ends the auction. Press now and win, or wait a second for a better price, but risk someone else jumping in.

Auctions are also used by CarBargains. However, instead of many buyers competing to buy a single good, the service organizes a competition among sellers—local car dealers—to sell to a single consumer. For one student, CarBargains persuaded six dealers to participate in an auction, and the bids ranged from $1,500 over factory invoice to $100 over invoice. Unfortunately, the dealer with the exact car (options, color, etc.) that the student wanted came in with the worst bid. But when the student showed the dealer the $100-over-invoice bid from another dealer, he matched the offer and took care of the deal himself. This cut out the salesman, which meant that the dealer didn't have to pay a sales commission. It also saved the student the time and hassle of negotiating with a salesman. She concluded that the service was well worth the service's cost.

In previous chapters, we examined various types of competition, like price competition and bargaining. In this chapter, we examine another type of competition, auctions. Not only do auctions identify the high-value bidder but they also set a price for the item, thereby avoiding costly bargaining. But, as the CarBargains example indicates, auctions are often used in conjunction with bargaining. In this case, the auction identified a potential negotiating partner, and the student used the outside alternative of rival bids to negotiate a deal.

18.1 Oral Auctions

A variety of auction formats are available, and we start with the most familiar.

In an **oral auction** or **English auction**, bidders submit increasing bids until only one bidder remains. The item is awarded to this last remaining bidder.

Since every bidder is willing to bid up to his value, but no higher, the high-value bidder wins the item as soon as the second-highest-value bidder drops out.

For example, if five bidders have values of $8, $5, $3, $2, and $1, the bidder with the $8 value will win at a price close to $5, right after the bidder with the next-highest value drops out of the bidding. In auctions, it is the losing bidders who determine the price; the stronger they are, the higher the price.

Consider a retail store with a single, unique item remaining in stock but with two interested customers. To illustrate the benefits of using an auction, we compare it to a fixed price. Say the store assumes that each customer values the product at either a high value ($70) or low value ($50), with each value equally likely. The four possibilities are listed in Table 18.1. In setting a fixed price, the store faces the familiar trade-off: price high and sell only if a high-value consumer shows up (a 75% chance), or price low and sell to everyone. A high price generates more *expected* revenue ($52.50 = $70 × 0.75) than a low price ($50 = $50 × 1.00).

TABLE **18.1**

Oral Auction with Two Bidders

Bidder 1 ($)	Bidder 2 ($)	Probability	Winning Bid ($)
50	50	0.25	50
50	70	0.25	50
70	50	0.25	50
70	70	0.25	70

Suppose instead that the store uses an oral auction among these two customers. The winning bid, listed in the last column of Table 18.1, is equal to the second-highest value. If the auctioneer is lucky, he'll get two high-value bidders, and the winning bid will be $70. However, this outcome occurs only 25% of the time. The other 75% of the time, the second-highest value is just $50. The *expected* revenue of the auction is the weighted average of these two outcomes, where the weights are the probabilities of each: $70 × 0.25 + $50 × 0.75 = $55. Compared to a fixed price of $70, the auction in this case gives the seller higher *expected* revenue.

Now suppose that three bidders show up at an auction. As before, they could be either high-value ($70) or low-value ($50) bidders. What is the *expected* revenue from the auction?

The possible outcomes of the auction are listed in Table 18.2. Again, if the auctioneer is lucky, two or more high-value bidders will show up, so the winning bid is $70. But this happens only 50% of the time. The other 50% of the time, we expect at most one high-value bidder, so the winning bid is $50. Expected revenue is $70 × 0.50 + $50 × 0.50 = $60.

TABLE **18.2**

Oral Auction with Three Bidders

Bidder 1 ($)	Bidder 2 ($)	Bidder 3 ($)	Probability	Winning Bid ($)
50	50	50	0.125	50
50	50	70	0.125	50
50	70	50	0.125	50
70	50	50	0.125	50
50	70	70	0.125	70
70	50	70	0.125	70
70	70	50	0.125	70
70	70	70	0.125	70

Comparing Tables 18.1 and 18.2, we see that more bidders raise the expected price because you are more likely to get more strong (high-value) bidders.

Stronger losing bidders lead to higher winning bids.

For example, eBay auctions that remain open for ten days return 42% higher prices than three-day auctions, presumably because the ten-day auctions attract a larger number of bidders.[1]

18.2 | Second-Price Auctions

A **Vickrey auction** or **second-price auction** is a type of sealed-bid auction in which bidders submit their bids without knowing the bids of other participants. The item is awarded to the highest bidder, but the winner pays the *second-highest* bid.

When Google revamped its online advertising platform in 2002, it replaced the traditional fixed price with an auction. To show an ad to a Web visitor, an advertiser had to be the highest bidder. However, instead of charging this advertiser how much they bid, they charged them the bid of the next-highest (losing) bidder. Why would an auctioneer use an auction that seems to leave money on the table? The answer is that a second-price auction induces bidders to bid more aggressively because their bid determines only whether they win, *not* the price they pay.

The optimal strategy in a second-price auction is to bid *exactly* your value. This is because a second-price auction is actually strategically equivalent to the English auction described earlier. In an English auction, everyone is willing to bid up to his or her value, and the highest-valued bidder wins at a price equal to (or just above) the second-highest value. That's precisely the outcome that a second-price auction achieves. A second-price auction allows the auctioneer to simulate what would have happened in an English auction, but without the need to have bidders show up at the same place and time.

William Vickrey shared the 1996 Nobel Prize in Economics for inventing the Vickrey auction and establishing its equivalence to oral auctions. Recently, however, economists have discovered that second-price auctions were used to sell rare stamps as early as 1893.[2] To accommodate bidders who didn't want to travel to participate in a live auction, stamp dealers held second-price auctions through the mail. So, Vickrey auctions predated Vickrey by nearly a century!

Vickrey auctions are also useful for auctioning off multiple units of the same item—say, 10 laptop computers. As in the second-price auction, the highest losing bid determines the price. In this case, the highest losing bid is the 11th highest. As in the second-price auction, it is optimal to bid your value.

18.3 First-Price Auctions

In a sealed-bid **first-price auction**, the highest bidder wins the item at a price equal to the highest bid.

In contrast to a second-price auction, in a sealed-bid first-price auction, you have to pay the amount you bid. Consequently, each bidder faces a trade-off: he can bid higher and raise the probability of winning, but doing so lowers his surplus (or profit) if he does win. Since bidding exactly your value guarantees zero profit whether you win or lose, each bidder *shades* his bid; that is, he balances these two effects by bidding below his value. In these auctions, experience is the best teacher. In general, you should bid more—shade your value less—if the competition is stronger.

18.4 Bid Rigging

Collusion among bidders is one of the biggest challenges for an auctioneer. To illustrate the effects of *collusion* or *bid rigging*, let's return to our simple oral auction in which bidders have values of $8, $5, $3, $2, and $1. Imagine that the two high-value bidders form a *bidding ring* or *cartel*. What is the winning bid?

A cartel earns money by eliminating competition among its members. Here, the two highest-value bidders (those willing to pay $8 and $5) decide not to bid against each other. To win the auction, they have to outbid the highest noncartel member, whose value is $3. Collusion reduces the auctioneer's revenue by 40%, from $5 (what the price would have been without the cartel) to $3 (the price with the cartel). The cartel members typically split this $2 profit between them.

This kind of agreement between bidders in an auction is a criminal violation of the antitrust laws of the United States and of most other developed countries. In addition, most countries offer amnesty to the first conspirator willing to testify against fellow conspirators. These amnesty schemes create a prisoners' dilemma among the conspirators. This "race to the courthouse" has led to the discovery and prosecution of a number of different cartels.

In one type of cartel, antique dealers refrained from bidding against one another at an estate sale. They met after the auction to "reauction" the goods they won at the estate sale. The difference between what the good sold for in the first auction and what it sold for in the second or "knockout" auction is the profit that the cartel members split among themselves. A more common type of cartel is the bid-rotation scheme where bidders refrain from bidding against one another in exchange for similar consideration when it's their "turn" to win.

The weakness of a bid-rotation scheme is that each cartel member must wait for his turn to win. And, cartel members can easily cheat by bidding slightly above the agreed-on bid. Grouping many contracts or items together into a single big auction raises the gains from cheating on the cartel. This leads to our first observation about bid rigging:

Collusion is more likely in small, frequent auctions than in big, infrequent ones.

In a sealed-bid auction, collusion requires the cooperation of *all* the cartel members; that is, the cartel members must figure a way out of the prisoners' dilemma. If any of the cartel members raises his bid above the agreed-on price, he could win the item for himself at a very low price. This temptation often leads cartel members to cheat on the cartel, which makes cartels more difficult to organize.

In an oral auction, however, cheating on the cartel offers no benefit. The cartel members know immediately if one of their own tries to bid higher than the agreed-on price. In retaliation, the other cartel members begin bidding competitively, and there is no gain to cheating. This leads to our second observation about bid rigging:

Collusion is more likely in oral auctions than in sealed-bid auctions.

For bidders to collude, they must devise a way to punish cheaters. But to punish cheaters, you have to know who they are. If cheaters don't fear punishment from other cartel members, then cheating is likely, and the cartel is unlikely to survive. This leads to our third observation about bid rigging:

Collusion is more likely when winning bidders and winning bids are identified.

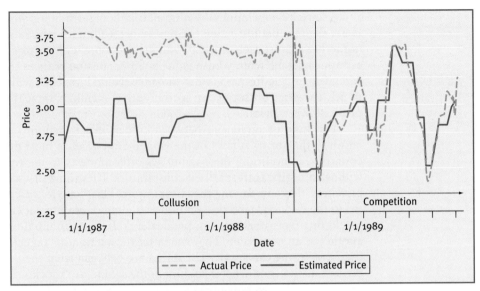

FIGURE **18.1** Collusion in Frozen Fish Bidding

Collusion can be quite costly for the auctioneer. The graph in Figure 18.1 plots the average winning price of a conspiracy that collapsed when a grand jury began investigating auctions to supply the U.S. Navy with frozen fish. The investigators computed the effect of the conspiracy by *backcasting* (the opposite of forecasting) from the competitive period into the collusive period (the darker line in Figure 18.1). This allowed them to determine that prices would have been 23% lower during the collusive period had bidders behaved competitively. The judge used this information to help determine how long the conspirators would go to prison.

Among the reasons for the conspiracy was a set of "domestic content" rules, which prevented foreign suppliers from bidding on new contracts. Without foreign competition, it was quite easy for the few domestic suppliers of frozen seafood to form a cartel. Another reason was the frequent (up to 10 each week) auctions, which made the bid-rotation scheme fairly easy to organize.[3]

18.5 Common-Value Auctions

So far, we have considered auctions in which each bidder has her own *private value* for whatever is being auctioned. Bidders for an unexplored oil field, on the other hand, have a *common value* because the amount of oil in the field determines the value of the field and it is the same for all bidders. In a **common-value auction**, the value is the same for each bidder, but no one knows what it is for sure. Each bidder has only an estimate of the unknown value.

Imagine that you are bidding on a suitcase of cash. You are more likely to win the auction if you overestimate the amount of money in the suitcase than if you underestimate it. But you are also more likely to lose money. Winning in a common-value auction is bad news: it means that your estimate was the highest and most optimistic. Since the highest and most optimistic estimate is likely to exceed the actual value, the winner will lose, on average. This is known as the **winner's curse**. The winner's curse does not mean you lost money in an auction (this is called bad luck). It does mean that you bid incorrectly, and put yourself in a position to lose money, on average. To avoid the curse, you must bid as if your estimate is the most optimistic in the first place.

To avoid the winner's curse, you bid as if everyone else thinks the value is less than your estimate.

For example, imagine that you estimate the value of the suitcase of cash at $500. If I were to tell you that everyone else (including some very smart people) thinks it is worth less than $500, would you revise your own estimate downward? This revised estimate—based on the assumption that everyone else is more pessimistic than you are—should serve as the basis of your bid.

How much you should revise your estimate depends in part on how many other bidders there are. Which would make you doubt your estimate more: if I told you that just one other person thinks it is worth less than $500, or 50 people all think so? It is easy to imagine that one other bidder is wrong and you're right, but it is harder to imagine that 50 other people are all wrong. The more competitors there are, the more winning is "bad news," and the lower you should bid.

To avoid the winners' curse, you bid less aggressively as the number of bidders increases.

The winner's curse is especially bad when rival bidders have better information about the value than you do. For example, some bidders for oil fields own neighboring fields and have better estimates of the amount of oil than those without neighboring fields. In this case, you will win only when others think the item isn't worth much, or when you overbid. It's seldom a good idea to bid in common-value auctions when rivals have better information than you do.

If you're the auctioneer, you want to encourage aggressive bidding by releasing as much information as you can about the value of the item. By reducing uncertainty about the value of the item, you mitigate many of the effects of the winner's curse, which encourages bidders to bid closer to their estimated values. Even if you have adverse information about an item, you should still release it. If you don't, bidders will correctly infer that the information is bad.

Oral auctions return higher prices in a common-value setting than sealed-bid auctions.

One way to release information in a common-value auction is to hold an oral auction. Each bidder can see how aggressively rivals are bidding, which reduces uncertainty and reduces the magnitude of the winner's curse. Oral auctions result in more aggressive bidding and higher prices in common-value auctions.

If releasing information is good for the auctioneer, it must be bad for the bidders. Since the value is the same for each bidder, everyone knowing that value leads everyone to bid away any potential profits. The source of profit in a common-value auction is the information that you have and that others do not.

SUMMARY & HOMEWORK PROBLEMS

Summary of Main Points

- In **oral** or **English auctions**, the highest bidder wins but only has to outbid the second-highest bidder. Losing bidders determine the price.
- A **Vickrey or second-price auction** is a sealed-bid auction in which the high bidder wins but pays only the second-highest bid. These auctions are strategically identical to English auctions, but easier to run and well suited for use on the Internet.
- In a **sealed-bid first-price auction**, the high bidder wins and pays his bid. Bidders must balance the probability of winning against the profit they will make if they do win. Optimal bids are less than bidders' private values.
- Bidders can raise profit by agreeing not to bid against one another. If collusion is suspected,
  - do not hold open auctions;
  - do not hold small and frequent auctions;
  - do not announce the winners or the winning bids.
- In a **common-value auction**, everyone has the same value but each has only an estimate of what it is.
- To avoid the **winner's curse** in common-value auctions, bid below your estimated value. Bid as if your estimate is the most optimistic and everyone else thinks it is worth less.
- Oral auctions return higher prices in common-value auctions because they release more information.

Multiple-Choice Questions

1. You are bidding in a second-price auction for a painting that you value at $800. You estimate that other bidders are most likely to value the painting at between $200 and $600. Which of these is likely to be your best bid?
   a. $1,000
   b. $800
   c. $600
   d. $400

2. Which of the following is true about different ways of conducting a private-value auction?
   a. A first-price auction is strategically equivalent to a second-price auction.
   b. A first-price auction is strategically equivalent to an oral English auction.
   c. A second-price auction is strategically equivalent to an oral English auction.
   d. None of the above.

3. Suppose that five bidders with values of $500, $400, $300, $200, and $100 attend an oral auction. Which of these is closest to the winning price?
   a. $500
   b. $400
   c. $300
   d. $200

4. In the above auction, if the bidders with the first- and third-highest values ($500 and $300) collude, which of these is closest to the winning price?
   a. $500
   b. $400
   c. $300
   d. $200

5. In a common-value auction, you should
   a. bid more aggressively the more competitors you face.
   b. bid less aggressively the more competitors you face.
   c. bid the same regardless of the number of competitors.
   d. bid more aggressively when others have better information than you.

6. If a seller is concerned about collusion among bidders, which of the following changes to the auction should the seller make?
   a. Hold frequent, small auctions instead of infrequent large auctions.
   b. Conceal the amount of winning bids.
   c. Publicly announce the name of each auction's winner.
   d. Hold an English auction instead of a sealed-bid first-price auction.

7. You're holding an auction to license a new technology that your company has developed. One of your assistants raises a concern that bidders' fear of the winner's curse may encourage them to shade their bids. How might you address this concern?
   a. Release your analyst's positive scenario for the technology's future profitability.
   b. Release your analyst's negative scenario for the technology's future profitability.
   c. Use an oral auction.
   d. All of the above.

8. Which of the following is true about the winner's curse?
   a. The winner's curse occurs primarily in private-value auctions.
   b. You successfully avoided the winner's curse if you made money in the auction.
   c. The winner's curse means that you bid incorrectly.
   d. The winner's curse means that you lost money in an auction.

9. A bidder's value for a good may be low ($2), medium ($5), or high ($7). There is an equal number of potential bidders having each value. Suppose two bidders participate in a second-price auction. What is the best estimate of the expected revenue from the auction?
   a. $4.11
   b. $3.99
   c. $3.56
   d. $5.00

10. In a first-price auction, you bid _____ your value, and in a second-price auction, you bid _____ your value.
   a. at; above
   b. below; above
   c. below; at
   d. below; below

Individual Problems

18-1 Effects of Collusion

You hold an auction among three bidders. You estimate that each bidder has a value of either $16 or $20 for the item, and you attach probabilities to each value of 50%. What is the expected price? If two of the three bidders collude, what is the price?

18-2 Reserve Prices

A reserve price is a minimum price set by the auctioneer. If no bidder is willing to pay the reserve price, the item is unsold at a profit of $0 for the auctioneer. If only one bidder values the item at or above the reserve price, that bidder pays the reserve price. An auctioneer faces two bidders, each with a value of either $30 or $80, with both values equally probable. What reserve price should the auctioneer set, and what is the expected revenue from auctioning the item with and without a reserve price?

18-3 Reserve Prices II

Consider the problem above, but now each bidder has a value of either $60 or $80. What reserve price should the auctioneer set, and what is the expected revenue from auctioning the item with and without a reserve price?

18-4 Asset Auctions in Sweden

In Sweden, firms that fail to meet their debt obligations are immediately auctioned off to the highest bidder. (There is no reorganization through Chapter 11 bankruptcy.) The current managers are often the high bidders for the company. Why?

18-5 Art Auctions

When a famous painting becomes available for sale, it is often known which museum or collector will be the likely winner. Yet, representatives of other museums that have no chance of winning are actively wooed by the auctioneer to attend anyway. Why?

18-6 Contractor Bidding

Moe Green estimates the cost of future projects for a large contracting firm. Mr. Green uses precisely the same techniques to estimate the costs of every potential job and formulates bids by adding a standard profit markup. For some companies to whom the firm offers its services, no competitors exist, so they are almost certain to get them as clients. For these jobs, Mr. Green finds that his cost estimates are right, on average. For jobs where competitors are also vying for the business, Mr. Green finds that they almost always end up costing more than he estimates. Why does this occur?

Group Problem

G18-1 Using Auctions in Your Business

Identify something you buy or sell that could be bought or sold using an auction. How would you run the auction? Do a benefit-cost analysis of the auction relative to how you currently buy or sell.

END NOTES

1. David Lucking-Reiley, Doug Bryan, Naghi Prasad, and Daniel Reeves, "Pennies from eBay: The Determinants of Price in Online Auctions," *Journal of Industrial Economics* 55 (2007): 223–233.

2. David Lucking-Reiley, "Vickrey Auctions in Practice: From Nineteenth-Century Philately to Twenty-First-Century E-Commerce,"

Journal of Economic Perspectives 14 (2000): 183–192.

3. The cartel and its collapse are described in Luke Froeb, Robert Koyak, and Gregory Werden, "What Is the Effect of Bid-Rigging on Prices?" *Economics Letters* 42 (1993): 419–423.

The Problem of Adverse Selection

With over one billion in annual sales, Zappos is the Internet's largest shoe retailer. Customer service is a key differentiator for Zappos, and its core value is to "Deliver WOW through Service." As part of the hiring process, new recruits participate in a four-week training program to introduce them to the company's strategy, processes, and culture.

Training alone cannot teach employees how to deliver WOW. In addition, it takes the right personality and attitude. But Zappos has not been able to figure out how to measure these intangible qualities. Instead, they use a clever plan to get the WOW employees to identify themselves. After the first week of training, the company offers $4,000 to any new hire who will quit that day. About 3% take the offer. The ones who are left are the ones with the ability to deliver WOW. Zappos has discovered that the $4,000 "screen" is a relatively inexpensive way to reduce the rate of bad hires, to decrease the costs of employee turnover, and to protect the company's reputation for service.[1] After acquiring Zappos, Amazon announced a similar "Pay to Quit" program in 2014, offering its fulfillment-center employees up to $5,000 to leave.

This story illustrates the problem known as **adverse selection**. It arises when one party to a transaction is better informed than another—in this case, workers know more about their work habits and WOW ability than does Zappos or Amazon. Because low-quality workers typically have worse outside options, they are more likely than good ones to accept an offer of employment. Unless employers can distinguish high- from low-quality workers, they are more likely to hire the wrong sort.

In this chapter, we show you how to anticipate adverse selection, how to protect yourself from its consequences, and, in some cases, how to get around it.

19.1 | Insurance and Risk

The adverse selection problem is most easily illustrated in the market for insurance. To understand the demand for insurance, we have to return to our discussion of random variables. A lottery is a random variable with a payment attached to each outcome. If I agree to pay you $100 if a fair coin lands heads-up and $0 otherwise, you face a lottery with an expected value of $50. Your attitude toward risk determines how you value this random payoff.

> A *risk-neutral* consumer values a lottery at its expected value. A risk-averse consumer values a lottery at less than its expected value.

Consider the possibility of trade between a risk-averse seller and a risk-neutral buyer. For instance, a risk-averse consumer might be willing to sell the $100 coin toss lottery for $40, whereas a risk-neutral consumer would be willing to pay $50 for the same lottery. If the two of them transact, say at a price of $45, they create wealth by moving an asset—the lottery—to a higher-value use. After the transaction, the risk-averse seller has $45, a sure payout that he values more than the lottery, and the risk-neutral buyer pays only $45 for a lottery that she values at $50.

Similarly, insurance is a wealth-creating transaction that transfers risk from someone who doesn't want it (the risk-averse consumer) to someone who is willing to accept it for a fee (the risk-neutral insurance company). The only difference from our lottery example is that the risk-averse sellers face a lottery over *bad* outcomes instead of *good* ones.

For example, suppose that Rachel owns a $100 bicycle that might be stolen. The possibility of theft means that the payoff from owning the bicycle is like that of a lottery: lose $100 if the bike is stolen and lose nothing if it isn't. If the probability of theft is 20%, the *expected* cost of the lottery is $(0.2)(\$100) = \$20$.

If Rachel purchases insurance for $25 that reimburses her for the value of her stolen bicycle, she eliminates the risk. By voluntarily transacting, both Rachel and her insurance company are made better off. Rachel pays to eliminate the risk, and the insurance company earns $5, on average, for accepting it. Note that the insurance company never earns $5. If the bike is stolen, it loses $75; if not, it earns $25, so the expected value of offering insurance is $\$5 = 0.2(-\$75) + 0.8(\$25)$.

Insurance is not the only way of moving risk from those who don't want it to those who don't mind it. One of the financial industry's main functions is to move risk from lower- to higher-valued uses. For example, farmers face uncertain future prices for their crops. To get rid of the risk, they sell forward contracts to grain companies or speculators. The buyer of the contract takes possession of the crop on a specified delivery date and accepts the risk that the crop may be worth less than the price. Selling crops before they are planted moves risk from risk-averse farmers to risk-neutral buyers.

19.2 Anticipating Adverse Selection

To illustrate the problem of adverse selection, we modify our bicycle insurance example by assuming that there are two different types of consumers, each facing different risks. One type of consumer lives in a secure area, where the probability of theft is 20%. The other type lives in a less secure area, where the probability of theft is higher—say, 40%. Each consumer is risk-averse and would be willing to buy insurance for $5 more than its expected cost; that is, the low-risk consumer would be willing to pay $25 for insurance, and the high-risk consumer would be willing to pay $45. If the insurance company could tell them apart, it would sell different policies, at different prices, to each.

But when the insurance company cannot distinguish between the high- and low-risk consumers, it faces potential losses. If the company naively offers to sell insurance at an average price of $35, only the high-risk consumers will purchase the insurance. They think it's a great deal because they'd be willing to pay as much as $45 for the insurance. In contrast, the low-risk consumers recognize a bad deal when they see it. They would rather face the possibility of theft than pay $35 for insurance that they value at only $25.

If only high-risk consumers purchase insurance, the insurance company's expected costs are $40, meaning it loses $5 on every policy it sells. This leads to the first important lesson of the chapter:

Anticipate adverse selection and protect yourself against it.

If the insurance company correctly anticipates that only high-risk consumers will buy, it will offer insurance at $45. At this price, only high-risk consumers buy the insurance, but the company does make money on the policies it sells.

To see what happens when you don't anticipate adverse selection, let's turn to a real example. In June 1986, the city of Washington, DC, passed the Prohibition of Discrimination in the Provision of Insurance Act, which outlawed HIV testing by health insurance companies. What do you think happened?

According to press reports at the time, the result was a "mass exodus of insurers from the city." Unable to distinguish low- from high-risk consumers, insurance companies faced the prospect of being able to sell only to high-risk purchasers. The insurance companies, if not the DC government, correctly anticipated adverse selection and realized they could not make money selling only to HIV-positive consumers.

When the law was repealed in 1989, the problem disappeared. Once companies were able to distinguish between consumers with HIV and those without, they offered two polices based on the costs of insuring each population. When you eliminate the information asymmetry—when the company knows who is high risk and who is low risk—there is no adverse selection. President Obama's signature health-care legislation uses a different solution. Like the Washington, DC, measure, it also prohibits insurers from distinguishing high- from low-risk patients, but by requiring everyone to purchase insurance, it prohibits low-risk purchasers from exiting the market.

In financial markets, adverse selection arises when owners of companies seeking to sell shares to the public know more about the prospects of the company than do potential investors. Potential investors should anticipate that companies with relatively poor prospects are the ones most likely to sell stock to the public. For example, small Initial Public Offerings[2] (IPOs) of less than

$100 million lose money in the long term, on average, whereas large IPOs have "normal" returns, equal to those of comparably risky assets. Economists find it puzzling that investors don't anticipate adverse selection by reducing the price they pay for these small IPOs.

Finally, we note that the winner's curse of common-value auctions is a kind of adverse selection. Unless the winning bidder anticipates that she will win only when she has the most optimistic estimate of the item's true value, she'll end up overbidding. Only if bidders anticipate the winner's curse—by bidding as if they have the highest estimate—will they bid low enough to avoid overpaying.

19.3 Screening

If our bicycle insurance company sells at a price of $45, the low-risk consumers will not purchase insurance, even though they would be willing to pay a price ($25) which is more than the cost of the insurance to the insurance company. This leads to the second point of this chapter.

The low-risk consumers are not served because it is difficult to transact with them profitably.

Adverse selection represents a potentially profitable, but unconsummated, wealth-creating transaction. **Screening** (the subject of this section) and **signaling** (the subject of the next section) are two ways to overcome the obstacles to transacting with low-risk individuals.

One obvious solution to the problem of adverse selection is to gather information so you can distinguish high risk from low risk. If, for example, the insurance company can distinguish between high- and low-risk consumers, it can offer two different policies to the two groups—a low-price policy to the low-risk group and a high-price policy to the high-risk group.

This isn't as easy as it sounds. Information gathering can be costly; moreover, privacy and antidiscrimination laws can prevent insurance companies from acquiring (and using) information that lets them sort customers into high- and low-risk groups. For example, your credit report is an excellent predictor of whether you'll be involved in an auto accident. If you give an insurance company permission to look at your credit report, you can get car insurance at a low price, provided your credit is good. But three states, California, Hawaii, and Massachusetts, prohibit car insurance companies from using credit scores to price insurance. This restriction reduces the amount of information available to insurance companies and raises the cost of insurance to good drivers.

Even when it's hard to gather information about individual risks directly, you can sometimes gather information indirectly. By offering consumers a menu of choices, you can get them to reveal information about themselves by the choices they make. Returning to our bicycle insurance example, suppose you offer two policies: full insurance for $45 and partial insurance for $15. Partial insurance would compensate the owner for just half the value of the bicycle. Typically, partial insurance involves a deductible or a copayment.[3]

If high-risk individuals prefer full insurance for $45 to partial insurance for $15, they will purchase the full insurance, whereas low-risk individuals will purchase partial insurance. At these prices, the insurance company can make money because the cost of insuring the high-risk group is $(0.4)\$100 = \$40$ and the cost of partially insuring the low-risk group is $(0.2)\$50 = \$10$. By offering partial insurance, the insurance company can transact (partially) with the low-risk consumers.

> *Screening* describes the efforts of the less informed party (the insurance company) to gather information about the more informed party (consumers). Information may be gathered indirectly by offering consumers a menu of choices. Consumers reveal information about themselves (risk) by the choices they make.

A successful screen has one critical requirement: it must *not* be profitable for high-risk consumers to mimic the choice of low-risk consumers. In our insurance example, the high-risk group must prefer full insurance at $45 to partial insurance at $15. If high-risk individuals purchase partial insurance, the screen fails, and the insurance company loses money.[4]

As a consumer, you can use this information to your advantage when purchasing insurance. If you're a low-risk individual, you may be able to lower your own *expected* insurance costs by purchasing a policy with a large deductible or copayment. This choice will identify you as a low-risk individual to the insurance company and allow you to purchase (partial) insurance for a lower price, albeit with a large deductible or copayment. Likewise, if you purchase insurance with a small deductible or copayment, you identify yourself as a high-risk consumer and pay a higher expected price. Buying a policy with a small deductible signals that you expect your insurance costs to be high.

Note that the software price discrimination scheme discussed in Chapter 14 is very similar to screening. By offering consumers a choice between a less expensive, disabled version of the software and a more expensive, full-featured version, the software company induced consumers to identify themselves as either high- or low-value consumers. This allowed the company to price discriminate. The scheme was successful because it was unprofitable for business users to mimic the behavior of home users (i.e., by purchasing the disabled version).

Let's apply these ideas to the used-car market, where adverse selection is known as the *lemons problem*. Suppose there are bad cars (lemons) worth $2,000 and good cars (cherries) worth $4,000. The information asymmetry is that each seller knows whether he or she owns a lemon, but the buyer does not.

What happens when an uninformed buyer tries to buy a used car from an informed seller? If a buyer offers a price of $3,000, only lemon owners would be willing to sell, so the buyer ends up paying $3,000 for a $2,000 car. If, instead, the buyer offers to purchase at a price of $4,000, both cherry owners and lemon owners would be willing to sell, so the expected value of any purchased car will be less than $4,000. In both cases, the buyer pays too much, on average, for what he is getting.

If the buyer anticipates adverse selection, he offers to pay just $2,000. At this price, only lemon owners will sell, but at least the buyer won't overpay for the car. Owners of cherries are analogous to low-risk consumers in the insurance market because they are unable to transact. Again, adverse selection represents an unconsummated wealth-creating transaction. Put yourself in the position of a buyer who wants to buy a cherry for $4,000, and try to design a screen to solve the lemons problem.

One option is to offer $4,000 for a car, but demand a money-back guarantee. Sellers of good cars will accept the offer because they know the car won't be returned. Lemon owners would be unwilling to offer guaranties like this. Warranties on products serve a similar purpose. Manufacturers of high-quality, durable products are more willing to offer longer warranties because they don't expect to have to make many repairs.

Screening occurs in a wide variety of contexts beyond the insurance and auto markets. For example, the state of Louisiana allows couples to choose one of two marriage contracts: a covenant contract, under which divorce is very costly, and a regular contract, under which divorce is relatively cheap. What is the screening function of this menu of choices?

Suppose there are two types of prospective partners: gold-diggers (those who want only a short-term relationship) and soul mates (those who want to stay together until death). Given a choice of contracts, you learn something about your intended by the choice he or she makes. Note that this screen works only if gold-diggers prefer the regular marriage contract to the covenant marriage.

Finally, as seen in our Zappos story, screens can solve the adverse selection problem in hiring. The $4,000 payment to quit made it profitable for low-quality workers to identify themselves as such.

Incentive compensation is another way that employers identify and avoid low-quality workers. Suppose you can hire two types of salespeople—hard workers who will sell 100 units per week in their territories and lazy workers who will sell only 50 units per week. The asymmetric information means that workers know which type they are but you don't. The employer could ask potential employees if they are lazy at the interview, but that is unlikely to be fully revealing.

Suppose hard and lazy workers alike expect to earn at least $800 for a week's work. If you offer a wage of $800 per month, you get a mix of lazy and hard workers. To screen out the lazy workers, offer a straight $10 commission. Hard workers will accept the offer because they know they'll earn $1,000. Lazy workers, who know they'll make only $500, will reject the offer. This is a perfect screen because the workers' own choices (accept or reject) identify their type (lazy or hardworking).

However, most incentive compensation schemes expose workers to risk. In addition to effort, there are factors beyond the salespersons' control that affect sales—like consumer income, rival prices, or interest rates. A screen that works just as well, but presents less risk, is a contract with a flat salary of $500 in combination with a $5 commission on each sale. This combination guarantees each worker a base salary of $500 without risk, and an expected compensation of $1,000 for good workers. If bad workers do not expect to sell at least 60 units, they will reject the offer. And the good workers get a compensation scheme that exposes them to less risk.

19.4   Signaling

Let's recap what we've learned so far. Even when we anticipate it and protect ourselves against it, adverse selection results in unconsummated wealth-creating transactions, such as those between

- insurance companies and low-risk consumers;
- car buyers and sellers with good cars; or
- employers and hardworking employees.

Screening is a tactic by the less informed party to consummate these transactions by getting rid of the information asymmetry. When consumers identify themselves by their choices, wealth-creating transactions can be consummated.

In this section, we discuss efforts by an informed party—the low-risk consumers, the hardworking employees, and the sellers with good cars—to get rid of the asymmetric information. This is called signaling.

> *Signaling* describes the efforts of the more informed parties (consumers) to reveal information about themselves to the less informed party (the insurance company). A successful signal is one that bad types will not mimic.

Signaling is closely related to screening. In fact, any successful screen that separates low- from high-risk consumers, good from bad car sellers, or lazy from hardworking employees can also serve as a signal. To signal, the informed party could use the mechanisms just described: low-risk consumers could offer to buy insurance with a big deductible, good employees could offer to work on commission, and sellers with good cars could include a warranty with the purchase.

The crucial element of a successful signal is that it must not be profitable for the bad types to mimic the signaling behavior of the good types.

For example, much of the value of education may derive not from what it adds to students' human capital but rather from its signaling value. Students signal to potential employers that they're hardworking, quick-learning, dedicated individuals (all these qualities are difficult to measure) by dropping out of the labor force and spending lots of money to pursue an education. Consequently, they receive high offers from employers. It's not profitable for lazy, slow-learning, or undedicated individuals to mimic this behavior because their type will be revealed before they can recoup the investment in education. Once employers realize that they are low-quality workers, they won't be promoted or retained. Further, the education itself is more arduous (expensive) for these types.

Advertising and branding can also serve as signals. By investing significant money into branding and advertising a product, firms signal to consumers that theirs is a high-quality product. Low-quality firms won't mimic this signal because even consumers who buy will soon learn of its low quality and avoid the brand in the future. For branding and advertising to serve as a signal, it must be the case that low-quality producers cannot sell enough to recover their advertising and branding expenditures. Consequently, consumers are willing to pay more for branded and advertised goods.

This type of advertising is often called "burning money" as the message of the advertisement is less important than the fact that money was spent on it. Burning money is used to signal in nature, too. The male peacock's colorful feathers serve as an expensive signal (they serve no apparent survival purpose) but reflect health and superior genes preferred by females. A less healthy peacock won't (or biologically can't) mimic this signal. For the same showy reason, before Federal Deposit Insurance Corporation (FDIC) insurance, banks were often built of granite. This served to reassure depositors that the bank owners were not looking to abscond with depositors' money. Doing so would not offset the building costs of the bank.

19.5 Adverse Selection and Internet Sales

In 2016, Amazon.com sued over 1,000 sellers using its own Amazon Marketplace. Amazon claimed that these sellers posted fake reviews about their products.[5] One suit claimed that 1,269 out of 2,242 reviews (54%) were fraudulent. Amazon and these sellers know that product and seller reviews are an important mechanism that consumers use to evaluate how satisfied they will be with the service. Sharing the experiences of third-party consumers has become a valuable signal for retailers and manufacturers. An additional star on Yelp! due to positive reviews is associated with a revenue increase of 8%.[6]

Amazon has an incentive to keep poor performing sellers from its Marketplace. It fears that dissatisfaction with one seller will reflect poorly on all sellers on the Marketplace. Sellers have an incentive to seek the Amazon Marketplace "seal of approval" whether the deserve it or not. Other ways Amazon discourages fraudulent behavior is to ban reviews "incentivized" by payments or free items, to develop algorithms that identify fake reviews, and to design a review system that gives fake reviews less importance by highlighting more recent and more helpful reviews. Amazon's continued efforts to address this adverse selection problem have helped make it the dominant online retailer in the world.

SUMMARY & HOMEWORK PROBLEMS

Summary of Main Points

- Insurance is a wealth-creating transaction that moves risk from those who don't want it to those who are willing to bear it for a fee.
- **Adverse selection** is a problem that arises from information asymmetry, or "hidden" information. Anticipate it and, if you can, figure out how to consummate the unconsummated wealth-creating transaction.
- The adverse selection problem disappears if the information asymmetry disappears.
- **Screening** is an uninformed party's effort to learn the information that the more informed party has. Successful screens have the characteristic that it is unprofitable for bad "types" to mimic the behavior of good types.
- **Signaling** is an informed party's effort to communicate her information to the less informed party. Every successful screen can also be used as a signal.
- Online auction and sales sites, like eBay, address the adverse selection problem with authentication and escrow services, insurance, and online reputations.

Multiple-Choice Questions

1. An insurance company offers doctors malpractice insurance. Assume that malpractice claims against careful doctors cost $5,000 on average over the term of the policy and settling malpractice claims against reckless doctors costs $30,000. Doctors are risk-neutral and know whether they are reckless or careful, but the insurance company only knows that 10% of doctors are reckless. How much do insurance companies have to charge for malpractice insurance to break even?
   a. $5,000
   b. $7,500

   c. $27,500
   d. $30,000

2. An employer faces two types of employees. Regular workers are 70% of the population and generate $100,000 in productivity. Exceptional workers are 30% of the population and generate $120,000 in productivity. Employees know their types and reject salaries below their productivity. If the employer offers a salary equal to the average productivity in the population, what will be the employer's per-employee profit?
   a. −$10,000
   b. −$6,000
   c. $0
   d. $4,000

3. An all-you-can-eat buffet attracts two types of customers. Regular customers value the buffet at $20 and eat $5 of food in costs to the restaurant. Hungry customers value the buffet at $40 and eat $10 of food. If there are 100 of each type in the market for a buffet dinner, what is the restaurant's maximum profit?
   a. $2,500
   b. $3,000
   c. $4,500
   d. $6,500

4. To combat the problem of adverse selection, _____ informed parties can employ _____ techniques.
   a. more; signaling
   b. less; signaling
   c. equally; screening
   d. equally; signaling

5. Which of the following can be an example of a signal?
   a. An air-conditioning manufacturer offers a 50-year warranty.
   b. A lawyer offers to be paid only if the client wins.
   c. A student pursues an MBA.
   d. All of the above.

6. Which of the following is not an example of adverse selection?
   a. A business bets the proceeds of a bank loan on the next NFL game.
   b. An accident-prone driver buys auto insurance.
   c. A patient suffering from a terminal disease buys life insurance.
   d. A really hungry person decides to go to the all-you-can-eat buffet for dinner.
7. The demand for insurance arises primarily from people who are
   a. risk-seeking.
   b. risk-averse.
   c. risk-neutral.
   d. None of the above.
8. Which of the following is a potential solution to the adverse selection problem faced by insurance companies?
   a. Offer plans with different deductibles so that higher-risk customers accept higher deductibles.
   b. Create a national database of customers that allows companies to look up each person's historical risk.
   c. Mandate that every person purchase insurance.
   d. All of the above.
9. An insurance company suffers from adverse selection if
   a. safe customers are less likely to insure than risky customers.
   b. customers know their willingness to pay for insurance but the company does not.
   c. a customer takes on much greater risk because he is insured.
   d. its customers are risk-averse.
10. Which of the following is an example of adverse selection?
    a. A safe driver taking greater risk in a rental car than his own car.
    b. A terminally ill person purchasing life insurance.

c. An employment contract encourages little effort on the part of employees.
d. All of the above.

Individual Problems

19-1 Leasing Residuals

In the late 1990s, car leasing was very popular in the United States. A customer would lease a car from the manufacturer for a set term, usually two years, and then have the option of keeping the car. If the customer decided to keep the car, the customer would pay a price to the manufacturer, the "residual value," computed as 60% of the new car price. The manufacturer would then sell the returned cars at auction. In 1999, the manufacturer lost an average of $480 on each returned car (the auction price was, on average, $480 less than the residual value).

A. Why was the manufacturer losing money on this program?
B. What should the manufacturer do to stop losing money?

19-2 College Degrees Required for Police Officers

Many police officer positions require the applicant to have a college degree even though the tasks of a police officer rarely call upon college course material. Why don't police departments increase their applicant pool by dropping this requirement?

19-3 Bicycle Insurance and Information Asymmetry

You sell bicycle theft insurance. If bicycle owners do not know whether they are high- or low-risk consumers, is there an adverse selection problem?

19-4 Job Auction[7]

When China reformed state-owned enterprises, it tried a new approach to choosing managers: it put managerial jobs up for auction. The bids for the jobs consisted of promises of future profit streams that the managers would generate and then deliver to the state. In cases where the incumbent manager was the winning bidder, firm productivity tended to increase dramatically. When outside bidders won, there was little productivity improvement. If incumbent managers were not generally more qualified, how can you explain this result?

19-5 "Soft Selling" and Adverse Selection

Soft selling occurs when a buyer is skeptical of the usefulness of a product and the seller offers to set a price that depends on realized value. For example, suppose you're trying to sell a company a new accounting system that will reduce costs by 10%. Instead of naming a price, you offer to give them the product in exchange for 50% of their cost savings. Describe the information asymmetry, the adverse selection problem, and why soft selling is a successful signal.

19-6 Hiring Employees

You need to hire some new employees to staff your start-up venture. You know that potential employees are distributed throughout the population as follows, but you can't distinguish among them:

Employee Value ($)	Probability
50,000	0.25
60,000	0.25
70,000	0.25
80,000	0.25

What is the expected value of five employees you hire?

Group Problem

G19-1 Adverse Selection

Describe an adverse selection problem your company is facing. What is the source of the asymmetric information? Who is the less informed party? What transactions are not being consummated as a result of the information? Could you (or do you) use signaling or screening to consummate these transactions? Offer your company some sound advice, complete with computations of the attendant profit consequences.

END NOTES

1. The payment has increased from $100 in 2008 to $4,000 now. For more on Zappos' use of this hiring practice, see Keith McFarland, "Why Zappos Offers New Hires $2,000 to Quit," *Business Week*, September 16, 2008.
2. An Initial Public Offering of stock describes the sale of a company by its private owners to the public who can purchase shares in the stock.
3. A *deductible* is a dollar amount the consumer pays (e.g., $50), while a *copayment* is a percentage of the total bill (e.g., 50%). In both cases, the insurance company pays the remainder.
4. Every time the insurance company sells partial insurance for $15 to a high-risk individual, it loses $5 (its cost is $0.4 \times \$50 = \$20$).
5. Sarah Perez, "Amazon Sues More Sellers for Buying Fake Reviews," *TechCrunch*, October 27, 2016 https://techcrunch.com/2016/10/27/amazon-sues-more-sellers-for-buying-fake-reviews/.
6. Michael Luca, "Reviews, Reputation, and Revenue: The Case of Yelp.com," Harvard Business School Working Paper No. 12-016.
7. Inspired by John McMillan, *Games, Strategies, and Managers: How Managers Can Use Game Theory to Make Better Business Decisions* (New York: Oxford University Press, 1996).

20 The Problem of Moral Hazard

Introduction

Progressive Snapshot

In 2004, the Progressive Direct Group of Insurance Companies introduced a new car insurance product called TripSense. Now called Snapshot, the service includes a free device that plugs into a car's diagnostic port and records mileage totals, the times when the vehicle is driven, and driving style, including if you slam on your brakes. Progressive uses this information to offer renewal discounts to customers who drive fewer miles during off-peak times. New customers earn an initial discount of up to 10% just for signing up. Renewal discounts vary from 30% to reported *increases* of 9%.

At this point, you should be thinking that this is another example of an insurance company trying to solve the problem of adverse selection by gathering information about the different risks faced by consumers who purchase insurance. But there is another factor involved. Some of the risky driving behavior is caused by the insurance itself. To see this, note that the decision of how much or how fast to drive is an extent decision. The marginal benefit of driving more or at faster speeds is obvious. The marginal cost is the cost of gasoline and wear on the car and the increased risk of accident. Once you buy insurance, the cost of getting into an accident goes down, so we would expect to see more accidents. We call this change in behavior **moral hazard**. Insurance companies anticipate that insured drivers drive less carefully, and they price policies accordingly. The Federal Communications Commission did not foresee the moral hazard, and therefore had many companies default on their risky winning bids.

Social Capital as a Motivator

Imagine you are a budding entrepreneur in a developing country. You probably don't have sufficient credit history to obtain a conventional loan. But you do have a presence on online social networks, and this activity online may provide insight into your level of integrity in real life. In 2011, Lenddo began using online behaviors to determine loan applicants' credit worthiness. Given permission to access to an applicant's social media accounts, Lenddo can develop a "Lenddoscore" much like a credit score. The difference is that, instead of a credit history, the Lenddoscore uses borrowers' online social network information to assess their loan riskiness. If your online presence looks like you have strong roots to the community, for example, then you are more likely to be worth the risk. Lenddo's algorithm seems to be effective because many lenders in developing countries have begun using the Lenddoscore. This helps with adverse selection.

But even the creditworthy can fall on hard times and have trouble making payments. Lenddo has a clever approach to help reduce the likelihood that these borrowers will default. Lenddo members nominate friends as references. If you are unable to make payments, it will affect *your friends'* ability to borrow. So, you have this extra incentive to not let your friends down. Also, your friends will tend to exert a bit of peer pressure on you to pay back the loan. These social sanctions put extra pressure on borrowers to make every effort to make repayments. This helps with moral hazard.

Moral hazard is ubiquitous. Researchers have found that improvements in risk-abatement technology create incentives for consumers to take more risks. For example, improved parachute rip cords did not reduce the number of sky-diving accidents. Instead, overconfident skydivers waited too long to pull the cord. Likewise, workers who wear back-support belts try to lift heavier loads, and wilderness hikers take bigger risks if they know that a trained rescue squad is on call. Public health officials cite evidence that enhanced HIV treatment can lead to riskier sexual behavior. And children who wear protective sports equipment engage in rougher play. The analogy to insurance is obvious. All these costly technologies reduce the costs of risk taking, which leads to more risk taking.[1]

The problem of moral hazard is closely related to the problem of adverse selection, and it has similar causes and solutions. Both problems are caused by information asymmetry: moral hazard is caused by hidden *actions* (insurance companies cannot observe your driving behavior), whereas adverse selection is caused by hidden *information* (insurance companies cannot observe the inherent risks that you face). Both problems can be addressed by getting rid of the information asymmetry.

20.2 Insurance

To illustrate the problem of moral hazard, let's return to the bicycle insurance example from Chapter 19. Assume there is just one type of consumer, the high-risk consumer whose probability of theft is 40%. Now, however, suppose that consumers can bring their bikes inside ("exercise care"), which reduces the probability of theft from 40% to 30%. If the cost of exercising care is low enough (let's say it costs $5 worth of effort to exercise care), then it makes sense to do so. Each uninsured consumer brings the bike inside because the *expected* benefit of doing so—the reduction in the probability of theft multiplied by the price of the bike, $(0.40 - 0.30) \times \$100 = \$10$—is greater than the $5 cost of exercising care.[2]

These owners still face the risk of theft and are willing to pay $5 more than the *expected* cost of insurance to get rid of the risk. In this case, the *expected* loss is $30 (or 0.3 × $100), and the bicycle owner would be willing to pay the insurance company $35 to insure against this risk. However, once consumers purchase insurance, any benefit from exercising care disappears.

Moral hazard means that insured customers exercise less care because they have less incentive to do so.

In our example, the consumer stops bringing the bicycle inside, and the probability of theft increases from 30% to 40%. This leads to the first lesson of moral hazard:

Anticipate moral hazard and protect yourself against it.

The insurance company should anticipate that the probability of theft will rise to 40% and price its policies accordingly; that is, it must charge at least $40 for the insurance, instead of $35.

What happens when an insurance company doesn't anticipate moral hazard? To answer this, let's look at the widespread introduction of modern antilock braking systems (ABS) in the late twentieth century. Insurance companies thought that ABS would make driving safer, and they offered discounts on cars with ABS.

What they didn't anticipate, ironically, is that drivers thought that ABS would allow them to drive safely on ice and in the rain. When insurers saw how much money they were losing on policies written for cars with ABS, they phased out the discounts, except in states that required them.

The second point of this chapter is that the problem of moral hazard can represent an opportunity to make money.

Moral hazard represents an unconsummated wealth-creating transaction.

If the insurance company could figure out how to get insured consumers to take care, then it could make more money. For example, if the insurance company could observe whether the customer was exercising care, then it could lower the price of insurance to those taking care. This is what Progressive's Snapshot system tries to do.

20.3 Moral Hazard versus Adverse Selection

Moral hazard and adverse selection often offer competing explanations for the same observed behavior. Consider the fact that before airbags were required equipment in cars, people who drove cars equipped with air bags were more likely to get into traffic accidents. Either adverse selection or moral hazard could explain this phenomenon.

The adverse selection explanation is that bad drivers are more likely to purchase cars with air bags. If you know you're likely to get into an accident, it makes sense to purchase a car with air bags.

The moral hazard explanation is that air bags are like insurance. Once drivers have the protection of air bags, they take more risks and get into more accidents. If you don't believe that people change behavior in this way, try running a simple experiment. Next time you drive somewhere, don't wear a seat belt. (Make this a thought experiment if a seat belt is required by law.) See if you drive more carefully. If you do, then this also means that you drive less carefully when you wear a seat belt. Although wearing a seat belt will protect you better in the event of an accident, seat belts also cause more accidents.

What distinguishes adverse selection from moral hazard is the kind of knowledge that is hidden from the insurance company. Adverse selection arises from hidden *information* regarding the type of person (high versus low risk) who is purchasing insurance. Moral hazard arises from hidden *actions* by the person purchasing insurance (taking care or not). Adverse selection is the problem of separating you from someone else. Moral hazard is the problem of separating the good you from the bad you.

More information can solve both problems. If the insurance company can distinguish between high- and low-risk consumers, it can offer a high-price policy to the high-risk group and a low-price policy to the low-risk group, thereby solving the adverse selection problem. Similarly, if the insurer can observe whether customers are exercising appropriate levels of care after purchasing insurance, it can reward people for taking care, thereby solving the problem of moral hazard. For example, insurance investigators devote a great deal of time trying to figure out exactly what happened in accidents in order to determine whether it faces a problem of adverse selection or a problem of moral hazard.

20.4 Shirking

Shirking is a type of moral hazard caused by the difficulty or cost of monitoring employees' behavior *after* a firm has hired them. Without good information, ensuring high levels of effort becomes more difficult.

Suppose, for example, a commission-based salesperson can work hard or shirk. Further suppose that working hard raises the probability of making a sale from 50% to 75%, but the increased effort "costs" the salesperson $100. How big does the sales commission have to be to induce hard work?

In Figure 20.1, we draw the decision tree of the salesperson who decides whether to work hard or shirk. The benefit of working hard is the increased probability of making a sale and earning a sales commission (C). The "cost" to the salesperson of expending effort is $100. The salesperson will decide to work hard if $25\% \times C > \$100$, where C is the sales commission. In other words, the commission has to be at least $400.[3]

Unless the company's contribution margin $(P - MC)$ is at least $400, the company cannot afford to pay a commission that big.[4] In this case, it doesn't pay to address the moral hazard problem with a simple incentive compensation scheme. Ordinarily, it's very hard for business students to accept that sometimes solutions cost more than the problem they are supposed to address. For these students, we leave you with a simple maxim:

If there is no solution, then there is no problem.

Note that the shirking problem arises from the same lack of information that leads to moral hazard in insurance: only the salesperson knows how hard

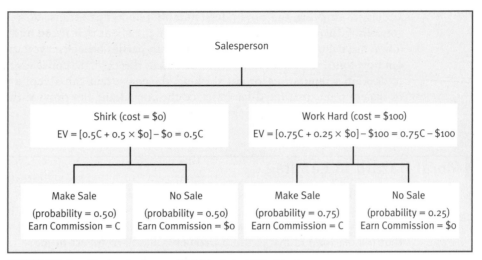

FIGURE **20.1**   **Choice between Shirking and Working**

she is working, just as only the insured driver knows whether he is driving carefully. The performance evaluation metric that the company does possess—whether or not a sale is made—is a noisy measure of effort because too frequently (50% of the time), the salesperson earns a commission for doing nothing.

Suppose we had a better performance evaluation metric than sales. In particular, suppose we could hire someone to monitor the behavior of our salesperson to verify that she was working hard. This could be done, for example, by tracking the salesperson's movements with a GPS device. How would you design a compensation scheme with this different metric?

Think of rewarding the salesperson for effort directly, with either a stick (work hard or get fired) or a carrot (work hard and earn a reward). If you have a performance metric like this, then almost any incentive compensation scheme will work. The new performance evaluation metric allows you to put the salesperson's entire compensation or job at risk. If the benefits of keeping a job and earning a salary are bigger than the costs of exerting effort, the salesperson will exert effort.

Another solution is to find a worker who has a reputation for working hard, regardless of whether she is monitored. Having a reputation for working hard without monitoring is valuable to the company and to the worker, who should be able to command a higher wage.

This leads directly to our last point about moral hazard—it hurts both parties to a transaction. Consider, for example, the case of a consulting firm that gets paid based on an hourly rate. Given the rate structure and the inability of the client to monitor the consultant's actions, the client expects the consultant either to bill more hours than the client prefers or to spend time on projects that the consultant values but that the client does not. Clients anticipate shirking and are understandably reluctant to transact, unless the consulting firm can find a way to convince the client that it can address the moral hazard problem. The point is this: both parties benefit if they can figure out how to solve the moral hazard problem. In this case, the consultant can try to develop a reputation for not shirking, the consultant can accept a portion of the contract on a fixed-fee basis, or the consultant can provide the client with information documenting the value of the work being done.

20.5 Moral Hazard in Lending

As a final example, let's consider the problems that banks face when making loans. The adverse selection problem is that borrowers who are less likely to repay loans are more likely to apply for them. The moral hazard problem is that once a loan is made, the borrower is likely to invest in more risky assets. Both of these factors make repayment less likely. Again, adverse selection arises from hidden *information*, whereas moral hazard arises from hidden *actions*.

To illustrate the moral hazard problem, suppose you're considering a $30 investment opportunity with the following payoff: $100 with a probability of 0.5 and $0 with a probability of 0.5. The bank computes the expected value of the investment ($50) and decides to make a $30 loan at a 100% rate of interest. If the investment pays off, the bank gets $60. But if the investment returns zero, the borrower defaults and the bank gets nothing. The expected return to the bank ($30 = 0.5 × $60 + 0.5 × $0) is equal to the loan amount, so it breaks even, on average. The borrower's expected profit is the remainder ($20 = 0.5 × $40 + 0.5 × $0).

The moral hazard problem arises when, after receiving the loan, the borrower discovers another, riskier investment. The second investment pays off $1,000, but has only a 5% probability of success. Although the expected payoffs of the two investments are the same, the payoffs for the parties are not. Compare the expected payoffs of the borrower and the bank in Tables 20.1 and 20.2. Because the borrower receives more of the upside gain if the investment pays off, he captures a much bigger share of the expected payoff. And if the borrower does much better, the bank does much worse. The bank's share of the expected $50 payout drops to just ($3 = 0.05($60) + 0.95($0).

TABLE **20.1**
Payoffs to a Less-Risky Investment ($30 Loan at 100% Interest)

	Investment Returns $100 ($p = 0.5$)	Investment Returns $0 ($p = 0.5$)	Expected Payoff ($)
Payoff to borrower	$40	$0	20
Payoff to bank	$60	$0	30

Note: p = that the investment is a success.

TABLE **20.2**

Payoffs to a More Risky Investment ($30 Loan at 100% Interest)

	Investment Returns $1000 ($p = 0.05$)	Investment Returns $0 ($p = 0.95$)	Expected Payoff ($)
Payoff to borrower	$940	$0	47
Payoff to bank	$60	$0	3

Banks guard against moral hazard by monitoring the behavior of borrowers and by placing covenants on loans to ensure that the loans are used for their intended purpose.

We can also characterize moral hazard as an incentive conflict between a lender and a borrower. The lender prefers the less-risky investment because she receives a higher expected payoff. The borrower prefers the more risky investment for the same reason.

Remember that moral hazard is a problem not only for the lender, but also for the borrower. If the lender anticipates moral hazard, it may be unwilling to lend. The incentive conflict between banks and borrowers is exacerbated when the borrower can put *other people's money* at risk.

Borrowers take bigger risks with other people's money than they would with their own.

Savings and loan institutions (S&Ls) are specialized banks that borrow from depositors and lend to homeowners. In the 1980s, in Texas, the real estate market collapsed and the value of the S&Ls' assets (the real estate loans) fell below the value of their liabilities (the money owed to depositors). But before the regulators could shut these banks down, they borrowed more money from depositors at very high interest rates and "bet" heavily on junk bonds—the riskiest investment available to them. Just as in our loan example, this increased the expected payoffs to the S&L, but decreased the expected payoff to the lender. When the risky bets failed to pay off, U.S. taxpayers were stuck with the $200 billion cost of repaying depositors.

To control this kind of moral hazard, lenders must try to find ways to better align the incentives of borrowers with the goals of lenders. They do this by requiring that borrowers put some of their own money at risk. If an investment doesn't pay off, the lender wants to make sure that the borrower shares the downside. This is why banks are much more willing to lend to borrowers who have a great deal of their own money at risk.

20.6 Moral Hazard and the 2008 Financial Crisis

Regulators can reduce the costs of moral hazard by ensuring that banks keep an equity "cushion" of about 10% so that they can repay depositors who want their money back. For example, a bank that raises $10 million in equity can accept $100 million in deposits and make $100 million in loans. Banks earn money on the spread between the interest they receive from their loans and the interest they pay to depositors. The balance sheet of this bank would have $100 million in liabilities (deposits that must be paid back) and $110 million in assets (loans plus equity).

When the value of the assets fall, the risk of moral hazard increases. In late 2008, economists voiced concerns that the U.S. Treasury's plan to guarantee short-term loans would give undercapitalized banks the opportunity to make risky "heads I win, tails you lose" investments (bets). If the bets paid off, then the bank would get most of the gain, but if they didn't, the taxpayers would absorb most of the losses.

A better alternative is to have the Treasury Department inject equity into banks. Not only does this get banks lending again but it also gives the bank owners a "stake" in the bank that mitigates some of the risk of moral hazard. In addition, it has the benefit of punishing bank owners by making them give up some of their ownership stake to the government.

Bailing out homeowners raises similar issues. Proponents of the bailout insisted that only "responsible families" would benefit from a foreclosure prevention program. But it was obvious that the plan would help tens of thousands of borrowers who made risky bets that house prices would continue to rise. Responsible borrowers, who didn't buy houses they clearly could not afford, watched as their less-responsible neighbors were bailed out by the government. Furthermore, expanding the rights of borrowers to renegotiate loans, which helps those with existing loans, makes new loans even more expensive. So responsible borrowers are punished twice—once by sharing in the bailout and again when they face higher loan rates.

SUMMARY & HOMEWORK PROBLEMS

Summary of Main Points

- **Moral hazard** refers to the reduced incentive to exercise care once you purchase insurance.
- Moral hazard can look very similar to adverse selection—both arise from information asymmetry. Adverse selection arises from hidden information about the type of individual you're dealing with; moral hazard arises from hidden actions.
- Anticipate moral hazard and (if you can) figure out how to consummate the implied wealth-creating transaction.
- Solutions to the problem of moral hazard center on efforts to eliminate the information asymmetry (e.g., by monitoring or by changing the incentives of individuals).

- Shirking is a form of moral hazard.
- Borrowers prefer riskier investments because they get more of the upside, while the lender bears more of the downside. Borrowers who have nothing to lose exacerbate this moral hazard problem.

Multiple-Choice Questions

1. Which of the following is an example of moral hazard?
   a. Reckless drivers are the ones most likely to buy automobile insurance.
   b. Retail stores located in high-crime areas tend to buy theft insurance more often than stores located in low-crime areas.

c. Drivers who have many accidents prefer to buy cars with air bags.

d. Employees recently covered by the company health plan start going to the doctor every time they get a cold.

2. In a bad economy, a CEO has a 4% chance of meeting earnings estimates at regular effort, and a 5% chance at extraordinary effort. Extraordinary effort costs the CEO $10,000 more than regular effort. How large a bonus should the CEO be paid for meeting estimates to encourage extraordinary effort?
   a. $100,000
   b. $200,000
   c. $250,000
   d. $1,000,000

3. A salesperson can put in regular effort (resulting in a 40% chance of sale) or high effort (60% chance of sale). If high effort costs the salesperson $20 more than regular effort, how large a per-sale bonus is required to encourage high effort?
   a. $12
   b. $20
   c. $33.33
   d. $100

4. Which of the following is *not* an example of a process designed to combat moral hazard problems?
   a. Banks include restrictive covenants in loan agreements.
   b. Universities have students complete evaluations of professor performance at the end of a class.
   c. Insurance companies require applicants to provide medical history information as part of the application process.
   d. Employers regularly monitor employee performance.

5. Which of the following is an example of moral hazard?
   a. High-quality products being driven out of a market by low-quality products.
   b. A local charity raising insufficient funds because no one contributes, expecting that their neighbors will.

c. A bakery defaults on its loan because of a new consumer fear of carbohydrates.

d. A corporation uses a business loan secured for one investment on another, higher-risk investment.

6. Which of the following is *not* an example of moral hazard?
   a. People are more likely to lock their own car than a rental car.
   b. Skateboarders attempt more difficult maneuvers when wearing a helmet.
   c. Bad salespeople are less drawn to commission-based jobs.
   d. People with fire insurance are less likely to install smoke alarms.

7. Which of the following is true?
   a. Moral hazard is primarily an issue prior to a transaction.
   b. Adverse selection is primarily an issue after a transaction.
   c. Moral hazard is the result of an information asymmetry.
   d. Resolving adverse selection also resolves moral hazard.

8. Restrictive covenants on loans are used to avoid
   a. moral hazard.
   b. adverse selection.
   c. free riding.
   d. none of the above.

9. Loan applications require a lot of information from applicants to avoid
   a. moral hazard.
   b. adverse selection.
   c. free riding.
   d. none of the above.

10. Which of the following is true about moral hazard?
    a. Moral hazard arises from actions that cannot be observed.
    b. Shirking is a form of moral hazard.
    c. Moral hazard refers to the taking of excessive risk.
    d. All of the above.

Individual Problems

20-1 Extended Warranties

Your product fails about 2% of the time, on average. Some customers purchase the extended warranty you offer in which you will replace the product if it fails. Would you want to price the extended warranty at 2% of the product price? Discuss both moral hazard and adverse selection issues.

20-2 Business Loan

A colleague tells you that he can get a business loan from the bank, but the rates seem very high for what your colleague considers a low-risk loan.

> Give an adverse selection explanation for this, and offer advice to your friend on how to solve the problem.

> Give a moral hazard explanation for this, and offer advice to your friend on how to solve the problem.

20-3 Locator Beacons for Lost Hikers

Lightweight personal locator beacons are now available to hikers that make it easier for the Forest Service's rescue teams to locate those lost or in trouble in the wilderness. How will this affect the costs that the Forest Service incurs?

20-4 Auto Insurance

Suppose that every driver faces a 1% probability of an automobile accident every year. An accident will, on average, cost each driver $10,000. Suppose there are two types of individuals: those with $60,000 in the bank and those with $5,000 in the bank. Assume that individuals with $5,000 in the bank declare bankruptcy if they get in an accident. In bankruptcy, creditors receive only what individuals have in the bank. What is the actuarially fair price of insurance? What price are individuals with $5,000 in the bank willing to pay for the insurance? Will those with $5,000 in the bank voluntarily purchase insurance? What is the effect of state laws forcing individuals to purchase auto liability insurance?

20-5 BPO Services

BPO Services is in the business of digitizing information from forms that are filled out by hand. In 2006, a big client gave BPO a distribution of the forms that it digitized in house last year, and BPO estimated how much it would cost to digitize each form.

Form Type	Mix of Forms (%)	Form Cost ($)
A	25	0.25
B	25	0.10
C	25	0.15
D	25	0.50

> Compute the average cost of digitizing a form.

> The client agreed to pay the average cost computed in A for each form that BPO processed, but BPO lost money on the contract. How much did BPO lose, on average, for each form that it processed?

20-6 Frequent Flyers

Frequent flyer programs are targeted more toward business travelers (who do not pay for their own tickets) than leisure travelers (who do). Explain their effect on each type of traveler. Why is there a difference?

Group Problem

G20-1 Moral Hazard

Describe a moral hazard problem your company is facing. What is the source of the asymmetric information? Who is the less-informed party? Are there any wealth-creating transactions not consummated as a result of the asymmetric information? If so, could you consummate them? Compute the profit consequences of any advice.

END NOTES

1   William Ecenbarger, "Buckle Up Your Seat-belt and Behave," *Smithsonian,* April 2009, available at http://www.smithsonianmag.com/science-nature/Presence-of-Mind-Buckle-Up-And-Behave.html.

2   We thank Mark Cohen for the bicycle insurance example.

3   Work hard = $0.75C - \$100 > 0.5C =$ shirk; equivalently, $0.25C > \$100$ or $C > \$400$.

4   Even if its contribution margin is greater than \$400, it still may find it more profitable to settle for shirking at lower commissions.

Organizational Design

21

Getting Employees to Work in the Firm's Best Interests

In the late 1990s, a large auction house, Auction Services International (ASI), employed art experts to manage ASI's business in various schools of art—French Impressionism, American Realism, and the like. Each expert's job was to persuade art owners to use ASI's auction services to sell their art. ASI earned money by charging the art owners a percentage of the final price at auction. The art expert negotiated this percentage rate with the art owners.

Art experts were given discretion to negotiate rates from 10% to 30%, depending on the art expert's assessment of the seller's willingness to pay and knowledge of competitors' offers. Instead, most of these negotiations yielded relatively low rates, much closer to the 10% minimum. Puzzled, ASI's CEO did some investigation and discovered that the art experts were discounting rates in exchange for gifts from the sellers—cases of fine wine, fur coats, even luxury cars. After she found out about these kickbacks, the CEO took away the experts' discretion to negotiate the rates.

The CEO's action ended the exchange of gifts for lower rates, but the experts had become accustomed to the kickbacks, considering them an important part of their compensation. Consequently, many of the art experts quit, leaving to set up their own independent galleries in direct competition with ASI.

To make matters worse, the CEO decided to set a 17% price by conspiring with a rival auction house. When the conspiracy was discovered, the CEO was sentenced to a year in jail, and the judge tacked on a $7.5 million fine, an amount calculated as 5% of the $150 million volume of commerce affected by the price-fixing conspiracy.

Had the CEO read this chapter, she would have known better how to motivate her employees to work in the firm's best interest, and she may have been able to avoid prison.

In this and the final two chapters, we come back to the original problem-solving framework of Chapter 1. Our goal is to show you the analytical roots of the framework to help you understand why it works in addition to how it works. To do this, we begin with principal–agent models.

21.1 Principal–Agent Relationships

When we study the relationship between a firm and its employees, we use what economists call *principal–agent models*.

> A **principal** wants an **agent** to act on her behalf. But agents often have different goals and preferences than do principals.

In the ASI story, for example, the firm or the CEO is the principal, and the art expert is the agent. We adopt the linguistic convention that the principal is female and the agent male.

Like the art expert, the agent often has better information than the principal. The problem the principal faces is that the agent has different incentives than does the principal, which we call an **incentive conflict**. In our example, ASI's CEO wanted her art experts to negotiate profitable commission rates, whereas the art experts wanted to increase personal income, including kickbacks from customers. In general, incentive conflicts exist between every principal and every agent throughout the management hierarchy—between shareholders and managers, between managers and subordinates, and between a firm and its various divisions.

Incentive conflict generates problems that should sound familiar:

> The principal has to decide which agent to hire (a problem of adverse selection). Once the agent is hired, the principal has to figure out how to motivate the agent (moral hazard).

We know (from Chapters 19 and 20) that adverse selection and moral hazard problems are costly to control. In fact, the costs associated with moral hazard and adverse selection are called **agency costs** because we analyze them using principal–agent models. A well-run firm will find ways to reduce agency costs; poorly run firms often blindly incur agency costs or unwittingly make decisions that increase them.

We also know that we can reduce the costs of adverse selection or moral hazard by gathering information about the agent:

> A principal can reduce agency costs if she gathers information about the agent's type (adverse selection) or about the agent's actions (moral hazard).

For adverse selection, information gathering means checking the background of agents *before* they're hired; and for moral hazard, information gathering means monitoring agents' actions *after* they're hired. This difference has led some to characterize adverse selection as a *pre*-contractual problem caused by hidden information and moral hazard as a *post*-contractual problem caused by hidden actions.

At ASI, for example, had the CEO known when agents were reducing rates in exchange for gifts, she might have devised a simple incentive-compensation scheme (a reward or a punishment) to stop it. But even without this information, she should have anticipated the art experts' opportunistic behavior, especially since she was paying them flat salaries—compensation unrelated to performance. Because ASI did not reward art experts for setting profitable rates, the art owners found it easy to bribe them to set unprofitable ones.

When the CEO decided to take away rate-setting discretion from the art experts, she compounded her initial mistake. This solution was costly because the CEO lacked information about what rates owners were willing to pay. Instead, she tried her "17% solution," the rate set collusively with her rival.

A better solution would have been to leave the rate-setting authority with the art experts but change to an incentive-compensation scheme—for example, to one that paid art experts a percentage of the revenue they brought to the firm. This kind of compensation scheme better aligns the agents' incentives with the firm's goals. If the agents set profitable rates, they'll increase both the firm's profit and their own compensation. If you think of the art experts as salespeople, this incentive-compensation scheme seems like an obvious solution—most salespeople are compensated with sales commissions.

This solution does have one drawback: like all incentive-compensation schemes, it exposes the agents to risk. In this case, should the economy decline, the firm would sell fewer art pieces, and the art experts' compensation would fall through no fault of their own.

If you are the principal, imposing risk on the agent may not seem like your problem, but we know (from Chapter 9) that people must be compensated for bearing risk. This raises the principal's cost of using an incentive-compensation scheme.

Incentive compensation imposes risk on the agent for which he must be compensated.

The risk of incentive compensation reminds us that most solutions to the problems of adverse selection and moral hazard involve trade-offs. We adopt incentive compensation only if its benefits (the agent works harder) exceed its costs (we have to compensate the agent for bearing risk). We measure these costs and benefits relative to the status quo or relative to other potential solutions.

21.2 Controlling Incentive Conflict

We don't have any hard and fast rules for the best way to control incentive conflicts between principals and agents, but we can identify the trade-offs associated with various solutions. Once you understand the basic trade-offs, it is easier to identify the costs and benefits of various solutions. In a well-run organization, decision-makers have (1) the information necessary to make good decisions and (2) the incentive to do so. To ensure that decision-makers have enough information to make good decisions, there are two obvious solutions:

Either move information to those who are making decisions or move decision-making authority to those who have information.

Typically, information enters a firm from the bottom so that subordinates (who are further down in the management hierarchy) are better informed than their bosses. In the case of ASI, the art experts, but not the CEO, knew how much clients were willing to pay. When the CEO *centralized* decision-making authority to set rates, her company lost the ability to price discriminate between high- and low-value customers.

When you centralize decision-making authority, you should also figure out how to transfer information to the decision-maker.

This is not as easy as it sounds. Information comes from self-interested parties who may have an incentive to manipulate the decision-maker. For example, sales agents often tell their marketing bosses that they have to reduce price in order to make a sale. They have an incentive to lie if they are paid predominantly based on the number of sales or, in the case of ASI, kickbacks.

The other solution, leaving pricing discretion with the art expert, *decentralizes* decision-making authority.

When you decentralize decision-making authority, you should also strengthen incentive-compensation schemes.

The logic is clear. Once you give an agent authority to make decisions, you want to make sure that he is motivated to make choices in the firm's best interest. At ASI, the weak incentives were obvious—the art experts were given no financial incentive to set profitable rates. The CEO should have adopted an incentive-compensation scheme to encourage more profitable rate setting.

Recall from Chapter 1 that incentives have two parts: before you can reward good behavior, you have to be able to measure it. You can measure performance informally, with some kind of subjective performance evaluation, or formally, using sales or profitability as performance metrics. Once you have an adequate performance measure, you create incentives by linking compensation to the performance metrics. Here, we speak very generally about compensation: compensation can be pay, increased likelihood of promotion, bonuses, or anything else that employees value. The link between performance and compensation creates the incentive for agents to act in the firm's best interest.

Designing good incentive-compensation schemes is challenging. Take a simple example of a fruit farmer trying to decide how to pay pickers. The obvious solution is to pay workers a piece rate for each piece picked. A complicating factor is that the rate has to be increased when pickings are slim to ensure that the workers earn the minimum wage required by law. Under this system, however, workers sometimes monitor each other to discourage fast picking, resulting in the piece rate being raised. This defeats the purpose of the incentive-compensation scheme. One solution to this problem is to gauge the difficulty of picking by having managers test-pick a field and then set the piece rate based on this test-pick.[1]

The lesson of this story is to realize that workers have an incentive to "game"-compensation schemes. Like a teacher rewarded for student test performance will often "teach to the test" rather than foster deeper understanding of the material, employees will often discover ways to maximize their pay or make themselves better off that don't improve or even hurt profitability.

To combat gaming, first try to anticipate the more obvious games and adjust the compensation scheme to prevent them. Second, monitor outcomes to ensure that you are getting the behaviors you really want. Monitoring gives the principal a better performance evaluation metric, which allows her to better align the incentives of the agent with the goals of the principal.

In the case of ASI, it looks like decentralization, but with stronger incentives, would have been the better solution. In general, the answer to whether centralization or decentralization is better depends on the relative cost of the two alternatives. If you want to centralize decision making, how costly will it be to transfer information from agents to principals? If you want to decentralize, how costly will it be to institute incentives that adequately compensate agents for bearing risk?

21.3 Marketing versus Sales

The conflict between the art experts and their employer is fairly typical of the general incentive conflict that arises in organizations with separate sales and marketing divisions. The two divisions rarely get along, and this is often due to the different incentives that they are provided. Marketing managers generally receive profitability bonuses as compensation, whereas salespeople receive commissions based on revenue. They disagree about what price to charge because the marketing principal wants to maximize profit—that is, by making sales where $MR > MC$. In contrast, the sales agent wants to maximize revenue by making sales where $MR > 0$. This means that the salesperson prefers more sales or, equivalently, lower prices.

If the marketing managers *know* when salespeople are making unprofitable sales, they can easily put a stop to it. Without that information, however, controlling the incentive conflict becomes costly.

To see why, put yourself in the place of a marketing manager who is overseeing a salesperson who tells you that he *has* to reduce price to make a particularly tough sale even though it will leave the firm with very little profit. Because you don't know how much each customer is willing to pay, you can't tell whether the salesperson wants to reduce price to make a particularly tough sale, which would be reasonable from the firm's perspective, or whether he has decided that the extra effort to sell at the higher price is not worth the small increase in commission, despite the big increase in profit for the firm.

Since it seems easy to design an incentive-compensation scheme that rewards the salesperson for increasing profitability rather than revenue, we have to wonder why this kind of incentive compensation is not more widely used. Most salespeople will tell you they prefer performance evaluations based on revenue because revenue is what they directly control. They may also perceive a change from a sales commission to profit commission as a sneaky way for the company to cut labor costs. Remember that profit is always lower than revenue.

You should be able to persuade the sales agent to accept the change to a profit commission if you design the profit-based compensation scheme to be "revenue-neutral" to the salesperson. For example, a 20% commission on profit is equivalent to a 10% commission on revenue if the contribution margin is 50%. Agents are guaranteed to earn the same under each compensation scheme, even if their behavior does not change. But because they can earn more money if they change behavior (by pricing less aggressively), their compensation should increase under a commission based on profit.

Companies often try to control incentive conflicts simply by asking sales agents to change their behavior—but actions (and paychecks) can speak much louder than words. Sales agents will change behavior when they have incentives to do so.

Another common solution is to require that sales agents obtain permission to reduce price below some specific threshold. The sales agent could do this by transferring enough information to the marketing principal to convince her that the price reduction is profitable.

21.4 Franchising

We can understand the growth of franchising in the United States over the past 50 years as a solution to a particular principal–agent incentive conflict. The principal is the parent company that owns a popular brand, like McDonald's. As the company grows, it has a choice—it can open up company-owned stores, or it can let independent franchisees open and run stores. The franchisees then pay the company a fee for the right to use the parent company's brand.

Suppose you are advising the owner of a fast-food restaurant chain. This chain's owner is trying to decide whether to sell one of its company-owned restaurants, currently run by a salaried manager, to a franchisee. If the chain sells the store, the franchisee will manage it and pay the owner a fixed franchise fee for permission to use the brand. Should the owner sell the store?

Of course, the answer is, "It depends." In this case, it depends on whether the franchise organizational form is more profitable than the company-owned organizational form. With the company-owned structure, managers don't work as hard as they would if they owned the restaurant (moral hazard), and the salaried management job may have attracted a lazy manager (adverse selection). The company must spend resources on monitoring managers' productivity.

These agency costs disappear once a franchisee owns the restaurant because the agent and the principal become one and the same. The franchisee works harder than a salaried manager because he gets to keep all profit after paying off his costs—including the franchise fee—and industrious franchisees will outbid lazy ones for the right to run a franchised restaurant. Running a franchised store can be thought of as a strong form of incentive compensation—you turn a manager into an owner (franchisee) when you give him the residual profit from running the store.

However, the franchisee faces more risk than does a salaried manager and, as a consequence, will demand higher compensation in the form of a lower franchise fee. If the franchisee demands too much for bearing risk, then the restaurant could be more valuable as a company-owned store than it is as a franchise.[2]

Jointly, the parties can split a larger profit pie if they can figure out how to balance these concerns. At one extreme, the company-owned store with a salaried manager leads to shirking on the part of the agent—a type of moral hazard. As mentioned earlier, it also leads to adverse selection because salaried jobs are more likely to attract lazy managers. The company may also incur costs to monitor the managers' actions.

At the other extreme, the franchise organizational form is analogous to an incentive-compensation scheme because the franchisee keeps every dollar he earns after paying off his costs. But if factors other than effort affect profit, this kind of incentive compensation also imposes extra risk on the agent for which he must be compensated.

Sharing contracts fall between these two extremes. Instead of a fixed franchise fee, the franchisor might demand a percentage of the revenue or profit of the restaurant. This arrangement reduces franchisee risk by reducing the amount the franchisee pays to the franchisor when the store does poorly. However, sharing contracts also increase agency costs (moral hazard, adverse selection, and monitoring costs).

21.5 A Framework for Diagnosing and Solving Problems

Understanding the trade-offs between information and incentives is useful, but it still doesn't tell you how to identify and fix specific problems within an organization. For that, you need to be able to find the source of the incentive conflict and come up with specific alternatives to reduce the associated agency costs. Then choose the alternative that gives you the highest profit.

To analyze principal–agent problems, we return to the problem-solving framework introduced in Chapter 1. First, reduce the problem to a bad decision, and then ask three questions:

1. Who is making the (bad) decision?
2. Does the decision-maker have enough information to make a good decision?
3. Does the decision-maker have the incentive to do so?

In principal–agent relationships, the source of the problem is almost always either moral hazard or adverse selection. The first question identifies the source of this problem. The second examines the employee's information and the nature of the information asymmetry. The third identifies how the decision-maker is evaluated and compensated. Remember that incentives have two parts: the performance evaluation measures whether the individual is doing a good job; the compensation rewards good performance.

Let's answer the three questions for the ASI example at the beginning of this chapter:

1. *Who is making the bad decision?* The art experts. They are negotiating rates that are too low.
2. *Does the decision-maker have enough information to make a good decision?* Yes—in fact, they are the only ones with enough information to set profitable rates.
3. *Does the decision-maker have the incentive to do so?* No. The art experts received a flat salary, making it relatively easy for art owners to bribe them with gifts.

In general, answers to the three questions will suggest alternatives for reducing agency costs in three general ways: by (1) changing decision rights, (2) transferring information, or (3) changing incentives.

In this case, we have two obvious solutions: leave rate-setting authority with the art experts, but adopt stronger incentive compensation; or transfer rate-setting authority to a marketing executive, and then transfer crucial information to her. The first is a *decentralization* solution, and the second is a *centralization* solution.

To see how well you understand how to use the framework, imagine that you are called in as a consultant to a large retail chain of "general stores" that target low-income customers in smaller cities. As the company has grown, the CEO and the stock analysts who follow the company have noticed that newly opened stores are not meeting sales projections. The CEO wants you to find out what's causing the problem and fix it.

In the course of your investigation, you learn that the company uses "development" agents to find new store locations and negotiate leases with property owners. The company rewards these agents with generous stock options, provided they open 50 new stores in a single year. Although agents are supposed to open new stores only if the sales potential is at least $1 million per year, this is obviously not happening. Newly opened stores earn just half that amount.

------------ *Before continuing, try to identify the problem.* ------------

Begin your analysis by asking the three questions.

1. *Who is making the bad decision?* The development agents. They are opening unprofitable stores.
2. *Does the decision-maker have enough information to make a good decision?* Yes. Development agents probably have access to information about whether the new stores would be profitable. This appears to be a moral hazard problem.
3. *Does the decision-maker have the incentive to do so?* No. The agents received stock options for opening 50 stores each year, regardless of the new stores' profitability.

The problem is not with information but rather with the incentives of the agent, who is rewarded for opening stores regardless of profitability. Before you continue, suggest at least two solutions to the problem and choose the best one.

------------- *Before continuing, try to fix the problem.* -------------

You have at least two obvious solutions:

1. (Decentralization) The company could change the incentives of the development agents by rewarding them for opening only *profitable* stores.
2. (Centralization) Alternatively, the company could take the decision to open stores away from agents and then gather its own *information* about the potential profitability of new store sites.

The decentralization solution would leave decision-making authority with the agents, who have specialized knowledge about the profitability of locations for new stores. But the agents would have to wait for a year of store operation before receiving compensation (at which point, they know whether the store made $1 million in sales). However, this solution exposes the agents to risk beyond their control—their compensation would depend on the behavior of the store manager, as well as on the state of the economy. The agent would have to be compensated for bearing this risk in the form of higher compensation, which is the usual trade-off between incentive compensation and risk.

In this case, the general store chain chose the centralization option. It developed a forecasting model to predict the profitability of new stores based on local demographic information and the locations of rival stores. Agents were allowed to open new store locations only if the model predicted sales exceeding $1 million.

If the model is good at predicting which stores are likely to be profitable, this solution will work well. But if the model cannot identify profitable locations, it will be a poor substitute for the agents' specialized knowledge or intuition about which new store locations are likely to be profitable. It will make both Type I errors (open unprofitable stores) and Type II errors (fail to open profitable stores). As you should recall from our discussion of minimizing expected error costs in Chapter 17, if the error costs are asymmetric (it is more costly to open an unprofitable store), "shade" your prediction threshold to avoid the more costly error (raise the predicted thresholds for opening stores). In this case, the model predicted well, and the problem disappeared.

SUMMARY & HOMEWORK PROBLEMS

Summary of Main Points

- **Principals** want **agents** to work in the principals' best interests, but agents typically have different goals from those of principals. This is called **incentive conflict**.
- Incentive conflict and asymmetric information lead to *moral hazard* and *adverse selection*.
- The costs of controlling incentive conflict (agency costs) go down if the principal can gather information about the agent's productivity (adverse selection) and about his actions (moral hazard).
- Three alternatives for controlling principal–agent conflicts are
  1. reassigning decision rights,
  2. transferring information, and
  3. changing incentives.
- In a well-run organization, decision-makers have (1) the information necessary to make good decisions and (2) the incentive to do so.
  1. If you decentralize decision-making authority, you should strengthen incentive-compensation schemes.
  2. If you centralize decision-making authority, you should make sure to transfer needed information to the decision-makers.
- Agents may try to "game" incentives, maximizing their own profit at the expense of the principal.
- Three approaches to controlling incentive conflicts are
  1. a fixed payment to the agent (akin to company-owned stores with salaried managers, giving rise to agency costs, and requiring monitoring costs to overcome them),
  2. incentive pay (akin to franchising, requiring no monitoring but requiring agents to be compensated for bearing risk), or
  3. sharing contracts, which blend the above two approaches (requiring some monitoring, some agency costs, and some risk compensation).
- To analyze principal–agent conflicts, focus on three questions:
  1. Who is making the (bad) decision?
  2. Does the decision-maker have enough information to make good decisions?
  3. Does the decision-maker have the incentive to make good decisions?

Multiple-Choice Questions

1. Your notebook computer's hard drive recently crashed, and you decide to take it to a local repair technician to have it fixed. In this relationship,
   a. you are the agent.
   b. the technician is the principal.
   c. the technician is the agent.
   d. no principal–agent relationship exists.
2. A good incentive-compensation scheme
   a. maximizes the agent's utility.
   b. anticipates how an agent will game the scheme.
   c. does not subject a risk-averse agent to risk.
   d. accompanies centralized decision-making authority.
3. Principal–agent relationships
   a. reduce monitoring costs.
   b. occur because managers have good information about employees.
   c. are not related to asymmetric information.
   d. are subject to moral hazard problems.
4. All of the costs associated with a principal interacting with an agent are called
   a. opportunity costs.
   b. agency costs.
   c. monitoring costs.
   d. sunk costs.

5. Principal–agent problems
   a. occur when firm managers have more incentive to maximize profit than shareholders do.
   b. would be reduced if firm owners had better information about the actions of the firm's managers.
   c. are made worse when executives own stock in their companies.
   d. are increased as more information is shared between the parties.
6. In order to create an effective incentive-compensation scheme, you must have
   a. adequate performance measures.
   b. unlimited funds.
   c. a flat management structure.
   d. none of the above.
7. Decentralization of decision-making authority is consistent with which of the following?
   a. A trend of stronger, more active CEOs.
   b. Shrinking costs of computing bandwidth, which allows information to be inexpensively aggregated from geographically diverse business units.
   c. Development of computing resources at the corporate, division, and employee level.
   d. Reduction in the use of incentive compensation.
8. A firm faces two kinds of employees, those able to sell 10 units/year, and those able to sell 5 units/year. High-productivity employees are willing to work for $100K/year, while low-productivity employees are willing to work for only $50K/year. To screen out the low-productivity employees, the firm should
   a. offer a salary of $100K.
   b. offer a salary of $75K plus $5K/unit commission.
   c. offer a sales commission of $10K/unit.
   d. offer a sales commission of $20K/unit on sales above 5 units.
9. You own a retail establishment run by a store manager who receives a flat salary of $80,000. If you set up another store as a franchise with incentive compensation to the franchisee, what would be a reasonable total compensation range that the franchisee could earn?
   a. $80,000
   b. $40,000–$80,000
   c. $60,000–$100,000
   d. $80,000–$100,000
10. In the magazine *Budget Travel*, a hotel maid admits, "I cut corners everywhere I could. Instead of vacuuming, I found that just picking up the larger crumbs from the carpet would do. Rather than scrub the tub with hot water, sometimes it was just a spray-and-wipe kind of day.... After several weeks on the job, I discovered that the staff leader who inspected the rooms couldn't tell the difference between a clean sink and one that was simply dry, so I would often just run a rag over the wet spots.... I apologize to you now if you ever stayed in one of my rooms." Which of the following organizational forms is more likely to have caused this kind of shirking?
    a. Franchising: where the hotel managers are the owners of the hotel (franchisee) and pay a fixed franchise fee
    b. Company-owned hotels
    c. Franchising with a sharing contract, where the hotel managers are the owners of the hotel (franchisee), pay a small fixed fee but share revenue with the franchisor
    d. None of the above

Individual Problems

21-1 Real Estate Agents

When real estate agents sell their own, rather than clients', houses, they leave the houses on the market for a longer time (10 days longer on average) and wind up with better prices (2% higher on average). Why?

21-2 Airline Departures

Planes frequently push back from the gate on time, but then wait 2 feet away from the gate until it is time to queue up for take-off. This increases fuel consumption and increases the time that passengers must sit in a cramped plane awaiting take-off. Why does this occur? What can be done to fix it?

21-3 Incentive Conflicts

Which of the following are characteristic of *principal–agent conflicts* that often exist in a firm?

a. Managers do not always operate in the best interest of owners because owners are generally more risk averse than managers.

b. Managers generally have a shorter time horizon than owners; thus, managers do not fully take into account the future long-run profitability of the firm.

c. Managers do not always operate in the best interest of owners because managers care about the noncash benefits of their jobs.

d. Firms can usually find solutions that reduce agency costs without increasing monitoring or incentive costs.

21-4 Public School Principals

Each year, public schools are rewarded with bigger budgets for achieving a rating of "excellent" or "recommended" and are punished for rating "needs improvement." These ratings are based on meeting thresholds on a broad set of measures such as attendance rates, graduation rates, standardized test scores, SAT scores, and so on. Discuss the incentives for school principals (who are the agents, in this case) under this scheme and how you might improve them.

21-5 Venture Capital

Venture capital (VC) firms are pools of private capital that typically invest in small, fast-growing companies, which usually can't raise funds through other means. In exchange for this financing, the VCs receive a share of the company's equity, and the founders of the firm typically stay on and continue to manage the company.

a. Describe the nature of the incentive conflict between VCs and the managers, identifying the principal and the agent.

b. VC investments have two typical components: (1) managers maintain some ownership in the company and often earn additional equity if the company performs well; (2) VCs demand seats on the company's board. Discuss how these two components help address the incentive conflict.

21-6 Meeting Milestones

A convenience store manager earns a base salary plus small bonuses for each of 10 different possible monthly milestones he meets. Typical managers can meet half of these milestones. Do they miss the others by a little or a lot?

Group Problems

G21-1 Incentive Conflict

Describe an incentive conflict in your company. What is the source of the conflict, and how is it being controlled? Could you control it in a less costly way? Compute the profit consequences of the change.

G21-2 Incentive Pay

Describe a job compensated with incentive pay in your company. What performance evaluation metric is used, and how is it tied to compensation? Does this compensation scheme align the incentives of the employee with the goals of the company? Estimate the profit consequences of the scheme relative to the next best alternative.

G21-3 Centralization versus Decentralization

Describe a decision that is centralized (or decentralized) in your company. How could you decentralize (or centralize) the decision? What would happen if it were decentralized (or centralized)? Compute the profit consequences of the change.

END NOTES

1. For more on the incentive compensation challenges and solutions in fruit farming, see Tim Harford, "The Fruits of Their Labors," *Slate*, August 23, 2008, http://www.slate.com/id/2197735/.

2. The variability of franchisee profit represents risk, and the franchisee must be compensated for bearing this risk. Note also that the franchisor needs to be aware of the incentive conflict regarding quality. Franchisees have an incentive to free ride on the brand name of the franchisor by reducing quality.

22
Getting Divisions to Work in the Firm's Best Interests

Black liquor soap is a by-product of the paper manufacturing process at Acme's Paper Division. The Paper Division normally sold the soap to Acme's Resins Division, which converted it into crude tall oil, an input into resin manufacturing. Since a low transfer price increased the Resins Division's profit, its managers spent a lot of effort lobbying for a low transfer price while the Paper Division pushed for a high transfer price.

The Resins Division won this lobbying battle when a relatively low price was set, but it turned out to be a hollow victory. Given the low transfer price, the Paper Division decided to burn the soap for fuel rather than sell it to the Resins Division, which was then forced to buy higher-priced soap on the open market. On net, burning the soap decreased overall company profit because its value as a fuel was below that of its value as an input into resin manufacturing.

To make matters worse, the Paper Division's burners were not designed to handle black liquor soap, leading to a potentially explosive situation. Fortunately, corporate headquarters recognized the danger; however, their "solution" was to spend $5 million for a special furnace to allow the Paper Division to safely burn the soap.

The moral of this story is that incentive conflict between divisions is costly to control. In this case, a low transfer price not only prevented the movement of an asset (black liquor soap) to a higher-valued use (resin manufacturing), but the parent company compounded its mistake by building a new furnace. In addition, lobbying by the two divisions diverted management attention from more important issues. All these costs could have been reduced, if not avoided, had the managers of Acme read this chapter.

22.1 Incentive Conflict between Divisions

Incentive conflicts arise in the normal course of business; however, these conflicts need not reduce a company's profit. With two simple modifications, we can apply the framework set up in Chapter 21 to make sure that the incentives of the various divisions are aligned with the goals of the parent company. The first is to "personify" the division as being controlled by a division manager. So when we ask the three questions, we are really talking about the division manager's decision rights, information, and incentives.

The most important feature of a division's incentive is the metric used to evaluate division performance. For example, we can have a **profit center** or revenue center, where the manager is evaluated on division profit or division revenue; a **cost center** where the manager is evaluated on division average cost; or an investment center, where managers are evaluated on the net present value of the investments they make. Understanding the separate concerns of the divisions allows you to figure out why problems arise. For example, incentive conflict between the paper and resin divisions is driven by the fact that each division is trying to maximize its own division profitability, without concern for the overall profit of the company.

The second modification relates to the first question asked in the framework. A complicating feature of applying our method to problems created by conflict between divisions is how to reduce the problem to a simple decision. For a principal with two agents, this is hard to do. In our introductory example, it is clear that the two divisions are not acting in the best interests of the parent company, but it is not clear whether one of the two is making a "mistake." Consequently, it is important not to "blame" one of the divisions for the problem, as that may falsely suggest an incorrect fix, but rather think about the incentive conflict as being driven by their separate concerns. The question, "Who is making the bad decision?" should be replaced by "What is the problem?"

OK, now that we have the analytic preliminaries out of the way, let's apply our modified framework to the problem.

1. *What is the problem?* The Paper Division is burning the soap for fuel, even though transferring it to Resins would increase the firm's profit.
2. *Do the divisions have enough information to fix the problem?* Between the two divisions, they have enough information to understand that soap has a higher value to the Resins Division.
3. *Do the divisions have the incentive to fix the problem?* No, each division is concerned only with division profitability. Incentive conflict between the two divisions is the core of the problem.

Treating divisions as profit centers and rewarding managers based on division profit has a number of benefits. First, it often makes sense to assign some decision-making authority to division managers because they have the best information about how to run their own divisions. As part of the assignment of decision-making authority, we also want to give these managers incentives to make good decisions. Another virtue of a profit center with delegated decision-making authority is that it doesn't require a lot of parent company involvement. The parent company looks at division revenue, subtracts division costs, and rewards managers based on the difference. Division managers are given a lot of discretion because the parent company has a good performance evaluation metric, and it's relatively easy to tie management pay to division performance. But, as we see with this example, running divisions as profit centers can lead to conflict between the divisions. And, this conflict can sometimes reduce company-wide profit.

OK, now that we understand the source of the problem, how do we fix it? There are three generic fixes to problems caused by incentive conflict between divisions: we can (1) reallocate decision rights to either the parent firm, or one of the two divisions; (2) change the information flow; and/or (3) change the incentives of one or both of the divisions.

One obvious solution is simply to give information to senior management that would allow them to set a better transfer price. But where does senior management of the parent company get the information necessary to set a good transfer price? If they have to rely on reports from interested parties, like those from the buying and selling divisions, they are likely to see only information favorable to one side or the other. This solution only shifts the divisions' attention away from lobbying for a favorable price to attempting to produce more favorable information.[1]

Another possible solution is to alter the incentives of the Paper Division so that it is evaluated based on parent company profit. Although this might eliminate the incentive conflict over the transfer price, it sacrifices the benefits of treating the division as a profit center. For example, it might create a free-riding problem. Division managers might exert less effort because they have less control over parent company profit compared to division profit.[2]

Another solution would be to change the decision rights by giving the Paper Division managers the right to sell black liquor soap to the external market if they couldn't negotiate favorable terms with Resins. With this simple organizational change, the Paper Division would burn the soap only if the Resins Division was not willing to pay very much. And this is exactly the decision that maximizes parent company profit. Additionally, this organizational change means that senior management doesn't need to spend time resolving disputes between divisions about the transfer price.

Choosing the best solution depends on the magnitude of all the costs and benefits of the various solutions. From what we know, this last solution appears to be the best.

This story has a happy ending (and no explosions). Soon after the company had the burners redesigned to handle black liquor soap, an increase in the price of energy raised the soap's value as a fuel, making it profitable for the Paper Division to burn it. So the company's initial mistake became profitable, thanks to an unforeseen increase in the price of energy. In other words, Acme got lucky. But once the price of energy falls, the problem will reappear, so it is still important to try to address it.

22.2 Transfer Pricing

Transfer pricing is a contentious issue for almost any company where divisions buy from or sell to each other. Together with corporate budgeting (a topic we'll cover later in this chapter), transfer pricing causes more conflict between divisions than almost any other issue. To illustrate a more typical transfer pricing conflict, let's return to our paper company and examine the transfer of paper from the upstream Paper Division to the downstream Cardboard Box Division. Paper is the most expensive input into box production.

When two profit centers negotiate a transfer price, sometimes the divisions bargain so hard that they reach an impasse. And sometimes, the downstream Box Division will purchase from an external supplier, even though the parent company would prefer that the Box Division purchase from the Paper Division. And finally, even if the divisions reach agreement, the cost of interdivision haggling may exceed any benefit the parent company derives from the transfer.

In this case, the two divisions agreed on a transfer price that was 25% higher than the marginal cost (MC) of the Paper Division. Although this price ensured that the Paper Division found it profitable to transfer paper to the Box Division, it also raised the costs of the downstream Box Division, making the boxes more difficult to sell.

To understand the effects of a high transfer price, look at Figure 22.1. The MC of paper production is $100. The Paper Division produces the paper and transfers it to the Box Division at a price of $125. The downstream Box Division counts the transfer price as part of its costs and then makes all sales where $MR_{Box} > MC_{Box} + \$25$. The $25 represents the markup that Paper Division builds into the transfer price, and MC_{Box} is the MC of producing boxes (and includes the $100 paper production cost). This is a higher threshold for making sales than the profit-maximizing threshold, $MR_{Box} > MC_{Box}$. In other words, under this scheme, the Box Division makes fewer sales, and charges higher prices, than would maximize parent company profit.

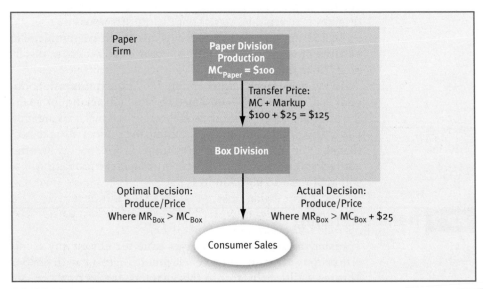

FIGURE 22.1   Transfer Pricing

Note that this problem is the opposite of the one faced by a marketing division in Chapter 21. There, the sales agents made *more* sales and charged *lower* prices than those that would have maximized company-wide profit.

Let's see how well our framework does in analyzing this problem:

1. *What is the problem?* The boxes are priced too high, so the company is not selling enough of them.
2. *Do the divisions have enough information to make a good decision?* Yes. Between the two, they have enough information to make a good decision.
3. *Do the divisions have the incentive to make a good decision?* No. The divisions are run as separate profit centers, so they work to increase profit of their own divisions, even if it means reducing parent company profit.

The analysis makes clear that the conflict arises because two profit centers are each trying to extract profit from a single product. For this reason, we call this the "double markup" or "double marginalization" problem. One way of solving it would be to turn the upstream Paper Division into a cost center.

Cost centers are not evaluated based on the profit they earn, so they don't care about the transfer price. If the Paper Division became a cost center, its managers would not object to transferring paper at marginal cost. And this would cause the downstream division to reduce box prices to their profit-maximizing level.

But cost centers have other problems. For example, the cost center may try to reduce cost by reducing quality, so the company may have to add a quality control and testing facility to the factory. As long as this kind of monitoring is not too costly, the cost center may be the best solution. As always, the right answer depends on the magnitude of the benefits and costs of the alternative solutions.

As we might expect, once our Paper Division became a cost center and began transferring paper at marginal cost, the Box Division began winning more jobs from its rivals. Ironically, though, the Box Division's success set off a price war in the industry that lasted for five years. The previous inefficient organizational form had the hidden benefit of softening price competition with rival box producers, the third of our generic strategies from Chapter 10.[3] This underscores another lesson for decision-makers—make sure that you also consider indirect consequences of changes before you make them.

22.3 Organizational Alternatives

Many firms are organized into functional divisions. Adam Smith's pin factory and Henry Ford's automobile assembly line are classic examples of production processes that divide tasks into narrow functional steps.

A *functionally organized firm* is one in which various divisions perform *separate tasks, such as production and sales.*

Functional organization offers firms the advantage that workers develop functional expertise and can easily share information within their division. This setup also helps firms realize any economies of scale inside the function because all the activities of a particular function are grouped together. For example, a global consumer products manufacturer might choose to centralize all its R&D activity in order to capture economies of scale and learning curve effects rather than have separate R&D facilities across the globe. Functional divisions also make it easy to tie pay to performance because performance is more narrowly defined and thus relatively easier to measure. *Piece-rate pay*—compensation based on the number of units a worker produces—is an example of such a simple performance evaluation metric.

The major difficulty in running a functionally organized firm is ensuring that the functional divisions are working toward a common goal.[4] Consider the problems faced by a functionally organized company when it designed a new turbine jet engine. The Engineering Division designed the engine, the Production Division manufactured it, and the Finance Division decided how much to charge for it. The engineers came up with a radical new design incorporating hollow fan blades. The award-winning design required less fuel than conventional engines, but the hollow fan blades were very difficult (and costly) to build. When the Finance Division computed the operating costs of the engine, it discovered that the new engines were much more expensive to buy and operate than rival engines, even after accounting for the expected fuel savings. The lack of coordination between the divisions resulted in a product whose total cost was higher than its value.

A similar coordination problem arose at a midsized regional bank divided into a Loan Origination Division (LOD) and a Loan Servicing Division (LSD). The LOD identifies potential borrowers, lends money to them, and then hands them over to the LSD. The LSD collects interest on the loan and makes sure that borrowers repay the loans as payments come due. However, the bank suffered an unusually high number of defaults.

Again, let's use our framework to diagnose the problem:

1. *What is the problem?* The LOD was making risky loans that resulted in a high number of defaults.
2. *Do the divisions have enough information to fix the problem?* The LOD had access to information on the credit status of the borrowers.
3. *Do the divisions have the incentive to fix the problem?* The parent bank evaluated the LOD managers on the amount of money they were able to lend. They had little incentive to restrict lending to qualified borrowers.

In other words, the LOD made loans regardless of their profitability.

We could change the incentives of the LOD so that its managers are rewarded for making only profitable loans. But this would be difficult to implement because it can take many years before a bank knows whether loans are unprofitable, and then only when borrowers don't repay them.

We could adopt a solution similar to the one used by the General Store from Chapter 21 where development agents were opening unprofitable stores. If we could design a good predictor of whether a loan would be profitable, we could let the LOD make loans only when the model predicts a good chance of repayment.

Another solution, and one that banks commonly use, is to put the origination and servicing personnel in the same division, essentially reorganizing the bank into an M-form or multidivisional company with process teams built around a multifunction task:

> An **M-form firm** *is one whose divisions perform all the tasks necessary to serve customers of a particular product or in a particular geographic area.*

Multidivisional or M-form structures have the advantage of higher flexibility to customize a firm's products or services to particular customer needs. They also improve coordination across functional departments and take advantage of expertise on servicing specific types of customers. This, of course, comes with the cost of having duplicate functional areas in each division.

In a bank, an M-form reorganization might consist of two divisions: one focused on both originating and servicing residential loans and the other focused on commercial loans. In each division, the profit of the loans originated and served would measure performance and subsequent compensation.

In fact, our bank decided to do just that—reorganize as an M-form. Not only did the number of bad loans decrease, but the speed of decision making increased. The M-form organization made it relatively easy for the divisions to respond to the changing conditions in local markets because its managers no longer had to coordinate with a sister division who shared responsibility for the customer. The bank also found it easier to develop long-term customer relationships because customers always dealt with the same person, whose responsibility included both origination and servicing.

The answer to whether it is better to organize as a functional or M-form organization is, of course, "It depends." Each form has particular benefits and drawbacks, and the right choice will depend on the magnitude of these costs and benefits in specific cases.

22.4 Budget Games: Paying People to Lie[5]

One of the functions of corporate budgets is to transfer information between divisions that need to coordinate with one another. Consider a toy company where the Marketing Division submits a budget that includes a forecast of the number and types of toys it expects to sell in the upcoming holiday season. The Manufacturing Division uses the sales forecast to plan production for the coming year. An accurate sales forecast means that the company will produce the right number of toys in time for the holiday demand. At least, that's how the process is supposed to work.

Put yourself in the place of a division manager who has good information about how much her division can earn. Regardless of her information, she always has an incentive to try to reduce the goal if her bonus is tied to reaching it. If her divisional budget goal is above what she thinks she can earn, she complains to senior managers that her goal is unreachable. The CEO understands her incentives and typically treats what she says with skepticism. They eventually hammer out a compromise that has more to do with the bargaining ability of the various divisional managers than with the information that they possess. As a consequence, the budget process often fails in its most basic function—transferring information from one division to another.

This lack of information can cause problems. For example, if the Marketing Division of the toy manufacturer lobbies successfully for a low sales budget, the Manufacturing Division may produce too little of a popular item just as the holiday season begins.

And the problems do not end there. Once the goal is set, a division may accelerate sales or delay costs to make sure that it can meet the goal. For example, a division's managers may ship products near the end of the year and record these shipments as sales. They do this even though they know that it is likely that the items will be returned later. This is sometimes referred to as "channel stuffing."

Alternatively, division managers who have already met their goals—or those who know they have no chance of meeting their goals—may delay sales or accelerate costs to make it easier to meet next year's budget goals. And these practices can generate real losses for the parent company. If, for example, a division tries to persuade a customer to delay purchasing a new piece of equipment, that customer might demand a discount or purchase from a rival instead of waiting to place the order.

Basing rewards on achieving specific target levels of performance can create problems. Let's run this problem through our framework:

1. *What is the problem?* The budgeting process takes an enormous amount of time and accurate information does not reach the CEO.
2. *Do the divisions have enough information to fix the problem?* Each division has good information about how much individual division profit it will likely earn.
3. *Do they have the incentive to fix the problem?* No. Each division has an incentive to say that the budgeted profitability goal is too high, regardless of whether this is true. Once budget goals are set, divisions have an incentive to accelerate or delay profit, or to stop work once the goal is reached.

Figure 22.2 illustrates the problem for a fairly typical compensation scheme that pays division managers a bonus when they reach a minimum

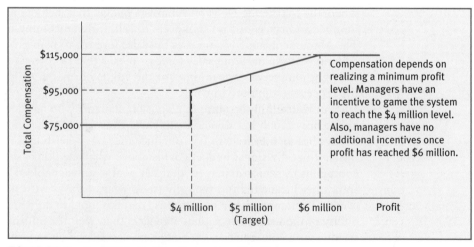

FIGURE **22.2** **Typical Incentive Compensation Scheme**

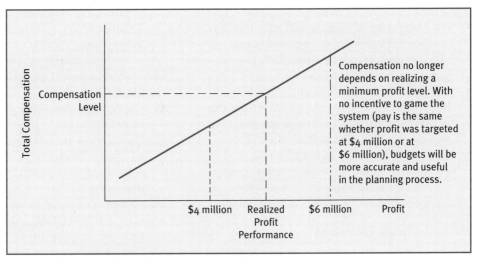

Compensation no longer depends on realizing a minimum profit level. With no incentive to game the system (pay is the same whether profit was targeted at $4 million or at $6 million), budgets will be more accurate and useful in the planning process.

FIGURE **22.3   A Better Compensation Scheme**

profit goal (e.g., a $20,000 bonus for reaching $4 million in profit). Note the kink in the compensation scheme. This kink gives division managers an incentive to lie about the information they have in order to make the goal easier to reach.

Figure 22.3 shows a simple solution to this budget-gaming problem: remove all kinks from the compensation schedule. Straight-line pay-for-performance functions eliminate division managers' incentives to lie about the budget because compensation does not depend on meeting a particular budget goal. Managers get rewards for doing more and punished for doing less, no matter where they are relative to the budget target. This compensation scheme eliminates managers' incentives to lie about the budget.

SUMMARY & HOMEWORK PROBLEMS

Summary of Main Points

- Companies are principals trying to get their divisions (agents) to work profitably in the interests of the parent company.
- Transfer pricing does not merely transfer profit from one division to another; it can stop assets from moving to higher-valued use. Efficient transfer prices are set equal to the opportunity cost of the asset being transferred.
- A **profit center** on top of another profit center can result in too few goods' being

sold; one common way of addressing this problem is to change one of the profit centers into a **cost center**. This eliminates the incentive conflict (about price) between the divisions.

- Companies with functional divisions share functional expertise within a division and can more easily evaluate and reward division employees. However, senior management must often coordinate the activities of the various divisions.

- An M-form or multidivisional structure has divisions that perform all the functional tasks to serve specific customer types or geographic areas.
- When divisions are rewarded for reaching a budget threshold, they have an incentive to lie to make the threshold as low as possible, thus ensuring they get their bonuses. In addition, they will often pull sales into the present, and push costs into the future, to make sure they reach the threshold level. A simple linear compensation scheme solves this problem.

Multiple-Choice Questions

1. A computer manufacturer has two divisions: one serving residential customers and one serving business customers. If an incentive conflict arises between the two divisions, how will overall company profits be affected?
   a. Profits will definitely fall.
   b. Profits will definitely rise.
   c. Profits may fall, but it depends on the nature of the conflict.
   d. The conflict has no potential to affect overall profit.

2. Which of the following changes might help solve a divisional conflict regarding a decision?
   a. Change who has authority to make the decision
   b. Transfer information to the decision-makers so they are better informed
   c. Change the performance evaluation and associated compensation of the decision-makers
   d. All of the above

3. Joe runs the Service Division for a car dealership. The overall dealership has a profit of $10 million on sales of $100 million and costs of $90 million. Joe's division contributed $9 million in sales and $7 million in costs. If the Service Division is evaluated as a profit center, what dollar amount is most relevant to Joe?
   a. $2 million
   b. $7 million
   c. $9 million
   d. $10 million

4. If you were a manager of a cost center, which of the following areas would be of most interest to you?
   a. Capturing potential economies of scale
   b. Increasing the quality of your product
   c. Hiring more marketing staff to figure out how to increase prices
   d. Adding additional features to your product

5. Transfer prices should be set at
   a. marginal cost of the selling division plus a reasonable profit amount.
   b. marginal cost of the selling division unless it is evaluated as a profit center.
   c. the opportunity cost of the asset being transferred.
   d. whatever price is negotiated between the selling and buying divisions.

6. Which type of organizational form has the benefit of closer coordination to serve a particular product or geographic area?
   a. Profit centers
   b. Functional organizations
   c. M-form organizations
   d. Functional and M-form organizations have the same benefits

7. Which of the following provides an example of divisions based on a functional organizational structure?
   a. Americas, Africa, Asia, Europe
   b. Research and development, production, finance, marketing
   c. Youth products, teen products, senior products
   d. Business users, home users, educational users

8. Which of the following organizational forms requires the strongest management oversight to ensure coordination of functions?
   a. Profit centers
   b. Functional organizations
   c. M-form organizations
   d. Functional and M-form organizations likely require similar oversight

9. Which of the following actions is consistent with a manager whose compensation depends on meeting a budget goal and who does not believe he can make that goal?
   a. Asking a vendor to preship and invoice materials for the following year.
   b. Discovering a "problem" in the order-taking process, thereby forcibly pushing sales into the ensuing year.
   c. Increasing accounting reserve estimates, leading to higher recognized expenses.
   d. All of the above.
10. One of the basic functions of the budgeting process is
    a. assigning decision rights.
    b. transferring information.
    c. evaluating managerial performance.
    d. implementing structural change.

Individual Problems

22-1 Transfer Pricing

Suppose that a paper mill "feeds" a downstream box mill. For the downstream mill, the *marginal profitability* of producing boxes declines with volume. For example, the first unit of boxes increases earnings by $10, the second by $9, the third by $8, and so on, until the tenth unit increases profit by just $1. The cost the upstream mill incurs for producing enough paper to make one unit of boxes is $3.50.
a. If the two companies are separate profit centers, and the upstream paper mill sets a single transfer price (the price the box company pays the paper mill), what price will it set, and how much money will the company make?
b. If the paper mill were forced to transfer at marginal cost, how much money would the company make?

22-2 Transfer Prices Set by Headquarters

List three reasons why it might be a bad idea to have corporate headquarters set transfer prices.

22-3 Chargebacks

Your local fast-food chain with two dozen stores uses the company's internal corporate marketing department to produce signage, print ads, in-store displays, and so forth. When placing an order, store managers are assessed a chargeback (transfer price) that reduces store profitability but increases marketing department profitability. Lately, the store managers have been ordering more and more marketing services; the marketing department is swamped, and it cannot afford to hire more staff. What does this indicate about the chargeback rates?

22-4 Divisional Profit Measure

Discuss the advantages and disadvantages of using divisional profit as the basis of incentive compensation for division managers compared to using company profit as the basis.

22-5 Furniture Forecasting

Futura Furniture Products manufactures upscale office furniture for the "Office of the Future." The sales division comprises regionally based sales offices made up of sales representatives and regional managers. Sales representatives—who report to the regional managers—conduct direct sales efforts with customers in their regions. As part of the sales process, representatives gather information about likely future orders and convey that information back to the regional managers. Regional managers use that information to create sales forecasts, which are then used as the basis for manufacturing schedules.

Sales representatives and regional managers are both compensated on a salary plus commission (percentage of revenue as pricing is centrally controlled). However, a regional manager's commission is adjusted based on regional sales that exceed the forecasted budget.

Corporate managers are concerned with one of Futura's key products, the "DeskPod." They worry that DeskPod forecasts are inaccurate, causing extreme havoc in the manufacturing process. How are the forecasts likely to be inaccurate? What do you think is driving this inaccuracy? How might this problem be solved?

22-6 Jet Turbine Design

This problem is mentioned in the text (see the section on "Organizational Alternatives"). Your task is to propose an organizational solution. To briefly recap, a manufacturer is trying to design the next generation of turbine engines for jet airplanes. The company is divided along functional lines. Engineering designs the engine, production manufactures it, and finance figures out how much to charge for it. The engineers invented a radical new design that used hollow fan blades. The award-winning design used less fuel than conventional engines, but the hollow fan blades were very difficult to build. When the Finance Division computed the marginal cost of an engine, it discovered that the new engines were much more expensive than rival engines, even accounting for the expected fuel savings. No one purchased the engine. How would you make sure that this problem does not recur?

Group Problems

G22-1 Transfer Pricing

Does your company use transfer pricing to "charge" divisions for the cost of the products they consume? Are these prices set equal to the opportunity cost of the product? Why or why not? Can you think of a better organizational architecture? Compute the profit consequences of changing the organizational architecture.

G22-2 Divisional Evaluation

Discuss a division or subunit of your organization and how it is evaluated (revenue center, profit center, cost center, etc.). How does the evaluation scheme affect performance? If it is optimal, explain why. Otherwise, explain why you think it is suboptimal, and recommend what you would do if you were free to change it. Compute the profit consequences of the change.

G22-3 Budget Games

Does your company tie compensation to meeting a budget? If so, what kind of problems does this practice cause? What can you do to fix these problems? Compute the profit consequences of changing the process.

G22-4 Functional Silos versus Process Teams

Is your company organized around functional divisions? If so, what kind of problems does this cause? What can you do to fix these problems? Compute the profit consequences of fixing the problem.

END NOTES

1. Using this solution would also require that you make sure senior management has the correct incentive to set a good transfer price.
2. This solution would also expose the managers to additional risk, likely requiring additional compensation.
3. See Mikhael Shor and Hui Chen, "Decentralization, Transfer Pricing and Tacit Collusion," *Contemporary Accounting Research* 26, no. 2 (2009): 581–604.
4. For one example of the challenge of organizing economists, see Luke M. Froeb, Paul A. Pautler, and Lars-Hendrik Roller, "The Economics of Organizing Economists," *Antitrust Law Journal* 76 (2009): 569–584.
5. This section was inspired by the ideas of Michael Jensen, "Paying People to Lie: The Truth about the Budgeting Process," HBS Working Paper 01-072, September 2001. An executive summary of this paper entitled "Corporate Budgeting Is Broken, Let's Fix It" was published in the *Harvard Business Review* November (2001).

23

Managing Vertical Relationships

When Jacques Papillon was appointed marketing manager for Argent Tobacco, one of the first things he did was commission a study of retail prices in the drugstores, supermarkets, and convenience stores that sold Argent cigarettes. What he found was disturbing. Whenever Argent reduced the wholesale price in order to promote its brand, fewer than half of the retail outlets responded with price cuts of their own. Instead, most retail outlets "ate" the price reduction, which increased retail profit but did nothing for Argent's sales or profitability.

M. Papillon traced the source of the problem to an incentive conflict between Argent, who is interested in the profit from sales of its own brand, and retailers, who are trying to maximize profit from sales of all the brands they carry. In other words, when a customer comes into a store, Argent wants the customer to purchase Argent's brand, while the retailer is content if the customer purchases any brand. As a consequence, retailers were reluctant to "pass through" Argent's price reductions because doing so would cannibalize sales of other brands they carried.[1]

As you should now be able to recognize, this is a type of a principal–agent conflict (Chapter 21) caused by moral hazard (Chapter 20). The manufacturer is the principal, the retailer is the agent, and the principal finds it difficult to control the pricing behavior of the agent. If the manufacturer could figure out which price the retailer should charge, it would be a simple matter to write a contract, offering the wholesale price reduction in exchange for a reduction in the retail price. The problem for Argent was that there were thousands of different retail outlets, each with different pricing strategies and each facing different demand elasticities. M. Papillon couldn't write and enforce contracts specifying a discount off the regular price because he didn't know what the regular price should be. He came up with a clever solution. In the contract, he specified the "regular" price as the price of Argent's closest rival brand. So, for example, when Argent reduced the wholesale price by two cents, the retailer would have to reduce the retail price of Argent by two cents below the retail price of the rival brand. This contract gave each retail outlet the flexibility to set the overall level of prices according to the demand they faced, while finding a way to get wholesale price discounts passed through to Argent's retail price. The contract raised the profit from selling and promoting Argent cigarettes, which was shared between Argent and its retailers.

This kind of incentive conflict between firms in the same vertical supply chain is quite common. This chapter is about how vertically related firms use a variety of informal and formal measures, like the Argent Tobacco contract, to control the incentive conflict to increase profit. We also discuss tax avoidance, and end the chapter with a discussion of the legal (antitrust) and financial concerns associated with vertical relationships.

23.1 How Vertical Relationships Increase Profit

To illustrate how a variety of contractual or organizational forms can increase profit in a vertical supply chain, let's return to the simple example of rent control. Suppose a rent-controlled apartment has a price ceiling of $1,000, meaning that city regulations limit the rent to less than $1,000 per month. If a renter is willing to pay $1,500 per month, the landlord has an incentive to evade the price regulation by **bundling** the apartment, say, with overpriced furniture or by **tying** furniture rental to the apartment rental. In the first case (bundling), the landlord offers a "furnished apartment" for $1,500; in the latter (tying), the landlord requires the renter to rent furniture from the landlord for an additional $500.

The general principle behind the profit-increasing effects of vertical contracts is easy to articulate:

> *If unrealized profit exists at one stage of the vertical supply chain, firms can capture some of the unrealized profit by adopting a variety of contractual or organizational forms.*

In the opening story, the unrealized profit is a consequence of incentive conflict between the upstream manufacturer and downstream retailers. In the apartment example, unrealized profit is a consequence of the price regulation. You can think of "furnished housing" as our vertical supply chain, which comprises two links, apartment rental and furniture. The solutions (tying or bundling) are contractual links that allow the landlord to extract some of the unrealized profit.

Exclusion can accomplish the same thing. If a building owner can make it costly or difficult for rival furniture sellers to sell to the tenant (by "excluding" them), the tenant is forced to purchase or rent furniture from the landlord. The landlord can then capture some of the unrealized profit through the sale of overpriced furniture.

Regulators usually anticipate these strategies and often require unbundled pricing, or they make it illegal to tie the sale of a regulated good to the sale of an unregulated one. To thwart exclusionary tactics, regulators mandate access for rival sellers, but this is often difficult to enforce.

Like regulatory evasion, multinational companies can use vertical integration to evade national profit taxes. A company manufacturing shirts in Mexico, for example, can transfer the shirts at a low price to a sister division located in the Cayman Islands, where they are marked up and shipped to the United States for sale to final consumers. The company reduces its tax burden by choosing to realize most of its profit in the Cayman Islands, which has lower taxes than Mexico or the United States.

Regulators in Mexico anticipate this strategy and force goods to be transferred at a price at least 5% over cost. This forces the company to realize at least some of its profit in Mexico.

23.2 Double Marginalization

The price paid to an upstream supplier is viewed by the downstream purchaser as part of its marginal cost (MC). Unless the upstream supplier prices at MC, the price of the downstream product will include multiple, successive markups. This is commonly referred to as "double marginalization" because the downstream firm sets prices where marginal revenue (MR) equals MC plus the supplier's markup. These successive markups result in prices that are too high (where MR < MC), higher than would maximize profit for the whole supply chain. This becomes a larger problem when both firms have more market power and each markups is larger. This is similar to the incentive conflict that occurs over transfer pricing (covered in Chapter 22).

If two "links" in this supply chain were to merge, they could increase total profit by coordinating their pricing. For example, the merged form could operate the downstream division as a profit center and convert the upstream division to a cost center, and transfer the input at MC. This would increase profit because the downstream firm would price at the optimal point, where MR = MC. Many vertical contracts aim to achieve the same end, reducing the price charged by the downstream firm, and sharing part of its profit with the upstream firm. Vertical contracts that aim to decrease final prices typically benefit all parties in the supply chain as well as the consumer.

23.3 Incentive Conflicts between Retailers and Manufacturers

Double marginalization is but one example of incentive conflict in a vertical supply chain. There are many others. In this section, we look at incentive conflict between manufacturers (the upstream supplier) and retailers (the downstream purchaser) over quality, promotion, advertising, and new product introduction. Both the manufacturer and retailer have an incentive to control these conflicts to increase the size of the profit "pie" that they split.

Quality Control

A manufacturer of perishable food may want her product kept fresh and at a controlled temperature. If not kept fresh, a consumer might mistakenly attribute an unsatisfying experience with the brand (at least partly) to the manufacturer. This would harm the manufacturer's reputation and reduce sales across all retailers that carry the brand. This incentive conflict arises because the retailer does not bear the full cost of the consumer response and may not have sufficient incentive to invest in refrigeration and inventory management. Recognizing this possibility, a manufacturer might "give" a refrigerator to the retailer to guarantee freshness. The gift might come with the stipulation that the retailer keep at least 60% of the refrigerator shelf space stocked with the manufacturer's product.

The same concern with quality control arises between manufacturers of copy machines and the firms that service them. If a machine breaks down, a consumer might mistakenly infer that it is due to faulty design or manufacture when, in fact, it is due to faulty service. To better protect its reputation, the manufacturer might "bundle" service with the sales of the machine, or try to "exclude" any but its own qualified technicians from servicing and repairing the machines. It can do this by refusing to provide diagnostic software and spare parts to third-party firms that service the machines.[2]

Promotional Activities

Advertising, service, promotion activities, and higher-quality service can increase customer interest, awareness, and sales. However, since the retailer earns only a fraction of the revenue from these sales, the retailer often does not have sufficient incentive to invest in these important demand-enhancing activities.[3]

To see this, consider a customer who adopts a new brand of cigarettes as a result of the promotional efforts of a retailer. This consumer will subsequently purchase the brand from many different retailers, and each of those sales benefits the manufacturer, but not the original retailer. Since the original retailer fails to realize the full benefits of its promotional activities, it will underinvest, at least from the manufacturer's point of view, and this reduces both their profit.

Consider, for example, an investment of $5,000 in a display cabinet that returns $8,000 of additional profit. Clearly, this is a profitable investment. However, if the profit is divided equally between the retailer and manufacturer, neither would have the incentive to make the investment on its own because each would realize only a benefit of $4,000 but pay a cost of $5,000.[4] Vertical contracts can provide the retailer with incentive to undertake these costly activities.

"Free Riding" among Retailers

Another reason why retailers do not find it profitable to engage in promotional activities is the ability of competing retailers to "free ride" on these efforts. If a retailer invests in promotional activities, displays, or expensive storage, the consumer is provided with a higher-quality product and a better ability to choose. However, since these activities are costly, a retailer that provides these services would need to charge a higher price than a retailer that does not. Retailers are reluctant to invest in these activities if they risk losing customers to lower-service rivals, who sell at lower prices.[5]

As an example, consider PING golf clubs. PING wants its retailers to spend considerable time and effort custom-fitting clubs to individual customers. But discount retailers can tell consumers to visit a full-service retailer to get a custom-fitting session, and then bring the specifications back to the discounter for a lower price. This kind of "free riding" by the discounters on the custom-fitting efforts of the full-service retailers weakens the incentive of full-service retailers to perform these services.[6]

Vertical contracts can often overcome this problem. For example, awarding retailers exclusive territories prevents consumers from going to discounters in the same area. Although these agreements can lead to higher prices (in accordance with service, quality, and promotional activity), they also result in higher sales, suggesting that consumer awareness and willingness to pay are both increased.[7] Recently the Supreme Court ruled that it may be okay for manufacturers like PING to set minimum retail prices to prevent this kind of free riding. This limits free riding from discounters because they are prohibited from selling at lower prices. However, in some U.S. states, and in foreign jurisdictions, contracts specifying retail prices are still illegal.

New Product Introduction

A similar kind of incentive conflict between retailers and manufacturers surrounds the introduction of new products. It is often quite costly to introduce and promote a new product. Sufficient resources must be invested in promotional pricing, advertising, and customer education. Ability to free ride on these investments by rival retailers reduces retailer incentives to invest in new products. Additionally, retailers often have very little information about a new product's sales prospects, while manufacturers, having invested in market research, are better informed. Various forms of vertical agreements reward the retailer for incurring the risk inherent in introducing a new product and the cost of managing an expanded inventory. Further, large lump-sum payments from the manufacturer to the retailer sometimes serve as a credible "signal" because only a manufacturer who believes in the likely success of her product would be willing to make such a payment.[8]

23.4 Price Discrimination

By itself, the upstream manufacturer cannot implement a price discrimination scheme against downstream consumers because downstream retailers can defeat it. To see this, suppose that home gardeners and farmers both use the same herbicide. Home gardeners are willing to pay $5 for a one-liter spray bottle ($5 per liter), whereas farmers are willing to pay $600 for a 200-liter barrel ($3 per liter).

If the manufacturer tries to price discriminate (by pricing at $5 per liter to home retailers and $3 per liter to farm retailers), the farm retailers could buy herbicide in 200-liter barrels, put it in small spray bottles, and sell it to home gardeners. By vertically integrating into retail operations, the manufacturer can prevent this kind of arbitrage. Note that the manufacturer has to integrate only into low-price retailing to accomplish this.

Use Vertical Integration When Contractual Solutions Aren't Enough

Sometimes, you can control the conflict only by buying your upstream supplier or downstream customer. By putting the two firms under the same corporate "roof," you eliminate the incentive conflict, but you also create a bigger firm that is more difficult and costly to manage. In addition, new incentive conflicts can appear in different parts of the organization. For example, if a manufacturing firm buys a retail outlet, and operates it as a separate profit center, the incentive conflict between two separate firms becomes a conflict between two separate divisions of the same company. These conflicts were covered in Chapter 22.

23.5 | Antitrust Risks

Most countries have antitrust laws governing vertical relationships between firms in the same vertical supply chain. The laws are generally focused on two types of anticompetitive risks. The first is that a dominant firm at one level of the supply chain will use vertical contracts to extend its market power to other levels of the supply chain. The second is that vertical contracts will reduce the intensity of competition and harm consumers. In the case of Argent Tobacco, for example, a competition agency sued Argent and its retailers because it thought that the contracts reduced the intensity of price competition among cigarette manufacturers. Eventually, Argent was exonerated by a court, but only after a long and costly trial.

It is instructive to compare the effects of horizontal agreements (like those between two retailers or two manufacturers) and the effects of vertical agreements. Horizontal agreements generally run contrary to the goals of consumers because they eliminate competition between firms selling substitute products, and this often results in higher prices. Vertical agreements, on the other hand, as seen earlier, are typically undertaken to control incentive conflict and reduce the costs of the firms that use them. In this way, they are much like agreements between firms producing complementary products, which often result in lower prices. What this means is that the antitrust risks from vertical restraints are typically smaller than those from horizontal agreements. But these risks are not negligible, especially for big or dominant firms.

For example, European authorities have prohibited Coke from purchasing refrigerators for retail outlets (a demand-enhancing investment) because the practice may exclude rival soft drink manufacturers from retail outlets that use Coke's refrigerators. In the United States, Dentsply has been convicted of excluding rival tooth manufacturers from its dealer distribution network, which forces rivals to use less efficient and higher cost ways of distributing their product. Similarly, 3M has been convicted of unfairly using discounts to encourage retailers to carry only 3M products. Again this makes it more costly for rival manufacturers to get into retail outlets that carry 3M products.

These practices are called abuse of dominance in Europe and monopolization or exclusion in the United States. Even though these practices can help manage incentive conflict, and thus reduce costs, they can also harm competitors, and sometimes consumers. To avoid running afoul of these laws, we repeat the following advice taken on antitrust law:

If you have significant market power, you should consider the effect any planned action will have on competitors.[9]

If your plans are likely to hurt your competitors, be sure that such a harm is a by-product of actions that have a sound business justification. These laws are in a state of flux right now, so be sure to seek legal counsel if your firm is dominant in your market and you are considering adopting contracts or practices that would disadvantage your competitors.

23.6 Do Buy a Customer or Supplier Simply Because It Is Profitable

We end this chapter with a warning—one that most of you will forget when you have the opportunity to buy a profitable customer or supplier.

Purchasing a profitable upstream supplier or downstream customer will NOT necessarily increase profit.[10]

Rather, it depends on what price you pay. The current owners know how much the company is worth, so you'll be paying a price exactly equal to the value of the company's discounted future profits. In addition, adverse selection is a potential problem because current owners typically have better information about the value of the firm than do potential buyers. They are likely to sell only when a buyer offers too much.

Without some kind of synergy that makes an asset more valuable to the buyer than it is to current owners, the acquisition will not be profitable. Based on the stock price reactions following acquisition announcements, it appears that about half of all corporate acquisitions are unprofitable. The shareholders of the acquired firm gain a little, but the shareholders of the acquiring firm typically lose a lot.

However, even if acquisitions turn out to be unprofitable, this doesn't necessarily mean that acquiring the company was the wrong thing to do at the time of the acquisition. In 1999, for example, AT&T purchased the cable assets of Tele-Communications, Inc. (TCI), for $97 billion, anticipating that the acquisition would allow them to offer local telephone service through TCI's cable lines. Three years later, the technology failed to develop as expected, so AT&T sold the old TCI cable assets to Comcast for $60 billion. AT&T purchased the company because it anticipated a synergy. After that synergy failed to materialize, it sold the assets and moved on. A lesser firm might have held onto the assets to avoid the embarrassment of publicizing a $37 billion mistake—a version of the sunk-cost fallacy.

SUMMARY & HOMEWORK PROBLEMS

Summary of Main Points

- If unrealized profit exists at one stage of the vertical supply chain—as often happens as a consequence of incentive conflict—a firm can capture some of the unrealized profit by integrating vertically, tying, bundling, or excluding competitors.
- Double marginalization problems occur in supply chains because the same input is marked up multiple times. Vertical integration or price contracts that keep marginal input prices closer to MC will raise total profit.
- Manufacturers typically want higher-quality, lower retail prices, higher sales effort, and higher levels of promotional activity than retailers want to provide. Manufacturers and retailers use a variety of formal and informal agreements to more closely align the incentives of retailers with the profitability goals of manufacturers.
- Vertical integration can facilitate downstream price discrimination schemes.
- Most countries have antitrust laws that regulate vertical relationships. To avoid running afoul of these laws, remember that if you have significant market power, you should consider the effect that any planned action will have on competitors.
- Do not purchase a customer or supplier merely because that customer or supplier is profitable. There must be a synergy that makes it more valuable to you than it is to its current owners. And do not overpay.

Multiple-Choice Questions

1. Alpha Industries is considering acquiring Foxtrot Flooring. Foxtrot is worth $20 million to its current owners under its existing operational methods. Because there are some opportunities for synergies between the two companies, Alpha believes that Foxtrot is worth $25 million as part of Alpha Industries. What do you predict for a sales price of Foxtrot?
   a. Less than $20 million or Alpha will not buy
   b. More than $25 million or Foxtrot will not sell
   c. Something between $20 and $25 million
   d. The different valuations make a sale very unlikely

2. All of the following provide a motive for vertical agreements *except*
   a. effective execution of price discrimination.
   b. elimination of free riding among retailers.
   c. quality control.
   d. diversification.

3. Which of the following is an example of vertical integration?
   a. A custom software company purchasing a competing software firm
   b. A soft drink producer buying a brand of iced tea
   c. A coal producer purchasing a nuclear power plant
   d. A gourmet cheese company purchasing a dairy

4. Why are contact lens manufacturers reluctant to sell their lenses through the Internet?
   a. The Internet price is too high due to double marginalization.
   b. Search costs are lower, so the Internet sales are too competitive.
   c. Doing so reduces the incentives of retailers to provide point-of-sale services.
   d. They are afraid of antitrust lawsuits.

5. In which of the following instances would an acquisition make the most sense?
   a. The target is a very profitable company.
   b. Synergies exist between the acquirer and the target.
   c. Integration costs are low between the two.
   d. Synergy benefits outweigh the costs of integration.

6. Why do vertical agreements typically pose less antitrust risk than horizontal agreements?
   a. Vertical agreements occur less often than horizontal agreements.
   b. Vertical agreements often result in lower prices, which are beneficial to the consumer.
   c. Vertical agreements are rarely profitable.
   d. Vertical agreements do not pose less antitrust risk than horizontal agreements.

7. CUS Pharmacy wishes to carry Pepgro blue pills. But Daisy Pharmaceuticals, the maker of Pepgro, will not supply CUS unless CUS agrees to carry other medications that Daisy makes. This is an example of
   a. exclusion.
   b. tying.
   c. territory restriction.
   d. bundling.

8. A multinational firm acquires many of its components preassembled from suppliers. One of these suppliers operates in a country with a much lower corporate income tax rate. How does this affect the vertical relationship between this supplier and the multinational?
   a. This will not affect the relationship.
   b. The multinational should stop working with the supplier.
   c. The multinational should consider purchasing this supplier.
   d. The multinational should move all its operations to the supplier's home country.

9. In which of the following cases might you expect to find a manufacturer granting exclusive territories?
   a. A pet supply chain that requires heavy local advertising to drive sales
   b. Custom computer sales that require a good deal of consultation
   c. A submarine sandwich chain that relies on its nationwide brand reputation
   d. All of the above

10. Local Spanish TV markets cater to individual cities by producing local content. This content can be produced in-house by a network or they can also purchase rights to third-party produced content. Recently, Spanish cities have erected barriers to entry in television content production that allows content producers more market power. How would this have affected vertical integration between content providers and TV networks?
    a. There is more vertical integration to limit arbitrage by price discriminating content producers.
    b. There is less vertical integration because point-of-sale services are less important.
    c. There is more vertical integration to reduce the double marginalization problem.
    d. There is less vertical integration because evading regulation is less important.

Individual Problems

23-1 Local Phone Companies

State utility commissions typically regulate local phone companies, but local phone companies also offer long-distance service to their customers. Rival long-distance carriers also connect to local phone lines to provide long-distance service to customers. Recently, the rival long-distance carriers have complained that the local phone company repair persons have put peanut butter on rival long-distance carriers' phone lines to encourage rats to eat through the lines. If true, why is this a profitable strategy?

23-2 Integration of Physician Groups and Testing Services

Under a proposed health-care reform, doctors' fees will be capped at 80% of their current rate, but doctors can order blood tests that will be reimbursed at 90% of the current rate. How does vertical integration of physician groups into testing services increase profits?

23-3 Online Cosmetics

Australian cosmetics maker, Eternal Beauty Products, pressures online retailers to either sell goods at prices charged by brick and mortar stores or risk being cutoff. If online retailers are paying the same wholesale prices, why would Eternal not want online retailers to charge lower prices?

23-4 Wedding Dresses

Stores that sell wedding dresses do not typically permit photos, and do not have tags in the dresses that would identify the manufacturer and style type. What is the purpose of these rules? Suggest one other way of accomplishing the same objective.

23-5 Herbicide Integration

Suppose the herbicide manufacturer mentioned in the chapter can vertically integrate only into home gardening retailing. Would this allow the manufacturer to price discriminate?

23-6 Loyalty Payments

Intel made large loyalty payments to HP in exchange for HP buying most of their chips from Intel instead of rival AMD. AMD sued Intel under the antitrust laws, and Intel settled the case by paying $1.25 billion to AMD. What incentive conflict was being controlled by these loyalty payments? What advice did Intel ignore when they adopted this practice?

Group Problems

G23-1 Managing Vertical Relationships

Identify a vertical relationship in your company and determine whether it could be managed more profitably by tying, bundling, exclusion, or vertical integration. Clearly identify the source of the profitability (e.g., regulatory evasion, elimination of double markup, better goal alignment, or price discrimination), and describe how to exploit it. Estimate the change in profit.

G23-2 Undoing Vertical Relationships

Identify a vertical relationship in your company, and determine whether it could be managed more profitably by outsourcing, untying, unbundling, inclusion of rivals, or vertical disintegration. Clearly identify the source of the profitability and describe how to exploit it. Estimate the gain in profit from the change.

END NOTES

1. We have simplified the theory for this example. In general, pass through depends not only on how many other competing brands a store carries, but also on things like the curvature of demand. See Luke Froeb, Steven Tschantz, and Gregory Werden, "Vertical Restraints and the Effects of Upstream Horizontal Mergers," in *The Political Economy of Antitrust*, edited by Vivek Ghosal and Johann Stennek (Amsterdam: North-Holland Publishing, 2007). Available at SSRN: http://ssrn.com/abstract=917897.

2. There may be some antitrust risks in doing this as we discuss later in the chapter.

3. See Benjamin Klein and Kevin M. Murphy, "Vertical Contracts as Contract Enforcement Mechanisms," *Journal of Law and Economics* 31, no. 2 (1988): 265–296; and Paul H. Rubin, "The Theory of the Firm and the Structure of the Franchise Contract,"

Journal of Law and Economics 21, no. 1 (1978): 223–233.

4. See, for example, Benjamin Klein, "The Economics of Franchise Contracts," *Journal of Corporate Finance* 2, no. 1–2 (1995): 9–37; and James C. Cooper, Luke M. Froeb, Daniel P. O'Brien, and Michael G. Vita, "A Comparative Study of United States and European Union Approaches to Vertical Policy," *George Mason Law Review* 13, no. 2 (2005): 289–308.

5. Brief of Amici Curiae Economists in Support of Petitioner, et al., *Leegin. v. PSKS*, 75 U.S.L.W.3207 (U.S. Nov. 3, 2006) (No. 06-480) (On Writ of Certiorari to the United States Court of Appeals for the Fifth Circuit).

6. See brief of PING, Inc. as Amicus Curiae in Support of Petitioner, *Leegin Creative Leather Prods., Inc. v. PSKS, Inc.*, 127 S. Ct. 2705 (2007), at 9–15 (noting PING, Inc.'s significant costs in operating a unilateral RPM policy), available at: http://www.abanet.org/antitrust/at-conversation/pdf/Leegin_PING_Amicus.pdf.

7. See Tim R. Sass and David S. Saurman, "Mandated Exclusive Territories and Economic Efficiency: An Empirical Analysis of the Malt-Beverage Industry," *Journal of Law and Economics* 36, no. 1 (1993): 153–177.

8. See Wujin Chu, "Demand Signalling and Screening in Channels of Distribution," *Marketing Science* 11, no. 4 (1992): 327–347.

9. John Shenefield and Irwin Stelzer, *The Antitrust Laws: A Primer*, 4th edition (Washington, DC: AEI Press, 2001).

10. For more on this topic, see Luke Froeb, "If Merger Is the Answer, What Is the Question?" *M&A Journal* 41, no. 3 (March 2006), reprinted in Owen Manager (2006) and in *Proceedings of the I Lisbon Conference on Competition Law and Economics* (Frederick, MD: Kluwer Law International).

SECTION 7

Wrapping Up

24 Test Yourself

24 Test Yourself

The preceding chapters have given you some tools to solve business problems. In this chapter, we give you an opportunity to use these tools to solve a set of problems faced by real businesses. After the question, pause and take a couple of minutes to identify the source of the problem. Then propose a solution to fix it.

24.1 Should You Keep Frequent Flyer Points for Yourself?

When Jimmy and Evelyn founded a new restaurant, they purchased supplies on company credit cards and used the points for personal travel. As the chain grew, they brought in a second investor, and the three of them shared the points among themselves, allowing them to purchase several business-class tickets to Europe each year.

As the chain continued to grow, two more outside investors were brought in. The new CFO who came with them insisted that the points be used only for company-approved travel. The relationship between the founders and the new shareholders began to sour, and, eventually, the new shareholders forced a buyout of the founders and terminated their employment with the company.

Question: Was the new CFO justified in forcing out the original owners?

Answer: Using the points for personal travel was OK when they were shared among the owners because they were essentially spending what they already owned. But when the new owners were brought in, the founders were spending the new shareholders' money on themselves.

This should be an easy question, as it represents the principal/agent incentive conflict of Chapter 21. The principals are shareholders, and their agents are the employees of the company.

But if you do not recognize that the CFO stopped what was essentially theft, please read Milton Friedman's article, "The Social Responsibility of Business Is to Increase Profit."[1]

24.2 Should You Lay Off Employees in Need?

Jorge Pine is a restauranteur who attributes success to three elements: great food, great operations, and enough capital to support them. However, after opening up a new restaurant, "Taco Love," he noticed a problem with operations. The profit margin (net income divided by revenue) was only 5%, well below the 20% required to cover the cost of capital.

After looking at the books, Jorge noticed that labor costs were unusually high. He spoke to his manager and discovered that she was reluctant to send workers home when demand was low, as on rainy days. "They need the money," the manager explained, pointing out several workers who supported young families, or sent money back to struggling parents in Mexico.

Question: What is the problem, and how do you fix it?

Answer: The cause of the problem is obvious: the manager was motivated more by compassion for her fellow employees than by whatever incentive pay scheme Jorge is using. An obvious solution would be to make her incentive pay stronger but, in this case, Jorge found a better solution.

Jorge sat his manager down and said, "Look, if you do not hold costs down, this restaurant won't earn a profit, and my investors will not fund our next one." Jorge had plans to open three more "boxes" under the same brand name.

Jorge continued, "Think about the families of the workers that I am not going to be able to hire, and what is going to happen to them if you don't earn a profit." The manager responded positively to Jorge's talk, and now Taco Love is so successful that Jorge plans to expand to other cities.

The moral of this story is still one of incentive alignment—successful businesses will find ways to give workers enough information to make good decisions and the incentive to do so—but incentives include more than just money. Great managers learn what motivates employees, and use that knowledge to get them to do the right thing.

This story also illustrates: (i) the zero-sum fallacy (when the restaurant makes more profit, workers also benefit), (ii) the consequentialist morality of earning profit, and (iii) the hidden-cost fallacy (the manager ignored the hidden cost of her initial decision—on the workers who were not going to be hired).

24.3 Manufacturer Hiring

When a manufacturing firm in South Carolina, Rivets & Bolts, Inc. (R&B), hires assembly workers, it wants employees whose work ethic is strong. But this is difficult to measure, so firms like R&B frequently hire workers who can be best described as "shirkers." Shirkers are difficult to manage and have high

---

[1]Milton Friedman, "The Social Responsibility of Business Is to Increase Profit," *New York Times Magazine*, September 13, 1970.

absentee rates. Shirkers also reduce worker morale, which ultimately raises production costs.

Question: How would you improve the quality of R&B's workforce?

Answer: R&B's human resources managers asked candidates to go through a prehire process (24 hours of classes over eight days during a four-week period). The HR managers told potential employees that this process would be the final step before full-time employment and that candidates would receive no pay for attending these classes. The candidates thought the prehire classes were an orientation to the company; however, the firm used the classes to screen out less motivated candidates. Candidates who missed a class—or showed up late—were sent home and not allowed to return. On average, R&B's managers dismissed 2 from each class of 30 people. Overall, this prehire screening has been very successful; the rate of bad hires has fallen from about 8% to less than 1%.

This question sometimes confuses students because they tend to think about shirking as moral hazard (Chapter 20), a post-contractual change in behavior caused by the difficulty of observing employee effort. However, in this case, the tendency to shirk is unobserved information about an employee's "type" that leads to the pre-contractual problem of adverse selection (Chapter 19).

Warning: This kind of screening may be illegal. Before trying something like it, consult an attorney to ensure that you are in compliance with labor laws.

24.4 American Airlines

In 1992, American Airlines (AA), the market share leader in the airline industry, announced a new pricing strategy—Value Pricing. AA narrowed the number of possible fares from 500,000 to 70,000 by classifying each into one of four classes (first class, coach, 7-day advance purchase, and 21-day advance purchase). It also began pricing based on flight length.

According to AA, the purpose of Value Pricing was to create "simplicity, equity, and value" in its prices. AA believed that Value Pricing would address customer complaints, stimulate demand by lowering prices, increase market share, and reduce costs by increasing load factors.

Question: Is this pricing program likely to be successful?

Answer: AA failed to anticipate its competitors' reactions to this new pricing plan. Competitors responded with aggressive price cuts, and industry profits plummeted. The Value Pricing initiative was abandoned within months of its launch. Had Robert Crandall, the CEO of AA at the time, understood the lessons of game theory, a devastating industry price war might have been avoided. Crandall should have tried a strategy that was less easily mimicked by his rivals.

24.5 Law Firm Pricing

In response to competitive pressure, a Chicago law firm (the "firm") created a program to move some of its best clients to a flat monthly fee instead of traditional hourly billing. The clients received unlimited legal representation in three practice areas: employment, litigation, and small transactional work.

Clients wanted the flat-fee billing to better predict and control their expenses, and the law firm thought it could profitably accommodate this request by utilizing lower-cost and younger attorneys at the firm.

Question: How well did this program work?

Answer: The new program resulted in big losses for the law firm.

Predictably, clients requested more assistance on relatively trivial matters because the marginal cost (to the client) decreased to zero. Although the requests and inquiries were minor on a case-by-case basis, in aggregate, they represented a significant outlay of attorney time and expense.

Harder to predict was another change in clients' behavior: they were less likely to engage in preventative measures and were more aggressive in settlement negotiations. For example, in the employment practices area, the clients did not perform supervisor training with the same frequency as before and were more confrontational when dealing with disgruntled employees—both potential areas of risk for employment discrimination claims. This change in behavior increased legal costs borne by the firm. After six months of losing money on the program, the law firm ended it.

Note that this is a kind of moral hazard (Chapter 20) that is difficult to control because it is hard to write a contract specifying exactly the kind of behavior you would expect.

24.6   Should You Give Rejected Food to Hungry Servers?

When customers order a meal at Taco Love, and what they receive isn't what was expected, they often send it back. If food gets returned, the restaurant has a rule to prevent the cooks and servers from eating it. On its face, this seems inefficient, as good food is discarded. Indeed, one of the managers at one of Taco Love's stores asked the new chief operating officer (COO) whether she would change the rules to allow the manager to give food to his staff

Question: Should the new COO let the restaurant manager give rejected food to his staff?

Answer: To answer the question, consider all the benefits and costs that vary with the consequence of the rule (Chapter 3).

- The obvious *benefit* of giving food to hungry servers and cooks is that you increase the attractiveness of working at the restaurant, which allows you to reduce wages, or to attract higher-quality workers (the "compensating wage differentials" of Chapter 9).
- However, the *hidden cost* of giving rejected food to the staff is that you create incentives for hungry staff members to deliberately mess up orders so they can get free food.

The new COO should also realize that if a restaurant has rules preventing staff from eating rejected food, the previous COO must have thought that the benefits of the rule were bigger than its costs. Unless the new COO has evidence that the existing rule should be changed, it is probably best to keep it as it is.

24.7 Managing Interest-Rate Risk at Banks

Banks are often functionally organized (Chapter 23), with a deposit division responsible for gathering deposits, and a loan division responsible for making loans. Banks make money by borrowing short (from depositors) and lending long (to homeowners). If the short-term rates they pay to depositors (costs) are lower than long-term rates they earn from mortgage loans (revenue), the banks make money.

Banks are often tempted to reduce costs by reducing the maturity of deposits (short-term deposits pay lower rates) and to increase revenue by increasing the maturity of loans (longer-term loans earn higher rates).

However, increasing the maturity on loans and reducing the maturity on deposits increases interest-rate risk: if interest rates rise (as they did in the early 1980s), bank borrowing costs increase quickly as depositors demand higher rates. However, revenue from loan payments does not increase at the same rate because rates are fixed for longer maturity loans. A regional bank was surprised to discover that it was exposed to a particularly high level of interest-rate risk.

Question: How could you better manage interest-rate risk at the bank?

Answer: Let's start by looking at the incentive conflict between the two divisions and the bank. The loan division raises its profitability by making longer-term loans while the deposit division raises its profitability by accepting shorter-term deposits. The resulting mismatch between the maturities of loans and deposits exposes the bank to interest-rate risk.

Another way of thinking about the problem is that the bank has two goals (increasing profit and reducing interest-rate risk), but it rewards each division for only one of the goals (increasing profit). If you can measure interest-rate risk, you can use it as a performance metric, and reward each division for reducing it. For example, since risk is closely related to mismatch between the maturities of the deposits and loans, you can reduce risk by rewarding the deposit division for *increasing* the maturities of deposits (e.g., 10-year certificates of deposit) and the loan division for *decreasing* the maturities of loans (e.g., 15-year instead of 30-year mortgage loans).

This solution relies on the ability of senior management to recognize that the two functional divisions are working at cross-purposes to each other and to adjust performance metrics to more closely match the riskiness of loans and deposits.

Another solution would be to put the deposit and loan decisions in the same division, and then tie division evaluation to interest-rate risk. This would move the responsibility down from the firm level to the division level.

24.8 What You Should Have Learned

If you've read and understood this book, you should now know how to do the following:

1. Use the rational-actor paradigm, to identify problems, and then fix them
2. Give employees enough information to make good decisions, and the incentive to do so (incentive alignment)

3. Use benefit-cost analysis to make profitable decisions
4. Use marginal analysis to make profitable extent (how much) decisions
5. Make profitable investment and shutdown decisions
6. Set optimal prices and price discriminate
7. Predict and explain industry-level changes using demand-supply analysis
8. Understand the long-run forces that erode profitability
9. Develop long-run strategies to increase firm value
10. Predict how your own actions will influence rivals' actions
11. Bargain effectively
12. Make decisions in uncertain environments
13. Solve the problems caused by moral hazard and adverse selection
14. Motivate employees to work in the firm's best interests
15. Motivate divisions to work in the best interests of the parent company
16. Manage vertical relationships with upstream suppliers or downstream customers

Now go forth and move assets to higher-valued uses.

Can Those Who Teach, Do?

by Luke Froeb

I finished the first edition of this book while managing 110 employees in the Bureau of Economics at the Federal Trade Commission. The experience taught me much about management that isn't in this book.

The government has no well-defined goals, few metrics to measure performance, and no sticks or carrots to align employees' incentives with organizational goals. In addition, most federal employees are lifetime civil servants, with better information and strong ideas about what the agency ought to be doing. And they can easily outlast the political appointees who come to manage them for just a couple of years.

In this environment, the rational-actor paradigm predicts that government employees would shirk or follow objectives of their own choosing. While this was certainly true of some, others put in long hours and take pride in their work. If you want to accomplish anything during a short government stint, you have to identify these employees and motivate them to work toward a common goal.

Before you can work toward a goal, you must have one. Set realistic goals during annual or semi-annual meetings that review past performance and outline what you hope to accomplish in the future. Be as specific as possible with timetables and measurable benchmarks. Refine and readjust your goals as new information becomes available. If you discover that a goal has become too costly to reach, drop it and replace it with another.

Constantly monitor progress toward your goals. Otherwise, subordinates will infer that your priorities have changed and, as a consequence, stop working to achieve them. To guard against this, require weekly reports from them or ask questions during weekly staff meetings to assure them that you still care about what they're doing. Remember that criticism is much easier to accept if it is framed as a question, e.g., for a late report, simply ask "how is the report coming?"

If the organizational structure is broken, fix it. Otherwise, respect the organizational structure you have, that is, figure out what you can do that no one else in the organization is capable of doing, and then do it. If you find yourself doing something that your subordinates can do, stop. In particular, let your subordinates manage their own people. If you jump over them to become directly involved in specific matters, you're implicitly telling them that you don't think they're capable of doing their assigned jobs. Every time I did this, I ended up creating more work for subordinates with no better outcome.

If you manage a functional division, meet with the managers of other functional divisions to ensure cooperation and to resolve conflict. If you manage a divisional organization, make sure that you recognize and reward functional expertise.

Manage yourself. Set goals, hold yourself accountable for meeting them, and adjust them as circumstances change or as you learn more. Importantly, do not let your inbox run your life. Put yourself on a schedule so that you do the routine tasks at the same time every day, like answering e-mail. Otherwise you can find yourself glued to your computer, putting out fires instead of accomplishing your goals.

Finally, learn to point the finger at yourself. When something goes wrong, it is human nature to blame others and react with anger or frustration. Often, however, it is more effective to try to understand the source of the problem from the point of view of those involved. When you begin like this, more often than not, the problem will resolve itself, as those involved come to understand its cause. Or you may find that the problem lies with your own attitude or assumptions, and not with other people's behavior.

GLOSSARY

A

Accounting costs costs that appear on the financial statements of a company.

Accounting profit profits as shown on a company's financial statements. Accounting profit does not necessarily correspond to real or economic profit.

Adverse selection refers to the fact that "bad types" are likely to be selected in transactions where one party is better informed than the other. Examples include higher risk individuals being more likely to purchase insurance, more low-quality cars (lemons) being offered for sale, or lazy workers being more likely to accept job offers. Adverse selection is a precontractual problem that arises from hidden information about risks, quality, or character.

Agency costs costs incurred in principal–agent relationships; these costs are associated with moral hazard and adverse selection problems.

Agent a person who acts on behalf of another individual (a principal). Principal–agent problems are created by the incentive conflict between principals and agents.

Aggregate demand curve describes the buying behavior of a group of consumers. We add up all the individual demand curves to get an aggregate demand curve (the relationship between the price and the number of purchases made by a group of consumers).

Arbitrage a means to defeat a price discrimination scheme; it occurs when low-value individuals are able to resell their lower-priced goods to the higher-value group.

Average cost the total cost of production divided by the number of units produced.

Avoidable costs costs that you get back if you shut down operations.

B

Break-even price the price that you must charge to at least break even (make zero profit). It is equal to average avoidable cost per unit.

Break-even quantity the amount you need to sell to at least break even (make zero profit). The formula (assuming that you can sell all you want at price and with constant marginal cost) is $Q = F/(P - MC)$, where F is fixed costs, P is price, and MC is marginal cost.

Bundling the practice of offering multiple goods for sale as one combined product.

Buyer surplus the difference between the buyer's value (what he is willing to pay) and the price (what he has to pay).

C

Common-value auction in a common-value auction, the value of the item being auctioned is the same for each bidder, but no one knows what it is. Each bidder has only an estimate of the unknown value, and the value is the same for everyone. In common-value auctions, bidders have to bid below their values in order to avoid the winner's curse.

Compensating wage differentials differences in wages that reflect differences in the inherent attractiveness of various professions or jobs (once equilibrium has been reached).

Competitive industry competitive industries are characterized by three factors: (1) firms produce a product or service with very close substitutes meaning demand is very elastic, (2) firms have many rivals and no cost advantage over those rivals, and (3) the industry has no barriers to entry or exit.

Complement a good whose demand increases when the price of another good decreases. Examples include a parking lot and shopping mall or a hamburger and a hamburger bun.

Constant returns to scale when average costs are constant with respect to output level.

Consumer surplus *See* **Buyer surplus.**

Contribution margin the amount that one unit contributes to profit. It is defined as price–marginal cost.

Controllable factor something that affects demand that a company can change. Examples include price, advertising, warranties, and product quality.

Cost center a division whose parent company rewards it for reducing the cost of producing a specified output.

Cross-price elasticity of demand the cross-price elasticity of demand for Good A with respect to the price of Good B measures the percentage change in demand of Good A caused by a percentage change in the price of Good B.

D

Decreasing returns to scale See **Diseconomies of scale.**

Demand curves curves that describe buyer behavior and tell you how much consumers will buy at a given price.

Difference-in-difference an estimator that identifies the causal effect of a treatment, like a special promotion, by comparing the periods before and after the treatment between an experimental group and a control group. The second difference is designed to remove selection bias.

Direct price discrimination scheme a price discrimination scheme in which we can identify members of the low-value group, charge them a lower price, and prevent them from reselling their lower priced goods to the higher value group.

Diseconomies of scale exist when average costs rise with output.

Diseconomies of scope exist when the cost of producing two products jointly is more than the cost of producing those two products separately.

E

Economic profit a measure of profit that includes recognition of implicit costs (like the cost of equity capital). Economic profit measures the true profitability of decisions.

Economies of scale exist when average costs fall as output increases.

Economies of scope exist when the cost of producing two products jointly is less than the cost of producing those two products separately.

Efficient an economy is efficient if all assets are employed in their highest-valued uses.

Elastic a demand curve on which percentage quantity changes more than percentage price is said to be elastic, or sensitive to price. If $|e| > 1$, demand is elastic, where e is the price elasticity of demand. If $|e| = 0$, demand is perfectly inelastic while if |e| is infinite, demand is perfectly elastic. If |e| = 1, demand is unit elastic.

English auction See **Oral auction.**

Exchange rate the price at which two different currencies are exchanged, for example, ¥10 to the dollar, or $.010 per yuan.

Exclusion the practice of blocking competitors from participating in a market.

Extent decision a decision regarding how much or how many of a product to produce.

F

First Law of Demand consumers demand (purchase) more as price falls (i.e., demand curves slope downward), assuming other factors are held constant.

Five Forces a framework for analyzing the attractiveness of an industry. Attractive industries have low supplier power, low buyer power, low threat of entry, low threat of substitutes, and low rivalry.

Fixed costs costs that do not vary with output.

Fixed-cost fallacy consideration of costs that do not vary with the consequences of your decision (also known as the sunk-cost fallacy).

Foreign exchange See **Exchange rate.**

Functionally organized firm a firm in which various divisions perform separate tasks, such as production and sales.

H

Hidden-cost fallacy occurs when you ignore relevant costs, those costs that do vary with the consequences of your decision.

I

Implicit costs additional costs that do not appear on the financial statements of a

company. These costs include items such as the opportunity cost of capital.

Incentives have two pieces: a performance evaluation metric, like sales, profit, or investment return, and a reward scheme that rewards better performance, like a bonus, the promise of a promotion, or a commission. Performance evaluation metrics can be objective or subjective.

Incentive alignment or **goal alignment** occurs when an employee has enough information to make a good decision and the incentive to do so.

Incentive conflict a situation where parties have different, competing goals. In agency relationships, the different goals of principals and agents is an example of incentive conflict.

Income elasticity of demand measures the percentage change in demand arising from a percentage change in income.

Increasing returns to scale See **Economies of scale.**

Indifference principle if an asset is mobile, then in long-run equilibrium, the asset will be indifferent about where it is used; that is, it will make the same profit no matter where it goes.

Indirect price discrimination scheme a price discrimination scheme in which a seller cannot directly identify low- and high-value consumers or cannot prevent arbitrage between two groups. The seller can still practice indirect price discrimination by designing products or services that appeal to groups with different price elasticities of demand.

Individual demand curve a curve that tells you how much an individual consumer will buy at a given price.

Inelastic a demand curve on which percentage change in quantity is smaller than percentage change in price is said to be inelastic, or insensitive to price. If |e| < 1, demand is price inelastic (where *e* is the price elasticity of demand).

Inferior goods for inferior goods demand decreases as income increases.

Interest the cost that creditors charge for use of their capital.

L

Law of diminishing marginal returns as you try to expand output, your marginal productivity (the extra output associated with extra inputs) eventually declines.

Learning curves a phenomenon in which experience leads to learning meaning that current production lowers future costs.

Long-run equilibrium when firms are in long-run equilibrium, economic profit is zero (including the opportunity cost of capital), firms break even, and price equals average cost (i.e., no one wants to enter or leave the industry).

M

Marginal cost the additional cost incurred by producing and selling one more unit.

Marginal profit the extra profit from producing and selling one more unit (MR – MC).

Marginal revenue the additional revenue gained from selling one more unit.

Market equilibrium the price at which quantity supplied equals quantity demanded.

Mean reversion suggests that performance eventually moves back toward the mean or average.

M-form firm a company whose divisions perform all the tasks necessary to serve customers of a particular product or in a particular geographic area (also known as a multidivisional company).

Monopoly a firm that is the single seller in its market. Monopolies have market power because they produce a product or service without close substitutes, they have no rivals, and barriers to entry prevent other firms from entering the industry.

Moral hazard post-contractual increases in risky or negative behavior. Examples are reduced incentive to exercise care once you purchase insurance and reduced incentives to work hard once you have been hired. Moral hazard is similar to adverse selection in that it is caused by information asymmetry; it differs in that it is caused by hidden actions rather than hidden types.

Movement along the demand curve change in quantity demanded in response to change in price.

N

Nash equilibrium a pair of strategies, one for each player, in which each strategy is a best response against the other.

Nonstrategic view of bargaining a view that does not focus on the explicit rules of the game to understand the likely outcome of the bargaining. This view says that the likely outcome of bargaining is determined by each player's gains to agreement relative to alternatives to agreement. Sometimes called "axiomatic bargaining" or "Nash bargaining."

Normal (goods) for normal goods, demand increases as income increases.

NPV rule if the present value of the net cash flows is larger than zero, the project is profitable (i.e., earns more than the opportunity cost of capital).

O

Opportunity cost the opportunity cost of an alternative is the profit you give up to pursue it.

Oral auction in this auction type, bidders submit increasing bids until only one bidder remains. The item is awarded to the last remaining bidder.

P

Perfectly competitive industry *See* **Competitive industry.**

Post-investment hold-up an attempt by a trading partner to renegotiate the terms of trade after one party has made a sunk cost investment or investment specific to the relationship.

Price ceilings price controls that outlaw trade at prices above the ceiling.

Price control a regulation that allows trade only at certain prices.

Price discrimination the practice of charging different people or groups of people different prices that are not cost justified.

Price elasticity of demand (e) a measure of how responsive quantity demanded is to changes in price. Formula: (% change in quantity demanded) ÷ (% change in price).

Price floors price controls that outlaw trade at prices below the floor.

Principal an individual who hires another (an agent) to act on his or her behalf.

Prisoners' dilemma a game in which conflict and cooperation are in tension; self-interest leads the players to outcomes that no one likes. It is in each player's individual interest to not cooperate regardless of what the other does. Thus, both players end up not cooperating. Their joint interest would be better served, however, if they could find a way to cooperate.

Profit center a division whose parent company evaluates it on the basis of the profit it earns.

R

Randomized Experiment of observations to treatment and control groups is designed to eliminate selection bias, any systematic difference between the two groups.

Random variables a variable whose values (outcomes) are random and therefore unknown. The distribution of possible outcomes, however, is known or estimated. Random variables are used to explicitly take account of uncertainty.

Rational–actor paradigm this paradigm says that people act rationally, optimally, and self-interestedly.

Relationship-specific investments See **Specific investments.**

Relevant benefits all benefits that vary with the consequence of a decision.

Relevant costs all costs that vary with the consequence of a decision.

Risk premium higher expected rates of return that compensate investors in risky assets. In equilibrium, differences in the rate of return reflect differences in the riskiness of an investment.

Risk-averse a risk-averse individual values a lottery at *less* than its expected value.

Risk-neutral a risk-neutral individual values a lottery *at* its expected value.

Robinson-Patman Act part of a group of laws collectively called the *antitrust laws* governing competition in the United States. Under the Robinson–Patman Act, it's illegal to give or receive a price discount on a good sold to another business. This law does not cover services and sales to final consumers.

S

Screening a solution to the problem of adverse selection that describes the efforts of a less informed party to gather information about the more informed party. A successful screen means that it is unprofitable for bad types to mimic the behavior of good types. Any successful screen can also be used as a signal.

Sealed-bid first-price auction a sealed-bid auction in which the highest bidder gets the item at a price equal to his bid.

Second-price auction See **Vickrey auction**.

Selection bias the difference between two groups, a treatment or experimental group and a control group, if both were given the same treatment. The observed difference between two groups is equal to the causal effect of the treatment only if the selection bias is zero.

Seller surplus the difference between price (what the seller is able to sell for) and the seller's value (what she is willing to sell for).

Sequential-move games in these games players take turns, and each player observes what his or her rival did before having to move.

Sharing contracts a type of franchising agreement under which the franchisee pays the franchisor a percentage of revenue rather than a fixed fee.

Shift of the demand curve a change in demand caused by any variable except price. If demand increases (shifts up and to the right), consumers demand larger quantities of the good at the same price. If demand decreases (shifts down and to the left), consumers demand lower quantities of the good at the same price. Shifts are caused by factors like advertising, changes in consumer tastes, and product quality changes.

Shift of the supply curve a change in supply caused by any variable except price. If supply increases (shifts down and to the right), sellers supply larger quantities of the good at the same price. If supply decreases (shifts up and to the left), sellers supply lower quantities of the good at the same price. Shifts are caused by factors like changes in costs, technological change, changes in capacity, and entry or exit of new firms.

Signaling a solution to the problem of adverse selection that describes an informed party's effort to communicate her type, risk, or value to less informed parties by her actions. A successful signal is one that bad types won't mimic. Any successful signal can also be used as a screen.

Simultaneous-move games in these games players move at the same time. Neither player knows prior to moving what the other has done.

Specific investment investments that are less valuable outside of a particular relationship. They are similar to sunk costs in that the costs are "sunk" in the relationship.

Stay-even analysis allows you to determine the volume required to offset a change in cost, price, or other revenue factor.

Strategic view of bargaining a view that focuses on how the outcome of bargaining games depends on the specific rules of the game, such as who moves first, who can commit to a bargaining position, or whether the other player can make a counteroffer.

Substitute a good whose demand increases when price of another good increases. For example, two brands of cola soft drinks are substitutes.

Sunk costs costs that cannot be recovered. They are unavoidable even in the long run.

Sunk-cost fallacy See **Fixed-cost fallacy**.

Supply curves curves that describe the behavior of sellers and tell you how much will be offered for sale at a given price.

T

Treatment effect is the causal effect of a treatment, like a promotion, on an outcome variable, like sales.

Tying the practice of making the sale of one good conditional on the purchase of an additional, separate good.

U

Uncontrollable factor something that affects demand that a company cannot control. Examples are consumer income, weather, and interest rates.

V

Value an individual's value for a good or service is the amount of money he or she is willing to pay for it.

Variable costs costs that change as output levels change.

Vertical integration refers to the common ownership of two firms in separate stages of the vertical supply chain that connects raw materials to finished goods.

Vickrey auction a sealed-bid auction in which the item is awarded to the highest bidder, but the winner pays only the second-highest bid.

W

Winner's curse arises in common-value auctions and refers to the fact that the "winner" of the auction is usually the bidder with the highest estimate of the item's value. To avoid bidding too aggressively, bidders should bid as if their estimate is the most optimistic and reduce their estimate accordingly.

Z

Zero-sum fallacy the fallacy of assuming that if someone is winning (e.g., making money) someone else must necessarily be losing (e.g., losing money).

INDEX